東京大學史料編纂所編纂

日 本 關 係 海 外 史 料

イギリス商館長日記
原 文 編 之 上

自元和元年五月　至元和二年十一月

昭和五十三年

東京大學史料編纂所刊行

NIHON KANKEI KAIGAI SHIRYO:
HISTORICAL DOCUMENTS IN FOREIGN LANGUAGES
RELATING TO JAPAN

(ORIGINAL TEXTS)
SELECTION II VOLUME I

A Publication
Edited by The Historiographical Institute *(Shiryō
Hensan-jo),* The University of Tokyo and
Published simultaneously
with the Series of Translation into Japanese.

DIARY KEPT BY THE HEAD OF THE ENGLISH FACTORY IN JAPAN

DIARY OF RICHARD COCKS, 1615–1622

Vol. I

June 1, 1615—December 31, 1616

TOKYO
1978

PREFACE

Since 1949 the Historiographical Institute (*Shiryō Hensan-jo*) has been functioning as one of the research institutes attached directly to the University of Tokyo. The primary objective of the Institute is the research, compilation, and publication of historical source materials concerning Japan. This work, however, was begun as early as 1869 in obedience to an Imperial request. During those earlier days, the Institute was under the direction of the executive department of the Government; and was assigned the task of compiling a general survey of Japanese history. In 1888, however, this office of compilation was transferred to a section under the Faculty of Letters of the University of Tokyo, after having experienced frequent name changes. Likewise, by 1893 its purpose had been Redefined, and the Institute was charged with the compilation of source materials concerning Japanese history. From 1901, the results of the Institute's efforts have been published yearly in various series of source books, among which the most famous are the "Chronological Source-books of Japanese History" (*Dai Nippon Shiryō*) (275 volumes as of March 1975), "Old Documents of Japan" (*Dai Nippon Ko-monjo*) (157 vols.), "Old Diaries of Japan" (*Dai Nippon Ko-kiroku*) (56 vols.) and "Historical Materials of the Edo Period" (*Dai Nippon Kinsei Shiryō*) (71 vols.) Today, the Institute is the country's leading centre for the study of Japanese history.

In the persuit of its assigned tasks, the Historiographical Institute has also collected primary and secondary materials, including hand reproductions and photographs. The present holdings include more than 335,000 items, having fortunately escaped damage from the great earthquake and fire of 1923 and the air raids during World War II. Today the collection is housed in a new 10 story library constructed three years ago. Of particular interest is the collection of microfilms of unpublished documents concerning Japanese history which were preserved in foreign countries and imported into Japan beginning in 1954, under the supervision of the Japan Academy's Centre d'Information d'Enquete et d'Echange and the Union Academique Internationale's Seventh Committee. The number of microfilms had reached 720,536 exposres, when The Historiographical Institute compiled and published a 14–volume inventory in 1963–1969 under the title *Historical Documents Relating to Japan in Foreign Countries*. To preserve the integrity of the originals, a set of duplicate films has been made. These are available for public use at the Institute. I am glad to add that the Union Academique Internationale has recently resumed its welcome support.

In response to the growing demands of native and foreign scholars, the Historiographical Institute decided in 1969 to publish a new series of documents, based on the above-mentioned tradition of historical editing and the new collection of foreign archives on microfilm. This new series is composed of two sections, one covering the foreign documents themselves, and a second containing the translations of these documents into Japanese. In 1973 this programme was inaugurated with publication of the diaries kept by the heads of the Dutch factory in Japan. Last year the Institute reached an agreement with the British Library to publish the diary of Richard Cocks, the cape-merchant of the English factory in Japan. This follows friendly negotiations between the Institute and the Japan Academy which had been also conceiving a joint plan to edit the same diary with the British Academy.

It is my great pleasure to announce the publication of this series to the public and at the same time to express my sincere gratitude for the personal and intitutional cooperation and advice which has enabled us to carry on this programme.

March, 1975.

T. Iyanaga

Teizo Iyanaga
Director and Professor

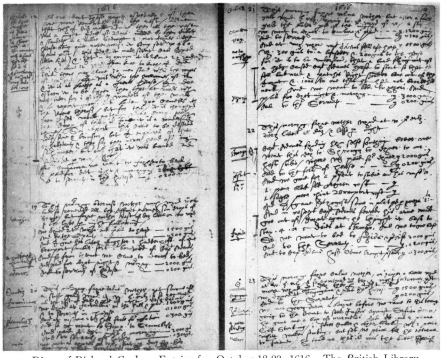

Diary of Richard Cocks. Entries for October 18-23, 1616. The British Library, Add. Mss. 31300. Fol. 149v.-150r. Microfilmed in 1974. (Size of a page: 35.0 cm. long and 22.5 cm. broad)

CONTENTS

INTRODUCTION

The First Anglo-Japanese Contact   A little before the founding of the United Dutch East India Company, but certainly under the stimulus of Dutch achievements in the Eastern seas, the "Company of Merchants of London trading into the East-Indies" was, on December 21, 1600 (o.s., or Julian calendar), incorporated by a charter of Elizabeth I, and on February 10 of the following year a royal decree laid down regulations for stationing its factories in the East Indies. From 1601 to 1612, the Company carried out twelve individual voyages in which profits were reckoned after each voyage, and thereafter developed a system in which profits were calculated after a series of voyages. During the seventeenth century, often characterised in the history of English overseas expansion as the "factory period," the Company opened more than sixty factories at over fifty places throughout the Far East before merging with the new United English East India Company in 1709. Bantam was the site of the first factory (1602–1619) and Hirado (Firando) in Japan, among those earlier established, was the northernmost (1613–1624, n.s.).

Anglo-Japanese relations first began, however, at an even earlier date. On April 19, 1600 (o.s.), just before the Tokugawa achieved their military hegemony over Japan, the *Charity* (*De Liefde*), a Dutch ship, drifted ashore on the coast of northern Kyūshū. On board the ship was the Kentish pilot, William Adams (1564–1620), who became a diplomatic advisor to Ieyasu, the first Tokugawa Shōgun, and who later rendered meritorious service to Japan after declining an opportunity to return home. The English became aware of Adams' story and the prospect of opening trade with Japan through reports from the Dutch, even before Adams' own letter of 1611 reached them. Capt. Anthony Hippon, commander of the seventh voyage of the London Company (1611–1615) was instructed to approach Japan, although he failed. Capt. John Saris (1579?–1643), commander of the eighth voyage aboard the *Clove*, eventually arrived at Hirado on June 12, 1613 (o.s.), still unaware of Adams' recommendation that Uraga was a better port of entry to Japan. Through Adams' mediation, Capt. Saris on September 8 visited Ieyasu, then in retirement at Suruga and known as Ōgosho Sama, to present him a message from James I. Saris then proceeded to Edo to see the current Shōgun Hidetada, and on his way back through Suruga received on October 8 a return message from Ieyasu, written in Chinese, and a license granting trading privileges, written in Japanese. The date of issue of this license was, according to Saris' journal, "the first daie of the nynth moneth" (October 5, 1613, o.s.; October 15, n.s.) though a Japanese register's date preceded this by three days.

A ship's council on November 26 decided to open a factory at Hirado, and Richard Cocks (1550?–1624) was appointed the cape-merchant in charge of mercantile management and consular jurisdiction. In Hirado the Dutch had already established their factory in 1609, trading with the native Japanese and the Portuguese in Nagasaki. The English were thus faced with a number of rivals, but the Matsura, Lord of Hirado, and his retainers welcomed the newcomers in a friendly manner. Capt. Saris then left Hirado on December 5 (o.s.).

The English Factory at Hirado Although the exact location is now not clear, the English borrowed a house from Andrea Dittis (Li Tan), head of the Chinese resident at Hirado, to use for Capt. Saris' lodge, and eventually purchased it for conversion into the English factory. The original merchandize which stocked the factory amounted to £5,650 in value. Under Cocks, seven Englishmen remainded at the factory: William Adams, Tempest Peacock, Richard Wickham, William Eaton, Walter Carwarden, Edmund Sayer and William Nealson. Later two others joined: John Osterwick in 1615 and Richard Hudson as a boy around the year 1617.

At the beginning of 1614, the central factory at Hirado established a representative agency at Nagasaki; despatched Wickham to Edo where he was to supervise the subordinate agencies at Suruga and Uraga; stationed Eaton at Osaka from where he was to oversee his

Japanese sub-agents at Sakai and Kyōto (Miaco); and commissioned Sayer to establish a post at Tsushima, for trading with Korea, a task at which he failed. Although the venture to Cochinchina by Peacock and Carwarden in 1614 was a complete disaster, the first three years at Hirado saw the English working hard to establish the factory, improve its facilities, and welcome three ships from England: the *Hozeander* in September 1615, the *Thomas* and the *Advise* in July, 1616, in addition to the junk *Sea Adventure,* which returned from her voyage to Siam with Adams and Sayer on board in July 1616.

For the second three years, however, the English factory, as Dr. Ludwig Riess once said, suffered from a state of humiliation. In 1616 the *de facto* ruler Ieyasu died and Cocks journeyed to Edo to seek from the new ruler Hidetada confirmation of the existing English trading privileges, only to learn that the shogunate had restricted the trading activities of the Dutch and English merchants to Hirado and Nagasaki. In the following year, the *Advise* came again from Bantam and brought a new message from James I to Ieyasu. Cocks visited Fushimi to present this message to Hidetada, who had come to see the emperor, and to petition to have the restrictions removed. But Hidetada chose not to reply either to the letter addressed to the deceased Shōgun or to the petition. Cocks was confronted with a "Hobson's choice." (Cf.: Letter dated October 1, 1616). Moreover, the Dutch, who at that time prevailed in the Eastern seas under the governorship of Jan Pieterszoon Coen, caught and *in bravado* brought to Hirado the English ships the *Attendance* (August 1618) and the *Solomon* and the *Swan* (September 1619). These events accelerated the Dutch-English rivalry at Hirado, and even led to occasional outbreaks of violence. Despite Cocks' repeated protests against the Dutch to Japanese officials at Edo (in 1618) and at Kyōto (in 1619), the shogunate would not meddle with the cases outside the country. In 1617, Adams, Nealson, and Capt. Whaw (Hua-u), the brother of Andrea Dittis and the person upon whom Cocks relied to obtain privileges for the China trade, died in Hirado.

The tension between the two nations in Hirado subsided temporarily when the English and Dutch Companies concluded a union against the Catholic nations in the East in July 1619. News of this reached their representatives in Hirado one year later, when in July 1620 the Fleet of Defence, despatched from Batavia, arrived off Japanese waters. This fleet, composed of five English and five Dutch vessels, used Hirado as its base and conducted two expeditions; the first from January to July, 1621, and the second from November, 1621 to July, 1622. This brought new life to the factory at Hirado. But the underlying rivalry between the two nations, which continued unabated and which saw the Dutch increasingly gaining superiority, caused the Batavian Council of Defence in August, 1622, to end their participation in joint fleet activities and to reduce the portion of commercial activity delegated to the English factory at Hirado. Upon receipt of that decision, the fleet at Hirado was disbanded, but Cocks hesitated to leave Hirado before receiving instructions from London and collecting debts which amounted to £3,200. When the Amboina Incident of February, 1623, suddenly forced the Englishmen to yield ground in the Eastern seas, the Batavian council decided on April 25, 1623 (o.s.), to dissolve the factory, and in July the *Bull*, captained by Joseph Cockram, arrived at Hirado with the orders, dated May 22. Cocks and the three remaining members closed the business of the factory on December 23, 1623 (o.s.; January 3, 1624, n.s.) after empowering the Dutch to receive the debts and entrusting to the Matsura the maintenance of the factory estates. On the following day, the four men left Japan on board the *Bull*.

Richard Cocks and his Diary The date and the place of Richard Cocks' birth are not known for certain, but from his own statements it seems likely that he was a native of Coventry, Warwickshire. He joined the London Company in 1600 and enjoyed the patronage of Sir Thomas Wilson. Before Cocks came to Japan he stayed at Bayonne in southern France from 1603 to 1608. He almost certainly must have been older than fifty at the time of his arrival in Japan in 1613, for in a letter dated November 30, 1613, he writes that he is now old and for years has been preparing to come home. Cocks was, more or less, a contemporary of Shakespeare (1564–1616).

Cocks remained in Japan until 1623(o.s.) when the council in Batavia, alarmed over his refusal to obey their orders to suspend activities at Hirado, summoned him to stand trial. In February, 1624, the Court at Batavia ordered Cocks to return to London to stand judgement in front of the Court of Directors, and further specified that all his property was to be seized upon his arrival home. Cocks left Batavia on board the *Ann Royall* early in 1624, but died on board ship on March 27, 1624 (o.s.).

In addition to his letters written from time to time, Cocks probably kept books at Hirado and those must have been brought back to Leadenhall Street in London. But almost all the records concerning the Japanese trade have been lost. As early as 1824, when Pieter Pratt of the Company compiled a history of Japan, the extant portion of Richard Cocks' diary, as at present, consisted of two portions; one covering June 1, 1615 to January 14, 1619, and the other covering December 5, 1620, to March 24, 1622. These two portions contain little information concerning the establishment of the factory at Hirado, the circumstances surrounding the death of William Adams, or the last days of the factory. Only copied extracts remain for the six days before his departure from Hirado. At some unknown time, the British Museum purchased the manuscript, bound in two volumes, and maintained it among their holdings (Additional MSS 31, 300 and 31,301). Recently it was transferred to the British Library. The volumes contain, respectively, the entries for June 1, 1615–July 5, 1617 on 210 leaves, and those for July 6, 1617–March 24, 1622 on 242 leaves of Japanese paper, 35cm long and 22.5cm wide. They bear no signature, but are obviously a holograph of Richard Cocks himself.

However much Cocks' conduct has been criticized since his own times, his honest character and assiduous and faithful observations make him a "not unamusing diarist" (Thompson), for both the general reader and the professional historian. As early as 1850 the first publication of the Hakluyt Society, Thomas Rundall's *Memorials of the Empire of Japan*, contained some excerpts from the diary, and thanks to the skilled efforts of Edward Maunde Thompson of the British Museum, a comprehensive edition was published by the same society in 1883 under the title *Diary of Richard Cocks, Cape-merchant in the English Factory in Japan, 1615–1622 with Correspondence,* in two volumes. This edition included an excellent introduction by the editor. (Burt Franklin in New York recently published an undated reprint edition.) In 1889 Naojirō Murakami reproduced Thompson's book and appended his own additional notes and documents. Many scholars have used these editions, and the Historiographical Institute in particular has relied on the Murakami edition for its publication of the "Chronological Source Books of Japan."

E. M. Thompson did not think it necessary to print the entire manuscript. He omitted those entries which had absolutely no interest to him and mentioned only once, in his "Preface," the memoranda of sales and purchases. In addition, Thompson omitted almost all entries on daily weather, many accounts on minor local events, and some words illegible or not fit to print, as well as all marginal notes except for those mentioned in his own footnotes. Perhaps in all, the Thompson edition contains only three fifths of the diary entries. Thus historians have long awaited the publication of a complete edition of the diary.

Since this present edition is prepared especially for scholarly use, the editors have adopted more strict conventions than suggested by the British scholars, as seen in the Remarks. In the preparation of new footnotes, those printed in the preceding editions have been consulted and many of them have been cited. However, the references to the relevant contemporary documents given by Murakami have been completely omitted, since they can be found in Murakami and Murakawa, *eds. Letters written by the English Residents in Japan 1611–1623* (Tokyo, 1900) and in other works.

Finally the editors wish to express their deep gratitude to Dr. Seiichi Iwao, Member of the Japan Academy, for his valuable advice before and during the process of editing of this transcription.

REMARKS

In this transcription, the editors have endeavoured to keep the original style and appearance of the manuscript and to retain the original spellings, although they have made some minor changes in the interest of uniformity. The following are the important editorial conventions.

1) Although the basic text is composed of a continuing series of daily entries and a year usually begins in late March, the editors, in the interest of clarity, have separated months by triple spacing and have separated the calendrical years with January.

2) Standard modern English punctuation is used throughout, even if the text frequently bears oblique lines and ambiguous periods.

3) The serial numbers appended by a librarian at the top of each folio have been deleted, and in their place, the end of an original page is indicated by unified marks such as [*fol. 110r.*]⏌. The spelling of the names of months given by the author as the running head differs from page to page, but the editors have adopted one of them for each month.

4) Standard modern English capitalization is used throughout, although the author indifferently used capitals or small letters at the beginning of words.

5) Efforts have been made to preserve the original style of abbreviation of words or parts thereof by using a special setting such as &, &c., cont'g, del'd, del'r, del'y Eng'sh, Eng'd, foll'g, foll'th, paym't, pos., viz., w'ch, w'th; Bantā, Cop̃, entertaynm̃t, fathō, grēt, marmā, etc.

6) The superscriptions and abbreviations of par, per, pre and pro are transcribed throughout by using an apostrophe without adding any appropriate vowels and brackets, *e.g.*: p'r, p'rte, p'rcell, y'rdes, pap'r, pepp'r, ap'reth, pr'sent, pr'vition, etc., except for such words as bettr, Hollandrs, lettr, remembr, ther, tymbr, etc.

7) Superscriptions have been neglected in many cases, *e.g.*: Capt., carp'ters, complem'to, Jor., pec., *pico.*, rec., Ric'd., S'r, w'ch, w'th,

(xv)

Wor'll, etc., but they are retained in the limited cases of acc?, Jn?, Matie, N?, N?erly, S?erly, Rs?, etc.

8) The letter y used for i and the (*e.g.*: yf, yt, yentent), and those of i, u and v used for j, v and u (reioice, subiection, cloue, cvntrey, vtterly) and the double f at the beginning of some words (ffayre, *ffoy ffone*) have been retained as they appear in the manuscript, except for i at the beginning of a word (Japon, *jurebasso* for Iapon, *iurebasso*).

9) The names of ships and the words of foreign origin have been italicized, *e.g.*: th'*Adviz*, the *Hozeander*; *bongew, caboque, Nifon catange; gantas, jurebasso, alias, vt svpra*, etc., with some exceptions such as armado, caualero, le, padre, poz., viz., etc.

10) Numerals and units of money, weight, measure, etc. have been faithfully transcribed, except for such Roman numerals as i, i0, ii, i00, iii, etc. used for 1, 10, 11, 100, 111, etc.

11) Identification of proper names or historical terms and research of terminology have been annotated in footnotes to a certain extent. Quotations from the two editions of the *Diary* of 1882 and 1899 and Yule and Burnell's *Hobson-Jobson: A glossary of colloquial Anglo-Indian words and phrases*(1903)are cited in the footnotes respectively as Thompson, Murakami and *Hobson-Jobson*. The proper names entered in the text have not been standardized in this transcription.

12) A special set of brackets [ ] has been employed in this transcription in order to indicate the editors' judgement on the incomplete words or entries as well as missing or illegible portions of the original text, *e.g.*: accompa[n]yng, brough[t], crue[l], Matt[ing]a, sin[c]e, the[y], v[i]-zet, etc., although some of the abbreviated words easily read are transcribed without this kind of addition (arivall, comition, Duch, mad, m'rchnt, milstons, ostis, wherin, wherof, etc.). The mark [*sic*] means the preceding word or words are transcribed as found in the text, although it seems mistaken or doubtful, *e.g.*: were [*sic*], sane [*sic*], bris [*sic*]. The repeated word at the beginning of a page is also treated in this manner.

13) The spaces originally left within the entries have been retained and indicated in the footnotes.

DIARY OF RICHARD COCKS
1615–1622
Vol. I
June 1, 1615–Dec. 31, 1616

[1]615

The Journall or dailye [b]ook of al[l] accurrant[es] happenyng, begvn at Firando in Japon, p'r me Ric'd Co[c]ks, le 1th day of June 1615, *stilo vetri*.[1]

---

1) Cocks used the Julian calendar while other nations in Japan had adopted the Gregorian. This date of June 1, 1615, *stilo vetri*, corresponds with June 11, 1615, *stilo novo*, or in Gregorian calendar, and the 15th day of the fifth month, the 1st year of Genna 元和元年五月十五日 in Japanese lunar calendar. This page bears, in addition to the original title, the signs "Book Letter C" by the same hand and "I" by a modern hand, and also an *ex-libris* seal of "British Museum," the former owner of the text.

[1615]

June 1615.

1. This mornyng littell wind N̊ erly, fayre wether all day, but a fresh gale most p'rt of day as aboue said, but calme p'r night.

9 carp'ters.
31 labo'rs.
1 mat maker.
5 gret postes.
1 bar gold.

This day 9 carp'ers and 31 labo'rs, 1 matt maker. And we bought 5 greate square postes of the kinges[2] m[aste]r car-p'ter; cost 2 *mas* 6 *cond'ns*[3] p'r peece. And I del'd vnto Nicholas Martyn one small bar gould, cost eight Riall of

6 *ta*. 8 *ma*.

eight[4] and a halfe, is six *taies* eight *mas*, for w'ch he is an-

1 bar gold.
55 *taies*.

swerable. Also I del'd a great bar gold, poz. fowre *taies* & fowre *mas* & two *condrins*, rated at fyftie and five *taies* as yt cost, & is to send to Capt. Whowe, the Capt. Chinas brother,[5] at Langasaque;[6] to geue in a pr'sent at a christn-ing as apereth p'r advice.

2 *mas*. 6 *con*.

Also I paid p'r Mr. Nealson for washing lynen, two *mas*

---

2) The then ruling Lord of Firando (Hirado 平戸) was Figena Samma, or Mat-sura Takanobu, *Hizen-no-kami* 松浦肥前守隆信. Hizen was the province, where Saga, Omura, Hirado and Nagasaki were located.

3) Cocks usually reckons in the Japanese currency as *taies*, *mas* and *condrins*, based on the Chinese and Malay weight and money. The *tael* or *liang* (*ryo* 兩) was the trade-name of the Chinese ounce, one sixteenth of a *catty* (*kin* 斤) and of the Chinese money of account. The *mace*, derived from Javanish and Malay *mas*, was adopted to designate the tenth part of the Chinese *tael* of silver, and *condrin*, from Malay *kanduri*, to designate the hundreth of the same. These two were called in Japan as *momme* 匁 and *bu* 分. Cocks puts the *tael* at five shillings.

4) The real of eight, often abbreviated as Rs. of 8, was a Spanish dollar of exchange.

5) The Captain China, Li Tan 李旦 by name, is mentioned by the English re-sidents as Andrea Dittis. Captain Whowe 華宇 was his brother.

6) Nagasaki 長崎.

5

June 1615

for washing
lynen.
ta. ma. co.
6: 8: 0
Mr. Wickam
arived at
Firando, &
junck at
Goto lost
voyage.

6 *condrins*, and I rec. back frõ Nicˢ Martyn the same day,
six *taies* eight *mas* in plate of barse for the small barr gould,
del'd as aboue said. And late w'thin night Mr. Wickham
arived here in company of Damian Marines, & brought
word the junck was at Goto,⁷⁾ they being put frõ Liquea⁸⁾
to haue proceeded on their voyage for Syam; but, being at
sea, the vnruly company would haue gon for Cochinchina,
& so Mr. Wickham standing against it, remembring our
former losse theare (as I gaue hym in comition), they retorned back for these p'rtes. Capt. Adames⁹⁾ hath wrot me
that the boateswaine and carpenter are in most falte, being
mvtenouse knaues, &c.

2. This mornyng faire calme wether, but after a fresh gale,
wind Nºerly most p'rte of the day, littell wind p'r night *vt
supra*; still fayre wether.

11 carp'ters.
39 labo'rs.
1 mat mak.
2 letters frõ
Capt.Adames
& Ed. Sayer.
Pr'sents.

Frõ Damian.

This day, 11 carp'ters and 39 labo'rs & 1 mat maker.

Capt. Adames & Ed. Sayer wrot me 2 lettrs frõ Goto of
30th May; & Mr. Adames sent me a bag of potatos, & Ed.
Sayer sent me a pece lik lynen (or rather silk) & the lyke to
Mr. Eaton & Mr. Nealson. & Mr. Wickham gaue me a jarr
of potatos. And Damian Marines brought me a dish of
plantians and an other of pottatos, &c.   [*fol. 2r.*]

A lettr frõ
Jnº de
Lieuano.
To Bongo
Dono.

I rec. a lettr frõ Jnº de Lieuano, the Spaniard. And Mr.
Wickham went & viseted Bongo Dono,¹⁰⁾ and carid hym a
pr'sent of 2 peec. Liquea cloth and a dish of pottatos; &
tould hym how matters stood about our junck, and w'thall
asked his counsell, wether it were best to let our junck stay

---

7) Islands of Gotō 五嶋.

8) Loo-choo or Ryūkyū 琉球.

9) William Adams (1564–1620), with the Japanese name Miura Anjin 三浦按針,
which meant a pilot enfeoffed at the Peninsula of Miura.

10) Matsura Nobuzane, *Bungo-no-kami* 松浦豊後守信實, Lord of Firando's great
uncle. *Dono* 殿 is a title of respect appended to the name.

at Goto to be trymbd, or else to bring her for Firando. & his opynion was (as may others are the lyke & among the rest my selfe)[11] that it is best to bring her for Firando,[12]

for diverse occations. We had news to day that Ogosho Samme[13] hath taken the fortres of Osekey[14] & overth[r]own the forses of Fidaia Samma.[15] Others say that most of the forses of Fidaia Samma issued out of the fortrese, & sallid out 3 leagues towardes Miaco,[16] but were encountred p'r the Emperours forses, & put to the worse, many of them being slaughtred and the rest driven back into the fortresse, &c.

Bongo Dono sent a bark this day to Crates[17] to bring hym the certenty of the news.

3.   This mornyng fayre wether w'th a fresh gale wind N°erly wind, so remeaned all day, the lyke p'r night; or rather calme, still faire wether, &c.

This day 13 carp'ters and 33 labo'rs.

I sent back the bark for Goto to the junck, & wrot 3 lettrs, viz., to Capt. Adames, Ed. Sayer, and Jn° de Lieuano and sent w'th it, viz.:–

4 barilles wyne . . . .[18]

---

11) This closing parentesis is put after "the lyke" in the original.

12) See 2) above.

13) Ōgosho Samma 大御所様 is Tokugawa Ieyasu 徳川家康, the founder of the Tokugawa shogunate created by order of the Mikado in 1603 (reign: 1603–1605). Samma, Samme or Sama is a title of respect also appended to the name. Cocks and other foreigners used to call the shogun "the Emperour."

14) Osaka 大坂. Cocks renders this place name as Osakay, Osekay, etc.

15) Toyotomi Hideyori 豊臣秀頼, son of the famous Hideyoshi 秀吉. Hideyoshi is better known as Taikō Sama 太閤様.

16) Miyako 都 or Kyoto 京都.

17) Karatsu 唐津.

18) Prices for this and the following articles are not entered. Hereafter, when the appropriate figure or word is wanting in the original, the editors leave the space as it is and put the words "Not entered" in the footnotes.

1 sack rise, cont'g 32½ *gentes* .... •
1 bundell canes, cont'g 32 .... •
25 matten to cover bark .... •

12 loves bread ⎱
1 pec. bacon ⎰ to eate way .... •

3 lettrs.

And I wrot 3 lettrs, viz., 1 to Capt. Adames, 1 to Ed. Sayer, and a therd to Jnᵒ. de Lieuano. And I thought good to note downe that a padre or Jesuist came to the English howse & said his name was Tomas and a Bisken p'r nation, & gaue it out he was a m'rchnt; & others gaue hym the name of Capt. Yet I knew what he was, haueing seene hym in this howse before, &c. He beged a littell allowaies of me, w'ch I gaue hym, [*fol. 2v.*]⏌ as I did the like when he wa[s here] before. For yow must vnderstand that these p[ad]res haue all the gifte of beging, & allwais answer:*"Sea, por l'amor de Dios."* This is a generall note to know them by, for they canot so counterfet, but that word will still be thrust out. This padre, Tomas (or Capt.), tould me that they stood in dowbt yt[19] the King of Shashma[20] would destroy Langasaque & bring all these p'rtes beloe Shiminaseque[21] vnder his subiection, as being geven hym p'r Fidaia Samme; but I beleeue it not, for now word is com on a sudden that all the streets must be made cleane, for that the King of Shashma is expected to be heare this night, he being bound vp w'th greate forces. And I receved 2 lettrs frō Jorge Duros & Capt. Garrocho frō Langasaque w'th wordes of complem'to. And ther was del'd to the China *jurebasso* p'r Capt. Chinas order, 1 *mas* w't in Priaman gould to pay 15 *mas* wight in silver. And I took 2 *mas* wight

Newes.
A lettr to
Jorge Durois
p'r Lv.
Martin.

A letter frō
Jorge Durois
& 1 frō Capt.
Garrocho.
1 *mas* w't
gould.
2 *mas* w't
mor. gould.

---

19) This "yt" must be "that," like "ye" for "the," while many others evidently represent "it," like "yf" for "if."
20) Satsuma 薩摩. The Lord of Satsuma was named Shimazu 嶋津.
21) Shimonoseki 下關.

out for my owne vse, but after put it in againe, &c.

Sonday.

4.   This mornyng faire calme wether, but after a stiffe gale, wind for a tyme at S? E'erly w'th rayne, after variable to N? W., yet faire wether all night.

13 carp's.
25 labo'ers.
40 bordes.
04 sq. postes.

This day 13 carp'ters and 25 labo'ers.

We bought 40 boardes at 5 p'r *mas*, small plate; and 4 *cacas*[22] at 12 *condrs*. peec. small plate. And about nowne we had news that the King of Shashma was coming into this road w'th 500 barks full of souldiers; soe we laid out a pr'sent for hym as followeth, viz.:–

A present to ye King of Shashma.

	ta.	ma.	co.
3 pec. rich damasks of Lankin,[23] cost			
16 *taies* p'r peec., is 48:	48:	0:	0
10 pec. byrams nill of 15 Rs. p'r *corge*,[24] is....05:	05:	6:	4
10 pec. red zelas, of 12 Rs. p'r *corg*, is.........04:	04:	8:	0
10 pec. whit baftas, viz., 6 of 11, & 4 of			
9 Rs. *corg*, is.............................04:	04:	0:	8
10 pec. of duttis,[25] of 12 Rs. p'r *corge*.........04:	04:	8:	0
Som totall amontes vnto 67:	67:	3:	2

Soe, Mr. Wickham accompa[n]ying me, we went and del'd the pr'sent, w'ch he took in good p'rte, offring our nation favorable entertaynm't yf we came to traffick in his domynions. I put out a word how the Liqueans refused to let vs trym our junk to haue pr'ceaded [*fol. 3r.*]] fr[om] thence on our voyag for Syam; but he said littll therto, but answered at his retorne he wold talke w'th me & geve me a pr'sent. I said I had receved suffition at his highnes handes in havinge the good hap to see the face of soe mightie a king as the King of Shashma; whereat he smiled. And soe

---

22) *Kakubashira* 角柱, or *kakuzai* 角材, a square post.
23) Nanking 南京 in China.
24) *Corge*, an Indian measure of "a score," or 20 pieces.—*Hobson-Jobson*.
25) This and other materials mentioned here seem to be Indian cotton goods.— Thompson.

June 1615

we craved lycence & retorned. Bongo Dono was w'th hym before and gaue hym a pr'sent, & came from hym as we went to hym; but we had byn w'th hym before hym, yf he had not sent a boate to call vs back till he had first vizeted hym. And at pr'sent a letter is com to Bongo Dono from Faccatay,[26] wherin he is advized that the Emperour hath overthrowne the forses of Fidaia Same, soe that he, his mother, and child haue cut their bellies; but that his wife is sent back to her father Shongo Samme,[27] King of Edo, & to succead in the Empire.

Newes.

5. This mornyng drowsie wether, w'th a fresh gale, wind at N? W., but after vered N?erly; fayre wether all day, and the lyke all night following, w'th a fresh gale of wind.

14 cap'ters.
13 labo'rs.
2 letters to
Jorge Durois.
2 bordes.
Newes.

This day 14 carp'ters, and 13 labo'rs. I sent 2 lettrs to Jorge Durois and Capt. Garrocho. We bought 2 long boardes, cost 3 *mas* the 2 bordes. And there came letters from the King of Firando to Bongo Dono, that it is true that the Emperoure hath ouerthrowne the forcese of Fidaia Samme, and taken the fortres of Osekey, & entred into it the 6th day of this moone, Fidaia Samme & his mother w'th his sonne having cut their bellies, &c. Mr.

To Oyen Dono.

Wickham went and viseted Oyen Dono,[28] and carid hym a dish of pottatos and a peec. of Liquea cloth. His brother retorned frõ aboue, whiles[t] Mr. Wickham was theare, &

2 pec.
candequis
nill of 4.
5 bas tyn.

confermed these newes to be true. And ther was taken to del'g [*sic*] mattes, 2 peec. candequis nill of 4 Rs? p'r *corg*. And the China Capt. had 5 bars tynne del'd to hym, poz. [29] rated at the cattie, &[c]. [*fol. 3v.*]⌋

---

26) Hakata 博多.
27) Shōgun Sama 將軍樣. The present shōgun was Tokugawa Hidetada 秀忠 (reign: 1605–1623), the son and heir of Ieyasu. Hideyori's wife and Hidetada's daughter was Sen-hime 千姫.
28) Ōi Dono 大炊殿, secretary to the Lord of Firando; surname unknown.
29) This space and the following one, not entered.

June 1615

6. This mornyng fayre wether w'th a fresh gale, wind N°er-
ly all day, but calme most p'rte of the night still faire
wether, &c.

12 carp'rs.
19 labo'rs.

This day 12 carp'ters, and 19 labo'rs.

And I wrot an other letter to Jorge Durois to look out for
a marchnt to buy our wheate, ʼas also of the confermyng
the newes from aboue. There was 1 of the King of Shashmas
barkes, cast away coming in, but all the men saved. We
bought 1 *caca* or squar post, cost 1 *mas*. We del'd or sent to
keep to Capt. China 51 bundelles great canes, cont'g in
each one 30 canes.

1 squar post.
51 bundes
cans.

7. This morninge faire calme wether, & after very littell (or
no wind) N° all day, and calme p'r night; still faire wether,
&c.

11½ carp'trs.
30 labo'rs.
2 til'ers.
50 *taies*.
A frire
called
Apolenario.

This day 11½ carp'ters and 30 labo'rs and two tilors.

And I del'd fyftie *taies* in plate bars to Mr. Nealso[n] to pay
carp'ters and labo'rs. And after dyner came a Franciskan
frire, called Padre Appolonario, whom I had seene 2 or 3
tymes in Firando heretofore. He was in the fortres of Osekey[30] when it was taken, and yet had the good happ to
escape. He tould me he brought nothing away w'th hym
but the clothes on his back, the action was soe sudden;
& that he marveled that a force of aboue 120000 men (such
as was that of Fidaia Samme) should be soe sowne overthrowne. He desired me for God's sake to geue hym somthing to eate, for that he had passed much misery in the
space of 15 daies, since he dep'rted out of the fortres of
Osekey. So, after he had eated, I gaue hym 15 *mas* in plate;
and soe he dep'rted. We had 1830 tiles this day for ston
walles.

15 *mas*.
1830 tiles.

30) In addition to this Franciscan friar, two Jesuit priests, Balthasar de Torres
and Giovanni Batista Parro, one Franciscan, one Augustin and two native
Japanese clergy were present in Osaka at the time of the fall of the castle.

11

June 1615

8. This mornyng fayre calme wether, & littell or rather no wind N̊.erly most p'rte day, but night calme, still faire wether, &c.

10 carp'ters.
28½ labo'rs.
1 tilor.
Shashmas retorne.

This day 10 carp'ters, 28½ labo'rs and 1 tilor.

Yt is said the King of Shashme hath geven order to his people to retorne back for their cvntrey; I meane the most p'rte of them, the rest he keepeth to carry along w'th hym

4 sqr. post.

to goe vizet the Emperour. We bought 4 *cacas*, cost 7 *condrins* p'r peec., small plate, &c.   [*fol. 4r.*]]

I sent to borow 4 or 5 *gantes*[31] of oyle of Yasimon Dono,

Nota.

because I could get non in any other place. But he reto'rd answer he had non, when I know, to the contrary, he

A lettr to Jo: Durois.

bought a p'rcell out of my handes the other day. And I wrot a lettr to Jorge Durois to take heed he gaue out no yll re-

20 spars.

portes of Safian Dono. We bought 20 spars (or rayles) at 5½ p'r a *mass* small plate, and the China Capt. lent vs

6 *gantas* of oyle.

6 great mesurs (or *gantas*) of oyle, to repay as much. And Semi Dones[32] steward came in the abcense of his m.ʳ

3 *tais* bar.

to borow a bar of plate of 3 *taies* w[igh]t, w'ch was lent hym.

9. This mornyng still calme fayre wether & littell wind, no (or rather) non at all, the rest of the day & the night calme; still faire wether, &c.

12 carp'trs.
23 labo'rs.
50 boardes.
A letter frō Ed. Sayer.

This day 12 carpenters and 23 laborers.

We bought 50 boardes at 5 p'r a *mas* small plates. Late w'thin night I receved a lettr frō Ed. Sayer, dated in the Roade of Casnora[33] in the Iland of Goto, the 7th currant, wherin he writ the junck wold com away for this towne of

---

31) *Gantes* or *gantas*, a dry measure equal to about the gallon, derived from Malay *gantan.—Hobson-Jobson.*

32) Sagawa Shumenosuke Nobutoshi 佐川主馬介信利, a minister of the Lord of Firando.

33) Kashi-no-ura樫ノ浦(?).

June 1615

Firand[o] p'r first wind. Jnº Japon brought this lettr, but
is sick of the French disease, & took vp his lodging at an
other howse.

10. This mornyng faire wether w'th a fresh gale, wind S'erly
all day, fayre wether till night & then som drops of rayne,
&c., but store p'r night, much wind.

carp'trs.
labo'rs. This day 10 carp'rs and 21 labo'rs.

A letter frō
Jorge
Durois. I rec. a lettr frō Jorge Durois, dated the 17th of June,
new stile, in Langasaque, w'th a baskit of aprecockes for
my selfe, and an other for Bongo Dono, & a therd for his
wife, w'th a p'rcell in a bag for the China Capten; all w'ch
were del'd according to advice. A Spa[niard] called Pablo
Garrocho de la Vega came to this towne of Firando to day
& brought Jorges lettrs. [*fol. 4v.*]⌡

Nota And before nowne word came that our junck was seene
w'thout. Soe I made ready to boate to goe out to Cochi to
see them put in harbor, & to vizet Capt. Adames, &c.

Sonday. 11. This mornyng much wind S'erly w'th store of rayne all
day, but not soe much p'r night, nether soe much wind,
&c.

*Sea Aduen-
tur* ariued
at Firando. Our juncke, the *Sea Adventure*, arived in the bay of
Cochi in Firando, at 10 cloth [*sic*] the last night, haveing
lost her voyage for Syam this yeare. I went abord, &
carid a barill of wyne, a quarter porke, & 10 loves bread,
w'th a box bankiting stuffe; &, p'r order of the gouerner,
carid 3 *bongews*,[34] to looke the mariners were all retorned
& had vsed their indeuours. Capt. Adames was vnwilling
we should bring any mans name in question, for geting vs
Nota. an ill report; soe I did let it pas for that tyme. But being

---

34) Perhaps *bugyō* 奉行, administrative officer or magistrate. *Bu* means "to
receive an order" and *gyō*, "to execute it." Usually the *bugyō* was the title
applied to a chief magistrate in the Tokugawa period, while in earlier times
it was widely used to describe sub-officials who conveyed masters' orders.

enformed that Damian Marines hath bought vp 8 or 10 *cattis*[35] of amber greese at Liqueas, forstalling all, that the Company could get non; whervpon I wrot a lettr to Capt. Adames to make stay of his chist, for that I wold bring the matter in question before the justice, & to same effect wrot an other letter to Damian hymselfe. And Capt. Garrocho, the Biskan, sent me a peare of crimson silk stockinges for present. And Mr. Nealson reconed w'th the carpenters, labo'rs & other mattrs bought for building since the 21th of May till this night, viz.:–

Frō Capt.
Garrocho.

ta. ma. co.
58: 1: 4.

con.

Pro tymb'r, oyle, & other mattrs as p'r
p'rticulers 14:   2:   6
Pro 457½ days labo'rs work, at 5 *con.*
p'r day 20:   4:   4
Pro carpenters wages, as p'r p'rticulers.......23:   4:   4

Som totall amontes vnto 58:   1:   4

[*fol. 5r.*]⌋

12.   This mornyng overcast wether & calme, but after a stiffe gale, wind Nº, all day fayre wether, but rayne in the later end of the night, calme.

Nota.

Damian Marines came ashore, & tould me Capt. Adames had staid his chist w'th the amber, & that he had rec. my letter, wherby he knew the occation. I answerd hym I did it for my owne discharg, he being a hired servant, & therfore, p'r the lawes of God & man, ought to look out for the benefite of them w'ch gaue hym meate, drynke, & wages. & by fortune Capt. Garrocho was in company when I debated the matter w'th hym. Soe I referred the matter to hym and Capt. Adames to make an end of it, & I to stand to what they ordayned; & soe wrot to Capt. Adames what was

---

35) 160 *mas* make a *catty* or *kin* 斤, 100 *catties* made a *picul*, to which the character 擔 was applied.

14

determened betwixt vs, but wished hym to take true notis how many *cattis* amber he had, & to keepe pocession of it, &c.

Nota.

I vnderstood Damian went after to Capt. Jacob Speck,[36] vnto whome (as it should seeme) he had offerd to sell all his amber; & soe he retorned abord the junck, and Capt. Speck followed hym w'th a pr'tence to vizet Capt. Adames, but rather to hvnt after amber greese. God grant Capt. Adams be not guld by them, &c.

16 barks wheate cont'g 1198 sackes, viz.:- 720 our lodg. 478 Capt. Chinas lodg.

9 labo'res.

100 Rs. 8.

I receaved 16 boates lading of wheate ashore this day, cont'g 1198 sackes, is 300 *gocos*,[37] wanting 2 sack laid out in henne meate. And Mr. Wickham brought all the m'rch'-diz ashore w'ch they had abord for the Syam voyage, but divers of our pikes had the heads stolne ofe. We had 9 labo'rs this day, viz., 6 all day & 3 at 2 *condr.* peec. And I rec. back 100 Rs. of 8 sent p'r Capt. Adames for Syam in same sort I del'd them.   [*fol. 5v.*]]

13. This mornyng calme raynie wether, or rather littell wind N.erly, after variable all pointes of compas but most p'rte of night calme; rayne all day & p'rte of night.

A lettr to Capt. Adames.

I wrot Capt. Adames how we receved 1198 sackes corne ashore yisterday, desiring hym to com ashore to end this matter of amber greese w'th Damian.

5 lobo'rs.

And we had 5 laborers to sifte white lyme.

And I receaved back of Mr. Ric'd Wickham a greate bag of plate in bars of Lucas Antonisons cont'g seven hvndred forty and eight *taies* in bars, and *fibuck*.[38] And I del'd fyftie *taies* in plate of barse to Mr. Nealson. And I rec. two *cattis*

748 *ta.*
50 *tais.*
For Company
2 *cat.* am'r.

---

36) Jacques Specx, the first head and president of the Dutch factory at Hirado, who took office from August 6, 1614 to January, 1621.

37) *Goku* or *koku* 石, a Japanese measure, equivalent to 4.96 English bushels.

38) *Haibuki-gin (haifuki-gin)* 灰吹銀, or refined silver bars. Bone ashes (*hai*) were utilized to smelt lead from ore containing gold or silver.

June 1615

Nota.
3 lettrs.

of amber greese of Mr. Ric'd Wickham, w'ch he bought for
the Wor. Company at Liquea: cost   39) the *catty*.
And I rec. 3 lettrs frō Capt. Adames, how Damian Marin set
hym at nought & wold not shew hym any amb'r; so I
retorned hym answer not to let hym cary his chist ashore,
but to bring it to the English howse, w'ch Capt. Adames

2½ cat.
am'r.

did, but Damian came not w'th it. Also I rec. 2½ *cat. cattis*
[*sic*] am. of Ed. Sayer, in halues betwixt hym & me; but he
willed me to take it all, for that he had need to vse money

Frō Mr.
Wickhā.

heare, the am. cost   40) the *catty*. Mr. Wickham
retorned me the peec. Liquea stuff I lent hym & gaue me
an other for a pr'sent & the China Capt.

18 sack
wheate.

Andrea had 18 bags whete wet [*sic*] to pay as we sell the
rest.

14.   This mornyng overcast calme wether, but after faire
sunshine wether most p'rte of the day, wind variable frō
N? to S. w'th som rayn at night, but greate store all night.

4 labo'rs.
Nota.

This day 4 labo'rs. Capt. Garrocho del'd Andrea Dittis,
the China Capt., his pap'rs of 1080 and od *taies* he owed
hym, as being suretie for an other, & left it to the said

A letter to
Jorg Daro.
& 4 sakes
whete.

Chinas discretion to pay or geue hym what he wold. I
wrot a lettr to Jorge Durois and sent hym it p'r Capt. Garrocho w'th 4 sackes of wheate to pay as we sell the rest,

ta. ma.
5: 4.
To Capt.
Garrocho.

and Mr. Nelson sent hym 5 *ta.* 4 *mas* p'r same conveance
for 2 per silck stockinges. And I sent a small bottell sallet
oyle to Capt. Garrocho. When we came to open Damians
chist, there was nothing to be fownd in it. He is a craftie
k[naue]. & soe let hym goe.   [*fol. 6r.*]⌋

Frō bot-
swaine.

The new botswayn of the junck brought me 2 Liquea
brushes, & a box of synamon of same place, the best that

---

39) Not entered.
40) Not entered.

Fro Jn.º
Japan.

ever I saw in my life. And Jn.º Japan, our *jurebasso*,[41) brought me a present of Liquea cloth, one peec. He hath byn in this place a wick, & never came into the English howse till now, but many tymes passed before the dore

Put away.

singing like a lunetike man. Soe I put hym out of the Companies service, or he rather put hym selfe out. And

8 *taies*.
ta. ma. co.
5: 4: 0.

Capt. Adames had eight *taies* in small plate del'd vnto hym p'r Mr. Nealson to lay out about reparing the junck, & Mr. Nealson put to his owne acc.º in plate bars 5 *taies* 4 *mas*.

15. This mornyng much rayne w'th littell wind S'erly, after variable, yet much rayne all day, & the lyke yet not so much p'r night, a stiffe gale wind N.º erly.

2 labo'rs.
3 *con*. pec.

This day 2 labo'res to clense the well at 3 *condrin* p'r peec.

Fro Jn.º
jurebasso.
A lettr frō
Capt.
Adames.

Jn.º Gorezan the *jurebassos* wife brought a present of Japan apels, or rather other frute lyke appelles. Capt. Adames sent me a lettr frō abord the junck at Cochi to haue the kinges m.ʳ shipp carpenter com to hym, to confer whether it were fitest to trym her at Cochi or bring her to

2 *catt*. amb'r.

Firando. Damian sent me 2 *cattis* amber p'r Capt. Adames, rated at 90 *taies* p'r *catty* resonable good, but had byn watered. And I rec. back two chistes money of Mr. Wick-

4400 *taies*.

ham, wherin he sayeth ther is aleven bagges Rs.º of 8, of 500 Rs. of 8 in eache bagg; but I opened not the chistes.

Roconguach.

16. This mornyng overcast wether w'th a stiff gale of wind N.º erly, but not soe much wind after, yet faire wether all day & forep'rte of night, rest rayne & calme.

A lettr to
Capt.
Adames.

I sent a lettr to Capt. Adames p'r m.ʳ carpent'r to Co-chi,[42) about finding out a place to trym our junck in. We took back the bar of plate, poz. 3 *tais* lent ye steward of

---

41) Interpreter; derived from Malayo-Javanese *jurubahasa*, language-master or expert of speech.

42) Kōchi-ura 河內浦, presently Kawachi in Hirado City.

June 1615

Semi Done le 8th curant and lent hym an other bar in place therof poz. 4 *ta*. 2 *ma*. 5 *con*. And I del'd 1 sack wheate to the baker, to pay in bread as we sell the rest. And I had 1 peec. Liquea cloth of Mr. Wickham to make Co. Jnᵒ of Goto a *catabra*.[43] We had much flying news to day, that

Newes.

Shongo Samme was [*fol. 6v*.]] dead. Others said it was Calsa Samme,[44] his brother. Others reported Fidaia Samme to be alive, and that many *tonos*[45] were gon to hym to take his part. But I esteem all this to be fables. Yet others geue out secretly that the Emperour ment to chang governm't of all these p'rtes, and put other *tonos* in their places. Soe that these of Firando dowbt the retorne of their

Tome, my
boy, put
away.

king. Tome, my boy, carid out his chist & thought to haue run away; but I preuented hym, yet turned hym out of dores w'th a *catabra* on his back as he entred in. He thought to haue pickt the lock of my money chist the other day, & had so wrong the wardes [*sic*] that I could not open the lock w'th my key, w'ch made me to trune [*sic*] hym out of my chamber. But he, misdowbting ferther disgrace,

Fro ye
juncks
purser.

thought to haue carid away all his ap'rell & haue geuen me the ship. The purcer of junck gaue me 10 Liquea trenchers for a pr'sent.

17. This mornyng calme rany wether, but sowne after a stiffe gale, wind Nᵒerly; but both rayne & wind ceased before nowne, & dry calme wether all night, &c.

A letter frō
Capt.
Adames.

I rec. a lettr from Capt. Adames frō Cochi, wherin he adviseth me that he hath taken counsell about the place most fittest to trym our junck in, and findeth Cochi to be the place. I del'd Mr. Richard Wickham the rich

Mr. Wickhā

---

43) *Katabira-ginu* 帷子衣, a thin summer garment.
44) Matsudaira Tadateru, *Sakonnoe-Shōshō* 松浦左近衞少將忠輝, formerly *Kazusa-no-suke* 上總介. The sixth son of Tokugawa Ieyasu.
45) *Tono* 殿. Equal to 'king' as referred to by the English residents.

18

cattan del'd
hỹ back.

cattan[46) he left in my custody at his dep'rture towarde Siam. The purcer of the junck gaue me a greate Liquea cock for a present, wh'ch I sent to Bongo Dono, he being desyrous to haue hym. I wrot Capt. Adames answer of his lettr rec. this day.

To Bongo
Dono.
A letter
to Capt.
Adames.

1175 sackes
wheate.

And I sould 1175 sackes wheate (brought frō the Liqueas) vnto Damian Marin, at 3 *mas* p'r sack, cont'g 25 *gantes* Liquea measure, to be paid in amber grees, at 115 *taies* the catty, to take 5 *cattis*, & pay the rest in ready money.

Not del'd.

	ta.	*ma.*	*co.*
The wheate amo[n]tes to 352:	5:	0	
5 *cattis* amb'r at 115 *tais* p'r *catty*,			
amontes to 575:	0:	0	
2 *cattis* amb'r at 90 *tais* p'r *catty*,			
amontes to 180:	0:	0	
Som totall, 7 *cattes* amber greese,			
amontes to 755:	0:	0	

[*fol. 7r.*]」

Sonday.

18. This mornyng calme overcast wether, but after littell wind variable w'th som rayne in the after nowne.

Frō Capt.
Adames.

Capt. Admes came ashore to dyner, having vnrigged the junck at Cochi. He gaue me a present of 3 nestes *gocas*,[47) w'th their trenchers & ladells of mother of perle, w'th 10 spoons same, and a peec. of white Liquea cloth. I rec. a

A lettr frō
Jor. Durois.

lettr frō Jorge Durois, dated in Langasaque, le 22th of June, new stile, wherin he advized me that no one man would buy all our wheate till the shiping came frō the Manillias. He wrot me that aboue 2600 persons are dead in Langasaque this yeare of the small pox, amongst whome his boy Domingo & a woman slaue are two, since he wrot

125 Rsọ 8.

me his last letter. And I del'd 125 Rsọ of 8 to Ed. Sayer w'th

---

46) *Katana* 刀, a sword.
47) *Gōki* 合器, or dishes which fit into each other.

June 1615

7 *ta.* 6 *mas* in 2 bars plate, is 107 *ta.* 6 *mas*, wherof he borowd 125 Rs? of Capt. Adames at Liquea to lay out for the amber greece.

19. This mornyng calme overcast wether, but after littel wind variable, fayre wether all day & the like most p'rte of night till towardes mornyng, & then som rayne, calme wether.

I wrot a lettr to Mr. Eaton sent p'r sea *bongew*. The contentes apeare p'r coppie. Also I wrot other 2 lettrs in Japon to our 2 hostes at Osekey & Sackey in kynd wordes, hoping they haue dealt well w'th vs in saveing our goods, though the towns be burned. I tooke a garden this day and

planted it w'th pottatos brought frō the Liquea, a thing not yet planted in Japan. I must pay a *tay* or 5 sh[illing]s

str. p'r ann? for the garden. And we bought forty *gants* of shark oyle for the junk, cost 1 *mas* and two *condrins*

the *gant*. And one of the mareners of the junck brought me 2 fishes for a present.   [*fol. 7v.*]

20. This mornyng overcast calme droping wether, most p'rte of the affore nowne littell wind N?erly, fayre wether after nowne, and the lyke all night calme.

And I del'd fyftie *taies* in plate of bars to Mr. Nealson, and ther was taken of the war'hōse to make Symon, the

negro, aparell & shertes, viz.:–

2 pec. rotten & roteaten dutis, of 10 & 12 Rs. *corg*.

1 pec. baftas, of 8 Rs? p'r *corg*, spoted.

2 pec. fitcas, of 4 Rs. p'r *corg*.

1 pec. alleja cottong, of 10 Rs. p'r *corger*.

Also Ed. Sayer had 2 pec. baftas of 12 Rs. p'r *corg* to make hym shertes of, rated to hym at 2 *taies* 5 *condrin*.

I sent a lettr to Capt. Adames to Cochi, w'th 6 lovs bread, desyring to know how much shark oyle we shall want for

our junck. We bought 11 square postes, cost 8 *mas* 2 con-

drin, and 18 *gantes* shark oyle at 1 *mas* 2 *con.* p'r *gant.* And we receaved

	ta.	mas
4 *cattes* 4 *taies* 2 *mas* wight		
amber greese, of Damian, cost 490:		1
w'th 2 *cattis* before rated at	180:	0
Som totall amontes, vnto	670:	1
	352:	5
	217:	6

I gaue hym a bill of my hand for soe much money owing hym, to rec. our wheate at price before made, & rest in ready money.

And news came frõ King Firando that he arived at Miaco the 18th of the last moone, and was admitted avdience w'th the Emperour the 20th, whoe vsed hym in all kindnes, w'ch causeth much rejoysing here. Also the Emperour hath geven order into all partes of Japon to look out for such as escaped out of the fortres of Osekey when it was burned. Soe that prive enquirie was mad in all howses in Firando what strangers were lodged in eache howse, and true notis thereof geven to the justice. Yt is thought the padres at Langasaque & else where will be narrowly looked after. The[y] say the taking of this fortres hath cost aboue 100000 mens lives [*fol. 8r.*]] on the one p'rte & other, and that on the Prince Fidaia Sammes p'rte no dead man of accompt is fownd w'th his head on, but all cut ofe, because they should not be knowne, to seek reveing [*sic*] against their frendes & parents after. Nether (as som say) can the body of Fidaia Samme be fownd; soe that many think he is secretly escaped. But I canot beleev it. Only the people of these Sothern parts speake as they wold haue it, because they affeckt the yong man more then the ould.

21. This mornyng fayre calme wether, & after littell wind

N.° W'erly most p'rte of the day, & calme most p'rte or all night; still fayre wether.

I sent a lettr to Capt. Adames in answer to one of his rec. yisterday frõ Cochi, wherin he advised he bought 200 *gantes* of shark oyle at Goto at 1 *mas* p'r *ganto*, wishing me to buy no more till he saw whether we had need of it or no.

I gaue Tome, my boy, a *wacadash*[48] & most p'rte of his clothes, w'th 5 *mas* in money, at the instigation of the China Capten. We had 2 labo'rs ½ a day. And Capt. Speck had 50 *cattis* tyn in 46 bars, to pay as wee sell the rest, or else to content. And Mr. Nealson paid for 23 mattes for rowmes 6 *ta*. 7 *ma*. 4 *con*., w'th 2 *ma*. 5 *con*. compr'hended for boate hier.

And I receaved a lettr frõ the *dico*[49] of Ikanoura[50] advising me he wold com or send to me to make price for plank or tymbr w'ch we should haue need of, vnto w'ch lettr I retorned answer.

Ed. Sayer put away his ould man, & entertayned Co. Jn.° my ould boy of Langasaque. One of the kings men came & tould me the p'rticulars of the news aboue, and that Fidaia Sammes mother was fownd dead, & his sonne aliue, being a child of 8 years ould, whoe was carid to the Emperour his grandfather; but the body of Fidaia could not be fownd, soe it is thought he was burned to ashes in a tower in the fortres burned. *[fol. 8v.]*

22. This mornyng fayre calme wether, and very littell wind after S'erly som p'rte of the day, the rest calme as the lyke p'r night; still fayre wether.

This day 20 labo'rs and two tilors.

---

48) *Wakizashi* 脇差, a short sword.
49) *Daiku* 大工, a carpenter.
50) *Inoura* 伊ノ浦 (?) in Ōmura 大村.

June 1615

We put Yoske the cook away, haveing ouer many laysy felloes in howse, & he 1 that could do littell or nothing, yet still rvning abroad. Mr. Nealson paid hym to cleare his

reconying, 8 ta. 7 ma. 7 condr. And we receved 50 greate tiles this day. And ther was a tay paid for a years rent potato garden. And Facheman our skullion had in [sic] p'rte of his wages paid p'r Mr. Nealson, three taies in small plate.

23. This mornyng faire calme wether, & after littell wind variable most p'rte of the day & lyke p'r night, fayre wether till break of day, and then som rayne.

This day 12 labo'rs. I sent a lettr to Jorg Durois p'r Symon jurebasso, in answer of his of 22th June, new stile, & how I had sould ye wheate to Damian Marine; & sent my clock p'r Symon to be mended; & gaue hym order buy som conserves, to invite the king at his retorne, we haueing made an end of building our howse. And ther was sould to

the China Capt. 4 per white baftas of 9 Rs. corg at one tay p'r peece.

And Miguel jurebassos wife brought Capt. Adames a catabra, a bar'll wine, & figges, for a present.

24. This mornyng droping wether w'th wind S'erly, & after much rayne all day w'th som thvnder, but littell or no rayne p'r night, yet much wynd as lyke most p'rte day.

Som of Firando barks retorned frõ Miaco, as others did the lyke into all p'rtes of Japon, only the tonos (or king) of each p'rte stay w'th the Emperour to take danco[51] or counsell of what shall be thought needfull; the souldiers being all sent home, the wars being ended. I receved my

skeane bark from the gouldsmith w'th 6 tais 6 mas in fibucq & plant [?], so now wantes 1 tay 2 mas plate in wight. Also I rec. a letter frõ our bungew Vshanuske Dono, dated in Mi-

---

51) Dangõ 談合, consultation.

23

aco le 24th of *Gongwach*[52] (or the moone past) wherin he writes me how well the Emperour receved the King of Firando his m.ʳ; & that a sonne of Fidaia Samme of 7 years ould, p'r a band woman, was put to death p'r the Emperours comand; & 100 *mas* & 150 *mas* a head [*fol. 9r.*]⌋ of all them w'ch were in the fortres; soe that dailie many are brought in and slaughterd.

Sonday.

25. This mornyng ouercast wether w'th a stiff gale, wind S'erly, rack frō W., yet fayre wether all day and the like p'r night following, &c.

Nota.

Ther passed divers boates w'th men from Fingo[53] & Shashma to goe to Osekey to make cleane the fortres, &, as it is said, they begyn to build the citties of Osekey & Sackay againe, the Emperour having geven order that yf the former owners will not forthw'th new build their howses, that any other may enter vpon the *chaune*[54] (or plot) and build vpon it.

26. This mornyng overcast wether, wind still S'erly, yet fayre wether all day and night following, littell or no wind p'r night.

8 labo'rs.
Fishmongr
run away.

This day 8 labo'rs. Our fishmong[er] is rvn away this night and hath stolne a boate of his neighbors. He was heare yisterday very ernest w'th our *jurebasso* to haue procured me to haue lent hym 10 or 20 *tais*, & in the end desyred hym to haue lent hym but one *taie*, but was deceaved of his expectation. And we bought 1 *c*. 9 *ta*. 8 *ma*. ambr greese of Mr. Wickham for the Wor. Company at 100 *catty* [*sic*] *taies* the *catty*. And soe we paid vp in 2 leaden boxes 9 *cattis* and 14 *ta*. ambr grise, viz.:–

c. ta. ma.
1: 9: 8.
ambr griser.

---

52) *Gogatsu* 五月, or the fifth moon. The 24th of *Gogatsu* corresponded to June 10, old style and June 20, new style.
53) Higo 肥後, a province next to Hizen in Kyushu.
54) *Chōnai* 町內, the neighbourhood in a town.

	c.	ta.	ma.	

N.º A.
  B.

in box N.º A: 5: 4: 2 ⎤
in box N.º B: 4: 9: 8 ⎦ is 9 *cattis* 14 *tay* wight.

Nota.

Bongo Dono sent to me to have had a jar of Liquea wyne (or rack) for that the Emperour hath sent for hym to com to Miaco, & therfore he sought for such matters to geue in present to greate men for a noueltie. All the kinges barks are com back w'th the souldiers; only the nobillety of all provinces stay w'th the Emperour. So it is dowbted ther will be trucking (or changing of kingdoms); & that w'ch maketh me the rather to belive it is the Empero'rs sending for this man who is the last man of the blood royall left behind the king, he being the kinges greate vncle and brother to the deceased King Foyne Samme,[55] [*fol. 9v.*]] and is a bursen[56] man & therefore not fit to be emploied

Nota.

in service, he being aboue 60 yeares ould. And ther was flying speeches how the Hollandrs had a man kild & much money taken in cominge downe frō Miaco; but Capt. Speck sent me word (I having first advize hym what I heard) that ther was no such matter, for that at instant he had receved a lettr frō their people that they were in a port neare vnto Shiminasaque, selling goodes, & expecting wynd & wether

A junck frō
Phillip.

to com for Firando. & ther is a Japan junk ariued at Langasaque frō Phillippinas, w'ch wintred theare the last yeare.

27.   This mornyng fayre calme wether, but after littell wind N.ºerly w'th calme all (or most p'rte) of the night; still same wether much heate.

9 labo'rs.
Foy fony.

We had 9 labo'rs. Also our junk *foney*[57] was sent to the

---

55) Matsura Shigenobu, *Shikibukyo* 松浦式部卿鎮信, posthumously named Hōin 法印.

56) Burst or ruptured.

57) *Fune* 船, a vessel; the marginal note suggests this was *hayafune* 早船, a swift boat.

June 1615

250 bags wheate.

Eng'sh howse w'th 18 ores, and seales w'th other provition as p'r p'rticulers. And we del'd 250 bages wheate to Damian

Matias frõ Miaco.

Marin and Matias the Flemyng retorned frõ Miaco to Firando; but we haue no lettr frõ Mr. Eaton, w'ch maketh me to dowbt legerdymeane. Also Chombo Donos man (a

Newes.

Caffro) came frõ Miaco w'th a lettr for Oyen Dono, and brought word his m[aste]r was coming downe for Langasaque, and that Safian Dono58) was ordayned *tono* (or king) of Arima.59) This Caffro I gaue lodging to in the Engl'sh howse w'th meate & drinke, because he was servant to such a m.r

28. This mornyng still fayre calme wether and soe remeaned all day & night following, littell or no wynd N.oerly.

[8] labo'rs.
ta. ma. con.
12: 5: 8.
50 *ta.*
500 saks
wheate.

This day 8 labo'rs and I del'd 4 bars plate to Mr. Nealson, poz. 12 *ta.* 5 *ma.* 8 *con.* And afterwardes a pap'r of 50 *ta.* plate of bars. We del'd 500 sackes of wheate to Damian Marin, viz., 440 out of our gedong & 60 out of that of Capt. China; soe we want 1 sack in our gedonge. [*fol. 10r.*]⌋

A paket lettrs frõ Syam.
2 suks frõ Syam.

And I receaved a packet of lettrs frõ Syam, viz., one from Mr. Lucas Antonison of 14th of Aprill, 1 frõ Mr. Jn.o Gourney of the 17th of Aprill.

Also 2 ould lettrs frõ Bantan, viz., 1 frõ Generall Saris of 6 February 1613, 1 frõ Georg Bale of 8th Marche, w'th an other humerous lettr to Mr. Tempest Peacock, & the lyke to Mr. Ric'd Wickham, as Mr. Bale is accustomed to doe. Ther were 2 juncks arived at Langasaque frõ Syam.

29. This mornyng still fayre calme wether, but after wind variable vering frõ N.o to S.o, & in the night a fresh gale N.oerly; still faire wether.

---

58) Hasegawa Sahyōe Fujihiro 長谷川左兵衞藤廣, governor of Nagasaki.
59) On the Shimabara 嶋原 peninsula in the province of Hizen.

June 1615

And vpon good consideration & p'r generall consent, I sent Jnº. Pheby to Mr. Eaton w'th lettrs & to accompany hym downe & procure the Emperours passe for hym, yf need required; w'ch I willed Capt. Adames to signefie vnto Codskin Dono[60] or Goto Zazabra Dono,[61] & gaue Mr. Eaton order to com away forthw'th, & bring in short endes what he could, & to chang the yello in white at Miaco. This lettr was dated the 27th, but kept till the 29th pr'sent. Also I sent 3 lettrs to our host of Edo, & hym of Shrongo,[62] w'th the 3d. for Sr. Andrea; as allso 1 for Miguel *jurebasso*.

And the brother of Sugien Dono of Vmbra[63] retorned frō the wars & brought me a pr'sent of 5 Japan fans.

And I sent an other lettr p'r Jnº. Pheby to Oshanusque Dono[64] in answer of his rec. 4 daies past frō Miaco.

Capt. Speck & Sr. Matias came to vizet me.

We had 4 labo'rs all day. Damian went for Langasaque.

30. This mornyng faire wether w'th a stiff gale, wind Nº.erly, variable to the E. and soe backwardes, but calme all or most p'rte of the night; still farie wether.

This day 2 labo'rs.

Mr. Nealson paid 10 *taies* plate bars to Jnº. Pheby, and I del'd hym my lettrs for Mr. Eaton, w'th the others for Caseror & Oshenosque Dono; & Capt. Adames wrot to Cogsque Dono & Goto Zazabra Dono, to renew or passe yf need

---

60) Honda Masazumi, *Kōzuke-no-suke* 本多上野介正純.
61) Gotō Shōzaburō Mitsutsugu 後藤庄三郎光次.
62) Suruga 駿河.
63) The word "Vmbra" (Ōmura) is written upon cancellation of another "Crats." In this diary, three persons bearing the same name Sugien Dono appear. This first one is a kinsman of a cavalero of Ōmura; the second, as seen in the entry of June 30 and others, is Matsura Shuzen Shigekata 松浦主膳重賢; and the third, is of "Crats" (Karatsu). The surnames of the first and the third are unknown.
64) Equal to Vshenusque, or Ushinosuke 丑之助, a *bongew*, surname unknown.

June 1615

Jnᵒ Yoosen.
Vnagense,
Sugien Dono.
3 pec. dittis.

require, as also to dispach Mr. Eaton away, if knaues stay hym. Jnᵒ Goosen[65] arived heare frõ Miaco, and Vnagense Dono[66] & Sugien Dono the lyke. And rec. back frõ Mr. Wickham of Syam cargezon 3 pec. rotten duttis of 12 Rs. p'r *corg*. *[fol. 10v.]*⌋

Nota.

And I sent our *jurebasso* to bid them welcom hom, as the lyke to Jnᵒ Yoosen. And sowne after Sugien Dono came to vizet me w'th a pr'sent of 10 fannes, & repeated the story of the wars, & how all the nobillety of Japon were joyned together at Miaco to viset the Emperour Ogosho Samme, w'ch was a marvelous thing to see the hudge nomber of them. Mr. Nelson rec. of Capt. Adames for m'rch'diz 4 pe. camdek mawy; 1: 3: 5.[67] And Mr. Nealson rec. 3 bars Shrongo & *nyshew*[68] plate, poz. ten *tais* 5 *mas*. And [I] del'd Mr. Nealson for his vse 1 pec. of white baftas of 12 Rs. p'r *corg* at 1 *tay* 5 *condrin*, & 4 pe. camdeque mawy of 4 Rs. *corg* for 1 *tay* 3 *mas*. 5 *condrin*.

ta. mas.
10: 5.
1 pec. bafta
4 pe. camd.
ma.

July 1615.

1. This mornyng fayre calme overcast wether; & littell wind after variable all day, still towardes night a fresh gale S'erly and so contynewd, all night much rayne.

To Bongo Dono

I went and viseted Bongo Dono, he being ready to goe for Miaco; and carid hym 2 barills *morofack*,[69] a basket of biskit, 50 roles drid bonita,[70] & 5 cords of drid cuttelfish,

---

65) Jan Joosten van Lodensteijn, named by the Japanese as Ya Yōsu 耶楊子.
66) Naizen-no-shō 内膳正 (?), captain-general of Firando, surname unknown.
67) This sentence is added between the lines by the author.
68) *Suruga nishu* or *nishū* 二朱, Japanese coins of silver or gold.
69) *Morohaku* 諸白, *sake* of finest quality.
70) *Bonito seco* (Sp.), or *katsuobushi* 鰹節.

28

he took it in good p'rte, w'th offer of many faire wordes.
I also envited Capt. Speak, Jn? Yoosen & the rest of the

Duch to
dyner.
A letter
to Figien
Samme, King
of Firando,
p'r Jn?
Pheby.

Duch to dyner to morrow. And wrot a lettr to Figien Samme,[71] the King of Firando, to Miaco, in complementall
sort, as also advising how our junk had lost her voyag to
Syam, & was retorned to Firando frõ ye Liqueo. Also, I
advised hym how ye King of Aua[72] of the race of Pegew, had
made wars 7 yeares, & in ye space gotten 8 other kingdoms,
w'ch in tymes past belonged to the Empier [sic] of Pegu;
& wantes now only to conquer Siam, Lanfu, and Camboia,
to make hym selfe a greater prince then ever any of his
ansesters was, & thought very easy to obtayne it, in respect of his valientnesse & mighty power.

Sonday

2. This mornyng much rayne w'th a stiff gale wind S'erly
but after variable, but dry wether befor it was nowne & so
contynued all day after, but rany wether p'r night.

2 lettrs.

I receved 2 lettrs frõ Capt. Garrocho, & Jorge Durois,
of the 8th & 10th currant, new stile, werin the[y] wrot
me as apeareth p'r their lettrs; but much falce news p'r
Capt. Garrochos lettr, yf my ame be not amis. And Capt.
Speck w'th Jn? Yoosen, Sr. Mat[ias], Jacob Swager, came
to dyner to day; & Jn? Yoosen told us a great history of
Ogo[sho] Samas good luck [fol. 11r.]] in pr'veling against
Fideia Samme, & that he verely thinkes he is dead in the
fortrese burned to ashes. Mr. Wickham deliverd me an

ta. m. co.
161: 2: 5.
For ambr.

accompt of Syam voyage, resting to ballance 132 ta. 3 m.
3 co., but del'd vp no money, as he spesyfied in his acc?,
becaus I owe hym for amber greese, for 1 cat. 9 ta. 8 m.
wight, at 100 taies catty T. 161: 2: 5.

3. This mornyng calme droping wether or rather a littell

---

71) See 2) above.
72) Ava, the capital of the Burmese Empire. The proper Burmese form is *Eng-wa,*
or "lake-mouth."

July 1615

wind N.ºerly, yet after variable to ye S.º yet wether much rayne, No.ʳ wind all day, but stor rayn p'r night.

2 carp'ers.
1 labo'er.
100 bordes.

This day, 2 carpenters, and 1 labo'r.

And we bought 100 boardes at 5 p'r *mas* small plate. Capt. Speck and the rest sent to thank me for their good entertaynm't, viz., *Nifon catange.*[73]

4. This mornyng fayre calme wether, but after a fresh gale,

2 carp'tr.
1½ labo'r.
Frō Jnọ
Yoosen.

wind S.ºerly most p'rte of the day, rest som small drops rayne, but dry calme wether p'r night.

This day, 2 carp'ers and 1½ laborer. Jn.º Yoosen sent me a drid salmon & divers peeces salmon in pickell for a pr'-sent.

5. This mornyng fayre calme wether, but after littell wind

2 carp's.
2 labo'rs.
2 lettrs,
viz,:-
1 to Jor
Durois.
1 to Capt.
Garro.
Nota.
6 bags rise.

variable, yet fayre wether all day & the lyke p'r night till an howre before day and then a great shewer of rayne.

This day 2 carp'ers & 2 laboreres.

I sent 2 letters to Jorge Duros & Capt. Garrocho dated yisterday, but kept till this day & sent p'r direction of Capt. China both enclozd to Jorge Durois. Jn.º Yossen came to vizet me to day, w'th 5 men wayting on hym. We bought 6 saks rise, p'r Capt. Ad. meanes, at 4 *gantos* p'r *mas* plate in bars. I and Ed. Sayer wayed the 3 *cattis* ambr we had in

7 *taies*,
want ambr.

halues, and fownd it wanted 7 *taies*, lacking 2 *mas* in wight.

.News.

Her was news (or repo'te) geven out that Tushma *tay*[74] hath burned Edo in the abcence of the Emperour, he haveing left hym pr'soner ther vnder the keeping of a yong man, for that he denied to fight against Fidaia Samme, the sonne of Ticus Samme[75] his m[aste]r. But I think this will proue a lye, as most Japon news comonly doe. [*fol. 11v.*]]

6. This mornyng calme raynie wether, littell wind after

73) *I.e.*, after the Japan fashion. *Katagi* 氣質 means turn of mind, or spirit.
74) *Tai* 隊, or troop.
75) See 15) above.

July 1615

variable most p'rte of day, much rayne but not for much p'r night, yet a stiff gale wind S'erly.

This day 2 carp'rs & 2 labo'rs.

A Japon telors wife brought me a pr'sent of pap'r. She spoake Spanish, & sought to pr'cur work for her husband.

7. This mornyng rayny wether w'th a stiff gale, wind at S. W'erly most p'rte of day, but after variable N°erly, but much rayne p'r night more then p'r day.

This day 2 carp'rs and 1 laborer.[76] Here is reports that the Emperour hath staid the King of Shashma & all the *tonos* of these p'rtes, & pr'tendeth to shifte them out of their governm'ts (or kingdoms), & put them into other provinces to the Northward, & them of the Northern parts in their places. But I rather (in p'rte) esteem it to be the escape of Fidaia Samme, whoe may ly in secret in som of their cvntreis expecting op'rtunety & their retorns; w'ch to pr'vent, he keepeth them by hym till he can vnderstand this certen

truth whether he be alive or dead. I del'd 50 *tais* in plate bars to Mr. Nealson to pay out for plankes for junk & othewaies w'ch wanted 2 *mas* in wight & had 1 bar strong & an other *nishew* plate. & is of that p'rcell sent frō Melchor van Sanfort[77] to be sent for Syam to Mr. Lucas Antoni-

son,[78] & rec. of Jn° Yoosen, we had newes that all men that entred into Langasaque were staid theare & not sufferd to retorne out of the towne. The reason is thought to be to look out for such as came out of the fortrese of Osekey; but I rather esteem it to be to serche out Fidaia Samme, w'ch is thought to be escaped.

Also, one of the king (or *tonos*) men of this place came &

---

76) The figure "1" before "laborer" is cancelled both in the text and the margin.
77) Melchior van Santvoort.
78) Lucas Antonissen.

July 1615

tould me that his mʳ had sent for 15 or 20 men of these p'rtes to com vnto hym, w'ch maketh me now yerely to think that he will be shifted out of his governm't, or kingdom.   [*fol. 12r.*]]

Extreme hot wether began.

8. This mornyng a stiffe gale, wind Nºerly w'th much rayne all the afore nowne, but dry wether after as the lyke all the night following.

Carp'ters.
20 tais.

This day 2 carp'rs, 1½ labo'rs. And ther was paid yisterday, p'r Mr. Nealson, to Yayemon Dono, the kinges ship carp'tr, in p'rte of paym't of 150 shething plankes for the junck at 4 *mas* p'r planck of 3 fathom & a halfe p'r peece. Also same tyme was del'd out of warehowse to Ed. Sayer for his vse, viz.:–

	ta.	ma.	co.
1 peec. duttis, of 12 Rs. p'r *corg*, is rated 1:		0:	0
1 peec. zela, of 12 Rs. p'r *corg* 1:		0:	00

1 pec. ditty.
1 pec. zela.

To Vnagense.

I sent Vnagense Dono 2 barilles wyne & 4 fishes, he being retoṛ frō wars, & now sick of small pox.

Sonday.

9. This mornyng fayre wether, wind still a fresh gale Nºerly most p'rte of day, but calme p'r night; continewall[y] fayre wether.

2 carp'trs

This day 2 carp'trs.

A lettr to Jº Dorois.
A Hollander slaue cut.

And I sent a lettr to Jorge Durois p'r Jnº Yoosen. I vnderstand that yisterday the Hollanders cut a slaue of theirs apeeces for theft, p'r order of justice, and thrust their *comprador* (or cats buyer) out of dores for a lecherous knaue, who, w'th hym that is dead, haue confessed of much goods (as cloues, mace, pepp'r, and stuffs) w'ch are stolne p'r consent of Jacob Swager; w'ch maketh much sturr in the Duch howse. Yet I think this cates buyer plaieth the knaue & defameth Jacob, because he was the occation he was thrust out of servyce, for haveing to do w'th his

Nota.

woman, the knaue being a marid man. Also Capt. Adames

32

July 1615

rec. a lettr frō Melchar van Sanfort frō Langasaque,
wherin he adviseth hym that a Japon wold sell vs an other
junck, & to that purpose conselled vs to lay vp ours. But I
had rather som man would buy her, for I had rather sell
then buy, for I haue enough of Japan juncks, yf I knew how
to bettr it.   *[fol. 12v.]*⌋

10.   This mornyng fayre calme wether, & very littell wynd
nether day nor night yet variable, & still faire wether.

2 China junk.   We had news of 2 China *somas*[79] arived at Goto. Soe the
China Capt. sent a boate to know whence they are.

Nota.   Also the China Capt. got Capt. Adames to write a lettr
to Damian to buy 400 sackes wheate for hym at price the[y]
cost, he haveing offerd it at same price to hym before, viz.,
at 3 *mas* p'r sack.

1 carp'ter.
5 labo'rs.
Newes.
This day 1 carp'tr and 5 laborers. And I was enformed
that Figen Samme, the king of this place, had sent a lettr
to Bunga Dono, how it was thought the Emperour would
make Chumbo Dono *bongew* of Arima, Langasaque, &
Firando, that is to say, of all these Sotherne parts. He w'ch

To Sugen
Dono.
sent me word of it was Sugen Dono of Vmbra, vnto whome
I sent a pr'sent of 2 barills wyne & 4 fishes *Nifon catange*.
And he sent his man afterwardes to thank me for it. Also

Damian frō
Langasaque.
Symon frō
Langasaque.
1 *cat.* tobaco.
Eong. Dono.
Damian retorned frō Langasaque, and Symon yt was our
jur. the lyke, & brought me my clock back. I gaue Mat. 1
[*cat.*] tobaco, cost 5 *condrins*. Bongo Dono went for Miaco
this day.

11.   This mornyng still fayre calme wether, but after littell
wind S'erly, but calme for most p'rte both day and night;
fayre wether &c.

ta. ma. co.
3: 1: 1.
1: 5: 5.
I del'd a bar plate to Jn? Gorchano *jurebasso* cont'g
3 *ta.* 1 *ma.* 1 [*co.*], wherof he paid for a *catabra* for Matinga

---

79) Small junks.—Thompson.

1 *ta*. 5 *ma*. 5 *co*.; rest due to me in great plate 1: 5: 6.

A lettr frō Capt. Garrocho.

Good news.

I rec. a lettr frō Capt. Garrocho, complementall, dated in Langasaque, le 18th of July, new stile.

The China Capt., Andrea Dittis, came to me and brought a lettr he had receaved frō his brother out of China; now our busynes consernyng procuring a trade into China was in greate hope to take effect, for that the greate men had taken 3000 *pezos*[80] pr'sented them to make way; & that at pr'sent the ould king was about to resigne vp his place to his sonne, & therefore best to let it rest a while till the ould man were out of place, or else it would be duble charg to geue to father and sonne. Also his cheefe kinsman, whoe is neare vnto the king, advised that in no hand it should not be geven out that we came out of Japon, for that [*fol. 13r*.]] that [*sic*] the hatred against Japons was worse then against any other nation; but rather to say we came directly out of England, or from Bantam, Siam, Camboia, or Cochinchina, &c.

2 labo'rs.

Newes.

Also there is a China com out of the Manillias from Cagallion, and reporteth that the Hollanders haue taken a place in the Phillippinas called Shibou; & that vpon this news, all the Spaniardes went frō Cagallion to defend Manillia, as being the place of most emportance. Also he reported that Don Juan de Silwa,[81] gouernor of the Manillias, was secretly slipt away, hearing an other was coming to take his place; but I esteem this a lye. Yet out of dowbt he is hated of the most p'rte, both Spaniardes & naturalls for his covetosnes, as having scraped a world of wealth together, he card not how, so he compassed it, as I haue byn tould by Spaniardes & others, &c.

Shibou.

12. This mornyng droping wether, calme, most p'rte of the

---

80) Dollars.—Thompson.
81) Don Juan de Silva, the Governor of the Philippine Is. (1609–16).

day, yet dry wether after a littell rayne in the mornyng, & soe fayre wether all night.

I rec. a lettr frõ Luis Martyn w'th a bar of plate cont'g 4 *ta*. 9 *ma*. 3 *co*. to bestow for hym in Azibar (or allowais Succatrin) the lettr dated in Langasaque le 18th of July,

new stile. And I sent a pr'sent to Taccaman Dono,[82] cheefe *bongew*, viz., 2 barilles wyne, 5 bundls dry cuttell, & 5 pcs. dryd bonita, w'ch he took in good p'rte.

13.   This mornyng fayre wether w'th littell wind S°erly, and soe remeaned all day and night following, faire wether.

I wrot a lettr to Mr. Eaton, p'r the purcer of our junck. Also I wrot 2 others to our hostes of Osekey & Sackey, p'r same conveance. We had much ado to apeace a dispute betwixt the Capt. China & Damian for wheate bought, but I entred pledg for China Capt.   [*fol. 13v.*]]

Capt. Speck went abord their junck to take vew of her, to sett her out before she rott. He seyeth he would send her for Syam; but I rather take it to be for the Molucos, to cary provition. He tould me also that a Portugez had wrot hym frõ Langasaque how the Viz Roy de Goa had byn at Surat w'th a power of 7000 men in many vessells, & had put all the English to the sword & spoiled the place; & this news he said came p'r way of Syam, & therfore I know it is a lye, having had lettrs frõ thence so late, and not a word thereof.

I borowd 200 *taies* in plate of bars of Capt. Adames to repay at pleasure, &c.

The Capt. China tould me his brothers greate junck was arived from Cochinchina at Langasaque.

Kitskin Dono's wife dyed this night past.

14.   This mornyng still fayre wether & wind S'erly, a fresh gale all day and the lyk p'r night, yet not soe much; still

---

82) Matsura Takuminosuke 松浦內匠助.

fayre wether.

This day 4 labo'rs to mend gadong and saw tymbr and Mr. Nealson reconed w'th smith till this day and paid hym

in small plate, 19 *taies*, 5 *mas*, 7 *condrin*.

And I del'd thre hvndred fyftie and eight *taies* to Mr.

Nealson, viz., 350 *taies* in bars & 10 Rs° of 8 is 8 *taies*. And he paid out to Damian Maryn 670 *ta*. 1 *ma*. O *co*. for 6 *cattis* 4 *ta*. 2 *mas*. whight ambr greese, viz.:-

	ta.	*ma.*	*co.*
1175 sack wheate, at 3 *mas* p'r sack, is	352:	2:	0
and in plate bars...........................	317:	9:	0
	670:	1:	0

Ther was reportes geven out that 2 shipps were seen ofe at sea neare Langasaque wherof Jn° Yooson advised Capt. Speck. Soe he sent out a penisse to look out for them; but I esteem it to be coṁon Japan news, w'ch most an end proue lyes. Yet the Duch expect a ship frõ Bantam or Molucos, besides the bark *Jaccatra* frõ Pattania & a junck.

[fol. 14r.]]

15. This mornyng still faire wether, wind S'erly, and so contynewd all day & night following; extreme hott wether.

This day 4 labo'rs as day before.

I sent Oyen Dono 2 small barilles wyne, 2 fyshes, and 30 pec. drid tuny, not having viseted hym since the king went frõ hence; but he was not at home when it came, yet sowne after came to the Eng'sh howse to geue me thankes for it, & tould me of the favorable axceptataion [sic] the king of this place had fownd in all his affares w'th the Emp'r.

Also I was advised p'r a frend in secret how the Duch were coyning falce Rs° of 8 at Langasaque, wishing me to take heede how I took any of them. & that w'ch maketh me to think it to be true is the tynne they bought of me the other day. It seemeth to me a dangeros matter, &c.

Sonday.

16. This mornyng still fayre hot wether w'th wind S'erly, all day but littell or no wind p'r night; still extreame hott weather.

2 labo'rs.
2 *taies.*

This day 2 laborers or sawyers.

I gaue a *tay* in small plate to two pore sick women of my money, the one to China woman, and the other a Japon.

8 pec. red zelus.

And ther was 8 pec. red zelas del'd & sould to Tonomon Sama[83] his man, at 1 *tay* p'r pec. 8 *tais*. And I wrot a letter

A leter to Luis Martyn.

to Luis Martin to Langasaque and sent hym a jar allowaies, N⁰ 1 poz. 6 *cat*. 4 *tay* wight gros, tare 1 *catty* 14 *taies*, rest net 4 *cattis* 10 *tay* wight, rated at 10 *tay* p'r *catty*, & sent the

1 pott allo.
No 1.

bar plate in the pott of allwaies. I meane the bar plate Luis Martin sent me to bestow in allowaies. The lettr & pott

Damian for Lang.

I sent p'r Sr. Damian, w'th som writing pap'r for Capt. Garrocho.   [*fol. 14v.*]⌋

17. This mornyng still fayre wether littell wind S'erly vering W'ward, extreme hott wether all day and the lik p'r night following, &c.

3 carp'ters.
2 labo'rs.
Frõ a
cauelero a
gvn.

This day 3 ship carp'ters and two labo'rs.

A cauelero of Vmbra came & viseted me, geving me thankes for the kindnesse shewed to his kinsman, Sugian Dono, & brought me a Japon hargabus (or gvn) for a present. He asked me many questions about the longnes of our voyag, w'ch I shewed hym in a globe. He also enquired whether I knew Rome. I answered I was never at Rome, yet I shewed hym the place where it stood. I p'rceaved p'r his questioning that he was a padre (or semenary prist) & therevpon gaue hym a tast, that we had nothing to doe w'th the Pope, but esteemed hym only bushop of Rome, having other bushops in England of as much authorety as he tuching spiretuall matters; & that we esteemed not much wheth-

---

83) Matsura Genshirō Nobutoki 松浦源四郎信辰, *alias* Tonomo 主殿.

er he were our frend or enemy, w'ch we left to his choise.
Lent Capt. Speck 1 barell gvnpolder out of junck, poz. 102
cattis duble barell and all.

18. This mornyng still faire hot wether, littell wind at N°·
W'erly, vering N°·erly in the after nowne, but calme p'r
night; still extreme hot wether.

carp'ters.
labor.
2 lettrs.

This day 3 ship carp'trs ½ labo'rs. I wrot 2 lettres to
Jorge Durois & Capt. Garrocho, advising the capt. I would
take the ambr greese, yf it were good, or else retorne it
back in saffetie; and to Jorge, to buy me 2 or 3 jarrs conservs & som candells. And ther was del'd vnto Capt. Ada-

202 *catt.* iron.
A letter.

mes 202 *cattis* iron, for vse of junck, of the ould iron out of
ston walles. Also I wrot a lettr in Japons to a seruant of
Mr. Lucas Antonison, a Japon at Langasaque, who I am
enformed hath the duble of my former lettrs & keeps them
by hym.

5 *taies.*

And ther was 5 *taies* in plate of bars lent vnto Sugien
Dono, the kinges kinsman, to be repaid at pleasure.

[fol. 15r.]

19. This mornyng still calme hot wether but after littell
wind variable all day frõ S. to N°, but calme most p'rte of
the night.

Carp'trs.
Labo·ers.

This day 8 carp'ers. and 4 laborers.

And I lent the China Capt., Andrea Dittis, viz.:-

2 bars gould.
200 Rs. 8.

	ta.	ma.	co.
2 bars gould of 55 *tais* p'r bar, is 110:		0:	0.,
w'th 200 Rs. of 8 in Spanish money, is 160:		0:	0

to be rapaid [*sic*] w'thin 8 or 10 dayes, at his retorne from
Goto, whit[h]er he is bownd to buy matters out of 2 China
junkes ther arived. This I doe in respeck I hope of trade
into China, w'ch now I stand in more hope of then eaver.

1 *cor.* duttes
of 12 Rs.

Also he had a bale or *corge* of duttis of 12 Rs° p'r *corge* to·
make a triall to sell them or more to the Chinas. Also Mr.

July 1615

Nealson had out of the warehouse for his owne acc? one

1 per red zelas. per red zealus of 12 Rs? p'r *corge*, rated at 1 *tay*.

5 *taies*. Capt. China to Goto. And Sugian Dono sent his man desiring to borow 5 *tays* in plate, w'ch on good consideration was lent to hym. The Capt. China dep'rted this day towardes Goto. We

40 rayls. bordes. bought 40 rayles at 2½ *mas* p'r eache 10 and [84] tables of *sugy* at   .

20. This mornyng still calme hot wether but after littell wind N? W'erly most p'rte of day, not soe much p'r night, vering againe S'erly.

4 carp'ers. 1 labo'rs. 2 *mas*. This day 4 carp'trs, 1 labo'rs.

I paid 2 *mas* to Torage for making 2 *kerimons*[85] for Tushma & Jn? Goblen, long ago. Tonemon Donos man came to haue borowed 20 *taies* of me in his m.ʳ[s] name,

Smith to work. but I had not a rag of money. The smigh [*sic*] began to work this day.

21. This mor[n]ing still hot wether, littell wind at S. W. and soe remeand all day and night following, yet more wind p'r day, then p'r night; extrem hot wether.

5 carp'trs. 1 labo'r coop'r. 1 junck fō Cochin China. This day 4 carp'ers, 1 labores & 1 coop'r.

I receved a lettr from Jn? de Lieuana, dated le 29th of July, new stile, in Langasaque, wherin he advised how Capt. Whaows greate junck was arived [*fol. 15v.*]⌋ frō Cochinchina; & he w'ch brought the letter tould me that other 4 are com frō that place in company w'th her, wherof he saw one coming in as he came away. Soe the former report of Whaous jonckes arivall was an vntruth.

14 bordes. Nota. We bought 14 bordes cost 3 *mas* & a halfe.

I forgot to note downe how Jn? de Lieuana advised that the report of the Hollanders being in the Phillippinas is falce, & that Don Jon de Silua was gon to keepe the straites

---

84) This and the following figures, not entered.
85) *Kimono* 著物, Japanese robe.

w'th a gale & a phriggat, attending the coming of shipping frõ Agua Pulca.

22. This mornyng still contynewed the hot wether w'th littell wind at S. W. as beforesaid, soe hot wether w'th som fey heate drops, & calme p'r night.

5 carp'ters.
1 labo'r.
A lettr to
Capt.
Adames.
10 spars.
Sonday.

This day 5 carp't, w'th the coop'r and 1 laborer. I sent Capt. Adames a barell of wyne, and loues of bread to Cochi, he being there about the juncks busynes. And wrot hym a lettr. We bought 10 spars, cost 2½ *mas*.

23. This mornyng still hott fayre wether, littell wind at S. W., but after a stiff gale as afforesaid all day, but littell wind (or rather calme) p'r night.

Ther was flying reportes that the Hollanders haue driven the Spaniardes out of the Molucos, and entred into the Phillippinas.

24. This mornyng still hott wether littell wind S. W'erly but after a stiffe gale the lyke most p'rte of the day. And littell or no wind p'r night; extrem hot wether.

This day 4 carp'ters and 1 laborer.

The China Capt. retorned this mornyng frõ Goto, and said that all the Chinas goodes were put into warehowses, & not sufferd to sell any till the king came or else order from hym to geue them leave. 		*[fol. 16r.]*⌋

I receved back the two hundred Rs? of eight frõ the China Capt.; but the 2 bars gould he left in pawne for a junck, to receve them back and pay other money in place, &c.

Also the China Capt. gaue me a peec. of China lynen to mak breeches of, &c.

And wee took eight peec. duttis of 8 Rs. p'r *corg* to make a saile for our bark. We entertayned a boateman this day at 18 *taies* p'r ano, named Sinzabra.

25. This mornyng still fayre calme extrem hot wether and so

July 1615

remeaned all day and night following, littell or rather no wind, but a breath variable.

This day 4 carp'ters, and 1 laborer.

Mr. Wickham being sick, Mr. Nealson, Mr. Sayer, and my selfe went to dyner to our frend Skeimon Dono, where we were well entertayned. And frō thence we went to Duch howse, where Capt. Speck tould me he receved a lettr frō Albartus yisterday, wherin he advised hym how Mr. Eaton arived at Miaco the first of this moneth. And the second went to Sackay to look out for the bark he sent from Edo w'th goods p'r sea, &c. He also tould me he expected news of 12 or 14 seale of their shipps to be in the Phillipinas this yeare, to cut ofe their China trade for the Manillias, as also to look out for the shipping from New Spaine (or Agua Pulca), and then to haue 3 or 4 of them to com for Firando to lade provition. Their plot is great &, yf it take effect, will vtterly ouerthrow the Spanish & Portingalle dissignes in these partes of the world, &c.

I bought 2 corse *catabras* for Ingoti, cost 1 *mas* 9 *condrins*

p'r peec.; paid out p'r Jn.º Gorchano, *jurebasso*, whoe put away his wife this day for trix.   [*fol. 16v.*]]

26.   This mornyng still faire calme extreme hot wether, & littell or rather no wind N.º W'erly most p'rte of the day, but night calme.

This day 5 labo'rs to sowe sayles.

I sent a lettr to Capt. Adames to Cochi w'th 3 iron stampers, 2 mattock, & a pickaxe, and a leg fresh pork & 5 loues of bread.

Also the China Capt., Andrea Dittis, sent me a legg of pork & an other of a goate, he feasting all the Chinas this day, and being ready to goe for Langasaque. I sent p'r hym for his brother, in respeckt his junck is retorned frō Cochinchina, hoping to heare the truth of our matters tuch-

To Whaw.

ing the losse of our goods & peeple, as I gaue hym in charg at my being at Langasaque; I say I sent hym, *Nifon catange,* 2 bottellelles [*sic*] of sallet oyle, & 100 pec. drid bonita;

To Capt. China. 80 Rs. 8.

and to Capt. Andrea Dittis hym selfe 1 barill wyne, and 25 pec. drid bonita. And I lent hym 80 Rs? of 8, at his request, he geveing me instance it was to geue to certan frendes &

China Capt. to Langasaque.

parentes com p'r way of Cochinchina out of China, & are to be emploid about our busynes in hand. The China Capt. went for Langasaque in th'after nowne.

27. This mornyng still hott calme wether, & very still wind after most p'rts of day at N? W'erly, but calme all night still hot wether.

6 lab'rs.

This day 6 labo'rs.

A letter frō Gonrock Dono.

I rec. a lettr frō Gonrock Dono, dated in Langasaque yisterday, wherin he wrot for stile & tynne for vse of the Emperour. And I receaved an other lettr frō Gorge Durois

3 lettrs receued.

of 2th August, new stile, w'th an other from Capt. Garrocho, & a therd frō Jn? de Liueano of complementos. And

A lettr to Gonrock Dono.

I sent a lettr to Gonrock Dono, & sent hym 1 bar tyn for sample, advising I had of the same som 190 *cattis* more, and had sould it at 4 *mas* p'r *catty,* & that this or what else was at the Emperours servis. [*fol. 17r.*]]

Frō Jn? Joosen.

Our hostis of Tomo came p'r this place, being bound for Langasaque, & sent her sonne to me w'th a pr'sent of 2 barilles wind, & other *recado,*[86] *Nifon catange.* Also Jn? Yosen arived from Langasaque, & sent me a pr'sent of peares. And our new botswan of jonck called [87]

Frō new botswain.

brought me a pr'sent of dry fish and 2 small barills of wyne.

A lettr frō

Also I rec. an other lettr frō Jorge Durois w'th 20 musk

---

86) *Regado* (Sp.), a present.
87) Not entered.

July 1615

millans; his 2 lettr dated [sic] lettrs dated the 2th & 5th day of August, new stile; he writes of much news of a flett of 5 seale, to be arived at Manillia frõ New Spaine, w'th men, money, & munition against the Duch at the Molocos; but I think it fabulose, as the rest of ther Goa forses to take & spoile Suratt. Also it is reported that Fidaia Samme is escaped into Shashma or the Liqueas; but I rest dowbtfull whether it be soe or no. I rec. the coopy of Mr. Luck. Anto. lettr this day, sent p'r his s'rvant frõ Syam.

28. This morning still hot calme wether, all the affore nowne, but the after a fresh gale of wind at N? W'erly, and calme p'r night; exstreme hott wether.

This day 2 corp'trs, and 5 laborers.

And I del'd 8 Rs. of 8 & 1 pec. *fibuck* per bill to our gouldsmith to plate my rapier & dagger. And ,88) a cheefe man, sent me a present of a barill of wyne, 2 chicking & 5 musk millions, & the lyke to Capt. Adames in respeckt his s'rvant is entertayned for a marrener in our junck voyage.

I receved a lettr frõ Lues Martin dated le 4th August, new stile, w'th the pot allowais sent hym hertefore, he desiring to haue no more then his bar plate amontes vnto, w'ch is the former retorned back. *[fol. 17v.]*⌋

29. This mornyng still calme hot wether, and after littell wind variable from S. to N?, most p'rte of the day, but night calme.

This day 2 carp'trs, and six laborers.

And I wrot 3 letters to Jn? de Lieuano, Jorgo Durois, and Capt. Garocho, & sent them p'r a Japon w'ch brought my lettrs from Jn? de Lieuana. This day Zenzebar's wyves brother sent for Jn? Gorezano, our *jurebasso*, to com &

---

88) Not entered.

July 1615

speake w'th hym, & laid to his charge that he had geven out bad speeches of hym that he had put men to death w'thout any reason (for yow must vnderstand this fello is the hangman, or execuseoner of this place, an office of reputation in these p'rtes of the world). But our *jurebasso* denied it that he spoake no such matter; yet that wold not serve his turne; but I was glad to send Capt. Adames to take vp the matter, I know this came p'r meanes of the Duch, or ther *jurebasso* Symon, whome I put a way. These are trix.

Frō Tome Dono. Sonday. Tome Dono sent me a baskit of egges for a present.

30. This mornyng still exstreme hot dry calme wether, and after a fresh gale, wind N°erly most p'rte of the day, but night calme.

2 carp'trs.
3 labo'rs.
To Capt.
Speck.
ta. ma. co.
35: 3: 1.
Wantes
4: 9: 1:

This day 2 carpenters and 3 laboer[s].

I sent Capt. Speck a quarter of beefe. And I del'd 35 *ta*. 3 *ma*. 1 *condrin* bars plate to Mr. Nealson, but it waied but 30 *ta*. 4 *ma*., soe ther wanted 4 *taies* 9 *mas* 1 *condrin*, and is of the money I rec. back frō Mr. Wickham sent to Lucas Antonison & opened p'r Mr. Wickham in the way, yet the lose fell vpon my selfe in rec. it w'thout waying. *[fol. 18r.]*

Nota.

Much a dow had I this day about clearing our *jurebasso* Goreson, whome Zanzebar & his wives rase thought to haue destroyed, and, as I take it, at the instigation of the Duch. For they sent me word as I was at dyner that for my sake they had saved his life, yet would haue hym to avoid the towne w'thin 5 or 6 dayes, I retorned them answer, I held them for no justices no judges, & that I had need of my *jurebassos* service; but the felloe w'ch came on the messadge was soe forward in his speeches that he tould me, yf I sent hym not away, that these fellowes servantes would kill hym as he went in the street. Yow must vnderstand his adversaries are the hangmen (or execusioners of

44

the towne). But I retorned answer that I was vnder the protection of Ogosho Samme the Emperour, & had it vnder his ferme, that no justice in Japon might meddell w'th me nor no servant in my howse, but p'r the Emperou[r]s p'rmition, & yet more larger then I spake it; and therefore I warned them vpon their heads, as they would answer it w'th their whole generation that the[y] should not tuch hym till the king of this place retorned. W'ch answer put them into such a quandare, that they sent me word that, for my sake, they were content to pardon hym of all matters, & to be his frend. This word was sent me p'r Capt. Adames, whome, before God & man, I must needs blame for taking part w'th that wild fello Zanzabar (*alius* Yasimon Dono), whom, p'r experience, I haue fownd to be an absolute cvning knaue, & thervpon haue donne all I can to make Capt. Wm. Adames to know it; yet he still esteemeth hym more then all our English nation, & said he would pawne [*fol. 18v.*]] his lyfe & soule for his honestie. And I canot chuse but note it downe, that both I my selfe & all the rest of our nation doe see that he (I meane Mr. Wm. Adames) is much more frend to the Duch then to the Englishmen, w'ch are his owne cvntremen, God forgeue hym. I leave it to his owne contience & to God & the world, to be judges w'th what respect I haue vsed hym ever since we came into Japan. An other matter is now set on foote, w'ch I never did heare of till this instant; and is, that we were cvzoned of 4 or 500 *taies* (yf not more) in the price we paid for our junck, & that it was p'rted betwixt Zanzaber, our host Andrea at Langasaque & other their copsmate,[89] wherof Miguel our *jurebasso* was one, & had 50 *taies* for his share; but as yet I can fynd no witnese of the truth, yet I

---

89) Copesmate, a partner, fellow-buyer.—Thompson.

verely beleeve it to be true, although Capt. Adames haue no hand in the matter. For w'ch their smoath speeches they make a childe of hym & so do what they list, & he will not beleeve any man that will speake to the contrary. & thus much thought I good to note downe, that it may be extant whether I live or dye.

Capt. Speck, Jn? Yoosen & Mr. Matias came vnlooked for to the English howse to supp'r. Capt. Spek tould me he vnderstood that Mr. Eaton was on his way coming from Miaco. God send hym well.

31. This mornyng still extrem hot calme wether. And after littell wind at N? W. som p'rte of day, but the rest w'th the night following call [sic] wether.

1½ labo'rs.   This day 1½ labores.

Frō Gonosco Dono.   Gonosco Dono, [90] our guardian's father in law, sent Mr. Wickham & me 2 peare pigions. This Gonosco Dono is lefte cheefe *bongew* or Viz Roy in abcense of the king and Nobasane.   [*fol. 19r.*]⌋

August   1615.

1. This mornyng still hot wether w'th littell wind at N? W. most p'rte of day; night calme.

1 labo'r.   This day 1 laborer.

The China Capt., Andrea Dittis, retorned from Langasa-

From Sr. Whaw China.   que & brought me a present from his brother, viz., 1 faire *kitesoll*, 2 spoutpotes or euers of tynn silverd, 2 pec. China

Capt. China frō Langasa-que.   lynen, & 1 peec. silk lane; & he hym selfe sent a white *cata-*

Nota frō Cochinchina.   *bra*. He sayeth, tuching our affares in Cochinchina, that the king denyeth that he never was consenting to the death of our people, nether knew of it till it was donne, it

---

90) Matsura Gonnosuke Nobutada 松浦權之助信忠

being donne p'r the Japons & not p'r his people; & that for the money he owed vs for the goods he bought of Mr. Peacock. He was willing to pay it, but non came to demand it; & for the rest of our goods it was retorned back in our junk it came in, &c., & offred to geue the China (our soliceter) his lettr or passe for any mans safe coming that I would send to receve it. But yow must vnderstand Capt. Speck sent a Japon about the lyke matter for the Hollandrs, w'th a pr'sent for the king, w'ch he receaved. But this Japon lodged in the howse of an other Japon theefe, where they handled the matter. Soe amongst them that the king retorned word of mouth to Capt. Speck that he would not make them restetution of any thing, &, yf they sent any more shiping, he would vse them as he did the other. & these Japon theevs, knowing how the king had promised to make vs restetution, went to hym & p'rswaded hym to the contrary, telling hym that, yf he made restetution to vs, he must doe the lyke to the Hollanders. Soe that when the China, [*fol. 19v.*]] our soliceter, went for the kinges letter, he denyed it hym. Thus the second tyme were we crost p'r the Hollanders. And I receved 2 letters, 1 from Jorge Durois and the other from Jn? de Lieuano of the 9th currant, new stile.

A letter
frō Jor.
Durois.
Nota.
China.

And I thought good to note downe that the China Capt., Andrea Dittis, came & tould me how his brother Whaw at Langasaque desired to haue it vnder my hand writing tuching procuring trade into China. For, as he sayeth, they haue laid out 3000 *taies* allready to make way, and make reconyng it will cost them 5000 *taies* more, is all 8000 *taies*, I say eight thousand *taies*; w'ch yf in case they procure vs free trade into China, we are to pay them the said eight thousand *taies* back, w'th what else shall be thought fiting. But yf they doe not procure vs free trade into China, then the losse to stand vpon them selues.

August 1615

Newes. I forgot to note downe how Jorge Durois wrot me how a greate Holland ship was cast away on the cost of Lucan in the Philippinas, out of the w'ch the cvntrey, people saved 5 greate peeces of ordinance, & that most p'rte of the men were cast away in the ship, & those w'ch escaped p'r swyming were taken prisoners and sent to Manillia to Don Juan de Siluas, whoe they say is ready w'th forcese to dep'rte to reskew them at the Molucas, but I can hardly beleeve it.

Nota. Also a frend of Capt. Adames tould hym that three daies past arived an emptie junck at Langasaque, w'ch came from Cagallon in the Phillippinas, & is one of the Japon junckes w'ch we thought was lost w'th ours w'ch Water Carwarden was in, & came out of Cochinchia 7 daies before our junck could be ready to dep'rte, & was driven on the cost of Cord [sic] p'r stormy wether, & after put among the ilands Liqueas, yet could not recover port in any of them [fol. 20r.]] them [sic]; yet after recoverd the iland of Lucan & put into the roade of Cagallan, having first lost their mastes and throwne all their goods overbord, being glad to escape w'th life; and frõ thence are now retorned w'th the emptie junck, but know nothing [of] what is becom of ours. Also this day we put away Fachman, our scullion, and

Fachman put away.

	ta.	ma.	co.
Mr. Nealson paid hym to cleare his accompt in small plate	3:	2:	8
And he had paid hym at 3 severall paym'tes before p'r accompt	7:	0:	0
Amontes all vnto	10:	2:	8

ta. ma. 10: 2: 8. 3 pec. red taffeties. And the China Capt. bought 3 pec. red China taffeties for me cost 6 mas p'r pece, is 1 ta. 6 ma. 0 [co.] paid my selfe, &c.

And I sent Capt. Adames to Cochi, viz:–

48

	ma.	con.
110 straw bag, cost	2:	8
50 peles, cost	1:	5
	4:	3

Nota

Also I sent hym 3 loves of bread and wrot hym the news of that junk w'ch was reported to hym came frō Cagallion is vntrew, for it is a junk belo[ng]ing to the China Capt. brother, & came not frō Cochinchina last yeare; so that is a lye.

Sayemon D.
a skullion,
entertaynd.

And we entertayned a new skullion named Sayemon D. at one *tay* p'r month.

2. This mornyng a fresh gale, wind at S. W. and soe by fittes contynewd both day and night following, &c.

14 ocs. black
silk.

I gaue Matinga 6 *taies* small plate to buy rise; and I had 14 onces black silk of China Capt., cost 2 *taies* p'r *catty*. I had nuch [*sic*] a dowe w'th Zanzabars desemuery.[91] who sent me word 3 or 4 tymes they would break my *jurebassos* boanes, yf he came to his owne howse; but as before, soe still I retorned them answer the[y] should take heed how they medled w'th [*fol. 20v.*]] any servant I had. And at night my *jurebasso* being desirous to goe to his howse, I gaue hym leave; where he fownd Jnọ Devins entertaynm't,[92] for Zamzabers wives brother w'th other consor'tes, set vpon hym in the streete, &, had he not by good fortune gotten into a howse, they had slayne hym. & about midnight, being garded p'r a gentelmans servant, my frend came hom againe, shakeing every joint of hym.

3. This mornyng still extreme hot wether, littell wind at S. W. all day, but more wind p'r night, *vt supra*.

120 Rs. 8 to

The China Capt. being ready to goe for Goto I lent hym

91) Decemviri, meaning his fellows.—Thompson.
92) It does not appear who was this John Davin, whose "entertainment" was so proverbial.—Thompson.

August 1615

China Capt..,
he going
ready to
dep'rt for
Goto.
4⅛ Rs⁰ 8.

our boate & wastclothes, and del'd hym back 120 Rs? of 8 w'ch was the rest of the 200 Rs. 8 lent hym before and retorned, the other being del'd hym after at his going to Langasaque, viz., 80 Rs. of 8. Also I paid hym 38 *mas* in Rs? of 8 for 1 *cattie* silk at 20 *mas*, and 3 pec. red China taffetie at 18 *mas*, is 4¾ Rs. 8.⁹³⁾

Nota.
2 pe. dutt.
to China
Capt. of 12
Rs. *corg*, for
ij to our
acc⁰.

And tuching the forse vsed against my *jurebasso* the other night, I thought good w'th the advice of the rest, to make it knowne vnto the cheefe justice in the kinges abcense, Mr. Wickham accompanying me. They all tould me I had greate reason in what I did, & that they would take order that this *bongew* should not offer my *jurebasso* any wronge; the w'ch I certefied Capt. Adames of in good termes by a letter sent hym to Cochi, where I heard he la sick. But he retorned me a very harsh answer, as all the rest of our cuntremen can witnesse w'ch saw it. He shewed hym selfe a fermer frend to Zanzaber and his consortes then to me and the rest of his contremen.   [*fol. 21r.*]⌋

Also Capt. Speck sent for Mr. Wickham to com and speake w'th hym, and complained much of my *jurebasso*, that he had a bad tonge, & had geven out vild reports of hym and his nation. I retorned hym answer, I never heard hym vse any such speeches, & yf he thought me his frend, he might think I could not endure neather hym nor any other vse such speeches, w'thout geveing hym notis therof, & chastesing the speakers, yf they were my servants. In fine, his desire was to haue me to send for these *bongewes* and to make an end of these matters in frendship; vnto w'ch I answerd that I knew not whether they would com or no, yf I sent for them, yet, yf their [*sic*] were any meeting, I desired that Capt. Adames might be present, and they

---

93) The marginal note beginning with "2 pe. ditt." must be an addition to the text.

should not fynd me out of reason. & soe I advised Capt. Adames, allthough he burdened me I went about to mentayne a theefe against all reason, w'ch all men may think that heare hym say soe that no honest man would doe it.

Cōsort w'th China.

And I had allmost forget to note downe, how I del'd a writing to Andrea Dittis, the China Capt., vnder my hand and seale witnessed by Mr. Ric'd Wickham, Mr. Wm. Nealson, and Mr. Ed. Sayer; wherin I consorted w'th hym and Capt. Whaw, his brother, & a therd brother w'ch they haue in China, that yf they procure vs trade into China, to repay them all such soms of money and money worth as they should lay out in procuring thereof; but yf it tooke not effect, then the losse to light vpon them selues. And they are to turne an other writing to me, to vse their best endevour in doing thereof only for Englishmen and no nation else whatsoever. And soe the Lord God grant a good suckcesse to our proceadings. I wrot 2 lettrs to Jorge

A lettr to Jorge Durois & Damian. A lettr Lieuano.

Durois and Damian Marin, and receved 1 from Jnọ de Lieuano of the 11th of August, new stile, of complementos. But I wrot Georg Durois to buy vs a peare of milstones and som candells, & send them p'r first [ship]. [*fol. 21v.*]]

4. This mornyng still extreme hot wether w'th littell wind S. W., but after a fresh gale most p'rte of day and night followinge.

Nata.

Capt. Adames sent me a more frendly letter then before. He is two much affection toward Zanzaber, & wholy led away by hym.

5. This mornyng still extrem hot wether w'th littell wind at S. W. most p'rte of the day, but most p'rte of the night calme.

4 labo'rs. Portingall shipps ariued at Langasaque.

This day 4 labores to make perry. Theare is reportes geven out that the Portingal shipp is arived at Langasaque from Amacan, and pr'sently after Capt. Speck wrot me a

August 1615

letter that it is the same greate shipp w'ch was there the last yeare; but as Jn? Yoosen hath advised hym, she is not soe well laden as she was the yeare post [*sic*], but as it should seeme, cometh more to fetch away the lagg they lefte heare the last yeare then for any thing else.

6. This mornyng still extrem hott wether & calme, yet sowne after a fresh gale of wind all or most p'rte of the day at S. W'erly, but night calme.

I hearing the sea *bongew* was gon vp to the king, & dowbting he might enforme vntruthes against my *jurebasso*, was determened to haue written 2 letters, 1 to the king and an other to Chumba Dono, my *jurebassos* ould mr, to desire them not to geue eare to his enemies falce reportes; but as I was about to haue donne it, Tackamon Dono, sent vnto me his cheefe man, he being accompanied w'th Skidayen Dono & Nicolas Martin for *jurebasso*. & his desire was that, for his sake, I would geue ouer the pursute of this matter, against the sea *bongew*, for that, yf it were followed, of force the said *bongew* must cut his bellie, & then my *jurebasso* must do [*fol. 22r.*]] the lyke. Vnto w'ch his request I was content to agree, and afterward went to geue hym thankes for the paynes he had taken in the matter, he haveing promised me that non should be, so hardy to meddell w'th my *jurebasso* hereafter, and that he would take the matter in hand to make the accord betwixt hym & his wife.

And frō Takamon Donos I went to the Duch howse, where, amongst other matters, we fell into discourse about the sea *bongews* proceedinges against my *jurebasso*, he taking the *bongews* part, & tould me he had donne well, yf he hat [*sic*] cut hym in peeces the other [day], & then their would haue byn no more words therof afterward. But I made hym answer that it might be he was dec[e]aved in

August 1615

that, for that I would haue brought the matter in question,
& it might he would haue cost both hym and others their
lives, for that all the justice of Ffirando said that the
bongew had donne that w'ch he could not answer. Once
I fownd my selfe agreeved that he had me in soe small
respect that he, w'thout geveing notis vnto me, sent craf-
tely for my *jurebasso* out of my howse, thinking to haue
put hym to death, w'thout any forme of pr'cesse; & he re-
plid and said that the *bongew* was a souldier, & stood vpon
his honer more then his lyfe, & car'd not to cut his belly
vpon such an occation. I answerd, I did not esteem this
bongew such a personage that he needed to take pepp'r in
the nose soe much as he did.

To Takaman
Dono.

I forgot to note downe how I carid a jarr of China beare,
& 5 stringes drid fish to Tacamon Dono for a pr'sent. This
bongew & Capt. Speck are all one, and I know this trowble
against my urebasso came, the begining of it, from the
Duch howse. [*fol. 22v.*]]

Nota.

6. Capt. Speck came late to the Eng'sh howse, & Sr. Matias
w'th hym, & desired my company to goe & see a peece of
ordinance cast; w'ch I did, but marveled at their workmanship. For they carid the mettell in ladells aboue 20 yardes
from the place where the mould stood, & soe put it in, ladel-
full after ladell, & yet made as formall ordinance as we doe
in Christendom, both of brasse & iron. Capt. Speck tould
me nether workmanship nor stuffe did not stand hym in
halfe the price it cost them in Christendom.

Capt. Speck tould me he receaved a barks lading of
copp'r this day frõ Sackay, and that his barke dep'rte[d]
from thence 3 daies after Mr. Eaton was dep'rted from
thence. God send hym hither in saffety. And we bought 22
bages rise of Zazabra Dono for 4 *gantes* a *masse*, and deliverd 12 bagges of them to our ship carpenters vpon

22 bagryse.
12 bages
rise to
carp'trs.

53

accompt. They beging to work vpon our junk to morrow. God be their good speed, &c.

7. This mornyng still extreme hot calme wether, but sowne after a small gale at S. W'erly, fayre wether till 4 a clock in the after nowne & then 3 or 4 showers of rayne, but dry all night, yet more wind then p'r day, &c.

Gonosco Dono came to the English howse, & amongst other talk tould me that the king had sent hym word to burne all the tobaco, & to suffer non to be drunk in his governm't, it being the Emperours pleasure it should be so; and the like order geven thorowghout all Japon. & that he, for to begyn, had burned 4 *piculls* or C. wight this day, & cost hym 20 *taies pico.*; & had geven order to all others to doe the like, & to pluck vp all w'ch was planted. It is strange to see how these Japons, men, women, and children, are besotted in drinking that herb; & not 10 yeares since it was in vse first. *[fol. 23r.]*

Tobaco defended.

We del'd 2 *piculles* 31½ *cattis* shething neales to the boteswaine of our junck.

2 pic. 31½ cattis neals.

8. This mornyng fayre wether w'th a fresh gale of wind S°.erly, but after nowne blew vp a stiffe gale, as it did the lyke all night w'th a few drops of rayne.

The China Capt., Andrea Dittis, retorned frõ Goto, for that the *bongew* would not let hym enter into that place, he haveing staid 4 daies a weating, & so retorned. Allso they of Goto staid 3 *somos*, or small junkes, theare of his, w'ch were bound for Firando, & would not let them passe, but send out boates to bring in by force all such juncks as passe w'thin sight. And for shark oyle, ther was but 25 littill jarrs, all w'ch was taken p'r Gonrock Dono & sent to Langasaque for his prop'r vse. And he adviseth me that 4 junks are arivd at Langasaque frõ Chanchew, w'ch w'th this ship frõ Amacan will cause all matters to be sould

China Capt. frõ Goto.

3 China junks at Goto.

No oyle.

4 junks at Langasaque.

August 1615

1 pec. whit damask.
cheape. The China Capt. of a junck at Goto sent me a peec. white damaske, pr'sent.

Newes.
We had newes this day that the Portingales of Amacan haue taken the bark *Jaccatra*.[94] And meane to set out 2 men of war every yeare to take all English & Duch that trade from Syam, Bantam, & Pattania for these p'rtes.

Jackatra arived w'th a prise.
But w'thin 2 howres after, the bark *Jaccatra* arived on the cost of Firando, and brought in a Portingall junck w'ch came from Champa, wherin both Chinas & Japons are marreners, but all the goods belong to Portingales. She took her on this cost 3 daies past, at an iland called Sta. Clare. Her lading is black wood, I think ebony. It is thought the Portingales will complaine to the Emperour, because the Hollanders take them w'thin his dominions.
[*fol. 23v.*]

9.   This morn'g a stiff gale wind S'erly till nowne, & then the wind slacked w'th som rayne & thunder most p'r day following, night calme dry wether w'th much lightnyng.

50 *ta.* to Mr. Nelson.
Cushcrom Dono lent vs 50 *taies* in great plate for a few daies, w'ch 50 *taies* Mr. Nealson receaved to lay out in necessaris for the junck.

2 Duch shipps a-riued at Firando.
And about midnight past the other Holland shipp called the *Ancusen*[95] of som 300 tonns arived in the roade (or harbor) of Cochi. The Capt. name being   96) and

To Duch ships.
the m.ᵣ his name   .97) And after nowne both shipps came into the harbor of Ffirando. And I went abord of them, and carid 2 barills wind, a hogg, 5 hense, and 10 loves bread to the greate ship; 1 barell wyne & the lyke quantety of the rest to the littell ship.

---

94) The *Jaccatra, jacht.*
95) The *Enckhuijsen, schip.*
96) Not entered.
97) Not entered.

August 1615

Oziander.

They tould me that the Eng'sh shipp w'ch is to com hither is called the *Oziander*, and the mastrs name Jn.º Hvnt; & that she would be ready to com after them w'thin 4 or 5 daies but haue brought no lettrs for vs, w'ch maketh vs to marvill. And I must needs condem Mr. Denton & them at Pattania of sloth, or else the Duch of legerdemeane. They report a p'rliament in England,[98] & that it is lyke we shall

Lady Eliza a sonne.

haue wars w'th Spaine; and that the Lady Elizabeth hath a yong sonne p'r the Palsgroue of the Ryne.[99] Also the[y] say that Capt. Dauid Midelton was generall of an other fleete to Bantam, and, vnderstanding of his brothers death, retorned for England. Oyen Dono sent me a present of 15

Frō Oyen Dono.

hense.   [*fol. 24r.*]]

10. This mornyng calm wether, but after a fresh gale variable but most an end S'erly all day and night calme, w'th a littell rayne at midnight.

2 lettres

I wrot 2 lettrs to Langasaque to Jorge Durois and Jn.º de Lieuana, of arivall Duch shipps. & that we had 1 in way, and sent that to Jn.º encloze to Jo.ʳ, p'r conveance of Capt. China.

Capt. China went out in our penise.

And I sent out our penisse w'th 16 men to roe, and the Capt. China, Andrea Dittis, in her, w'th an English flag & wastclothes & a letter, to lye ofe & on 8 or 10 dayes, to put a pilot abord our shipp yf she com on the cost. He had a

4 *tay* 1 *co.* bar 1 *tay* small.

bar plate, poz. 4 *taies* 5 *condrin*, & 1 *tay* in small plate, to lay out in provition for rowers, and a barrill of wyne, &c.

11. This mornyng raynie wether w'th littell or rather no wind S'erly, but after a gale most p'rt of the day; rayne lastet but till 9 a clock, rest day dry, but night calme w'th littell rayne.

Pr·sent.

Our neighbour of Faccatay sent me 2 hennse; and Ton-

93) In April 1614.—Thompson.
99) Henry Frederic, born on January 2, 1614.—Thompson.

56

August 1615

Nota

cho Samma sent to envite me & the rest of our nation to
dyner, but I exskewsed it till an other tyme. And Taccamon
Dono sent his man to me to tell me that he had donne what
he could to make peace betwixt our *jurebasso* Gorreson &
his wife, but that shee would not in any sort retorne back
vnto hym, allthough she should suffer death; and that
Bongo Donos wife had taken her vnder his protextion, and
said he should not haue her againe.   [*fol. 24v.*]]

12.   This mornyng overcast droping wether w'th lightnyng
and thunder, & a fresh gale, wind at S. W'erly, but after a
stiffe gale variable, w'th extreme lightning & thunder w'th
store of rayne most p'te of the afore nowne, yet calme p'r
night w'th rayne.

To Capt.
Adames.

I sent Capt. Adames 3 hense & 6 love bread, he having
written for charcole, lyme, & oyle for the junk, but could

Hempe &
rottonees
frō Langa.

not be sent p'r meanes of the rayne. And we rec. hempe &
rattones from Langasaque cost   100) & od *taies* as
p'r p'rticulers sent from our host Andrea.

2 lettrs frō
Joȓ & Jnọ

Also I rec. 2 lettrs from Langasaque frō Jnọ de Lieuana
& Jorge Durois, of the 19th and 20th currant, new stile,

Newes.

wherein the[y] write me much news, viz., that Don Jnọ de
Silua hath a fleet of 15 gallions, 8 or 9 gallies, w'th many
friggates & China *somas*, to transport an army of 3000
souldiers to the Molucos against the Duch; & that 3 gallions came frō Aguapulca to the Manillias w'th halfe a mil-
lion of plate for the setting forward of these affares against
the Hollanders; & that a new Viz Roy was sent to Goa,
called Don Jeronimo de Torres, & knight of the order of
Sạ Yago, & is likwaies ordayned governor of the Phillippinas, & carrieth 200 substantiall Spaniardes w'th hym
to Goa, amongst whome 1 is apointed for visetor, being

_____

100) Not entered.

well assisted w'th other Spaniardes, a thing never seen in the Portingall Indies befor; and that no matter may passe but p'r his p'rmission; & that he hath sent away Don Diogo de Basconçelos, the former Viz Roy (in cheanes) for Portingale till he be out of sight of land, & confiscat all his goodes, w'ch vallued aboue 200000 Rialles of 8, because he denied to send succors the last yeare to Don Jnᵒ de Siluas to haue gon against the Hollanders at Molucos, for w'ch it is thought he will loose his head, yf he live to com into Portingale. [fol. 25r.]]

Many other matters they write me, as of the duble mariadg betwixt the Princese of France & Spaine; & that the King of Spaine hath marid the Duke of Savoies doughter;101) & that the said Duk was generall in an armado p'r sea against the Turke, where the Christians tooke 150 of the Turks gallis; & that the King of France hath made 12 new gallions & sent them to the sucker of his father in law, the King of Spaine, w'th such forcese, that they and the Archduke haue taken 20 seale of Holland shipps w'ch were prepared to goe for the East Indies, and also haue taken 3 *catties* or townes from the Hollanders; but I esteeme this a fable, for this Holland ship now com for Firando came out of Holland but 14 moneths past. Many other matters they wrot of, w'ch is overlong to set downe, namely, that the King of Spaine was sending an embassador to the Emperour of Japan w'th a greate present, in respect of his favour to Christians. So it seemeth he did littell know how he hath formerly banished all Christians out of his dominions: I meane all fryres, monkes, Jesuists & priestes.

---

101) Margaret, daughter of Charles Emmanuel, Duke of Savoy, had married Francis III, Duke of Mantua. She was then a widow, but did not marry the King of Spain.—Thompson.

August 1615

13.   This mornyng fayre calme wether yet somthing overcast,
yet after dry wether, w'th a small gale N? W'erly most p'rte
of the day, but night calme, yet dry.

Nota.   And I sent Mr. Nealson w'th our *jurebassos* to Taccamon
Dono, to desire his Lordship that Goresonas wife might be
forthcoming at the kinges retorne to Firando, to answer to
what her hvsband would aleadg against her, for that her
proceadinges were a dishonor both to hym & me; w'ch he
retorned me word was true, & that yf she had byn a man,
as she was a woman, he would haue taken an other course
them yet he had donne. For that in som sort, women haue
more privelege then men.   [*fol. 25v.*]]

        And sowne after, Taccamon Donos man wrot a lettr to
Gorison to com & speake w'th hym, w'ch he did, and was
p'r his m'sters order, whoe tould Goresano, that he had better considered of the matter, and that, yf he would, he
would make his wife retorne againe to hym, whether shee
would or no; or else, yf I would, he would cause her nose to
be cut ofe and banish her out of the cvntrey. This new
change is p'r reason that, yf this matter of his wife be
brought in question before the king, the other of the sea
bongew must be the lyke, w'ch would be nothing to the
lyking of Zanzabar and his rase, &c.

Frō Capt. of   And after nowne the capten and masters of the 2 Duch
Duch shipp.   shipps came to the English howse and brought me a
present of 2 baricas of Spanish wine, 3 Hollandt cheeses,
2 small pottes of butter, and a bundell of stockfish. And
Mr. Eaton   about midnight Mr. Eaton arived (at Firando) frō Miaco,
frō Miaco.   and, as he tells me, hath lent 100 bars of gould to the King
of Firando, to be paid againe at 3 months; w'ch is such a
greefe vnto me in respect of the present vse we haue of
money, that I know not what to doe, I did littell think Mr.
Eaton would haue served me so, I haueing writen hym

59

expresly to the contrary. Mr. Eaton sayeth the comon report is that Fidaia Samme is yet living, w'th 5 or 6 other princepall men, & thought to be in Shashma.

5 letters.

Mr. Eaton brought me 5 letters as followth, viz.,

1 from King of Firando w'th 2 *catabras*, from Miaco.

1 from Vshenusque Dono, our *bongew*, frō Miaco.

1 from our host of Osekey, Yasozama Amanoia Dono.

1 from Gilbert Cunings wife from Edo.

1 from Andrea, Capt. Adames brother in law, frō Edo.

Mr. Eaton tills me how this Andrea & Mickmoy, our host, dealed Judasly w'th hym at Edo.   [*fol. 26r.*]

14. This mornyng overcast droping wether, calme, but after proved fayre dry wether all the rest of the day & night following; littell wind p'r day at N? W. but night calme.

Frō Sugien.

Sugian Dono sent me a pr'sent of new rise (*Nifon catang*) and Mr. Eaton brough[t] me 2 *catt.* & 2 gerd. for Matt. &

2 *catt.*
2 lettrs.

I rec. 2 lettrs of Mr. Eatons dated in Edo, le 27th Aprill & le 8th of June but kept till this tyme, &c.

15. This mornyng fayre calme wether & very littell wind, after N? W. most p'rte of day, and the lyke p'r night; fayre dry wether but not hot as before.

2 lettrs
Jorge.

I wrot 2 letters to Jorge Durois & Jn? de Lieuano in answer of their 2 rec. of 19th & 20th pr'sent, new stile. Also I receved of Mr. Wm. Eaton, for goodes sould for my owne

ta. ma. co.
569: 1: 5.
1250 *ta.*

account in Japan, plate barse, fyve hvndred threescore and nyne *taies*, one *mas*, & five *condrines*; and in plate barse, for accō of the Wo'll Company, one thousand two h'd and

10 *ta.* wight
Pri. gold.

fiftie *taies*; and in Priaman gould poz. ten *taies*, I say ten *taies* wight Priaman gould, & is the rest of a greater som del'd vnto hym at his going vp to Osekey heretofore. And I

1 pec.
grogren.
1 per silk
stock.

gaue hym a peec. ashculler grogren of my owne cost me 11½ *taies*, as also a paire of blew silk stockinges, cost me 3 *taies*.

August 1615

Jnº Yossen retorned frõ Langasaque & sent me a pr'sent of grapes. And I wrot a lettr to Capt. Adames, of the kna-

very of Miguel, our *jurebasso,* how Judaslyke he dealt w'th Mr. Eaton at Edo, & since his coming still abcentes hym selfe night and day, thinking I will beare w'th his fooleries as well as Mr. Eaton did, w'ch he did of meare necessetie, not knowing how to mend hym selfe. Yet I am in no such need, but meane to put away the knaue for his knauery.

And I rec. a lettr frõ Capt. Garrocho, dated in Langasaque, le 22th of this month, new stile, wher inclozed came an other for the China Capt. Alsoe he wrot me to buy a case of bottells, a lookinglas, and 2 Holland cheeses for hym, &c. *[fol. 26v.]]*

There was geven to the owner and mʳ of the boate w'ch

brought downe Mr. Eaton two peces of white baftas, of 10 Rs. p'r *corge,* in regard of the paines they took in bringing hym downe, &c.

And I sent a barell of wine and a bundell of pap'r to Gonosque Dono, & the lyke to Taccamon Dono, p'r Mr. Eaton newly retorned frõ Miaco; w'ch they tooke in good

p'rte, & in the after nowne Semi Dono retorned frõ aboue, and sent his man to advise me therof (*Nifon catange*). Soe I

went to viset hym, in company of Mr. Wickham and Mr. Eaton, & carid hym 2 barilles of *morofack* & 51 pec. of drid bonita. Also I sent a barill of wyne & millions to Jnº Yoosen, p'r Mr. Eaton, in respect he holpe hym at Edo, his *jurebasso* playing the knaue, viz., Miguel. He took it in good part, & envited me to breakfast the next morning w'th [him]. Jnº Yoosens brother envited hym abord the greate shipp, & had 7 pec. ordinance shot afe at his retorne ashore.

16. This mornyng littell wind at Nº W. overcast wether yet faire, and so remeaned all day & night following except som

61

August 1615

few drops of rayne.

To Oyen
Dono.
50 *ta.*
I sent a barell wyne & a bundell of pap'r to Oyen Dono
p'r Mr. Eaton, whoe took it in good p'rte. And I paid fyftie
taies in greate plate (or bars) to Cushkron Dono lent vs few

100 *ta.*
Nota.
daies past, and del'd one hvndred *taies* lyke plate to Mr.

To Capt.
Adames in
small plate
7 *ta.* 7 *m.* 5 *c.*
17 *tais* 6 *ma.*
to Zazbra
for 22 *catt*
rise clans.
30 saks rise
to Capt.
Adames,
Nealson to lay out about junck. And Mr. Eaton & I went to
dyner to Jn.º Yoosen, where we met capt. of the ships, w'th
Jn.º Yoosens brother. And at our retorne, we found Mr.
Wickham & Mr. Nealson a littell intostecated [*sic*], but Ed:
Sayer stark drunk; & he & Mr. Nealson fell together p'r
the eares w'th daggars drowne in every vild sort, & Mr.
Wickhams tong ran at large.

cost, 33 *ta.* 7 *mas* paid p'r Mr. Nealson in plate bars.

[*fol. 27r.*]⏌

And Bongo Donos wife in his abcense sent me a pr'sent
Frō Bongo
Dono.
of millans. And   , 102) our *bongew*, sent me a lettr
of complemento from Miaco & the like to Capt. Adames.

Nota.
Lues Mart.
And Jn.º Goreson our *jurebasso* brought his wife to the
English howse, where we made them good frends, & Lues
Marting came to Firando.

17. This morning overcast droping wether w'th littell wind
at N.º E., yet dry after all day, and the lyke p'r night;
calme.

8½ os. lalo.
And I sent 8½ onces or *tay* wight allowais soccatryn to
Lues Martyn, for a bar of plate poz. 4 *ta.* 9 *ma.* 3 *con.* And
Albaro
Monues.
after a Spaniard called Albaro Monues and [*sic*] brought
me a letter from Capt. Garrocho, w'th 14 onces of amber
grees, w'ch he wrot me cost hym 95 *taies* the *catty* & es-
teemd it worth 110 *taies* the *catty*. But I retorned it back
by the same bringer, as not being worth the price he wrot
me it cost.

102) Not entered.

August 1615

And Capt. Whaw the China sent me bundells net poz.

11½ pik net
12 bar'll olyle. 11½ pik., cost 10½ *taies*. And 12 barills oyle shark cont'g
325 *gantas*, w'ch he lends vnto me to reply as much oyle
1 jar of
conserues. hereafter when he shall need it. And I receved a jarr of
conserues frõ George Durois w'th 25 peares, w'ch the
China Capt., Andrea Dittis, took p'r way. I was advised to
Nota. send to Andrea our host at Langasaque to buy 5, or 600
gantes of shark oyle, at the price of 10 *taies* the C., as he
advised Capt. Adames he could haue as much as we stood
in need of. This I meane to doe to try conclutions, to see
whether wordes and deeds are alyke.   [*fol. 27v.*]]

18. This mornyng overcast wether w'th som few drops of
rayne, littell wind at N? E. or rather calme, & som littell
rayne p'r fittes p'r day, but much more p'r night w'th a
stiff gale at S. N.

I went to Cochi to vizet Capt. Adames and see how our
junck work. Went forward & carid hym a bottell Spanish
wyne, 2 hens, 1 duk, a pec. pork, 8 loves bread & 6 mill'ns,
Nota. and retorned to Firando to dyner, haveinge invited Albaro
Monues, whoe tould me the Duch mariners vsed hym ill
yisterday in wordes, calling hym *Cornudo*, he being a
marid man. Whervpon grew som quarrell, for w'ch 4 or 5
Duch mariners were duckt at yard arme & each one 40
China Capt.
retor. strips at capstayn. Also the China Capt. retorned, &, haveing geven order along the cost, to sent [*sic*] our pilotes yf
our ship came in sight, he sent to Langasaque & staid halfe
a day, and bringeth word that his brother tould hym that
the common report amongst both Spaniardes and Portingals was that now they took the English to be their enimis,
as well as the Hollanders, and therfore would take all our
shipps w'ch traded into these p'tes of the world, &c. But
Nota.
Wikham. I remembr the ould proverb, that "God sends a curst cow
shot hornes." I find on a sudden that Mr. Wickham growes

63

very sullen humorous and, as I am informed, geveth out that he is not the Companies servant, but at will, & therfore will rather seek out for his retorne for England in som shiping frō Langasaque to Syam or Pattania. I think the reason is that he hath fingerd 5 or 6 *cattis* of good amber grees in the Liqueas, & thinketh to make an India voyag for hym selfe & to retorne capt. or generall for the Company at his pleasure. Once truly I, & I think all the rest of the English in these partes, desyre rather his rowme then company. He is turbulent.   [*fol. 28r.*]]

19.   This mornyng overcast calme wether, but sowne after a littell rayne, w'th an extreme gale of wind N?erly, w'ch contynewed all day & the night following; rather a storme then othewaies, yet dry.

From Tacca-
mon Dono.
Nota.

Taccamon Dono sent me a present of 8 hense. And I wrot a letter to Capt. Adames how the China Capt.'s brother had lent vs 325 *gantes* of shark oyle, & therfore wished hym to send a man to Andrea, our host, to buy 4 or 500 *gantes* oyle at 10 *tais* p'r 100 *gantes*, as he enformed vs their was enough to be had, to the entent we may pay what

50 *taies*.

we owe & haue to serve our turne. And I deliverd fyftie *taies* plates bars to Mr. Nealson to lay out about charg of junck. And I wrot a lettr to Capt. Garrocho, & sent hym, viz.:–

a case bottells, cost .... Rs. 4⅜
2 Hollands cheeses, cost .... Rs. 6
1 loking glas, cost .... Rs. 1¼

11 Rs? ⅜,
Capt.
Garrocho.

Som totall amontes vnto ....Rs. 11⅜

Sent both lettr & thinges p'r Albara Monues.

And Mr. Nealson paid Yaiemon Dono, our junk carp'tr,

170 plank.
48 *tais*.

forty 8 *taies* in plate of bars, and is in full paym't for 170 plankes for the junck at 4 *mas* p'r peece; the rest being 20 *taies*, was paid p'r hym before.

August 1615

20. This mornyng still an extreme gale, wind Nºerly, yet fayre dry wether all day and the lyke p'r night, still much winde at Nº E.

Newes. I rec. a lettr frō Capt. Adames frō Cochi, dated this day, how a bark w'th Spaniardes frō Langasaque put into that roade, & came frō Mallia¹⁰³⁾ in shiping. The[y] say Don Lues de Fashardo did fight w'th 20 seale of Hollanders bound for the East Indies, & hath svnk (or taken) 12 of them, and the rest escaped by flight. Also the[y] say the King of Spaine hath wars w'th the Turk, & that this news is com frō Madrid in 6 months p'r way of New Spaine.

[*fol. 28v.*]]

Spaniards. And, after all, the Spaniardes came to the Eng'sh howse, viz., Miguel de Salinas, Capten Medina, and a Jerman called Marcus, w'th Alferis *Tuerto*, & Lues Martin, & Albora Monues accompanid them. They vsed many complementos & tould me of Don Lues Fachardos discomforting the Holand flete going for the East Indies, but after such a divers sort that I can scarse belleve it to be true; as also that 4 sayle of Eng'sh shipps were passed the Straits of Magilanus into the south sea. Capt. Speck sent

10 bars tynne. for 10 bars tynne, poiz. 9 *cattis* 4 *tay* wight.

21. This mornyng still a stiff gale, wind at Nº E., fayre wether and soe remeaned all day and the lyke p'r night, but the later p'rte yet calme.

To Capt. Adames. I sent Capt. Adames a barill of *singe*,¹⁰⁴⁾ 3 hense, and 6 loves of bread, w'th peares. And I wrot a letter to Andrea, our host at Langasaque, & sent it p'r a man called Miguel, an offecer of our junck apointed p'r Capt. Adames; & sent

150, *ta.* p'r hym one hvndred & fiftie *taies* in plate of bars, (this

---

103) Probably "Manillia."
104) Sing wine.—Thompson.

August 1615

To acc? Mr.
Nealson.

800 *gantes*
oyle.
A lettr to
Jorge
Durois.
Nota.

ta. ma. co.
7: 7: 4.
for lyme.

20 taies
Semi Dono.

50 *taies.*

Nota.

Also.

Parser.

150 *taies* made rec. p'r Mr. Nealson)[105] to pay for such hempe, sayles, & canes, as Andrea had bought for ye junck before, & 800 *gantos* of oyle. Also I wrot to Jorge Durois how I had rec. the milstones, a jar of conserve, & 25 pears w'thout lettr; and desired hym to buy me an other jar conserue of citrons, or lemons. And at night the Spaniardes envited them selues to our *fro*,[106] whom I entertayned in the best sort I could. Also Semi Dono had envited hym selfe to our *fro* before, but after sent me word he could not com, being sick of the sullens, because I would not lend hym money, being well experienced of his paym't before.

Paid China Capt.'s brother for 172 saks whit lyme at 4½ *condrin.*   [*fol. 29r.*]⌋

22. This mornyng faire calme wether, but after a small gale, wind N?erly, most p'rte of the day but calme all night, &c.

Semi Done being necessitous & in cheefe office in the kinges abcense, and now demanding but 20 *taies*, I haue, w'th generall consent, lent hym 20 *taies* to be repaid at a month as apeareth p'r his bill. And I del'd 50 *taies* I say fiftie *taies*, to Mr. Nealson, to lay out in charges of junck the 20 *taies* to Semi Dono, being paid p'r Mr. Nealson.

Semi Done came to our *fro*, accompanyd w'th Gonosque Dono, & divers other caueleros, whome (as I think) I entertayned to content.

And Capt. Adames came frõ Cochi in a great rage, against my *jurebasso*, Jn? Goresano, sayinge he was the occation the carpenters went not to work vpon our junck. But this (I know) was an vntruth, and the m? carpenter and Zanzabers knauery. And Capt. Adames scrivano or purcer of our our [*sic*] junk retorned from Miaco. And towardes night Capt. Adames fell into an extreame fevar w'th vomet-

---

105) These 8 words are written between the lines without any indication.
106) *Furo* 風呂, a bath.

66

Capt. Ada-
mes sick.

ing, and could not make water, soe he went to Zanzabars to take phisick. God send hym his health.

23. This mornyng still calme wether, but sowne after a fresh gale, wind N°.erly most p'rte of the day, but most p'rte (or rather) all night calme.

ta. ma.
6: 5:
2 lettrs
for Langa.

Nota.

I del'd Jn° Corezan, our *jurebasso*, 2 bars plate poz. 6 *taies* 5 *mas* to chang into small plate. And I rec. 2 lettrs frõ Jnọ de Lieuana & Jorge Durois of 30th & 31th pr'sent, new stile. Our scriuano of the junck tells me that Ogosho Samma sues to the *Dyrie*[107] to haue the name of *Quambaco*,[108] w'ch as it should seeme, is as the names of Ceaser or Augstus amongst the Emp'.s of Rome, w'ch is held an honor to all suckceadors. But he denies it till he know Fidaia Same is dead. [*fol. 29v.*]」

24. This mornyng fayre calme wether as lyke all the affore nowne, but after nowne littell wind at N° W., but calme all night, &c.

17 *cacas.*

30 row
postes.

3 lettrs
to Langa.

ta. ma.
6: 3:
mas.
5: 8:

We bought 17 *cacas* or square postes at 1 *mas* p'r peece, and 30 rownd postes, 2 for a *mas*, to send to Cochi, to make skaffolds to repare our junck. And I wrot 3 lettrs to Langasaque p'r Sr. Damian, viz.:-

1 to Jorge Durois w'th 6 *tais* 3 *mas* plate bars for stocking.

1 to Diego Farnando Rigota, in answer of his, to sell oyle.

1 to Jn° de Lieuana, in answer of his of 30th pr'sent.

A lettr to
Capt. Spek.

Also I wrot an other lettr to Capt. Speck in Spanish, tuching the retornyng of my slaue Tome, he not haveing yet answerd my former, & sent this p'r Capt. Adames. But his agew took hym againe, soe he del'd it not this day.

Nota.

And there came a greate man of Crates to see our Eng'sh howse, whome I entertayned in good sort.

---

107) The *Dairi* 內裏, or Mikado.
108) *Kwanbaku* or *Kanpaku* 關白 (lit. to concern in and advise), the regent for a *Mikado*, first appointed in A.D. 880.

August 1615

25. This mornyng still fayre calme wether, but after littell wind at N? W. most p'rte of the day, but littell or (rather) no wind at S. W. p'r night.

100 Rs? 8.

I del'd one hvndred Rialles of eight to Mr. Nealson to employ in stuffs w'th Duch marenars, whoe, as it should seeme, haue mett w'th som prize p'r way, otherwaies they

A man kild.

could not afford to sell soe good cheape. Also this night past a sentenell was slayne in this towne, & thought Taccamon Donnos men dyd it, yet no certentie.

And I del'd (or paid) to Mr. Wickham, in plate of bars, paid p'r Mr. Nealson; vpon acc?, his his [sic] yearly wage

20 ta.

or sallary, twentie taies.

Tome, boy, retorned.

Capt. Speck retorned my boy Tome hom, yet wrot me a pricking letter, to w'ch I answered as apereth p'r coppie. And I rec. back the 6 ta. 5 mas. of Jn?, w'ch w'th ex. amontes

ta. ma.
7: 5: 4.

to 7 ta. 5 ma. 4 con. and paid out 1 tay 1 mas for cattabr mat slaues, and 1 tay to her self and 1 tay to 50 Jn? & 2 mas for dying Jeffres keremon and 1 mas for knife sheathe, is all 3

ta. ma.
3: 4.
Frö Sugen.

ta. 4 ma. and Sugen Donos father sent a pr'sent of peares, & envited hym selfe to our fro a day or tow [sic] hence.

[fol. 30r.]]

1 pec. Cant. damask.

The China Capt. Andrea Dittis, gaue me a peec. of Canton damask for the peec. of Cochinchina silk I gaue hym before. And the Japan feast of All Soles being com,

1 pec. Lank. damask.
7 pec. duttis of 12 Rs. cor.

the China Capt. afforsaid sent me a peec. of Lankin damask for a present. And ther was 7 pec. duttis of 12 Rs? p'r corg, at 1 tay p'r pec., to a man w'ch came in company of Ske-

7 taies.

yemon Dono, is 7 taies, w'ch 7 taies Mr. Nealson receaved.

And Mr. Nealson paid the carpenter for od works the

ta. mas. co.
3: 8: 7
ta. n a. co.
3: 5: 0
1 pic. tyn.
40 taies.

som of 3 ta. 8 ma. 7 co. Also he paid a smith for making 2 piculls neals for junck, 3 tais 5 mas. And ther was one picull tyne sould cont'g 103½ bars at 4 mas the catty, amontes vnto forty taies, w'ch forty taies Mr. Nealson rec. in barse & kept

August 1615

it to lay out in charges about junck.

Also ther was a pink culler, N⁰ 85, & a primerose, N⁰ 125, w'th 6 other remnentes broad cloth measurd, as apereth p'r p'rticulers in the wast book; w'ch broad cloth was retorned from Edo & Shronge, and brought back p'r Mr. Wm. Eaton.

Broad cloth retorned.

26. This mornyng fyre wether w'th littell wind at S⁰ W., but after newne vered to N⁰ W. but at night to S. W. againe lettell wind, both day & night.

I bought & paid for my selfe two javelen or speare hedes, cost 8 *mas* & 8 *condrins*. And the China Capt., Andrea Dittis, bouth two *tattames*109) & a halfe broad cloth, viz.:-

m. con.
8: 8:
2 ½ *tat.*
broad cloth

1¼ *tat.*, cynamond culler, N⁰ 125, at 12 *ta.*   *ta.*   *ma.*   *con.*

tatt. amontes 15:   0:   0

1¼ tat., sad blew, N⁰ 98, at 12 *ta. tatt.*..........15:   0:   0

30 *ta*

                                                    30:    0:   0

And ther was therty *taies* in plate bars paid to the wrangling ship carpenters vpon acc⁰ of their wages p'r Mr. Nealson; and Migell *jurebassos* wife brought me a pr'sent of 3 hense, 20 egges, and pearse. And I reconed w'th Jnọ Goresano, our *jurebasso*, for triffling mattrs laid out for me till this day, haveing formerly del'd a bar plate to hym, so now all is cleuzed till this day, as apereth p'r a note on the phile.   [*fol. 30v.*]⌋

Frō Miguels wife.

Clered w'th Jnọ *jurebasso* as p'r note on file.

27. This mornyng still faire calme wether, yet after a fresh gale, wind a greate p'rte of the day, but calme all the night followinge.

This day at night all the st[r]eetes were hanged w'th lantarns, & the pagons vizeted all ther *futtaquis*110) and places of buriall w'th lantarns and lampes inviting their

Feast of dead.

109) A *tattamy*, the length of a *tatami* 疊 mat, equals to 1 *ken* 間 (ikken), about 1.818m. or 5.96 feet. Thompson gives a length of 6¼ feet.
110) *Hotoke* 佛, or Buddha, and the souls of dead men.

August 1615

dead frendes to com & eate w'th them, & so remeaned till midnight & then each one retorned to ther howses, having left rise, wine, & other viands at the graues for dead men to banquet of in their abcense, & in their howse made the lyke banquet, leving p'rte on an altor for their dead frendes & kindred. This feast lasteth 3 daies, but to morow is the solomest fast day.

28. This mornyng still faire calme wether, but after a small gale, wind Nºerly, most p'rte of the day, but calme p'r night.

100 *ta.*
And I del'd one hvndred *taies* in plate of bars to Mr. Nealson, to lay out about junk & other matters. And Mr. Nealson paid vnto Capt. Adames for charges laid out at Cochi about junck therty eight *taies* three *mas* and seven *condrins* in plate of bars, and in small plate six *taies* two *mas* and five *condrins*. And our ould *jurebasso*, Jnº Japon, groing into pouerty p'r his folly and lewd expences, came this day, seeking new e'tertaynm't; but we had no need of hym.

ta. ma.
38: 3: 7.
6: 2: 5.

Nota.

5 pec. for
2 *taies*
Mr. Nealson rec. of Capt. Adames for 5 pec. candeque mawy of 4 Rs. *corg*, 2 [ ]s.

29. This mornyng still fayre calme wether, but sowne after a fresh gale, wind most p'rte of the day S. W'erly, and the lyke all night following, &c. I wrot a lettr to Capt. Adames how his scrivano tould me our carp'trs said they would not work a stroake on the junk, except I gaue them a bill of my hand to pay them as they were paid the last yeare; w'ch I think is a *trampo*[111] of the Duch to get our carpenters from vs, to serve their owne turnes [*fol. 31r.*]] turnes [*sic*], they now pr'tending to set out their rotten junk for to carry provition to the Molocas. So I willed Capt. Adames to content them w'th bill or what else, so our busynes may goe forward; and w'th all advised hym that two

Nota.

111) *Trampa* (Sp.), trap.

70

August 1615

English men might be spared to assist hym in looking to these Japons we lying 4 or 5 of vs idell heare, for that the Wor'll Company would condem vs for lying idell & to suffer strangers to look to ther busynes.

A lettr from Capt. Garocho.

And I rec. a lettr from Capt. Garrocho of the 2th Sept., new stile, wherin he advised me of the recept of former mattrs sent, & to buy hym a jar Spanish wyne. Also I rec.

1 frō Aluaro Manos.

an other lettr frō Aluaro Monos, w'th a pr'sent of 10 water millons, 10 wreathes of bread, and a basket of grapes, w'th offers of much frendship.

Nota.

I vnderstand that the Hollanders haue offred Damian Marines to goe mr in their junk for the Molucos; but I know not whether he will accept of it or no. But they haue emploid hym to provid biskit for them.

And the China Capt., Andrea Dittis, bought ⅖ p'rts *tattamy* grene cloth, N⁰ 64: 95 at 12 *taies* p'r *tattamy*, 9 *ta.*

15 *corg* duttis.
½ *tat.* N⁰ 95 popinge
½ *tattamy.*
News of an Eng. ship.

3 *ma.* 7½ *co.* And 15 *cordg* dutty at 1 *tay* pece, is 300: 0: 0. And ther was halfe a *tattamy* of same cloth geven to his brothers sonne at Langasaque to make hym a cloake of.

And about midnight I had news that an Eng'sh shipp was on this cost, & that 2 daies past she was som 20 Japan leagues from Goto where 5 Japans were left abord to pilot her for Firando. So, herevpon, I sent out our pinis w'th Mr. Wm. Eaton in her, the Capt. China accompanying hym, to meet them, & sent them 2 barills wyne, 50 loves bread, 2 hoggs, 12 hense, 2 duckes, 10 water millans, and a baskit of pearse; and wrot a letter to Capt. Adames of the newse.

5 carp'rs.
3 lab'rs.

And 5 carp'rs & 3 lab'rs this day to glace garden hows window. *[fol. 31v.]]*

30. This mornyng still a stuff gale, wind S. W'erly, faire wether, but after a few drops of rayne, and p'r night wind at N⁰ W. littell wind.

Nota.

I sent our *jurebasso* to adviz. Semi Dono, Taccamon

71

August 1615

Dono, Oyen Dono, and Gonosque Dono of the newes our ship was w'thout the harbour neare Goto; of w'ch it seemed they were glad, & sowne after sent their men to congratulate or reioyce w'th me, &c.

A letter frō
Jor. Durois.
2 jars of
conserue.
70 candels.

And I receaved a letter frō Jorge Durois, dated in Langasaque, le 7th of Sept'br, new stile, w'th a jar of conserve of citrones, bought & cost 5 *taies*; also an other jarr conserve w'ch he sent me for a present, and 70 candells w'ch cost one *taies*.

And the man I sent to buy oyle retorned from Langasaque, & brought but 241 *gantes* oyle, w'ch cost 12½ *mas* p'r ten *gantes*, but could get no more at prise, and so retorned

241 *gantes*
oyle.

the rest money back, yet, Jorge Durois writes me a Portingal hath a good quantety brought from Amacan, w'ch he offerd hym to sell. So I must now send this foole back againe w'th the money; and Mr. Nealson noted downe in

Frō Langas-
aque.
ta. ma.
62: 1
to Mr. Nelson
before 21th
ditto.
A lettr
frō Goto.

accō frō Langasaque frō Andrea, for w'ch he paid hym selfe for rattons, hempe, oyle, sayles, jarrs, as p'r p'rticulers, amont vnto 87 *ta.* 7 *ma.* 4½ *co.* And he rec. in ready money of the fello. 62 *ta.* 1 *ma.*

Also I rec. a lettr frō the *bongew* of Goto, wherin he advised me of our ships being neare vnto Goto, & that he had put 3 or 4 men into her to pilot her to Firando. And towardes night Capt. Adames wrot me a lettr frō Cochi how they had discoverd the shipp to be w'thin 4 leagues, and

Our ship
distard.

that he imagened she would be at Cochi this tide. And I wrot a lettr to Jorge Durois in answer of his rec. this day,

3 lettrs to
Langasaque.
5 carp'rs.
5 labo'rs.

willing hym to buy me 700 *gantes* of oyle & an other lettr to Aluaro Munos w'th a Holland cheese, & a therd to Capt. Garrocho in answer of his sent p'r boy.   [*fol. 32r.*]]

31. This mornyng fayre wether w'th littell wind N?erly, but after a stiffe gale most p'rte of the day, and the lyke all night.

August 1615

I caused store of boates to goe out to tow in our shipp, & wrot a lettr to ye capt. p'r Mr. Ed: Sayer, dowbting Mr. Eaton hath missed of them. But sowne after our bote retorned & the Capt. China in her w'th a lettr frō Mr. Eaton how the ship was at an ancor 3 or 4 leagues frō Firando, & that [t]he shipps name was called the *Hoziander*, the Capt. or Cape m'rchantes name Mr. Raphe Copingall[*sic*]. So I retorned forth w'th p'r the said bark & went abord, where

I rec. these lettrs foll'g, viz.:–

1 generall coppy of a lettr frō Wor'll Company.

1 copy of theirs in p'rticuler to Capt. Jurdain, Bantā.

1 frō Capt. Jourden in Bantam, 15th April 1615.

1 frō Mr. Westbie in Bantam, 10th ditto.

1 frō Jnọ Beamond in Bantam, ditto 10th.

1 frō Harnando Ximenes in Bantā, le 9th ditto.

1 frō Mr. Adam Denton in Pattania, le 5th July.

1 frō Generall Saris at Souldania, 1th June 1614.

1 frō Sr. Thomas Smith in London, 30th Novembr 1613.

1 frō Sr. Thomas Smith in London, 26th April 1614.

1 frō my brother Walter Cockes in London, 6th April 1614.

And Mr. Raphe Copendall came ashore w'th an other yong man called Jnọ Osterwick, but the wind was soe extreame that all the barks were forced to retorne & leave the ship riding at an ancore. & it apeareth p'r the Wor'll Compˢ lettrs that all the voages now are put into one generall company in adventure. God be pr'sed for it. And as Capt. Copendall tells me, their is an other company made to adventure 120000 *lb*. str. p'r ano for 4 yeares ensuing, but to what places not openly knowne; & that 4 seale great English shipps weare entred into the Straites of Magelanus, but for what entent not knowne. [*fol. 32v.*]⌋

73

September 1615

1. This mornyng still a stiff gale wind N°erly all day, and
the like p'r night till midnight, and then it slacked and was
calme before day.

A lettr frō
Chubio Dono.

I rec. a lettr frō Chubio Dono deted in   ,[112] le
, wherin he wrot me much cumplimento, and
sent an other as from the Emperour to Capt. Adames, that

Nota.
3m. 3c. pd.
300 duttis.
10 Rs. corg.
10 China
Capt. at 1
tay p'r peec.

he should forth w'th com vp to the Emperour. What the
reason should be I know not; yet I suspect it was a plot laid
before p'r Capt. Adames hym selfe, & the Duch, to the
entent he might goe vp to serve their turnes; & truly I
esteem he loveth them much better then vs that are of

Bought 543
gantas oyle,
cost
ta. ma. co.
69: 3: 7½
pd. p'r Mr.
Nealson.

his owne nation; or else it may be he seeketh occasion to
get the Emperour to comand hym to stay & not to procead
forward on the Syam voyag, his tyme of service to the Company being out w'thin 2 months. Once the end will shew
what is the occation, but Capt. Adames hym selfe esteem-

20 taies
paid canks
vpon acc°
p'r Mr.
Nelson plate
bars.

eth it is to enquire of hym about a fortresse newly built
at the Liqueas, vnto w'ch place it was thought Fidaia
Samme would retire after his losse of Osekey. Capt. Speck
came to Eng'sh howse being ready to go vp to Miaco. And

50 ta.

I del'd 50 ta. in plates of bars to Mr. Nealson.

2. This mornyng calme wether, but sowne after an extreme
stiff gale, wind all day following & all the afore p'rte of the
night, but after midnight calme.

I gott barks to goe out to tow our shipp into harbor, yf
it were possible, much fearing a tuffon; & Capt. Copendall
& Mr. Eaton went abord to hasten matters forward &, yf

---

112) The name of place and the date, not entered.

74

September 1615

the shipp came not in, to bring aland our Cambaia cloth &
other comodetis, to the entent to lay out the pr'sent for
the Emperor, & make as much hast vp as we can, not to be
overlong behinde the Hollanders. But the wind proving so
hard, we could nether get ship into harbor nor bring goods
ashore, Capt. Copendall & Mr. Eaton remeanyng all night
abord. God send vs wether to bring her in this dangerous
tyme of the yeare.   [*fol. 33r.*]]

We looked out for a bark to goe vp in to the Emperour,
but could find non but ould rotten ons, all being aboue
w'th the king but one w'ch the Hollanders had gotten before
we asked. So we sent to Sanguro Dono, Foins[113] sonne a
bark of his. And Mr. Nealson paid for 218 *gantas* oyle for

ta. ma. co.
19: 3: 7¼.
Sonday.

our junck w'th 15 jars to put it in, cost all 19 *ta.* 3 *ma.* 7½*co.*
3.   This mornyng fayre calm wether, but sowne after a stiff
gale N? E'erly all day and all the fore p'rte of the night,
but rest calme as before.

Nota.

I got barkes to goe out againe to tow ship into harbour,
yf it remeaned calme, or else to bring good ashore; but

To ye m?

the wind was so stiffe all day that the[y] could doe nothing.
And I wrot a lettr to Mr. Jn? Hunt to send his carpentr to
tell what plank and tymber he needed to sheath and repare
the *Hoziander;* and w'th all sent hym a pig, 6 hense, 10
loves of bread, w'th peares, redish, cowcombers, & bell

A lettr to
Goto.

engenios. And I wrot a letter and sent a pr'sentt to ye
bongew of Goto for puting pilot a bord & sending me word
therof, so the pr'sent was, viz.:–

India cloth.

1 pec. white baftas, of nyne Rs., *corg*..............   114)
1 pec. blak bafta died, at 9 Rs., *corg*..............

---

113) Matsura Sangorō Nobumasa 松浦三五郎信正, later renamed Kurōdo 藏人
     (Matzrea Crodze Do in Vol III).
114) This and the following prices, not entered.

75

September 1615

1 pec. duttis, of 10 Rs. p'r *corge* ....

1 pec. blew byram, of   Rs. p'r *corg*.............

1 pec. red zelas, of 12 Rs? p'r *corg* ....

And geven the fello w'ch brought present, viz.:–

1 duble pec. burall of   Rs? *corge* ....

A pr'sent.

And the mr of the bark w'ch brought downe Mr. Eaton came frō Langasaque & brought me a pr'sent of pearse, & offerd to bring his bark hither, yf I had need to fraight her. And about midnight Capt. Adames went out in a bark ab-

2 pottes quicksilvr.

ord the *Hozeander* w'th many other barks to tow her in, we fearing a tuffon. And Capt. Copendall brought 2 bras vessells of quicksilver a shore out of the *Hoziander*. [*fol. 33v.*]]

4. This mornyng still faire calme wether, but sowne after a fresh gale wind N? E'erly som p'rte of the day, rest variable & calme w'th som rayne after midnight.

Ye *Hosiandr* cam to an ancor in Firando.

And about 9 a clock the *Hoziander* came to an ancor in the harbor of Firando, being towed in w'th boates and shot ofe ii pec. ordinance; and the Duch answerd them w'th 2 peec. out of the howse, and 5 out of the greate ship. &

Capt. Spek went for Miaco.

Capt. Speck w'th other m'rch'nt came abord her, he being ready to dep'rte for Miaco; & he pr'sently did, & had 3 pec. ordinance for a farewell, and we the lyke when we re-torned ashore. & they shot 3 pec. more after out of the

For my Boy.

Duch howse. And I make Tushma, my boy, a new *kerimon* of damask of Canton, w'th a cloake or gaberdyn of stript

6 *taies*.

taffete. And Mr. Nealson paid 3 *taies* to Toma, the boy, & 3 *taies* to Jnọ Moure, the boy, vpon reconyng of ther wages

50 *taies*.

at 1 *tay* p'r peec p'r month. And I del'd 50 *taies*, I say fifty taies, plate bars to Mr. Nealson; and he paid 10 *taies* like

10 *taies*.

plate to pilottes that brought our ship the *Hozeandar* from Goto to Firando. And we receaved ashore this day out of the *Hoziandr* 4 chistes gvns or fowling pec. N?   115)

115) This and following figures, not entered.

September 1615

cont'g   guns. Also two fardelles stile cont'g 166
gades,[116) w'th 4 fardeles cloth Choromandell, viz., N?
[117) from   .   [*fol. 34r.*]⌋

5. This mornyng a fresh gale, wind S'erly w'th store of
rayne, but after cleared vp, wind vering Noerly, & soe p'r
night No W'erly; faire wether.

carp'rs.
labo'rs.

Frō ye China
Capt. frō
Langasaque.

4 lettrs
frō Langa.

Nota.
Jorge.

Nota.

We set carpenters a work to make chistes for to carry
vp our goods, and   [118) laborers to make mat sackes
to put our pep'r in. Also the China Capt., Andrea Dittis,
retorned frō Langasaque, & brought me a pr'sent of a blew
peec. of damask frō his brother Capt. Whaw, & gaue me an
other hym selfe w'th an embrawdred velvet cushin. And
I rec. a lettr frō Capt. Garowcho of 12 of September, & an
other frō Jn? de Lieuana of 10th ditto, w'th 2 others frō
Jorge Durois of 3th and 7th ditto. And Jorge sent me 2
hampers cont'g 5 pec. wroght black velvet, 9 pec. black
taffeties, & 24 pec. sattens, wroght & plane, as also 3 pere
silk stockings, & 1 peare thrid, as p'r adviz. And Vshenos-
que Dono, our ould *bongew*, sent me a pr'sent of frute, &
came hym selfe & visited me offring his service to goe vp
in our bark as before, if need weare. Also we had newse the
king of this place was w'thin 13 leagues, & would be heare
to morrow. Yet I was secretly enformed by a frend that he
is in towne, secretly com in, & ment to retorne out to his
barks to morrow, & so to enter at pleasure.

Soe we gaue order to our ship to sute offe her ordenance
as he past by, being determend to goe out to meete hym.
It is said that the King of Shashma is lykwais retorned to

---

116) Bars. Hence the term gad-steel—Thompson.
117) This number and the following name, not entered.
118) Not entered.

his contrey p'r the Emperours p'rmition; soe it is thought som exploit is in hand.

Also the China Capt. tells me that Damian Marin & Jnº de Lieuana are taken pr'soners & carid about the greate ship, & is in dispite of the service they did to the English. [*fol. 34v.*]]

Capt. Sp'k to Miaco. Capt. Speck dep'rted towardes Miaco, & had 2 vollers small shot out of the *Jaccatra*, & 5 pec. ordinance out of their greate ship, & charged againe and gaue 3.

6. This mornynge fayre wether w'th littell wind at Nº W. most p'rte of the day & lyke p'r night or rather calme, &c.

Nota. We laded most p'rte of our goodes abord a bark, to goe for Miaco, Capt. Copingdall, going vp w'th Capt. Adames and Mr. Wickham. The p'rticulers goodes appeare p'r invoiz.

4 pec. chint. 2 pec. And ther was 4 per chint amad, rated at 15 Rsº p'r *corg.*, sould vnto Gonrock Donos man for for[*sic*] 1 *tay* p'r peec. w'th 2 pec. at ½ *tay* pec.; and ther was geven hym in a pre-

5 pec. chint. sent p'r Capt. Copendalls consent 5 pec. of same chint, cost 15 Rs. *corge.*

100 *tais.* 120: 9: 5 st. del'd or made rec. p'r Mr. Nealson for iron work frō Miaco or other matter. Nota. And I del'd (or paid) one hvndred *taies* to Capt. Adames of money borowed of hym. And som 2 howrs before day littell Antony the *bongew* came & advized me how the king was arived, & was glad our Eng'sh ship was in saffety in the port, & desired that yf we shot affe any ordinance, that it might be doone when he was landed or had sett foote ashore. The botswen, the gvner, and the carp'tr misvsed the mr., offring to haue let malefactors out of prison w'ch were punished p'r the mr.

7. This mornyng still faire calme wether, but after a fresh gale of wind Nºerly most p'rte of the day, but littell or rather no wind 'pr night.

The King of Firando ariued frō Very erly in the mornyng, the king entred into Firando, & the Duch shot ofe 3 small pec. ordinance as he passed by

ye Court.

out of the howse, & 20 pec. ordinance out of the great ship, & 6 out of the small, w'th 2 volle of small shot out of Duch ship. And our shipp, the *Hozeander* shot affe 11 pec. ordinance. And sowne after I sent our *jurebasso* to Oyen Dono, to desire hym to exkews me towardes the king, for that I came not to kisse his handes in respect I thought he was awery of his voyage p'r sea. He said he would adviz the king thereof, & that I had reason in not coming for that he was overweryed. [*fol. 35r.*]⌋

50 *taies.*
150 *taes.*
50 *taies.*

I del'd fiftie *taies* to Mr. Nealson, and one hvndred and fiftie to Mr. Wickham, in p'rt of his cargezon, and 50 *taies* to Capten Copendall.

1 pec. blak taffete Mr. Wickham.
1 bar gold poz. 55 *taies.*

And Mr. Wickham had a peec. fine black taffete, cost me 29 *mas.* And Andrea Dittis, the China Capt., brought back a bar of *oban*[119] gould, sent his brother before to geve to a godchild, but now retorned, and poz. fyftie and five *taies.*

Nota.

And *Tono* Sa� me, the king, sent for me to com & speak w'th hym; w'ch I did, accompanied w'th Capt. Copendall. He tould me that Shongo Sa� me was gon for Edo before he came away, & that he thought the ould Emperour was gon for Shrongo before this tyme. Soe he offred me his lettrs of fauour to Codskin Dono & Safian Dono, because (as he said) to Spaniardes & Portingals were reiected & not suffred to com in the Emperours pr'sence, nether would he vouchsafe to receve any pr'sent they sent hym. Also he said that he thought this junck w'th the Holladrs had taken was good prise, because they had not the Emperours passe; & therefore he would not meddell in the matter. I could not forgot[*sic*] to note downe how Mr. Hunt, the m.͘ of the *Hozeander*, fell out w'th Roland Romas, the purcer. Soe they went togethr by the eares. I condeme them both

Mr. Nealson rec. an accompt of 120 *ta.* 9 *ma.* 5 *co.* for iron work & other mattrs frō Mr. Eaton.

Nota.

119) *Ōban* 大判, a gold coin, usually 10 *ryo* 兩, or ten *kobans* 小判.

September 1615

very much; but surly they were drunk, espetially the m.^r,
& I think he is crazed in his witts.

45 pec. chint new cargeson.

And Gonrock Donos man bought 40 pec. of chint amad
at one *tay* p'r peec. & 5 of the same were geven hym in a

Nota. Damian pr'soner.

present. Also I wrot a letter to Gonrock Dono how the
Portingals had taken Damian Marin, and Jno de Lieuana
pr'soners abord there great ship at Langasaque, desiring
restetution of them, or else I would complaine to the Emperour.   *[fol. 35v.]*

8. This mornyng faire overcast calme wether, but after
store of rayne all day; wind at S. W., but vered N.^oerly at
night contynewing a stiff gale, yet dry.

50 *taies*.

And I del'd 50 *taies* plate bars to Mr. Eaton & is p'rte of
money sent in cargezon, Mr. Wickham having 150 *tais*

Invois goods del'd.

before. And I del'd the invoiz or cargezon of goodes sent
vp into the custody of Mr. Ric'd Wickham and Mr. Wm.
Eaton, to accompany Capt. Raphe Copendall, to goe vp to
the Emperour w'th a pr'sent & other goodes to sell. Mr.
Wm. Adames accompanyng them; Mr. Wickham & Miguell
jurebasso to goe for Edo, and Mr. Eaton & Tome to re-

Nota.

meane at Miaco or Osekey. And I would not want to note
downe that we had much a dow this day about the masters
faling out w'th the purcer, all the shipps company being
against the purcer; the m.^r aledging he followed hym & sett
vpon hym vnawares at advantage, & took two gould ringes
frō hym, & threw hym downe a hill, & thought to haue
stobd hym w'th his owne knife, haveing taken it frō hym
p'r force. Out of dowbt this Rowland Thomas is an idell
braned foolish felloe.

5 pec. chint.

Alsoo Gonrock Donos man bought 5 pec. of same chint
of that yesterday at 1 *tay* p'r peece. And I paid p'r to Juan
5 *mas* for a hat I gaue formerly to Sangero Sama, ould
Foynes sonne, few daies past. And I rec. two hvndred Riall

80

September 1615

of eight back frō Mr. Wickham of money del'd hym in Syam voyage, viz., 150 Rs? sent p'r hym for my selfe & 5 *taies* p'rte of 150 Rs? more lent hym, so that 100 Rs? remeanes yet in his handes.

I wrot a lettr to Gonrock Dono about the taking prisoners of Damian Marin & Jn? de Lieuano, desiring hym to procure their liberty, for that they belong to our junck, & therfore haue nothing to doe nether w'th Spaniard nor Portingall, whome I hould no justises in Japon. [*fol. 36r.*]⌡

9. This mornyng overcast wether w'th a stiff gale, wind at N? E'erly, or rather N? E. all day, but not alltogether soe much by night.

I wrot 2 lettrs to Jorge Durois and Capt. Garrocho in answer of theirs of the 7th & 12th Septembr, as also advising them I would geue knowledg to the Emperour how the Portingall had taken Damian Marin & Jn? de Lieuana pr'soners, they being our servantes, as I had advised the lyke to Gonrock Dono p'r lettr yisterday. These 2 lettrs I sent p'r conveance of Capt. China. Also I del'd one hvn-

dred *taies* plate bars to Mr. Nealson, to lay out for the needfull.

The king sent 2 barelles *morofack*, 6 bundelles drid cuttel fish, and a hogg, for a present to Capt. Copendall before he went vp. And Semi Done sent to me for a bottell of Spanish

wyne, w'ch I sent hym out of that littell the Hollanders gaue me. And Capt. Copendall had 2 pottes of sweet meats of ginger, citrons, & oringes, &c.

10. This mornyng still a stiff gale wind at N? E? and soe remeaned all day, but not soe much p'r night, but rather calme after midnight.

Semi Done sent for som sweet meates, haveing invited the king. Soe I sent hym of 3 severall sortes. Thus these noble men vse to doe in these p'rtes.

81

September 1615

Capt.
Copendall.

Capt. Copingdall had w'th hym vp 2 sivell[sic] spownes, 2 silver forkes, & 1 silver salt & cover of Companis w'th 2

Nota.

littell silver boles lyke half grapes of my owne. Capt. Adames now came & tould me how we want about 1000 *cattis* of ould net to calke our junk w'th all. Out of dowbt his skrivano is a falce knaue; yet I may not say soe to Capt.

2 bages
pepp'r.

Adames, for then all the fatt would be in the fire.

And ther was 2 baggs pep'r sould to Skidayn Dono, to pay as rest is sould, poz. 131 *cattis* nett.   [*fol. 36v.*]

We made consert this day w'th Skidayen Dono and the China Capt. for plank for the *Hoziander* as foll'th:-

600, 1 inch plank at 3*ma*. 6*co*. p'r plank.
100, tow[sic] inche pl'te at 6 [*ma*.] 6 [*co*.] p'r pec.
010, 5 of 3 inch & 5 of 4 inche at 17*mas* pec.

100 *taies*.

And I del'd them one hvndred *taies* in plate bris[sic] w'ch Mr. Nealson paid them. Mr. Nealson made rec. And I wrot

2 lettrs
to Jnº &
Damian.

2 letters to Jnº de Lieuana, 1 p'r a Japon, & the other enclosed to Gonrock Dono, both to one effect that I will vse the best means I can to procure their libertis, I meane Damian Marins & his, or else will mak it known to the Emperour.

11.   This mornyng fayre calme wether, but after a fresh gale, wind Nº. E'erly all day, but most p'rte of the night calme.

Capt.
Copendall
for Miaco.

Capt. Copendall, Capt. Adames, and Mr. Wickham & Mr. Eaton dep'rted from Firando this mornyng towardes Miaco; and ther was 11 pec. ordinance shot affe for a farewell. But as we were at dyner, ther came a lettr to me frõ

Nota.
Andrea
Dittis pid
40 *tais* for
p'rchs howse
on north
side for
Comp.

Capten Copendall, wherin he wrot me that Capt. Adames was gon before & would not stay for them, & that their bark was so pestred that it was ready to sinck. Wherevpon he wrot me to send them an other bark to lighten them, w'ch I did w'th all expedition; & p'r Mr. Rowland Thomas,

82

September 1615

the bringer of his letter, I sent hym, viz.:-

> 2 cases bottells of his owne w'th Spanish wyne.
> 2 barrelles *morofack*.
> 40 loves bread.
> 01 great *kitesoll*.
> 01 bras candellstick.

Nota.

And I wrot an other lettr to Capt. Copendall p'r the bark, advising how I vnderstood Migell *jurebasso* had in speeches misvsed a man of Gonrock Donos, whome went passinger

Turkish History.

in the bark. Also I sent my Turkish History p'r the bearer of this lettr to Capt. Coꝑ to passe away the tyme p'r the way.

ta. m. co.
245: 8: 8.

17 sows leed del'd Andrea Dittis poz. 40 *pic.* 98 *cat.* at vj *taies* pec.:– 245: 8: 8.   [*fol. 37r.*]]

12. This mornyng still fayre calme wether, but after a fresh gale wind at N? W. most p'rte of the day, but night calme, &c.

Cordag & seales landed.
100 *tais*.

We landed yisternight & this day all the cables cordage of *Hoziander* in our yord vnder a shed and the seales at China Captens howse. And I del'd one hvndred *tais* plate barse to Mr. Nealson to lay out about ship & junck. And

218.

wee rec. pep'r ashore yisterday in 4 boates, and this day 218

Frō Soye.

bagges pep'r in cloth sacks made. Also Soyemon Dono sent a pr'sent of 2 pewter cups and 10 Japon *sequanseques*[120] (or dishes), looking for greater mattrs, w'ch needes must

Nota.

be retorned to hym & others w'ch are in place. And towards night our carpenters that wrought vpon the junck came to Firando frō Cochi, to morrow being a festiefall day, as also to receave more rise. I find Gingro, Capt. Adames scrivano, left to look to our workmen, to be but an eypleasing prowd knaue. They thought to haue pickt a quarrell to fall out,

---

120) Sakazuki 盃.

September 1615

yet I geue them content.

13. This mornyng still faire calme wether, and soe remeaned all day and night following; not wether, but rather a small breath wind somtyme W. Nọerly.

Yaimon.

Yaimon Dono, the mͬ ship carpenter, brought me a present of pears, &, in the end of many compemental speeches, took exceptions that land carpenters were sett to work abord our shipp. I answered hym, he & others were occation therof, in vsing and out of reason heretofore & making me to pay them what they list, &c. And we carid

A prᵉsent to ye king.

Tome[*sic*] Samme, the King of Firando, a prᵉsent as foll'th, viz.:–

```
1 pec. black wrought velvet, cost.............020:  0:  0
3 pec. grogren at .................................121)
10 pec. whit baftas at 20 Rsọ corge ...........008:  0:  0
10 pec. red zelas, of 12, corg...................004:  8:  0
10 pec. blew byrams, of 15, corg ...............006:  0:  0
10 pec. chint amad, of 20, corg ................008:  0:  0
10 pec. cours tapis, of 04¾, corg ..............001:  9:  0
10 pec. chader pontado, of 09, corg ...........003:  6:  0
```

[*fol. 37v.*]

brought frõ other side:–

4 cakes wax, poz.122)
5 bages pep'r, poz.
2 sows lead, poz.
1 damaskt gvn.
1 chast gvn.
10 knyves.

14. This mornyng still fayre calme wether, and soe remeaned all day, and the lyke p'r night.

Nota.

The King of Firando compassed in most p'rte of the har-

---

121) Not entered.
122) This and following figures, not entered.

84

September 1615

bor w'th nettes & hedges to ket[c]h fish to morrow; and
sent me word to com & drink w'th hym to night, w'ch I
exskewsed till to morrow mornyng.

And towardes night Mr. Jnọ Huntt, the mᵣ of the *Hoziander*, came & tould me that 2 of the shipps company had
byn abcent 2 daies, viz., one Doughtie, a quarter mᵣ and an
other called Wadden, a rich mans sonne of Plymouth,
whome is fownd to be a very cheater. & at very instant I
had notis of Daughtie where he was drunken in a howse;
soe I took hym & sent hym abord w'th a lettr to the mᵣ,
&c. And there was one hund[r]ed *taies* receved of Andrea
Dittis, the China China[sic] Capt., vpon accọ, w'ch money
Mr. Nealson rec. in plate of bars. Also 15 sowes of leade
were sould & del'd to the China Capt. for his brother Whaw
of Langasaque, poz. 3628 *cattis* wantes 372 *cattis* to make vp
40 *piculls* to pay for it, as the Emperour doth rest[sic] the
rest. The mᵣ sent me word that one Piter Waddon was
ashore & had byn the lyke 2 daies & nightes together, &
that he had stolne & pawne his companions ap'rell, & laid
it to pawne in whorehowses and was gon vpon the score
in divers howses, & determened to run away to som other
place. So I laid out to look for hym. [*fol. 38r.*]」

15. This mornyng still fayre calme wether, but after nowne a
stiff gale, wind at Nọ W'erly all rest of day, but calme most
p'rte of night.

The walle or neting the king caused to be made to fish
was borne downe in the night w'th the force of the tide,
&c.

I went betyme in the mornyng to vizet the king, accompanid w'th Sr. Ed. Sayer, Mr. Jnọ Osterwick, and Mr.
Jones the chirurgion. He entertayned vs kindly; & soe we
retor'd.

Also we sent 18 *picolles* a *cattis* net abord the junk at

85

This 100 *ta*.
mad. rec. of
China Capt.
11th Septbr.
100 *ta*.

15 sows
leade.
Lead made
rec.
11th pr'sent.
17 sons.
Nota.
Waddon.

Nota.

September 1615

Chochi, w'th iron and sacks charcoll.

And ther was bought of Andrea, the China Capt., & his

4 *cattis* muske, 86 cods.

60 Rs.

2 *taies*.

Kings fishing.

brother Whaw foure *cattis* musk, being in 86 codds, cost twelue *taies* p'r *catty*, in China; & so let vs haue it to pay in Realles of eight 60 Rs. And I bought and paid for 4 peare lether pvmps & 3 peare velvett *pantables*,[123] two *taies* to a China shewmaker. And in the after nowne the king and all his nobles came a fishing before our dore, haveing laid duble nettes fist cres[124] over the haven at a hie water. I made ready 2 piges, 2 duckes, 2 hense, & a loyne pork, all rosted, w'th a banket sweetmeates, enviting them ashore, but fownd them vnwilling; & soe carid it abord the kings boate, where they did eate what they pleased. & soe they dep'rted along p'r our shipp, where they had 7 pec. ordi-

Nota.

nance shot affe at their landinge. And, in my absence, a fello came w'th a lettr from Jorge Durois & a peare silk stocking (as he said); but standing gaping at the fishermen, a knaue stole both stockinges & lettr frõ hym, or else, as som crastie knaues doe, did rob hym selfe, &c [*fol. 38v.*]]

16. This mornyng still calme faire wether, but sowne after a stiff gale most p'rte of day S'erly, but littell of[sic] not wind p'r night, some drops rayne.

A letter to Jorge. China. Nota.

I wrot a lettr to Jorge Durois of loosinge his lettr and stockinges. And I gaue my peare knives to the China Capt. to send to his brother (or rather kinsman) in China, vpon hope trade; as also he had 4 looking glasses for same pur-pose, bought of Duch, and 4 pec. *chowters*[125] of 20 Rs⁰ p'r *corg*, w'th knyves; & [it] is thought fit to geue 50 Rs⁰ 8 to the man w'ch carrieth the letter, to pay his charges

---

123) *Pantuflos* (Span.), slippers.
124) Perhaps a slip of the pen for "fixed across."—Thompson.
125) Or, *chowtars*, cotton cloth. Cocks uses *casho* for the same thing in the entry for December 1, 1615. Cf. *Chudder* in *Hobson-Jobson*.

86

September 1615

p'r way, & to send a greate gould ring of myne w'th a white amatist in it, cost me 5 *lb* str. in France. This ring to be sent to one of these 2 men, named Ticham Shofno, an evenuke. God grant all may com to good effect. Amen.

2 son dialls. Amen. Also 2 ivery son dialls, cumpas lyke, del'd hym.

Sonday. 17. This mornyng overcast calme wether, but after wind variable, & not much p'r day, but more wind p'r night N°. W., some drops rayne.

To kinges brother. And we carrid a pr'sent to Genshe Samme,[126] ye kinges brother, as followeth, viz.:–

	ta.	[ma.]	[co.]
1 damaskt pees., cost	5:	0:	0
5 pec. white baftas, cost	04:	0:	0
5 pec. chint, cost	04:	0:	0
1 peec. wrought satten, cost			[127]

60 Rs. 8. And I paid 60 Rs°. of 8 to China Capt. for the fowre *cattis*

50 Rs. 8. muske, is forty 8 *taies*. Allso I paid fiftie Rialles of eight more to geue the post (or man) that caries a letter & tokens into China, to' pay his charges p'r the way. And del'd hym my

Gould ring. great gould ring w'th the white amatist, cost me 5 *lb* str.

20 Rs. 8. And I lent twenty *pezes* to Andrea Dittis, to send to a frend, for w'ch he is to be accomptable in other plate. [*fol. 39r.*]⌋

Nota. I thought to haue carid pr'sentes to Takkaman Dono

Kinge on progres. and Semi Dono, but they were gon out of the towne to their lands to meete the king in his progresse, he now going vizet his cheefe placesse, being his granfather dying, he is soly com to governe, & had noe tyme to doe it till now by meanes of Japan warse. I must of necessety please this Takkamon Dono & Semi Dono, because I expect to procure 2 *chawnes* (or howses) to build gadongs vpon neare our English howse.

---

126) *Alias* Tonomon Samme. See 83) above.
127) Not entered.

September 1615

To Oyen Dono. And I went to Oyen Dono, the kings secretary or governor, & carid hym a pr'sent of

1 pec. rich wrought taaffety, cost			128)
5 pec. white baftas, of 20 Rs., cost	4:	0:	0
5 pec. chint amad, of 20 Rs., *corg.*, cost	4:	0:	0
5 knives, cost			129)

He tould me he would assist vs in getting these *chawnes* althought it displaced men that paid daylie tribute to the king, it being in the hart of the towne, & therfore gaue me counsell to get Taccamon Dono & Semi Dono to frendes; but hereafter when our busynes was well setled, then not to geue giftes to any one but to the kinge. This was his coun-

Nota. sell, &c. He also adviced me to envite the king to dyner at his retorne back, for that yet he was not invited since we came into Japan.

18 *pi'ls* 41 *catt.* nett 20: 3:5. And Mr. Nealson paid for 18 *piculles* 41 *catty* wight ould nettes to cawke our junk at 11 *mas* p'r *picull*, plate in bars, is 20 *ta.* 3 *ma.* 5 *co.*

Nota. Their came a Portingall prisoner to the Eng'sh howse in campany of Hollanders, haveing lycense to walk abroad. He was taken p'r the Hollanders in this junk, & is the 5th tyme the[y] haue taken hym at sea.   [*fol. 39v.*]⌋

18. This mornyng a stiff gale, wind Noerly w'th rayne som p'rte of the forenowne, rest of day dry, but much rayne most p'rte of the night & great windes.

And ther was sould one hvndred fyfty and nyne peeces duttis at 1 *tay* p'r peec. plate of barse receved p'r Mr. Wm. Nealson, & 3 peec. geven hym in for wett or staynes in som

162 pec. duttis 12 Rs? 159 *tais*. of them is 162 pec. duttis for 159 *taies* plate bars paid (as I said) to Mr. Nealson.

Nota. Jn? Gorezan, our *jurebasso*, fell out w'th Andrea Dittis,

---

128) Not entered.
129) Not entered.

September 1615

the China Capt. This *jurebasso* hath a fowle tong & fallth out w'th all men, & the China Capt. was overmuch hasty, &c.

19. This mornyng much wind at Nᵒ somthing E'erly w'th store of rayne, and soe contynewd most p'rte of the day; extreme wind p'r night but littell or noe rayne.

Frō Sugen Dono.

Sugian Dono came & brought me a present of 2 bagges sweet powlder to lay amongst ap'rell, & said they were geven hym p'r the kinge & formerly geven to the king p'r the Emperour.

20. This mornyng still much wind Nᵒerly, overcast wether; but yet dry all day and night following, except som few drops rayne at tymes; littell wind p'r night.

Nota.

We sent certen tymber, coles & other matters, to Cochi to Capt. Adames scrivano, for our junck.

21. This mornyng calme overcast wether w'th som drops of rayne, but after wind variable, yet fayre wether both day & night following, &c.

1 logg lead to Toma Dono.
China Capt. for Goto.

Ther was sould & del'd to Tome Dono, our next neighbour, 1 logg leade del'd to hym poz. 225 *cattes* to pay as rest are sould. The China Capt., Andrea Dittis, went for Goto this mornyng, to meete Capt. Whaw his brother, to send away a small *soma* for China about our pr'tended & hopefull pr'curing trade in China, w'ch God, of his mercy, grant may take effect, &c.   [*fol. 40r.*]]

22. This mornyng still faire calme wether, but sowne after a fresh gale, wind at Nᵒ E. most p'rte of the day, but more wind p'r night, yet dry wether.

18 sows lead.

We rec. 18 sows lead ashore at English howse, poz. 4250 *catties* Japan wight.

To Soyemon Dono.

And ther was 3 presentes sent as foll'th, viz.:-

To Soyemon Dono,[130) ye kinges receaver,

130) Minami Sōemon 南總右衛門, Lord of Firando's steward.

89

September 1615

1 pec. satten, cost	6: 0: 0
3 peec. white baftas, cost of 20 Rs?	131)
5 knyves, cost	

To Sifian Dono.

And to littell Ontony, *alis* Sifian Dono,

5 pec. white baftas, of 20 Rs? ....

5 knyves, cost ....

To Sugean Dono.

And to Sugean Dono,

1 damaskt peec. (or gvn), cost ....

18 sows lead.

And we rec. 18 sows leade more ashore, w'ch way 4115 *cattis*, and sould 15 pec. chint amad, of 15 Rs? *cor.* for 11 *ma.*, is 26 *ta.* 5 *ma.* 0 *co.*

15 pec. chint.

23. This mornyng a stiff gale, wind at N? E'erly, overcast wether, dry wether all the forenowne, but rayne after, as lyke most p'rte night.

64 sows lead poz. 14649 *cattis.*

We receaved 64 sows lead more ashore w'ch is the rest of 120 sows sent p'r *Hoziander*, w'ch 64 sows, poiz. 14649 *cattis*, whereof 1 sow of 202 *cattis* was retorned back for ships provition. And I went to Cochi to see how our junck work went forward, being accompanid w'th Mr. Huntt whoe lyked reasonably well of their work, only thought them laysie, as all men else doe. But it is the cuntry fation, &c. We carid 2 barills wyne, w'th 2½ *mas* in fish, and 10 loves of bread. And I rec. a letter frō Gonrok Dono, dated in Langasaque, 9 dais past, wherin he answerd me tuching myne sent about Damian, that he was in pr'son for misdemenor, [*fol. 40v.*] the capt. of the Portingall haveing taken hym as a man nothing ap'rtenyng to me nor our English nation. Nobesane retorned this day frō Miaco & sent me word thereof, & that the Emperour was gon for Edo before he came frō Miaco; for w'ch I am sory, for that Capt. Coppendalls jorney will be longe.

I went to se juncke at Cochi.

A letter frō Gonrok Dono.

Bongo Dono retorned frō Miaco.

---

131) This and the following costs, not entered.

Sonday. 24. This mornyng overcast wether w'th rayne & a stiff gale, wind at N? E'erly, but after broke vp & was fayre wether rest of day & night foll'g, not so much wind p'r night.

A lettr to Capt. Adames.

I wrot a lettr Capt. Adames to make knowne to the Emperour how the Portingalls haue taken Damian Marin and Jn? de Lieuana, prisoners; or, in his abcense, Mr. Richard Wickham, to procure in all he may to geue the Emperour or the King of Edo notis thereof. This lettr is directed to Mr. Wm. Eaton at Osekay or Miaco, in abcense of Capt. Adames, to send after hym, first having takyn coppie thereof.

A lettr to Gonrok Dono & an other to capt.moro.

Also I sent 2 other lettrs to Gonrock Dono & Martin de Quinia, *capt. more*[132) of the Amacan ship, as apereth p'r coppies of this date.

25. This mornyng fayre calme wether and littell wind after N?erly p'r day, but rather calme p'r night.

Rest wax ashore.
To Damian & his host 2 lettrs.

We receaved all rest wax ashore, but not wayd. I sent an other lettr to Damian enclosed to his host w'th an other to his host in Japon, in answer of his.

Yosque a sonne.
To Bongo Dono.

Yosque our butlers wife was brought to bed of a a[sic] boy. We sent a pr'sent to Bungo Dono as foll'th:–

5 pec. white baftas, of 11 Rs? p'r *corg.*

5 pec. chint amad, of 15 Rs? p'r *corg.*

1 damaskd gvn or peec., cost ....133)

Wax.
1 pec. zelis.
1 pec. dutties.

And we rec. all our wax ashore out of *Hozeander.* And ther was 1 pec. red zelas & 1 pec. rot eaten duttis taken out of gadong to lyne cushins, &c.   [*fol. 41r.*]⏌

2 *taies* Magdalina.

Magdalina Marias doughter paid me two *taies* I lent her a yeare past, & I gaue it to Matinga.

To Genemon Dono.

And ther was geven in present to Genemon Dono, the admerall, 5 pec. baftas of   134) Rs. *corg.*, and 5 knyvs, cost

---

132) *Capitão mór* (Port.), Captain-in-chief.
133) Not entered.
134) Not entered.

September 1615

.135)

200 bagges lyme.
10 *cacas*.
cattis iron.
We bought 200 bagges white lyme of Skidayen Dono, at 4 *condrins* p'r bag, & sent them to junck at Cochi w'th 10 *cacas* or square postes, cost 136) p'r peec., & 137) *catis* iron, cost .138)

100 plank of 2 inch.

Pc. ordinan. ashore.

Kinge retorned.
Also we rec. aland at Eng'sh howse 100, 2 inche planck of Skidayon Dono; and we brought the *Hoziander* to a key (or wharfe), & put all her ordinance ashore, to bring her aground to trym or sheath to morrow mornyng, God willing. And w'thin night littell Antony, *allies* Sifian Dono, sent me worde the king was retorned to Firando.

26. This mornyng still fayre calme wether, but sowne after a fresh gale, wind at N.⁰ E'erly all day, but a stiff gale all night fare wether.

A lettr to Jorge Durois.
And I wrot a lettr to Jorge Durois, to haue a reconyng of velvettes, sattens, & other matters, as of Jorge the Caffro, & the 100 *tais* retorned I lent hym; this lettr sent p'r a m'rchnt of Tushima.

From Semi Done.
To Semi Don.
Semi Dono sent me a hanch of venison. And I went and viseted Semi Done & Tackamon Dono, and carid eachr of them a pr'sent as foll'th, viz.:–

1 chast peec., cost .... 139)
5 pec. white baftas, of   Rs.⁰, *corg.*
5 pec. chint, of   Rs.⁰., *corg.*

To Takamon Dono.
1 chast peec., cost ....
5 pec. white baftas, of   Rs.⁰, *corg.*
5 pec. chint, of   Rs., *corg.*

A lettr frō Jorge Durois.
And I rec. a lettr frō Jorge Durois, dated in Langasaque,

---

135) Not entered.
136) Not entered.
137) This figure and the other in the margin, not entered.
138) Not entered.
139) This and the following figures, not entered.

September 1615

1th of Octobr, new stile, wherin he advised me how the
Spaniardes had taken Damian Marin & Jn.º de Lieuana pr'-
soners, saying they were bound to serue the King of
Spaine, & that they gaue it out they would take hym
pr'soner, because he was frend to vs & the Hollanders, &c.
[*fol. 41v.*]]

Hoseander
broght
aground.

We vnladed all the *Hozeanders* ordinance ashore, and
brought her agrownd before the English howse to sheath
her. And ther was sould for ready money as foll'th, viz.,
to Safian Donos man,

03 pec. chint, of 15 Rs. p'r *corg.*   *ta.   ma.   co.*

30 tais.

16 pec. tapis, of 15 Rs. p'r *corge*, at 1 *tay* pec., is: 30:   0:   0
11 pec. buxshaws,   140) Rs., *corg.*

Nota.

W'ch money Mr. Nealson receaved.

And Soyemon Dono sent me word that one of the kinges
men was now com frõ Miaco, & mett Capt. Adames & our
people at Osekey, & that the Emperour was dep'rted towardes Shronge 2 daies before they arived. But mens

A lettr frõ
hostis of
Tomo.
buxchaw.
5 pec.
5 pec. tapis.

words are so divers that I know not what to beleeve, espetially because I rec. noe letter. I rec. a complementall
lettr frõ our hostis at Tomo; & 5 pec. buckshaws & 5 pec.
tapis Suras sent to Nangasaque to Gonrockes man.

27.   This mornyng a stiff gale wind N.ºerly, overcast wether,
yet remeanes dry all day, and the lyke all night following,
but littell or no wind p'r night.

King envited
to Eng.
house.

I invited the King of Firando & his nobles to dyner to the
Eng'sh howse on Mvnday next; but he sent me word it
might bettr be on Sonday, for that he expected the King
of Crates one Mvnday.

A lettr to
Jorge
Durois.

And I sent a boate express to Langasaque to buy thinges
necessary, & sent 12 *taies* plate p'r hym w'ch went, & wrot

---

140) Not entered.

93

September 1615

Nota.

Jorge Durois to assist hym, & to send me 2 jars or pottes conserue; and sent 2 Hollandes chises to Jorge & Bartolomea de la Rocha. Also I sent to procure the kings lettr to Gonrock Dono about the setting free of Damian & Juan, w'ch he granted me, & sent it away p'r one of his owne servantes to Langasaque, as he promised me he would.

20 plankes.

And Sr. Matias lent me 20 plankes w'ch were sent to our junck & laid by 10 more yf wee needed to vse them.

[fol. 42r.]⌋

28. This mornyng close overcast calme wether w'th som few drops of rayne, & after drisling or rayny wether all day & most p'rte of night, som wynd N?erly.

Men sick.

The 2 carpenters & on m.ͬ carpenter, the m.ͬ mate, fell sick, & were brought ashore to the English howse. And, finding thay[sic] king had not sent his lettr to Gonrok

Ed: Sayer to Langasaque.

Dono yisterday (as he promised me), I sent Ed: Sayer w'th it express, & agreed w'th a boate & 7 men for the voyag for

To Gonrock Dono.

6 *ta.* 4 *ma.* And sent a present to Gonrock Donon:-

	ta.	ma.	co.
2 damaskt fowling pec., cost 10 *ta.*	10:	0:	0
5 pec. white baftas, of 20 Rs. *corg*, is	04:	0:	0
5 pec. tapis Suras, of			141)
5 pec. chint amad, of 15 Rs? *corg*	03:	0:	0
5 pec. blew byzams, of 15 Rs. *corg* is	03:	0:	0
5 pec. red zelas, of 12 Rs. *corg*, is	02:	4:	0
5 pec. buckshaws, of			
Som totall pr'sent amontes vnto			

Nota.

This pr'sent is sent to hym as cheefe *bongew* of all goodes brought into Firando, Langasaque, or any of these p'rtes of Japan. And Ed. Sayer had 20 *taies* deliv'r hym p'r Mr. Nealson to buy candells & other necessaris for howse. Also

20 *tais*.

---

141) This and two other prices below, not entered.

September 1615

Ambr.   I del'd back the 3 *catt.* ambr I had of Ed. Sayer to hym to
A lettr to   make it away at Lang., yf he can; and wrot a lettr to Jorge
Jorge Durois
p'r Ed. Says.   Durois to helpe hym in his affaires. The Duch envited the
Kinge   King of Firando to dyner abord their ship and gaue hym 3
envited
abord ye   pec. ordinance for a wellcom at entrance & 5 or 6 for
Duch ship.   healthes, and 15 out of both shipps at his going ashore. &
a Duch marenar, in charging a peec. that was honycombd,
A man hurt.   had his hand shott offe & his face all batterd. Soe our chirurgion was sent for to assist the Duch chirurgion to saue
the man, yf it were possible.   [*fol. 42v.*]]

29.   This mornyng a fresh gale, wind at N? E'erly overcast
drissling wether, but after store of rayne espetially in the
after nowne, as lyke all night, w'th much winde.

100 *tais.*   I del'd 100 *taies* to Mr. Nealson w'ch he paid in plate
barse to Skidayen Dono vpon acc? of plank & tymber for
4 lettrs frō   the *Hoziander.* I receaved 4 letters, viz.:-
Vshimando.

1 frō Capt. Raphe Coppendall.

1 frō Capt. Wm. Adames.

1 from Mr. Richard Wickham.

1 from Mr. Wm. Eaton.

All dated in Vshmando (40 leags short of Osakay) the 19th
of this pr'sent month of Septembr, where they were we-
therbound, yet heard of the Duch (or Hollanders) arivall
theare 4 daies before the date thereof, & that as then the
Emperour was at Miaco, & thought would stay till the end
of this month. Also Mr. Eaton wrot that they had news
of Mr. Jn? Gurneis death at Syam w'th one Jn? Dench,
& that Mr. Lucas Antonison was gon for Pattania or Bantam, and Mr. Shipard left cheefe at Syam. This was tould
to our trumpeter, by a Japan that is com frō Syam, who
served in the English house at Syam. Taccamon Dono
Nota.   sent me word that I might buy the China womans howse
& make a gedong in the place at my pleasure.

95

September 1615

30. This mornyng overcast wether, w'th a stiffe gale, wind
N?erly, but after brok vp; fayre wether all day, & lyke p'r
night, but not so much wind.

ta. ma.
13: 5
2: 5
_____
16: 0.

To Sangero
Samme.

Mr. Nealson paid 13½ *taies* to a man assigned by Andrea,
our host at Langasaque, for rest due for sayles for junck, is
in plate bars, 13 *ta.* 5 *ma.* 0 *co.* And in small plate for fraight
sayls, 02: 5: 0. And we sent a pr'sent to Sangero Samme yt
lent vs a barke to carry our goodes to Osekey, viz.:-

	ta.	ma.	co.
1 damaskt fowling peec., cost	5:	6:	0
1 pec. alleia,142) of 30 Rs., is	1:	2:	0
2 pec. tapis Suras, of 143) Rs., ...			

[*fol. 43r.*]]

October 1615.

Sonday.

1. This mornyng fayre calme wether but after a fresh gale,
wind at N? E'rly most p'rte of the day, but calme most
p'rte of night, faire wether.

Frō Tacamon
Dono.
100 *tais.*

Smiths
howse on
fire.

Bark frō
Langasaque.

Taccamon Dono sent me a dish of fresh fish, I of fresh
water, &c. And I deliverd one hvndred *taies* plate barse
more to Mr. Wm. Nealson to lay out in necessaries for
junck and shipp & other waies, &c. The kinges smiths
house was set on fyre this night p'r the neglegence of his
servantes, but sowne quenched. Yet his dores were shutt vp
p'r order frō the king, because they looked no bettr to
matters; it being strictly looked vnto, and they banished
or put to death that haue their howses burned. In the after
nowne the boate I sent to Langasaque to buy provition to

_____

142) *Allegeas* or *allegias*, an Indian stuff, made from cotton or grass.—Thompson.
143) This and the following figures, not entered.

envite the king to dyner, retorned, & brought that she went for, w'th 2 jarrs conserves frõ Jorge, bought for me. And Susanna, his wife, sent me a box of conservs, w'th a baskit of peares & an other of figges, & a small box of conservs for

A lettr frõ Jorge Durois.

China Capts doughter, w'ch I sent vnto her. Jorge lettr was dated in Langasaque, le 9th of Octobr, new stile, in w'ch he advised me that Damian Marin & Jnọ de Lieuana were taken prisoners p'r meanes of Capt. Garrocho, w'ch truly I doe belleeve. [*fol. 43v.*]⌋

2. This mornyng fayre calme wether & very littell wind, after all day somthing variable, yet most an end Nọerly, lyke p'r night still fayre.

Tho. Davis died.

Thomas Davis, the carpenter, died this mornyng at break of day of the small-pox, he being choaked w'th them.

King of Firand at diner.

And I envited the king w'th his 2 brothers & Nobesane, Seme Dono, Sangra Same, Taccaman Dono, Sugean Dono, & 5 other cavelleros to beare them company at the kinges choise. They dyned after the Japon manner, and supped after the English. And, as he was at supp'r, word came that

King of Crates arived at Firando.

the King of Crates was arived, w'ch made hym to make short, & soe went to meate hym at landing. Soe the great Holland shipp shot afe 3 pec. ordinance as he passed by, & the littell shipp 3 others at his landinge. Soe after he sent

Piter Waden.

me word of his arivall, & envited hym selfe to our *fro* to morrow in the after nowne. I vnderstood Peter Wadden went 3 tymes over the walle in the night; so I turned hym abord againe. He is a graseles fello & vnlykly to amend.

3. This mornyng still faire wether w'th a fresh gale, wind Nọerly, most p'rte (or rather) all day, but not soe much (or rather calme) most p'rte night.

Frõ ye king.

The King of Firando sent me a buck, knowing the King of Crates came to supp'r, & gaue me many thankes for his kind entertaynm't yisterday.

King of
Crattes &
King of
Firando to
suppr

And after nowne the King of Crates came according as he said, being accompanid w'th the King of Firando & 3 other noble men of Crates. Vnto whome I gaue the best entertaynm't I could & to ther owne contentes. & after, they went abord the great Holland shipp, & at retorne ashore had 6 pec. ordinance shot out of her & 3 peeces out of the littell shipp. *[fol. 44r.]*]

Nota.

And towardes night 2 Hollander mariners w'ch had comited som falt were laid out for having byn abcent 2 or 3 daies frõ shipp; & 1 of them came to the English howse, desiring me on his knees to get his p'rdon. Soe I wrot a word to the capt., & sent our chirurgion along w'th hym. & they were no sowner gon but others brought the other Duchman, & he desird the lyke favor of me; but whiles I was writing the letter, he gaue them that kept hym the slip & soe escaped for the tyme.

Frõ King
of Crates.

The King of Crates gaue me a present of 2 *langanacko*[144] and a *cattan*, and desird to see the experience of a fyry arrow shot out of a slurbo[145] & a burnyng pike, w'ch is referd till his retorne frõ a province of his w'ch he is now bownd to vizet.

4. This mornyng faire calme wether, but after littell wind at Nọ E'erly most p'rt of day, & littell wind or rather calme all night.

The King of
Crates
dep'rted frõ
Firando.

A lettr
frõ Ed.
Sayer.

The King of Crates dep'rted frõ Firando this mornyng, & the great Holland ship shot afe 3 peec. of ordinance as he passed by them. And I rec. a lettr frõ Ed. Sayer, dated in Langasaque, le 30th of Septembr, how he had del'd the present to Gonrock Dono w'th the lettrs, & that he willed hym to stay 2 daies, & he would vse his endevor for vs in

144) *Naginata* 薙刀, a lance or halberd with a sword-like head.
145) A slurbow, a kind of crossbow.—Thompson.

2 lettrs to
Jor. & Capt.
Garocho.

what he could. And I wrot 2 lettrs to Jorge Durois & Capt. Garocho.

And vpon councell of frendes, having remeander of

Caueleros of
Firando
invited to
dyner.

thinges bought for inviting of 2 kinges, I invited to dyner to morow 9 caualeros, viz.:–

Gonosco Dono.	Oyen Dono.	Shosque Dono.147)
Vnagense Dono.	Toresamon Dono.146)	Otonagen Dono.148)
Matasabra Dono.	Soyemon Dono.	Sifian Dono.

I had thought to haue envited Vchenusque Dono, our *bongew* & ye kinges secretary, but they were out of towne.

[fol. 44v.]

5. This mornyng still fayre calme wether, but sowne after a stiffe gale, wind N？ E'erly all rest of the day, but much more p'r night, a very storme yet dry.

China Capt.
frō Goto.
Gold ring
retornd.

The China Capt., Andrea Dittis, retorned to Firando frō Goto, & brought me back a gould ring, del'd hym the 7th Septembr last, to haue byn sent for a present to an eunuke in China, valued as it cost 5 *l*. str.; but, vpon bettr consideration, not haveing two ringes. & 2 principall men emploied about the affares, they thought it better to buy 4 *cattans*, or Japan sables, and to send 2 to eache one.

A musk cod.

Also the Capt. China gaue me a musk cod for a present, and was sent frō a China vnknown vnto me. & he doth

Nota.

assure me on his life that our pretence to gett trade into China canot chuse but com to good effect; w'ch God grant.

Nota.

The caueleros envited to dyner came, being 8 in nombr, as apeareth on the other side. And as they were at it, Bongo Saм̃es adopted sonne (w'ch is the kinges youngest brother) came by, & they called hym in. & after dep'rted all cont[en]t.

---

146) Tarozaemon 太郎左衞門 (?).

147) Shōsuke 庄助 (?).

148) Naizen Dono 內膳殿 (?).

October 1615

Gonosquo Dono brought a pr'esnt of 10 bundells Japan
pap'r.

6. This mornyng dry wether, but an extrem stiff gale of
wind at N? N? E., & soe was all the night past and still
endured all this day and night following.

*Chawn
bought.*

We bought our next neighbors *chowne*, or howse place,
to the N?wardes, to pay 40 *taies* for it, and she carry away
the howse, but geue it out we pay but 25 *taies* for it, she
being far in debt, & therfore the money seazed vpon. The
other 15 *taies* she hath secretly to mentayn her & her chil-

ta. ma.
60: 5.

dren. Also Mr. Nealson paid the scrivano of the junk 60 *taies*
4 *mas* plate bars, for to pay carpenters and mareners; &

150 bag
lyme.
40 Rs. 8.
4 *mas* w't
Pri: gold.

sent 150 bages lyme to Cochi. And I del'd 40 Rs. 8 to China
Capt. to buy, or rather gar[n]ish 4 *cattans*, to send into
China. Allso I del'd hym 4 *mas* wight Priaman gould for
same purpose.   [*fol. 45r.*]

1 pec. alleia.
100 *tais.*

And ther was sould p'r Mr. Nealson 1 pec. alleias of   149)
Rs. p'r *corg* turnd back frō aboue, & sould to scrivano of
the junk for som of 2 *taies* 5 *mas*.

And I del'd one hvndred *taies* plate bars to Mr. Nealson
to pay for howse & other matters of junck & ship. Also Mr.
Nealson paid sixteen *taies* small plate to China Capt., viz.,

16 *tais.*

12 *taies* in bars for blads, and 4 *taies* in small plate of workmanshipp. Also he paid for things sent to Cochi for junck,

ta. ma. co.
6: 2: 2.

as apeareth p'r p'rticulers, 6 *tais* 2 *ma.* 2 *co.* as doth appeare
p'r p'rticulers.

7. This mornyng still a stiff gale, wind at N? E., and so
remeaned all day, encreasing a very storme & yet dry, as
lyke p'r night yet some rayne.

Nota.

The China Capt., Andrea Dittis, came & tould me that
the capt. moure of the ship of Amacon & other Spaniardes

---

149) Not entered.

October 1615

& Portingales had hired 2 barkes for 100 *taies*, to com from Langasaque to Firando, to vse meanes to steale away a Portingall w'ch is capt. of the junk they Hollanders took; & that ther was divers Spaniardes and Portingalls armed secretly in the said barkes, w'ch matter was revealed by 3 Chinas w'ch fled out of the said junk to Langasaque & made report hereof to other Chinas, 1 of whome wrot thereof to the China Capt. So I went to the Duch howse and made it knowne to the Hollanders, whoe gaue me harty

A lettr to our host of Tushima. thanks for it. And I wrot a lettr to our host at Tushma, p'r a m'rchnt of that place, desyring to heare frõ hym of sale of our pepp'r, w'ch I vndrstand was sould long since; & that vpon his advise I would send more, desyri[n]g hym to bring or send the money for this p'r first sure conveance.

[*fol. 45v.*]]

Sonday. 8. This mornyng still a stiff gale, wind at N? E'erly, overcast wether, but rayne after p'r fitts most p'rte of day, but littell or non p'r night, nether soe much wind.

3, barkes frõ Osekay.   This day, before nowne, our 3 barks we sent to Osekay w'th Capt. Copendall & his company retorned, from whome

2 lettres frõ Capt. Copendall & Mr. Eaton. I rec. a letter, dated in Osekay the 23th vltimo, w'th an other of same date frõ Mr. Eaton, wherin they adviz me the Emperour was dep'rted frõ Miaco 8 daies before their arivall, & that Capt. Adames went post after hym, being geven to vnderstand that he ment to stay in a place at halfe way, hoping by this meanes to dispach busynes theare, & so to retorne; the Duch haveing dispached theirs before he went frõ Miaco. Also I rec. 11 barells *morofack*, 5 big & 5 lesser & 1 halfe barell, w'ch the m.r of our bark bought p'r order of Capt. Copendall, for the doing, whereof Mr.

tais ma. 10: 5. Eaton del'd hym 10 *tais* in plate & 5 *mas* to buy hym rise. & they thought it fitt to retorne back all 3 barks, because they knew not how long it wold be before they retorned.

101

October 1615

Also they both writ me that pack N? 116 is wanting in ye cargezon, w'th 5 bambows black paynting, & 5 small peec.

Frō our host at Sakey.

wax. Also our host of Sackay came to Firando, and brought me a pr'sent of a barrell of wyne, making much mone that all he had was burned when our comodeties were burned, so that now he is new to enter into the world, & to that entent meanes to goe purcer in a junk of Gonrock

Nota.

Donos for Syam. I sent our *jurebasso* to thank Songero Samme & Sifian Dono, for the lent of their barks to carry vp our men and marchandiz.   *[fol. 46r.]]*

Capt. Copendall advized me he gaue 2 *taies* to the mŗ

3 *tais.*

of the great bark & 1 *tay* to the purcer.

Pr'sentes.

And ther was geven away in pr'sentes as foll'th, viz.:–

	ta.	ma.	co.
To Gonosqo Dono, governor,			
1 pec. black satten, cost	6:	0:	0
3 pec. whit baftas, of 8 Rs. *corg*			150)
5 knives of p'r dozn.....................			
To Shosqo Dono, ye kings chamberlen,			
1 pec. alleias, of 15 Rs. p'r *corg*			
3 pec. baftas, of 8 Rs. p'r *corge*			
3 pec. tapis Suras, of *corge*			
To Vnagense Dono, capt. generall,			
1 demask peec. cost			
To Skiamon Dono, prouedor,			
1 pec. alleias, of 15 Rs. p'r *corge*.............			
1 pec. white baftas, of 8 Rsọ p'r *corge*			
1 pec. duble borall, 151) of 7 Rsọ p'r *corge*			
1 pec. tapis Surat, of Rs? *corge*			
To kinges cheefe cooke,			
1 pec. alleias, of 15 Rs? p'r *corge*			

---

150) This and the following figures, not entered.
151) *Borel,* coarse woolen cloth.—Thompson.

October 1615

To kinge[s] vnder cooke,
1 pec. white bafta, of 8 Rs? p'r *corge* ....
To kinge[s] sumaker for cookry,
1 pec. white bafta, of 8 Rs? p'r *corge* ....
To an other ould cooke,
1 pec. white bafta, of 8 Rs? p'r *corge* ....
To 5 neighbours maid servantes for cookry,
3 duble peeces of burrall, of 7 Rs. *corge* ......

A lettr frō Ed. Sayer. I rec. a lettr frō Ed. Sayer, dated 6 days past, wherin he wrot me Gonrock Dono drivs hym of w'th delaies, & as yet hath not sett the men at liberty, but rather that the Portingals haue put Jn? de Liueana in irons beloe in the shipp, as well as Damain, for that no man should com to speake w'th them. *[fol. 46v.]*⌋

9. This mornyng a fresh gale, wind at N? E'erly, fayre wether, and so remeaned all day & night following, but not so much wind p'r night.

Nota. We searched our warehouse for pack N? 116, but canot find it; & examenyng ouer packing bill & wast book, find that the said pack w'th the wax & 5 bambows painting were all sent along in the great bark of Sangero Samma; soe it must rest vpon the m.ͬ, the purcer, and vpon Jn? Pheby to answer for those mattrs.

A lettr frō Gonrock Dono. Ed. Sayer retorned frō Langasaque, and brought answer frō Gonrock Dono that he had donne what possibly he could but could not get the 2 men set a liberty. So I went & tould the king thereof, & tould hym I ment to send away a bark in all hast w'th letters to Capt. Adames to adviz the Emperour thereof, desiring to haue his Highnes letters of favor to Safian Dono, & Goto Zazabra of the truth of the mattr, w'ch he promised me, so I made ready the bark & wrot my letters: a generall lettr to Capt. Adams, Mr. Eaton, & Mr. Wickham, as apeareth p'r coppy, but antedated

A lettr to Capt. Ad. & 1 to Capt. Coꝑ.

103

to morow; & also a lettr to Capt. Copendall, advising of losse of pack N⁰ 116 w'th wax & paynting; & at any hand advised Capt. Adames to vse all meanes possible to set

Frō Gonrok Dono. these 2 men at liberty. Gonrock Dono sent me a pr'sent p'r his man of a peare *bubes*,[152] and 2 chist *mach*,[153] cont'g in each chist 200 roles, cotton *mach*.

10. This mornyng fayre wether w'th littell wind N⁰erly, and so remeaned all day, yet som rayne towardes night, wind vering S'erly, & store rayne p'r night, wind ver'd N⁰erly.

Nota. As I was about to send away the bark & sent to the king for his letters, he retorned me word that he had taken counsell about the matter, & wished me once more to stay a littell & he would send 1 of his owne men to Gonrock Dono, not dowbting but to pr'cure the men to be set at liberty. So, much against my will, I was constrained to desist from my purpose. *[fol. 47r.]*

4 lettrs frō Langasaque. I forgot to set downe how I receaved a lettr frō Martin de Quinia, the capt. of Amacan shipp, w'th an other from Capt. Garocho, & a therd frō Jorge Durois, all dated le 15th pr'sent, new stile, & a forth lettr frō Albaro Munos, of 14th

2 pere silk stockinges.
400 candls.
Frō Mel. a lettr. ditto. And Jorge Durois sent me 2 pear of silk stockinges, cost, as he said, 7 *taies*, w'th 400 candells at 7½ for a *mas*, paid for p'r Ed. Sayer. Also I rec. a fifte lettr from Melchar van Sanfort, dated in Langasaque, le 12th current, new stile, only of comendacons; & he retorned me a Duch cronocle w'ch I lent hym. And ther was a bag of Pattainia pepp'r, sould to Gonrock Dono for the Emperour, poz.

155 *cattes* pepp'r to Empror.
A pr'sent. grose 160 *cattis*, is net 155 *cattis*, at 8 *tais* p'r *picull*. And Gonrocks man w'ch brought the pr'sent from hym had geven hym 1 pec. whit bafta of 11 Rs⁰ *cor.*, 2 Eng'sh knives, cost .[154]

---

152) *Byōbu* 屏風, folding screen.
153) *Machi* 襠. Cf. *Vocabvrario da Lingua de Iapam*. Nagasaki, 1603. f. 148r.

October 1615

And about one a clock after midnight Tho. Heath, the carpenters mate of ye *Hozeander*, dyed of a lingaring disease, w'ch began w'th a blody fflix.[155]

11. This mornyng overcast wether w'th a stiffe gale, wind N?erly, vering to W., fayre wether all day and lyke all night, littell wind or rather calme.

Junk
lanched.
Mr. Hunt
said all is
well done.
Lettrs to
Miaco.

Our junck, the *Sea Adventure*, was lanched this day at Cochi, & I got Mr. Hvnt to goe see her yf they carpenters had donne their partes, Ed. Sayer accompanying hym. I sent the letters I wrot of 10th current to Mr. Eaton p'r a bark of Firando & put 5 *mas* port on it, & in that lettr 2 others for Capt. Copindall, 1 frõ Mr.   [156] & an other frõ Mr. Osterwick, & a therd from my selfe, dated as to morow, le 12th pr'sent, advising w'th all speed to send them to Capt. Adames to speak to the Emperour to procure the liberty of Damian & Jn?. Also I sent an other letter to Mr. Eaton, to enquir whether Twan[157] is apoynted to make warse against the Chinas, & to send me word.   *[fol. 47v.]*⌋

12. This mornyng faire calme wether or rather a littell wind N? W'erly, but a fresh gale after most p'rte of the day, but calme most p'rte of night.

I forgot to note downe yisterday that, when the ships company went to bury Thomas Heath in the place where they formerly had buried his mate, Tho. Davies, they

fownd that som villanouse people had diged vp the cooffin & stolne the winding sheete & his shert, & lefte the karkasse naked vpon the grownd, —a villanouse acte. So they soonke the other coffin into the sea.

The kinges eldest brother Guenche Samme, *alius* Tono-

---

154) Not entered.
155) Blood flux.
156) The name, not given.
157) Murayama Tōan 村山東安, regent of Nagasaki (d.1618).

October 1615

20 *cattis*
wax.
14 carp'ters
of junk.

Samme, had 20 *cattis* wax, to pay as the rest is sould. 14 of the junks carpenters began to work vpon the *Hozeander* this mornyng, counting the m.^r for one, all ship carpenters.

Nota.

I had much adow this about a boy w'ch Mr. Jn.º Osterwick had entertayned, named Antony, whome (as it seemth) is servant to a Spaniard that sent a Japon into our howse, a mallapert knaue, whoe, w'thout speaking a word vnto me nor no man else, went vp into Mr. Osterwicks chamber and laid handes on the boy to haue drowne hym out of the howse p'r force; yet he went w'thout hym. But sowne after the King of Firando sent me word to del'r the boye into his handes, w'ch I did, he promising to send a man w'th hym that yf in case it be a falce brauado of the Spaniardes (as I alead[g]e it is) that then the boy may be retorned back, &c.

A pitifull
spectacle.

Also, the m.^r, Jn.º Hvnt, & Mr. Osterwick going to a lodg the king had lent vs, fowned a yong gerle of som 11 or 12 years of adge, dead on the back side vnder the walle, & doggs feeding on her, having eaten both her legges & her lower partes, w'th one hand, being newly kild but a littell before. It is thought som villen had ravished her & after kild her, or else, being a slaue, her m.^r had kild her vpon som displeasure & cast her out to be eaten of dogges, an ordinary matter in these p'rtes, the lives of all slaues being in the m.^rs handes, to kill them when he will, w'thout controle of any justice.   [*fol. 48r.*]]

13.   This mornyng still faire calme wether, and not much wind after at N.º W. or rather W. most p'rte of the day, but night calme.

Skiffe
stole[n].

This night past, about midnight, our small skiffe of the *Hoziander* was stolne away &, as the shipps company sayeth, p'r a Holladr w'ch ran away from the greate shipp, being one of the two I wrot in favor of hertofore, & that

106

October 1615

they saw hym vpon our bridg in the night about midnight; so out of dowbt I think they let hym goe away w'th the boate, one knaue helping or winking at an others escape.

Orders For truly I neaver saw a more frow'rd & bad leawd company then most of them are, & the cheefe ringleader a m.ʳ mate called   158) Dorington. So that, seeing contynewally their leawd courses, in going abroad night & day w'thout leave, the offecers them selues being worst of all, we were forsed to make orders & set them vp at meane mast, sortinge the company into therds, one whereof might take their pleasure p'r day, retorning abord before sonne setting, & theother — to look to shipps busynes & that

Nota. carpenters doe their labour. This Dorington hath said in open company amongst them all that nether capt., m.ʳ, nor no other had authorety to punish men w'th ducking nor whiping, geving it out w'th othes that he and the rest would haue victuels as they list, w'thout controle. Once he is a drunken, vnruly, mutenouse fello, & not fitt to serve the Wor'll Company. I sent word to the Duch howse how that fellow had stolne away our skiffe; as also I sent word of the lyke to Taccama Samme and the admerall, whoe haue sent to look out after hym. The China Capt. brought

Gota [sic]
burned. me word that all Goto is burned, the kinges howse as well as rest, not one howse left standing of som 300. It is thought the Japans sett it on fyre of purpose to haue the riffling of the Chinas goods w'ch came in 7 or 8 junks, but the fyre was so vehement that littell or nothing was saved, 5 Chinas being burned that adventured to saue their goods.

[*fol. 48v.*]]

And in the after nowne the kinges man, w'ch he sent to
Nota. Langasaque about the setting of Damian and Jn.º at

---

158) The first name, not given.

October 1615

Skiff
retornd.

Nota.

2 lettrs for
king to Goto
Zazabra or
Safion Don.

1 from me
to Chubio
Dono.

12 *taies*.

A lettr to
Mr. Eaton
Capt. Ad. &
Mr. Eaton.

Jonk to
Firando.

Nota.
5 pico. pep'r.

liberty, retorned w'th a sleeveles answer, they Portingales answering, as they did before, that they would not deliver them vpon noe tearmes. And on the way, as the kinges man retorned, som 7 leagues from Firando, he met the Duch man w'ch had stolne our skiffe, and so brought both hym & it back againe. Soe I sent the Duchman to the Hollands howse, for w'ch they gaue me many thanks. I went to the king to sertefy hym, (or rather) to know of hym, what answer he had receavd frõ Gonrock Dono; w'ch was as I said before. Wherevpon I desire his Highnesse to lett me haue his letters of fauour to Safian Dono, and to Gota Zazabra, testefying how these 2 men were entertayned into the service of Englishmen to goe in our junck for Syam; w'ch lettrs the king granted me & sowne after sent them for the English howse. And I wrot an other to Chubio Dono, in the Japan tonge, to desire his assistance in this matter to the Emperour, to get these 2 men sett free. So we hird a light bark w'ch rowed w'th 4 ores & a fellow to cary these lettrs, & pid 12 *taies* small plate for the voyag, to del'r the lettrs to Mr. Wm. Eaton at Osekay, or Miaco; in doing whereof they are to rowe night and day.

14.   This mornyng still fayre wether w'th littell wind W'erly, vering N?erly som p'rte of day, but calme all or most p'rte of night.

I sent away the kinges lettrs & wrot a generall lettr to Capt. Adames, Mr. Wickham, and Mr. Eaton, & sent it p'r light horsman as before, advising at large, as I did in my former lettrs 2 daies past. And I sent out 6 barkes to tow in our junck from Cochi, w'ch brought her into harbor at Firando about nowne.   [*fol. 49r.*]」

I del'd back the writing I had of Capt. Whaw for 550 *pezos* adventured to China the yeare past. I del'd it back to his brother Andrea. And ther was five *piculles* Bantam

108

pepp'r sould to Tomo Dono, to pay as well sell the rest.

Two Caffros of the king came frõ Langasaque & advised me that an English gentleman was kept captive in cheanes abord the ship of Amacan, & that they saw hym he being a yong man of 24 or 25 years of adge. But I did enter into opinion that might be som tramp of the Portingals & Spaniardes to make me to write to the Emperour vpon such a slight speech w'thout other proofe, wherby to geue the Emperour distast, their being no such matter at all. Yet I haue geuen order to frendes that may goe abord the said shipp, to look out whether ther be any such matter or no, &c. And pid Tamon Dono carpenter vpon acc° work abord

16 *ta.* *Hoziander* p'r Mr. Nelson 16 *ta.* small plate.

Sonday. 15. This mornyng still fayre calme wether, but after a fresh gale at N°. E., and so remeaned all rest of the day and night following, fayre wether.

In this burnyng of Goto Goto[*sic*], the post, or man w'ch carid the kings letters, lost all that he had to the vallue of 700 *taies*, being an ould man but well spoaken & therfore chosen to goe about this busynes. Wherevpon the China Capt. said vnto me, that out of his owne he would send hym 50 *pezos*, is forty *taies*, & wished me to ad 20 *pezos*

70 Rs. 8. more to it, to make it vp 70 *pezos* and that he would send it all to hym in my name, as a largesse in respeckt of his losse, being sorry for it, promising greater matters, yf pleased God to prosp'r hym in his proceadinges to get vs trade into China. Also the China Capt., Andrea Dittis,

40 *ta.* del'd 40 *taies* in plate barse to Mr. Nealson for the 50 pec. or Rs. 8, I now del'd to the said Capt. China.   [*fol. 49v.*]⌡

And ther was sent 2 presentes to Whaw, the China Capt.

To Chinas at Langasaque. brother, and an other China of Langasaque called Leangu I say Leengv, both w'ch are emploid about our busynes to procure trade into China, viz.:–

109

	ta.	ma.	co.
6 pec. whit baftas, of 16 & 17 Rs? 8, *corg*	04:	0:	4
6 pec. blew byrams, of 15 Rs., *corg*	03:	6:	0
6 pec. red zelas, of 12 Rs., *corg*	02:	8:	8
6 pec. tapis Suras, 159) Rs., *corg*	00:	3:	3½
6 knyves, cost	00:	3:	3⅛
Som totall all amontes vnto................			

    To be devid [*sic*] 3 of each sort to each man.

Hous lent.

    And Jn? Dono lent vs his howse over way to put our junks provition in, till she be rig̍de. And I sent a lettr p'r

A lettr to Jorge Durois.

China Capt. to Jorge Durois, how I had rec. the 2 peare si[l]k stockinges, & kept the case bottells ffor hym till he

China Capt. to Langasaque.

came. Also I gaue order to the China Capt. to look out for 3 China carpenters, to goe in our shipp for Bantam, as also to buy 150 grate bamboes for vs, yf their be any, & to enquire whether the Portingals haue an Englishman prisoner abord their shipp or no. And Mr. Nealson paid

10 *tais.* Nota.

Chongro, scrivano of junck, ten *taies* in small plate vpon acc? junk charges. We brought all the tymbers & other matters ymploid about the junk frõ Cochi to Firando, having hired Tome or Jn? Donos howse to put them into.

16.   This mornyng still faire wether w'th a fresh gale, wind at N? E'erly, encreasing all day & so re[me]aned most p'rte of night, vering W. S'erly.

King of Crates retorned to Firando.

    The King of Crates retorned to Firando & sent to desire to see a fyre arrow shot out of a slurbo, w'ch was donne before hym & the King of Firando to their greate content twise. He desird to haue the slurbo to take a sample by to make an other, w'th a reseapt how to make the compownd for the fyre work. And about midnight dep'rted towardes Crates; w'ch saved the geveing a present of 2 damaskt fowling peeces, yf he had staid till morninge.   [*fol. 50r.*]⌋

---

159) The figure and the last total, not entered.

October 1615

Sould to
Tancho.

Tancho Samme, the kinges kinsman, bought two pec. Cambaia cloth, viz.:–

	ta.	ma.	co.
1 pec. chint amad, of 15 Rs. *cor.* for	001:	00:	0
1 pec. duble tapis Suratt, of 160) Rs. *corg* for	001:	00:	0

18 sakes
rise.

We rec. 18 bagges rise of the kinges, cont'g 53 *gantos* p'r sack, w'ch were del'd to the mareners of the junke, and were rated at 15 *ta.* 0 [*ma.*] 9½ [*co.*].

17. This mornyng overcast wether w'th littell wind W. S'erly, as the rack hath gone the lyke 3 or 4 daies, but after a fresh gale Noerly all rest of day & night followinge.

Capt. Jacob
Speck
retorned to
Firando.

And before nowne Capt. Speck retorned frõ Miaco, & had 3 pec. shot out of Duch howse & 6 out of great shipp, for a welcom. I went to the Duch howse to vizet hym, & he tould me, yf he had wanted but 2 howers tyme at his arivall at Miaco, that the Emperour had byn gon before he had

Nota.

com; & that he w'th his owne mouth tould hym that the Portingall junck they had taken was good prize, both men and goods, and all other they took hereafter to be the lyke, both of them & Spaniardes, yf they had not his passe, but

3 lettrs
frõ Miaco.

having it not to meddell w'th them. He also del'd me 3 lettrs frõ Capt. Copendall, Mr. Wickham, & Mr. Eaton, dated in Miaco the 28 & 29th Septembr, and 1 frõ Mr. Eaton of 2th

L'r from
Osekay.

Octobr, w'th 2 others frõ our host Osekay & Tome *jurebasso.* And Jorge Durois ariued heare & tells me, that the capt. more of the Amacan shipp sayth that, yf Gonrok Dono will, he is content to sett Damian and Jnọ at liberty, for p'r his p'rmison he took them pr'soners, & at his demand he will [*fol. 50v.*]] set them free. But I answerd hym that I had his lettr to shew to the contrary, once the end will try all. I think there be legerdymeane. And we receved 150

150 plank

bordes or planks of 1 inche of Skidayen Dono, and I paid

---

160) Not entered.

wherof 3
of 2 inches.
30 bordes or
planks.
Frõ Jorge.

the Hollanders the 30 lent me before. Jorge sent me a present of a bottell Portingall wyne, 12 greate peares and 2 boxes craknells & littel tarts.

18. This mornyng ourcast droping wether, w'th a fresh gale, wind N?erly, and soe remeand all day much rayne & encrease of wind, & lyke p'r night, & sõ rayn, I say som rayne.

A lettr frõ
Mr. Eaton.

Symon, *jurebasso*, brought me a lettr frõ Mr. Eaton, dated the 8th Octobr, wherin he writes he hath opened all the packes cloth Cambaia & findes most of the baftes, viz., ¾ of them, spotted & rotten, so that no man will looke on them, he offerd them all together to our host for 6 *mas* p'r peec., but he would not buy them answering he thought they would never be sould for any thing. Also he saieth their wantes 10 pec. chaddr pintado of them were put into the cargezon.

19. This mornyng overcast wether w'th stiff gale of wind N?erly, & soe remeaned most p'rt of the day, but littell or no wind p'r night; yet fayre wether both day & night.

To King of
Crates.

And Semi Done sent me a lettr how he met the King of Crates whoe willed hym to writ to me to send hym these p'racelles foll'g & he would send money p'r they w'ch brought them so I del'd them to Semi Donos man.

	ta.	ma.	oc.
20 pec. white baftas, of 20 Rs. *corg* at 1 ½ *tay*....	30:	0:	0
20 pec. tapis Suras, of Rs. p'r *corg* for 1 *tay* pe...	20:	0:	0
05 pec. alleias, of 30 Rs. p'r *corg* for 2 *tay* pe.....	10:	0:	0
Som totall amontes vnto	60:	0:	0

20 baft.
20 tapis.
05 allia.

From
Skidian
Dono.

ta. ma.
204: 5.

Skidian Dono sent a beefe for a pr'sent.   [*fol. 51r.*]]

I rec. two hundred and fowre *taies* five *mas* of Ed. Sayer vpon acc? ambr betwixt hym and me, w'ch 204 *taies* 5 *mas* I del'd to Mr. Nealson to lay out in shipp & junck charges; it beinge, in 4 pap'rs, viz., 63 *ta.* 1 *ma.* 5 *condrins*, 41 *ta.* 5

October 1615

condrins, 50 *ta.* 2 *mas*, & 50 *ta.* 1 *mas.*

And Jorge Durois mad acc? for these thinges, foll'g:-

	ta.	*ma.*	*co.*
4 jarrs conserves, at 5 *tais* p'r jar, is ..20:	0:	0	
2 milstones to grind malt or wheate ..01:	0:	0	
70 tallow candells, cost 01:	0:	0	

<table>
This is for the howse, & amont   *ta.* *ma* *co.*
vnto ....T. 22: 0: 0..22: 0: 0
</table>

More, 1 pere silk stockinges for
Capt. Cop., at 04: 0: 0
Mor., 1 per. thrid stock., for hym, at ..00: 6: 0
More, 1 per. gren silk stocking for
Mr. Osterwick.....................03: 5: 0
More, 2 pere silk stockinges, at
7 *tay*, for Capt. Copingdall or
Mr. Osterwick ....07: 0: 0..15: 01: 0

More due to hym p'r rest of velvettes ..15: 01: 0

& sattens com frō Amacan besids
profitt 27: 2: 0

Som totall amontes vnto.....................# 64: 3: 0

w'ch som of 60 *ta.* 8 *ma.* 0 *co.* goeth vpon the reconinge of
100 *ta.* lent hym le   161), as apeareth.

20. This mornyng faire calme wether, but sowne after a
stiff gale, wind Nºerly most p'rte of the day, and the lyke
p'r night, yet fayre wether.

I wrot a lettr to Albaro Muños in answer of his and an
other to Diego Farnando Rigote to geue 3 or 4 *gantos*
candy oyle to Jorge Durois & sell the rest as he can. Taccamon Dono sent me a beefe for a present and ther was a
pec. bafta Deher of 17 Rs. p'r *corg*, sent to Jorge Durois

Side notes:
Recons w'th Georg Durois.
ta. ma.
60: 8: 0.

2 lettr to Langasaque.

Frō Taccamon Dono.
1 pec. bafta Deher, of

---

161) The date, not given.

113

October 1615

17 Rsọ *corg*.
1 bafta of 8 Rs.

wife, in respect of frute & swetmeates she sent to vs at divers tymes w'ch was spent in the howse, &c. And Mr. Nealson had a peec. of w't bafta of 8 Rs. p'r *corg*, rated at 00:8:0.

21. This mornyng a stiff gale, wind Nọerly but after slacked, and littell or noe wind p'r night; yet fayre wether both day and night.

Pr'soners escaped.

This night past 2 of the Hollanders pr'soners ran away out of great shipp, viz., both Portingales, 1 being capt. of junk they took, and the other a m'rch'nt whome they had taken 5 tymes before. And Sticamon Dono sent me 2 ducks & a dish of peares for a pr'sent. He is a comedian or a jester to geue delight to the king. [*fol. 51v.*]」

From Sticamon Dono.

Sonday.

22. This mornyng fayre calme wether, but after a littell wind S'erly w'th som drops of rayne, wind vering Nọerly w'th a great shower of rayne at 5 clock after nowne, but dry p'r night.

Portingall prisoners brought back.

50 *ta*.

This night past both the Portingalls w'ch escaped out of the Holland shipp, were taken & brought back p'r such as the King of Firando sent out after them. And Jnọ Gorezon, our *jurebasso*, rec. fyfty *taies* plate bars w'th som small plate among, of the servant of Safian or Gonrock Dono in p'rte for good bought by hym heretofore w'ch amont to 55 *taies*, but he would haue 5 *taies* rebated w'ch I deny these are pedling people, &c.

4 per tapis Surat retorned.

The servant of Gonrock Dono retorned back 4 pec. tapis Suras of 1 *tay* peec.—thus these pedling fellows vse vs—& thinketh to stop the other 2 *taies*.

A lettr to Mr. Eaton.

I wrot Mr. Eaton to Miaco of recept of his 2 lettrs of 2th & 8th curant p'r Capt. Speck, & sent it p'r a servant of Gonrock Dono. Also Capt. Speck sent to buy our junk ould rother[162] w'th 2 great ores belonging to it, w'ch prise was

Junk rother sould for 110 *tay*.

162) Rudder.—Thompson.

114

October 1615

13: 1: 6.

made of at 110 *taies* p'r endifferent men on both p'rtes. Mr.
Nelson paid 13 *ta.* 1 *ma.* 6 *co.* to purcer of junck, I say.

23. This mornyng fayre wether w'th a fresh gale, wind
N?erly, & soe remeaned all day & the lyke all night foll'g,
or rather not soe much wind p'r night, faire wether.

294 pe. bux-shawes.
A lettr to Capt. Copindall.

Matsinda Saccozo Dono, servant to Gonrok Dono,
bought 294 pec. buxshaws[163] at 1 *tay* p'r peec. to pay at 2
months. And I wrot a lettr to Capt. Coppindall in answer
of his of 19th vltimo frō Miaco, & sent it p'r Gonrok Donos
man, that bough[t] buxshawes & is he w'ch paid the 50
taies yesterday.

460 *ta.*

The China Capt., Andrea Dittis, retorned frō Langasaque
and brought me 400 *taies* in plate sent frō his brother Capt.
Whaw, lent me also 60 *taies* more to chang for Rs? to send

Frō Capt. Whaw.

into China, is all. And Capt. Whaw sent me a peec white
damask for a present, and the Capt. Andrea gaue the m.ͬ a
pec. damask & a peec. China lynen I meane to Mr. Jn?
Hvnt for a present, & sent me a baskit of pearse, &c.

[*fol. 52r.*]⌋

Bambows 150.
10 *taies.*

I consorted w'th a Japon called Sinemon Dono for 150
great bambowa (or canes) for junck sayles, to pay 19 *taies*
p'r c'nto, and he had ten *taies* paid hym in plate bars p'r
Mr. Nealson vpon the bargen the rest to be paid at, del'd
in same sort of plate.

24. This mornyng a fresh gale, wind at N? W'erly, fayre
wether, and soe remeaned all day and the lyke all night
followinge.

Junk *Rother* retorned.
110 *tay.*
A lettr to Garocho.

Capt. Speck came & tould me the carpenters had begild
hym about his junk *Rother*, they being good, so that he had
no need of ours at 110 *taies*, but retorned them back againe.
I wrot a lettr to Capt. Garroche in answer of one of his

---

163) Some kind of Indian piecegoods, not identified.–*Hobson-Jobson.*

115

Rs. 11⅝
Garrocho.

20 bu'dls
rattons.
400 *tais.*

rec. this day, wherin he wrot me that Andrea Dittis, the China Capt., would pay me 11 *pezos* and 5 *mas* w'ch the said Garrocha owed me, w'ch the China Capt. is content w'th all. The Duch had 20 bundelles rattons to pay as we paid at Langasaque, rec. of China Capt. vpon severall acc⁰ som of 400: 0: 0.

25. This mornyng fayre cold wether w'th a fresh gale of wind N⁰erly, and so remeaned all day & the lyke all night, but not soe much wynd p'r night, cold wether.

Nota.

I wrot a lettr to Capt. Speck to desyre hym to lett vs caryne our shipp against their small shipp called the *Jaccatra,* we finding it impossible to trym her agrownd where she is, we not being able to com to the keele of her w'thout endangering the shipp. The servant of Calsa Samme,[164] the Emperours youngest sonne, came to the Eng'sh howse & bought for his m̃ as followeth:-

	ta.	ma.	co.
2 damaskt fowling peeces at 15 *taies* peec. 30:		0:	0
2 peec. buralles, of 165) Rs., *corge* for 02:		0:	0
1 pec. alleia amad of Rs., *corg* for 02:		0:	2
Som totall amontes vnto 34:		0:	0

2 fowling
pec.
2 pec. borall.

1 pec. alleia.

34 *tais.*
Frõ Nobsane.
30 pec. tapis.
24 *taies.*

9½ *cattys*
wax.

And Nobesane sent vs a beefe for a pr'sent.

Also sould to the China Capt. for a frend of his 30 pec. tapis Suras of 166) Rs. *corg* for 24 *taies* plate in barsse, w'ch he paid to Mr. Nealson. Also the China Capt. had 9½ *cattys* wight wax to pay for it, as the rest is sould, & I changed hym 60 *tayes* plate bars rec. of hym before.

[*fol. 52v.*]⌋

75 Rs. 8.

And paid hym 75 Rs⁰ 8 for it, wherof Mr. Nelson pad hym 70 Rs. out of the 100 Rs. I del'd hym hertofore. The other

---

164) Ma⸴sudaira Tadateru 松平忠輝. See 44) above.
165) This and the following prices, not entered.
166) Not entered.

5 Rs. I paid hym my selfe.

Nota.

Capt. Speck sent me a lettr how they could not lend vs the small ship to caryn against, for that they must bringe her aground this spring to trym her; & 1 pec. tapis or chaddr Cambaia to Capt. China at 1 *tay* sould to hym.

1 pe. tapis
at 1 *tay*.

26. This mornyng fayre cold wether w'th littell wind N°.erly, but sowne after blew vp a stiff gale, most p'rte of the day at N°. E'erly, but calme most p'rte of the night.

A lettr to
Mr. Eaton &
rest.

I wrot a lettr to Mr. Eaton how I find he put downe 1 pec. alleias at 2 Rs. peec. amontes to 22 *tais*, I esteeming he sett downe 1 for 11 as also to write the acc°. for what m'rch'-nidiz the money was he rec. of acc°. of deb. & cred., w'th eache paid to host & others for changing the moneis into plate barse. Also I adv[i]sed of the speeches ther is that Fidaia Samme is alive in Shashma, & much provition of barks a making ready, & that it is said the Emperour pr'tendeth to make warse against a great lorde in the North; wishing them (I meane the Eng'sh) to keep keepe [*sic*] this to them selues & look out in tyme to pr'vent the worst, yf need be, and to send me downe the true acc°. of all matters of ould, to the end I may send a true ballance to the Company & to keepe no monies by them, but send it downe in respect of our want as also to avoid danger, what-soever may happen. This lettr I sent p'r the servant of Gon-rok Dono, whoe staieth for a wind.

From Jorge
Durois.
Kinge
envited ye
Hollanders.

Georg Durois sent me a pr'sent of 2 pottes of mangeas & 20 great peares frõ Langasaque, but noe lettr came w'th them. The king envited the Hollanders to dyner to day, & sent me word he would haue had the English but that he stayeth for the retorne of Capt. Coppindall.   [*fol. 53r.*]]

27. This mornyng still cold wether & noe wind, yet sowne after a fresh gale at N°. E. most p'rte of the day, but the night calme fayre cold wether.

October 1615

We set the mastes of our junck the *Sea Adventure* this day; at the doing whereof were 3 or 400 men p'rsons, all the neighboures (or rather all the towne), sending their servantes & came them selues (them that were of accointance) and brought pr'sentes (*Nifon catange*), after Japon maner, of wyne & other eating comodety, abord the junk, wishing a prosperouse voyag, all the offecers haveing eache one a pr'sent of a littell *barso* of wyne, & should haue had lykewiaes each one a bar of plate advanced on their wagese, but I referd that till the coming of Capt. Adames. & sould vnto the King of Fushemis servant 40 peeces white baftas of 20 Rs. p'r *corg* for 14 *mas* p'r peece, amontes vnto som of 56 *ta*. 0 *ma*. 0 *co*., w'ch money Mr. Nealson receaved. The king sent me a buck for a pr'sent. And del'd 150 spikes for shipps vse of 2 handfull long, bought at Bingana Tomo for the gadonge.

40 pec. baftas.

56 *tais* to Mr. Nelson.

A buck frõ king.

150 spikes.

28. This mornyng fayre calme wether, but sowne after a fresh gale, wind N? E'erly, encreasing a very stiffe gale and soe remeaned all night following, dry wether.

We receved 150 inche plank of Skidayen Dono this day. Also we receaved of Soyemon Dono for acc? of the king 19 sack of rise of 53 *gantos* p'r sack, rated at 111[?] *ta*. 6: 6½.

150 inch planks.

19 sack rise.

And Goresanos wife brought her doughter of 20 daies ould to the Eng'sh howse, w'th a pr'sent of a *barsoe* of wyne, figges, & oringe, desiring a name to be geven her, w'ch was p'r consent Elezabeth. And Calsa Sammas man brought the money for the gvns and stuffs he bought the other day, amonting in all to 34 *taies* plate bars, w'ch Mr. Nealson receved. Also we receved 19 sacks rise for 20 at the request of Soyemon Dono, whoe is to make 1 sake more good in place hereafter, &c. Calsa Saman[167] tould me he had rec. lettrs frõ his m.ʳ that the Emperour was to retorne to Ose-

Eliza.

34 *tais*.

Nota.

Nota.

167) Perhaps a slip of the pen for "Calsa Sammas man."

key, & his m.ʳ w'th hym, to fortifie the ruenated fortresse &
put garrison into it; w'ch is a signe that warse are like to
ensue. God grant all may fall out for the best, &c.[*fol. 53v.*]

Sonday.

29. This mornyng overcast wether w'th an extreme stiffe
gale, wind at N.ᵒ E'erly, but not be cold as before, dry
wether all day but som rayne p'r night; warme wether.

15 hogges.
8 *taies.*

We bought 15 hogges of Bongo Samme, cost all 8 *taies*
plate of barse.

30. This mornyng overcast wether w'th a stiffe gale of wind
at N.ᵒ E'erly as before, but after nowne vered S. E'erly w'th
rayne rest of day & night following p'r fittes, extreme windy
p'r night vering to S.ᵒ W.

Frō a
gouernor
of Goto.

The governor of an island at Goto, he w'ch sent the pilot
abord our shipp *Hoziander*, came this day to see our Eng'sh
howse, and brought a pr'sent of a beefe & 10 hense. He is
going to the hott bathes in Issue[168] for dollar (or greefe)
he hath in his boanes.

Nota.

The China Capt. tells me that this night past his brother
sent hym a pot overland, to tell hym that Gonrok Dono
hath staid a small *somo* (or junk), at Langasaque, w'ch they
had thought to haue sent to China about our affares, but
now is said to carry souldiers into an island neare vnto
China called Tacca Sanga, [169]but I rather think it will
prouve the Liqueas, in w'ch place it may be the Emperour
doth think that Fidaia Samme lyeth lurking.

26 sakes
rise.

And we rec. 26 sackes rise of the King of Firando, whereof one is of the former acc.ᵒ, & the other 25 cost.[170] I wrot 2

2 lettrs to
Langsaque.

lettrs to Langasaque, viz., 1 to Jor. Durois to send sample
of pitche as also making re[cep]tion of pr'sent of mangoes

---

168) Ishū 壹州 or the province of Iki 壹岐, an island located close to Firando
island and belonging to the Lord of Firando.

169) Takasago 高砂 or Takasagun 高山國, Formosa.

170) Not entered.

October 1615

& peares sent; 1 to Melchar van Sanfort w'th musters of 4
sortes of spikes or neales to be made at Langasaque, viz.:-

1000 great spikes, of	171) inches.
1000 lesser, of	inches.
1500 lesser, of	inches.
2000 smallest, of	inches.

10 *tay.*

And Ed. Sayer had 10 *taies* in plate barse alowd hym on
his wagese, paid p'r Mr. Nealson, and Mr. Nelson del'd Mr.

50 *ta.*
8 *taies.*
4 *mas.*

Osterwick 50 *taies* plate bars, & 8 *tays* 4 *mas* small plate, of
smiths accº, the other 50 *taies* to be emploid about provition for the *Hozeander.*   [*fol. 54r.*]]

31. This mornyng extrem windes at S. W. w'th rayne, most
p'rte of the day, but not soe much rayne nor wind p'r night,
&c. Warme wether.

A lettr to
Mr. Eaton.
To the front
of Calsa
Samme.

And I wrot a lettr to Mr. Eaton to send the petty charges
of his voyag to Edo w'th other mattr, as doth apeare p'r
coppie, & sent it p'r Calsa Samme man. And in respect the
servant of Calsa Samme may doe vs good aboue hereafter,
as p'r words he offers lardgly, I gaue hym a fireloct petre-
nell for a present, w'ch Mr. Hvnt formerly gaue me. We

164 plants.

rec. 164 plantes of Skideyen Dono, viz., 155 inch plank & 9
others somthing thicker.

November   1615

1. This mornyng a fresh gale, wind Nº W. over[c]ast wether warme wether, but after broke vp, fayre wether all day
& night following, but a stiff gale, wind p'r night; cold
wether.

Feast of
Japon.

This day was a festifall day amongst the Japons, & the
horsruning day, to shewte at marckes w'th bowes & ar-

---

171) This and the following figures, not entered.

November 1615

rowes.

2. This mornyng cold wether w'th a stiffe gale, wind at N?
W., and soe remeaned all day & night following, very cold
wether not the lyke this yeare till now.

A lettr to
Mr. Gurney
to Syam.
I wrot a lettr to Mr. Jn? Govrney to Syam p'r way of
Langasaque, p'r a China, advising how *Sea Adventure* lost
her voyag last yeare & put into Liquea, & now is ready to
com w'th a cargazon littell more or lesse as the last year,
Ed. Sayer & Capt. Adames going in her. Also that the *Hozeand?* arived heare, Mr. Raphe Copindell, cap., & Mr.
Jn? Hvnt, m?; & he & Capt. Adames gon to the Japon
court. And how the Duch took a prise at sea, a junk laden
w'th ebony, the Emperour geving them leave to make good
prise both of shipp & goods.

3 pec.
buxshawes.
The King of Firando sent for samples of buxshawes &
had 3 pec. sent hym.   [*fol. 54v.*]]

3. This mornyng still very cold wether w'th a gale, wind
N?erly, but afterward varied divers wayes w'th som rayne
towardes night, & the lyke the fore p'rt of night, yet after
Nota.
dry and calme, not so could as before. The King of Firando
banished on of our marenars of our junck, because Takamon Dono had banished a yong gentelman for geving hym
a cut w'th a *cattan*. So the gentelman was recalled & the
marener banished, & Takamon Dono checked.

Also a yong yowth was cut in peeces for thefte.

4. This mornyng fayre calme wether & but littell wind, after
betwixt the N? & & [*sic*] the E., but calme most p'rte or all
the night not so cold as before, &c.

50 sackes
rise.
180 bam.
We rec. 50 sack rise more of the king vpon acc?, cost .[170]

Also we rec. 180 greate bambows or canes for our junck

---

172) The cost, not entered.

121

November 1615

seales & other vses of junck, bought at 19 *taies* p'r c'nto or hvndred, & Mr. Nealson del'd 50 *taies* plate barse to Mr.

Osterwick vpon the ship *Hozeanders* accompt.

5. This mornyng fayre calme wether, but sowne after a fresh gale, wynd at N? W. most p'rte of day, but calme p'r night.

And ther was sould the King of Firando 30 pec. white baftas, of 20 Rs. *corg*, at a *tye* & a halfe p'r peece, 45 *taies*.

Also we rec. 50 sackes rise more of King of Firando, cost 42 *ta*. 3 *ma*. 3 *co*., cont'g 51 *gantes* p'r sack. A servant of Gonrok Donos came frō Miaco this day, & tould me Capt. Coppindall was retorned frō Shrongo & that he was to com away for Firando forth w'th.

6. This mornyng fayre calme wether, but after a small gale, wind N?erly most p'rte of day, but littell or noe wind p'r night, fayre wether.

We bought Jn? Donos howse & *chawne* over the way for 170 *taies*, & are to pay noe rent for it in lending it the last yeare & this yeare lykewaies, it being a great howse standing ap'rte neare to our howse, over the way, fitt to put shipps store or any thing else. & he is to bring vs 30 boates lading of ston on the bargen, to make walls before it.

[fol. 55r.]]

I receved 2 lettrs frō Capt. Coppendall, 1 dated in Micao le 24th, & the other in Osekay le 28 October; & other 2 frō Mr. Eaton, 1 in Miaco le 23th, & the other in Osekay le 28 ditto; wherin Capt. Copindall adviseth me how well the Emperour did rec. the pr'sent he carid hym, & gaue hym an other of 5 *kerremons*, 10 pike heades, 100 arow heades, & three *waccadashes*, & hath geuen vs his letter to the King of Shashman for trad into all his dominions. He also writes he, the Emperour, sent Capt. Adames to Edo to the padres, to know wherefore they are com into his dominions, he

122

November 1615

haveing formerly banished all of their coate out of his dominions. He also hath made pr'clemation, in payne of death, that no Japon shall goe into New Spanine frõ henceforward. These padres are com now out of New Spaine in a shipp to. And we receved 166 baggs rise of the King of Firando vpon acc?, at 6 measures or *gantas* p'r *mas* amontes vnto the som of 138 *ta*. 3 *ma*. 3.3 *co*.

166 bages rise of King Firando.

7. This mornyng fayre calme wether, & but littell wind, after N?erly som p'rte of the day & night, calme fayre wether not soe cold as it was 3 or 4 dais past.

A lettr to Mr. Gourney to Syam.

I wrot a lettr to Syam to Mr. Gurney, as appeareth p'r coppie, & sent it to Langasaque to Melchar van Sanford to send it p'r first junck w'ch goeth from thence, advising Mr. Gourney, or any other in his place, to pr'vid lading in tyme, knowing before of her coming. Also I wrot other 2 lettrs, p'r Capt. China conveance, to the said Melchar and Geroge Durois, to Melchar to buy 8000 neales, and Jorge to buy 5 or 6 *piculls* rosen. The China Capt. had 1 peec. white bafta, of 20 Rs., to pay xiiij *mas*.   [*fol. 55v.*]]

2 lettrs to Langasaque.

1 pec. of bafta.

8. This mornyng still fayre calme wether, & but littell wind after N?erly to W'ward all day, but calme p'r night, warme wether.

A lettr from Jorge Durois.

I rec. a lettr from Jorge Durois, dated in Langasaque, le 14th of Novembr, new stile, wherin he wrot yt the King of Shashma was making ready 400 barkes of warr w'th all hast, but for what purpose it is not knowne; & that themperour had somond all the kinges or *tonos* in Japon to be at Shrongo in the moneth of M'rche next. He wrot me of pitch he would buy at Langasaque at 3½ *taies* p'r picull. And deliverd vnto Mr. Nealson fyftie *taes* in plate barse to lay out about junck. The w'che 50 *taies* he del'd or paid out instantly to Yaimon Dono, the ship carpenter, vpon acc? carperters wagese working vpon the junck. A Japon

50 *tais*.
50 *tais*.

November 1615

called Martin, w'ch Mr. Wickham imploied at Liqueas when he put Jnọ Japon away, did stieale a *wacadish* or dagger w'th 10 *gocos* or dishes, & being taken was condemned to be cut in pec. Yet the kinge saved his lyfe in respect he was of Langasaque, but banished out of his dominiones for ever in payne of death yf ever he were fownd heare again.

20 pec. baftas of 20 Rs.

The King of Firando had 20 pec. whit baftas, of 20 Rs., to pay a *tay* & a halfe p'r peece.

9. This monryng calme wether, but lowringe yet remend fayre all day, wind but littell vering S. E'rly, yet som drops of rayne p'r night.

A lettr to Jorge Durois

Ther was 169 planckes of inch thick rec. of Skidien Dono for vse of *Hozeander*. I wrot answer to Jorge Durois of his

186 plankes.

lettr receved yisterday, and we receaved 186 planks more for vse of junck, wherof 3 were 3 inch plank, & rest inche;

Portingal pr'soner escaped.

& of the inche plank 35 short planks. The Portugese, that was capt. of the junck w'ch the Hollanders took, escaped againe out of the shipp *Ankewsen* w'th fetters on his legges, &, as it is thought, could not be donne but the wache must

111 bag rise to junk maren'rs.

know thereof. And we delivered 111 sackes rise of 50 *gantes* & 18 *gantes* ouer to our mareners of junck. Yt was not the Portingale capt. w'ch escaped, but 10 other slaues, Chinas & Caffros, w'ch did belong to the junck. The king the king

23 pec. buckshaws.

[*sic*] had 20 pec. buckshaw at 1 *tay* p'r peece, & the 3 before is 23 in all, w'th the 3 he had for munsters[173] before.

[*fol. 56r.*]]

Gon Rock Dono wrot the King of Firando that he had donne what he could to set Damian & Jnọ at libertie, but that the Capt. would do nothing; yet before the shipp went out, he would goe and fet[c]h hym out hym selfe. This

173) *Monster* (Dutch.), sample.

124

is Gon Rock Donos suttiltie, because he now vnderstandeth the Emperour hath geven order to sett them at liberty; otherwiaes he had rather they were hanged, to haue Damians goodes.

10. This mornyng lowring wether, wind S'erly & sowne after rayne w'ch contynewd all day, wind vering N?erly after nowne & so contynewd all night, a stiffe gale littell rayne.

A lettr frō
Mr. Eaton.

I rec. a lettr from Mr. Eaton, in Osekay, le 31th vltimo, w'th 2 other lettrs frō Safian Dono, 1 for the King of Firando and the other for Gonrock Dono. About the delivering (or setting Damian & Juan at liberty) w'ch acc? dated sayeth he promised hym would be p'rformed at sight of his letter.

Nota.

The China Capt. rec. a lettr frō his brother in Langasaque, of a China junck (or *soma*) w'ch dep'rted frō thence for China w'th 77 or 78 men in her, but were met by theevs at sea, who cutt all their throtes & carid away all that was good, & soe the junk was driven vpon the cost of Goto w'th 7 or 8 dead men in her, the rest being throwne over board.

2 lettrs from
Langasque.

Also I rec. 2 lettrs, 1 from Albaro Munos of 17 & the other frō Capt. Garrocho of 5th Novembr, new stile, w'th a pap'r

ta. *mas*
9: 3.

w'th 9 *taies* 3 *mas* in it w'ch Capt. Garrocho owed me. And ther was paid the *mas* w'ch brought downe the letter frō

1 *tay.*
5 *maes.*
Oto ran
away.

Mr. Eaton one *tay*. And Gorezon, our *jurebasso*, paid Pedro five *mas* on my acc? to buy hym shewes. Oto, Mat[ingas] slaue, ran away; but her surties brought her back againe. I enquired wherfore she ran away, and she answered because she would occvpiing & that she could not endure it. *[fol. 56v.]*⌋

11. This monryng cold wether w'th a stiffe gale, wind N?erly and soe contynewed all day, and the lyke p'r night cold wether, yet dry.

50 *tais.*

I del'd 50 *tais* plate barse to Mr. Nealson, to pay out to

November 1615

marreners of junk to buy them fish & other pr'vition I say
I del'd hym 40 *ta.* in plate barse, and he paid out vnto them.

3 lettrs to
Langasaque.

And I wrot 3 lettrs to Langasaque, to Capt. Garocho,
Albara Muños & Jorge Durois, & retorned Garrocho the

ta. ma.
9: 3.

9 *ta.* 3 *mas* he sent me, accepting paym̃t in Andre Dittis,
the China Capten.

201 [*sic*] pec.
duttes at
201 *taies.*

The China Capt. rec. a lettr from his brother to buy 200
peeces dutts of vs & he would send money for them, & buy
them to geue to pore Chinas, to clothe them, that were in
2 junckes w'ch were cast away, one on the Liqueas and
the other on cost Shashme, som being d[r]owned, & them

Nota.

w'ch escaped were stark naked. He tells me they will geue
these duttis to these Chinas, w'ch dwell most of them neare
Lanquin, & tell them it was the gift of the English, because
they should speake well of our nation in respeck of the
matter they haue in hand to procure trade into China.
They must pay a *tay* p'r pece for these duttis.

1 barell
polder.
ta. ma.
33: 4.

And we rec. a rest of a barell gvnpold'r very bad w'ch
remened in Zanzabrs howse, & put it into our new lodg.
Also Mr. Nelson pad to the scrivano of junck 33 *taies* 4 *mas*,
small plate for marrenis fish for voyage, according to
custom; and the rise they had the 9th day, rated, as it cost,

ta. m. co.
93: 2: 4.

93: 2: 4. And the China Capt., Andrea Dittis, had 24 *cattis*

24 *catt.* wax.

wax more to pay as rest are sould.

Sonday.

12.   This mornyng cold wether w'th a stiff gale, wind N̊·erly
or rather N̊. E. &, so remeaned all day & night following,
very cold wether.

Nota.

I went to the King of Firnado & tould hym that Mr.
Eaton had advised me that Safian Do[no] said that yf the
men were not sett at libertye vpon sight of his letter, that
then I should advise hym thereof, & he would vse other
meanes. So the King tould me he would send to Gonrock
Dono, to know whether they would sent them at liberty

or no. Gonrok Donos man came to viset me, yet willed me I should not say he was heare. There is duble dealing w'th them. [*fol. 57r.*]]

13. This mornyng cold wether w'th a stiff gale, wind still at N̥̊ E. most p'rte of the day but towardes night calme, & so remend all or most p'rte night.

100 *tais.*

And I del'd 100 *taies* plate barse to Mr. Nealson, to pay for rest of plankes for the *Hozeander*, 200 *taies* being advanced before as followeth:-

Pro 114, 2 inch plankes at 6 *mas* 6 *con.*

	ta.	ma.	co.
peec., is .... T. 075:		2:	4

Pro 632 inch plank goe for 600, at 3 *ma.* 6 *con.*

pece, is .... T. 216:	0:	0

Pro 010 of 3 & 4 inches at 17 *mas* peece, is T. 017: 0: 0

Som totall pais both now w'th 200 *taes* before, is .... T. 308: 2: 4

ta. ma. c.
108: 2: 4.

Wherof Mr. Nelson paid now 108 *tais* 2 *mas* 4 *condrin.*

4 bages poz.
190 *tt.* for 11
ta. 9 *ma.* 7 *co.*

And we sould the   174) or *sancu*, being 4 bagges poz. grose 194 *cattis* tare 4 *cattis*, rest net 190 *cattis* at 6 *tais* 3 *mas* the *pico.* amontes vnto *T.* 11 *ta.* 9 *ma.* 7 *co.*

Del'd Mr.
Osterwick.
A lettr frõ
Jorge
Durois.

Also I rec. a lettr frõ Jorge Durois, in Langasaque, le 20th curr't, new stile, w'th a pere silk stocking for Mr. Nealson and a pere clamps or challipas for Ed. Sayer. And 6 *pico.* 80 *tt.* rozen, cost 3 *tais* 1 *mas picull.* Also Melchar van Sanford sent me a lettr w'th an other enclozed to Capt. Speck w'ch I sent hym. Melchar wrot in this lettr that he would send the neales I wrot for in the next bark, that came & sould 2 pec. tapis Suras sould for one *taies* p' peece.

6 *p'co.* 80
tattes inch
21: 0: 8.
A lettr frõ
Melchr.

2 pec. tapis
Suras.

14. This mornyng fayre wether w'th lettell wind at S. E'-erly, but sowne after much rayne all day littelle winde, but much wind p'r night N̥̊erly, still rayne a very storme.

---

174) The name, not given. *Sancu* must be *sanshō* 山椒, a spice.

November 1615

15. This mornyng a stiff gale, wind Nºerly overcast lowrying wether, & sowne after rayne all day, but calme p'r night, most p'rte littell or no rayne.

50 *tais*.

I del'd fyftie *taies* plate barse to Mr. Nealson to pay carpenters of the *Hozeander*, w'ch he del'd to Mr. Osterwick

ta. ma. co.
656: 7: 1.

whoe keepeth reconyng of shipp charges. And Mr. Osterwick made a reception wastbook for som of 656 *tais* 7 *mas* 1 *condrin* plate barse, w'ch he hath rec. of Mr. Nealson at severall tymes for to lay out about charges of *Hozeander*.
[*fol. 57v.*]]

8 peces
snaphanne.

And Figean Samma, King of Firando, sent for 8 damaskt snaphanne fowling peeces, to send to Safian Dono for the

A lettr to
Safian Dono.

Empetour. The price I sett at 20 *taies* pec., & I wrot a lettr to Safian Dono therof, as also to thank hym for writing to Gonrok Dono about seting Damian and Jnº at libertie.

2 p. chade.

And 2 pec. chade Cambaia sould this day at 1 *tay* peec. money rec. p'r Mr. Nealson.

16. This mornyng littell wind Nº E'erly lowring raynie wether, but sowne after brok vp faire wether all day, but som rayne p'r night, s'th a stiff gale wind at Nº W'erly later end of the night.

A lettr to
Jor. Durois
A let. to
M'lchar.
A lettr to
Mr. Eaton
dated to
morow.
4 pec.
buckshaw.

I sent a lettr to Jorge Durois and an other to Melchar van Sanford to Langasaque in answer of theirs. Also I wrot to Mr. Wm. Eaton how I had sent 8 gvns to Safian Dono p'r King Firandos order for themperour, price at 20 *tais* peec. And ther was 4 pec. buckshaws, of   175) Rs., sould for a *tay* p'r pec. is 4 *tais* rec. p'r Mr. Nealson.

17. This mornyng lowring wether w'th a stiff gale, wind at Nº W'erly, cold wether, but wind slacked before nowne, & tow'rdes night vered to S'ward of W., littell wind & so rayne p'r night.

---

175) Not entered.

128

November 1615

100 *taes.*

There was one hvndred *tais* plate Japon receved of Andrea Dittis, the China Capt., in bars, and instantly paid out againe to Tome Done in p'rte of paym't of a gadonge over the way bought at 170 *taies* & now paid in p'rte of

100 *tais.*

paym't one hvndred *taies*, this 100 *tais* mad rec. p'r Mr. Nealson.

18. This mornyng lowring wether w'th littell wind at W. S'erly, and so remeaned most p'rte of the day, but in the night turned to the N̊ W., a stiff gale most p'rte of night.

1 sow lead poz. 220 *tt.*

Capt. Speck sent for a sow of lead, poz. 220 *tt.*,[176] to pay for it as rest are sould.

Sonday.

19. This morning could wether w'th a fresh gale, wind N̊ W'erly most p'rte of day, & lyke p'r night vering E'erly; coulde wether, but before day to N̊ W.

20. This mornyng cold wether w'th a fresh gale, wind at N̊ W., and so remeaned all day, but not soe much wind p'r night, fayre wether.

50 *tais.*
4 *ta.* 6 *ma.*

I del'd 50 *taies* plate barse to Mr. Nealson for expenses and 1 bar & 2 lettll pe. to Matinga, poz. 4 *tais* great plate, is 4 *tais* 6 *mas.*   [*fol. 58r.*]

160 sakes rise.

We rec. one hvndred three score sacks rise of the kinges cont'g 50 *gantes* p'r sack, price set at 6 *gantes* p'r *mas*, amontes vnto in plate of barse T. T. 133: 3: 3⅜.

21. This mornyng fayre calme cold wether or rather a littell wind, N̊ W'erly, and so remeaned all day, & the lyke p'r night or rather calme.

5 pc. dutt 12 Rs̊ *cor.* Junk.
1 pc. duttis 14.
1 *tay* plate.

And there was del'd out warehouse 5 pec. dutts to make (or mend) junk, sayes: *Sea Adventure*, at 12 Rs̊ p'r *corg*, is 2 *tais* 4 *mas*, and sould 1 pec. duttis of 12 Rs̊ *corg* for 1 *tay* money rec. p'r Mr. Nealson. A cauelero, on of the kinges men, sent me 5 hense for a pr'sent, & Skite & a

---

176) The mark *tt.* is evidently for cattis, as seen in the margin of the entry for November 13, 1615 above.

Corean, each of them a baskit oringes.

22. This mornyng fayre calme cold wether, but sowne after a fresh gale, wind most p'rte of day S'erly to W'ward, and store of rayne som 2 howrs before day.

Our hostis of Bingana Tomo retorned frõ Langasaque & came to see thenglish howse & brought a pr'sent of pearse.

I sent a lettr p'r her to Mr. Eaton, to same effect as my former 5 *taies* past p'r kings man. Also I wrot 2 lettrs to Nangasauque to Melchar van Sanfort and Jorge Durois for the 8000 heales & 8 barill China oyle frõ China Capt. brother to trym *Hozeander*, & sent a boate expres for it.

23. This mornyng rayny wether w'th a stiffe gale, wind at S. W., but brok vp fayre wether before nowne, & so re-meand all rest of day & night following.

50 taies. And I del'd fyftie *taes* plate bars to Mr. Nealson to pay

30 tais. cawker of junck. And he paid 30 *taies* of it to the scrivano: Gingro vpon acc? of cawkers. The king sent me a lettr that he rec. frõ Gonrok Dono, wherin he advised hym that he wõld sett Damian & Jn? de Liuano at liberty.   [*fol. 58v.*]⌋

*A lettr to
Chubio Dono.* Also I wrot a lettr to Chubio Dono p'r his man, & sent hym my former lettr in it, w'ch was retornd frõ Langasaque

6 tais. w'th other complementos. Also I del'd 6 *taies* in great plat to Jn? Gorezano, *jurebasso*, to chang into small plate.

24. This mornyng wind vered N?erly, fayre wether, all day wind enclynyng W'erly, or rather N? W., a stiffe galle all or most p'rte of night, dry wether, &c.

*A lettr to
Mr. Eaton.* I wrot a lettr to Mr. Eaton dated to morrow and sent it p'r Pedro, our porters kynsman, how the Holl'rs were

*Nota.
Lead stolne.* bound vp in all hast for Edo. Ther was, to the vallew of 150 *tt.* wight, lead stolne out of the *Hozeandr* the night past, out of gvners cabben, w'ch were the covers for the tucholes of great ordinance & other ould lead rypt of shipp sids in tryminge her. It was taken out of Jn? Clough the gvners

cabbyn, & dowbtfull he was of consentt; yet on Robyn, a Scott, is brought in question, he haveng offerd to sell som before, as also neales w'ch he stole, & was taken w'th them. Ther is, as Mr. Hunt sayeth, aboue 200 *tt.* lead more stolne out of store rowne [*sic*], w'th this Skot w'th an othe[r] Jocky, his cvntreman, are thought to haue at severall tymes made away.

25. This mornyng a stiff gale wind at N? W., cold wether, and so remeaned all day & most p'rte night following, & then fell calme or rather a littell wind ver. S?.

Nota.

We met a knave Japon, a marrener, whoe ran away frō junck at Liquea. Soe, seeing hym pas the street in Firando, & entertayned into service of the Duch, whoe ordenarely entertayne all they know to haue byn formerly enter-tayned p'r vs (this is Jacob Speckes humor), yet I layd handes vpon this fellow & brought hym before the justice, whoe put a sureties to be forth coming to answer to what should be aledged against hym. [*fol. 59r.*]

Sonday

26. This mornyng fayre calme wether, or rather a littell wind S'erly, but sowne after vered N? E'erly, & so re-meaned all day, & rather at N? E. a stiffe gale in the after nowne, but calme all or most p'rte of night.

The king sent for a bottell Spanish wyne, & desird to buy Mr. Osterwickes cloake, being of culler du Roy,[177] w'ch

Nota.

he sent vnto hym at price of 20 *taies*, and, as I am enformed, the Portingall capt. is escaped out of the great Holland shipp swying abord to 4 barks w'ch had layne secretly at-tending for hym this monthe; for w'ch it is said Capt. Speck is much offended w'th Derrick de Vris, the m.ͬ

3 pe. duttis
of 12 Rs.
corg.

And ther was 3 pec. duttis sould to 3 Chinas of 12 Rs? p'r *corg* at 1 *tay* p'r peec., is 3 *taies* plate bars.

---

177) Royal colour.—Murakami.

November 1615

27. This mornyng fayre calme wether & very littell wind after at N? E'erly rest of day, but rather calm p'r night, still fayre wether.

About break of day I rec. a lettr frō Capt. Adames, dated in Cocora, the 17th pr'sent, how he hoped to be heare w'thin few dayes, & that he left Capt. Coppendale at Miaco not very well, & that he bringth *recaudo*[178] frō themperour to set Damian and Jn? de Lieuana free. And I wrot hym answer forthw'th, & sent it p'r Gingro, the purcer, w'th

20 *taies* in 5 plates bars, to spend, yf occation served, for hym to com overland, becaus he wrot me he had non; w'ch

plat Mr. Nealson paid out. Capt. Adames arived a littell after dyner, & we went to the kinges pallace to haue del'd hym the lettrs came frō thempror p'r Gota Zazabra & Saffian Dono; but the kyng was gon a hawkyng, & so we retorned, leaving the lettrs w'th Oyen Dono, his governor.

I rec. 2 complementall lettrs frō Stibio, our host at Shrongo &   ,[179] our host at Osekay. Also I rec. a lettr frō Mr. Wickham p'r Capt. Adames, dated in Edo, le 23th of October, w'th the acc? of Andrea, & a note of pr'sentes geven out to each one in p'rticuler. [*fol. 59v*.]] Also I

receaved 2 lettrs fro Jorge Duros & Capt. Garrocho, dated in Langasaque, le 5th and 4th December, new stile, lettrs complementall only. Jorge Durois writ he del'd the money

& lettr to Capt. Garrocho I sent hym before. And I rec. a lettr frō Melchar van Sanfort w'th a cheese & that the smiths went frō their word to make neales.

28. This mornyng still fayre wether, littell wind N?erly, but after a fresh gale at N? E. w'th rayne in thafter nowne, as also p'r fittes p'r night much wynde.

Capt. Adames went for Langasaque, accompand w'th

---

178) *Recado* (Span.), message.
179) The name, not given.

November 1615

Adames to Langa.

3 lettrs to Langa.

Letters frō Mr. Wick. & Mr.Eaton.180)

Capt. Coṗ arived at Firando 1 barell polder.

Nota.

frō Osekay.

Ed. Sayer & Mr. Jnº Osterwick, & carid the Emperours authorety to set Damian Marya & Jnº de Lieuana at liberty. & I wrot 3 lettrs p'r hym, viz., 1 to Jorge Durois, 1 to Capt. Garrocho, & the therd to Melchar van Sanfort, in answer of theirs receaved yisterday. Capt. Coppendall ar[i]ved heare before nowne, & brought me 3 lettrs, viz., 1 frō Mr. Wickham, dated in Shrongana, le 13th of October, and one frō Mr. Eaton in Miaco, le 15th November, & an other in Osekay, le 18th ditto, both p'r Capt. Coppendall. And we rec. a barill of gvnpolder p.r Capt. Adames poz. 43 *tt.* frō Shrongo 6 *ta.* 0 *m.* 8 *co.*

29. This mornyng fayre wether w'th a stiffe gale, wind at Nº E., and soe remeaned all day w'th the fore p'rte of the night, but afterwardes calme or very littell wind Nº.

The 2 barrilles *morafack,* w'ch my host of Osekay wrot me he had sent me, are not to be fownd in the bark that Capt. Coppendall came in, & a chist w'ch Mr. Wickham sent w'th *kerimons* & other thinges in it, to the vallew of 20 *taies,* is lykewais lost in same bark, or else the one nor other was never put into it. & we rec. back frō Osekay, viz.:–

Brod cloth 3 rem pink culler Nº 185, cont'g 13½ *tat.*

	cor.	pe.	
Cassidy nill181)	0:	02, of 12 Rsº., corg ......T.	182)
Byram183) nill	1:	08, of 15 Rs., corg ....T.	
Camsam nill	0:	03, of 10 Rs., corg. ....T.	
Candeque mawy	0:	18, of 4 Rs., corg ....T.	
Rangins	0:	12, of 5 Rs., corg ....T.	
Duttis	0:	08, of 12 Rs., corg ....T.	

180) This marginal note must be put after the next one.

181) *Anile* or *neel,* borrowed from Portuguese *anil,* deriving from Arabian *al-nil* and Sanskrit *nila,* indigo or indigo blue colour.–*Hobson-Jobson.*

182) This and the following prices, not entered.

183) Beiramee, a kind of cotton stuff.–*Hobson-Jobson.*

November 1615

> 14 *pico.* copp'r.
> 3 *pic.* iron
> 5 barelles gvnpolder.

And ther was sould Nobisana, or rather to his adopted sonne ,[184] the kinges yongest brother, zelas red 3 pc. of 8 Rs. p'r *corg* for 1 *tay* p'r peece, is 3 *tay*.

3 pc. zelas.

30. This mornyng fayre calme wether, or rather a littell wind at S? W'erly, but after was a fresh gale all day, but much wind after midnight.

100 *tais.*

We rec. one hvndred *taies* plate bars of Andrea Dittis, China Capt., w'ch money Mr. Nealson receaved.

Capt. Ad. frō Langa. w'th Damian.

And in the after nowne Capt. Adames retorned frō Langasaque, and brought Damian Marin w'th hym; but Jn? de Lieuana remeaned at Langasaque, sick ashore, they hauyng set both Damian & hym at liberty the day before Capt. Adames arrived at Langasaque; but, as Damian tells me, they had condemned them both to die the death, & sent hym word to confesse hym & make hym selfe ready, for dye he must. This passed som moneth agoe, he looking still when he should die, till the instant they set them at liberty. & then the capt. thought to haue p'rsawaded hym to haue gon along w'th hym, pr'mising hym mountaynes, &, when he could not pr'veale, pr'curd hym to sweare he should not goe w'th the English nor Hollanders. Capt.

Capt. Cop. petty chars 283: 8: 0

Coppendall gaue me in his petty charges laid out going vp to Emp? amonting to 283 *taies* 8 *mas.*

---

184) The name, not given.

December 1615.

01. This mornyng fayre wether w'th a stiff gale of wind at S.W. and so remeaned all day w'th som drops of rayne now & then, but littell wind p'r night.

Nota.

I rec. back frō Capt. Coppendall the sylver salt, the 2 spoones, & 2 forkes of silver, lent hym vp, w'th the 2 littell silver cups or tasters I lent hym. Also he gaue me a pr'sent

A pr'sent.

A lettr to Mr. Eaton p'r a China.

of 1 of the *kerrimons* the Emperour gaue hym, as also a peece of fine casho, or chowter. And I wrot a lettr to Mr. Eaton & sent it p'r a China in answer of recept of his 2 lettrs, w'th th'other frō Mr. Wickham p'r Capt. Adames & Capt. Coppendall. Capt. Copindall del'd to Mr. Nealson

12: 0: 6 *co*.

in bars 12 *ta*. 0 *m*. 6 *co*. [*fol. 60v.*]]

2. This mornyng fayre calme wether but sowne after a fresh gale, wind most p'rte day S. W'erly, w'th rayne p'r fittes in th'after nowne, but mere p'r night p'rte calm[e].

4 lettrs to Langasaque.

I wrot 4 lettrs to Nangasaque, 1 to Jorge Durois & 1 to Diego Farnando Rigote to del'r or sell a jarr of the zant oyle to Andrea Bolgarin & Marcus, the German, also an other lettr to Jnº de Lieuana, and a 4th to Melchar van Sanford, w'th a Hollandes cheese, all sent p'r Damian Marin. I rec. 12 *ta*. 6 *m*. *taies*[*sic*] in plate bars of Capt. Coppendall for thinges foll'g, viz.:–

	ta.	*m.*	*co.*
1 pear silk stockinges .... T. 04:		0:	0
2 pear silk stockinges, cost .... T. 08:		0:	0
1 pear cotton stockinges or wosted .... T. 00:		6:	0
	12:	6:	0

Nota.

And Lues Martin came to Firando & brought me a pr'sent of diet bread, w'th many wordes of complemento, telling me that I was praid for of many for the charetable deed I did in setting Damian & Jnº at liberty, & that the capt. of the shipp was in no falt about the matter, but the

135

December 1615

Castillianos; in fyne, they are all our enymies, deadly yf it la in their poweres. I was advised he hath byn 8 or 10 daies in towne, & la in his lodging secretly, but for what occation I know not. I tould hym I heard he had byn in towne som tyme before, w'ch he denyd not, but said it was to sell silk.

300 tais.

Andrea Dittis, the China Capt., paid vs 300 *taies* this day in plate bars rec. all p'r Mr. Nealson, & he paid to Capt. Adames to cleare junk mareners wages & calkers, as by

ta. m. co.
250: 5: 0.

p'rticuler, is 250: 5: 0.   [*fol. 61r.*]

Sonday.

3. This mornyng lowring wether, littell or no wind at all, but after a small gale E'erly all day w'th rayne now & then, but much rayne p'r night.

100 tais.
This 100 ta.
Mr. Nealson
mad rec.

I del'd 100 *taies* to Mr. Osterwick for to lay out about shipp charges. And betyms in the mornyng the king sent to envite vs to supp'r, because he vnderstood our junck was ready to dep'rte towardes Syam. Our entertaynm't was good, only the dryncking was overmuch. The Eng'shmen that went were, viz.:–

Capt. Cappendall,
Capt. Adames,
Mr. Nealson,
Ed. Sayer,
Jnº Osterwick,
and my selfe.

And Mr. Nealson reconed w'th Capt. Adames about the junck, and del'd hym   185) in plate of bars to pay the rest carpenters and cawkars wages.

4. This mornyng fowle raynie wether, wind Nº W. and soe remeaned all day, but not soe much rayne p'r night, but more winde.

100 taes to
Mr. Nealson
paid.

I del'd one hvndred *taies* to Capt. Adames p'd p'r Mr.

185) Not entered.

December 1615

Nealson in full paym't of two hundred *taies* borowed of hym at his coming frõ Liqueas, wherof the other 100 *tais* was

100 *taes.*

50 *taes.*

paid hym at his going vp to Miaco. Also I del'd 100 *taies* plate bars to Mr. Nealson and presently after fyftie more, is all 200 *taies*, to Mr. Nealson, to pay reconyinges for

10 pc. duks.

25 *tt.* wax.

junck & shipp. And ther was 10 pec. dvks, of 12 Rs, *corg*, w'ch were rot eaten to mend junk sayles, & 25 *cattis* wax to make candells del'd 50 sackes rise to China Capt. cont'g

50 sakes rise.

50 *gantes* sack, rated at 6 *gantes* p'r *mas*, is 416.0 [*fol. 61v.*]]

5. This mornyng fayre cold wether, w'th a stiff gale, wind at N̊. W. all day, &c.

I del'd six hvndred powndes str. this day to Capt. Adames wherof forty powndes, ten shilling, was in *fybuck* of Tush-

2400 *taies.*

81 bages pep'r.

ma and the rest in Rs̊. of 8, w'ch maketh 2400 *taies*. Also 81 sakes pep'r del'd China Capt. cont'g 55 pec. 81½ *cattis*, tare 3 pec. 64½ *cat.*, rest net 52 pec. 17 *tatt.* at 6 *ta. pic.*

6. This mornyng cold wether w'th a stiff gale, wind at N̊. E'erly all day, and lyke p'r night following.

Sea Adv'nt'r dep'rted toward Syam.

I sent 20 jarrs bisket & the 500 sheetes pap'r abord the junck, and deliv'rd lettrs to Capt. Adames for the Syam voyage, viz.:–

1 to Mr. Jn̊. Gourney, agent at Syam.

1 to Capt. Jn̊. Jourden, agent at Bantam.

1 to Mr. Adam Denton, agent at Pattania.

& put into the packet directed to Mr. Jn̊. Gourney a bill of lading & cargezon of all goodes sent, also 3 jars bisket sentt,

1 to Mr. Gvrney ⎫
1 to Mr. Shapp'rd ⎬ my owne gifte;
1 to Mr. Denton ⎭

w'th a memoiall del'd Capt. Adames & Ed. Sayer, how to vse busynes, yf they canot attayne Syam.

Soe the *Sea Adventur* went of of roade, & the Duch shot

December 1615

of 6 pec. ordinance at her dep'rture. And pr'sently after
Jnº Yoosen went for Miaco; & the Duch shot affe 9 pec.
ordinance at his dep'rture. So I went abord the junck to
Cochi & carid a barill wyne, a baskit orynges, & an other of
pears, & a therd of biskit & so drunk to the health of the
company *Nifon catange*, & retorned, deliverd to Andrea Dittis, China Capt., 3 *nukis*[186] or post or rather called *cakas*

3 cacas.

of *finuque*[187], cost 3 *mas* great plate p'r peec.   [*fol. 62r.*]]

7.   This mornyng still cold wether littell wind at Nº E'erly,
but sowne after a fresh gale all day but not so much p'r
night, fayre wether.

A lettr to
Ed. Sayer.

Ed. Sayer sent me a lettr vnto w'ch I made answer
p'r Chongro, the junk being vnder seale, & sent hym 5 *ta*.
7 *mas* in plate frõ China Capt. for a *pico*. pep'r he sould

2 *pico* 17
cat. wax.

hym; and ther was 2 *picos* & 17 *cattis* wax sould Andrea
Dittis, China Capt., to pay as rest was sould. And we gaue

6 pec.
duttis.

6 pec. dittis rot eaten of 12 Rs, *corg*, vnto a China for lod-
ghier of our pepp'r.

Junk set
sayle

The wind & wether being very fayre, the *Sea Adventure*
sett sail frõ Cochi towards Syam, this mornyng. God send
her a prosper's voyag.

8.   This mornyng littell wind Nºerly cold wether, but in the
after nowne vered more W'erly w'th some rayne towardes
night, & after droping.

1 tonne wax
wait.

We wayed out the wax w'ch came in the *Hozeander*, &
fownd it want a tonne. As also we paid the pepp'r, & it

2 tonne
pep'r wait.

wanted aboue 2 tonne; w'ch out of dowbt the mareners
haue embezeled and stolne. And I sent Niquan, the China

Lettrs to
Tushma p'r
Niquan.

Capt. kynsman, to Tushma, to bring the money for the
pep'r, & wrot hym a lettr, I meane to our host, to del'r hym
the money, &, yf in case he would not, I sent a lettr to the

---

186) *Nuki* 貫, a rail or a thin plank to connect pillars.
187) *Hinoki* 檜, Japanese cypress.

December 1615

King of Tushma to desyre justice. Also I sent our host a

2 pec. bafta.
2 pec. byram.

pr'sent of 2 pec. white bafta of 8 Rs? p'r *corg*, & 2 pec. blew byrams of 15 Rs? p'r *corge*; & I del'd our host bill vnto Niquan for 61 *pco*. 70 *cattis* pep'r & 305 bufflos honrs.

[fol. 62v.]⌋

9.   This mornyng droping wether wind N? W. but after vered N? E'erly, a stiff gale most p'rte of the day, fay[r]e wether.

Hoseand.
out.
8 Rs. 8.
40 sews
lead.
30 bales
wax.
50 bages
pep'r.
Sonday.

We got the *Hozeander* aflote & carid her out w'ch we could not doe in 2 Springs past. And there was eight Rialles of 8 lent to the China Capt., Andrea Dittis, to make hym a silver cup, paid hym p'r my selfe.

We laded 40 sowes lead 30 bales wax & 50 bagges pepp'r abord a bark to send for Osekay.188)

10.   This mornyng fayre cold wether, wind at N? E., and so remeaned all day, but blustring wether p'r night w'th rayne.

We put abord a barke to send for Osekay to Mr. Eaton, viz.:-

100 bages pep'r, poz. gros 6598½ *cat*. tare
    450 *catt*. net.

Pepp'r 6108½
cattis.

6108½ at 4²³⁄₄₄ *pico*. amontes vnto ....*T*. 0242: 9:   4 189)

65 bales wax, poz. 6497 *catt*. tare 436 *catt*. net

Wax 6061
cattis.

6061at *cattis* 24 Rs. 8 p'r *picull*.

6180 at 24 Rs. p'r *piico*. amontes vnto .....*T*. 1163: 7:   1

lead 9170
catt.

40 sowes lead, poz. 9170 *cattis* at 6 Rs.
    pico. ....*T*. 0440: 1:   6

1846: 2: 1
whole cargo.

Som totall cargezon amontes to .....*T*. 1846: 2:   6

The China Capt. sent Mr. Eaton a jar conserves. And we

---

188) In a space after this entry is a later remark, reading: "*Hozeander* got afloat."

189) Thompson corrected these figures as 0242: 3: 4⅛ on the basis of contemporary records. Thus the total becomes 1846: 2: 1⅛.

December 1615

rec. two hundred *taies* plate bars of Andrea Dittis, China
Capt, w'ch 200 *taies* he deliverd to Mr. Nealson to lay out
about shipps charges. But he paid Quiamo Dono 10 *taies* of
it, in p'rte bote hier to cary these goodes aboue to Osekay,
the rest to make it up 35 *taies* Mr. Eaton is to pay at Osekay. The m'rchnt that bought pep'r last yere offred 6½ *tais
peco.* lead, but went frõ his word & offred but 6 *tais pico.*

200 tais.
10 taes.

[*fol. 63r.*]]

11.　This mornyng cold lowring wether w'th a stiff gale wind
at N? W'erly most p'rte of the day, but calme most p'rte of
the night.

And there was sould vnto Kyng of Crates by

60 baftas.
5 tapis.

60 pec. w't baftas of 11 Rs, *corg,* for ....*T.* 90:	0:	0
5 pec. tapis Suras of 190) for ....*T.* 05:	0:	0
Som totall amontes vnto ....*T.* 95:	0:	0

del'd to Jubio Dono & a bill of his hand taken.

12.　This mornyng fayre cold calme wether, but after a stiff
gale wind all day, but not soe much p'r night, w'th som
rayne.

A lettr to
Mr. Eaton.

．wrot an other lettr to Mr. Eaton to haue effect littell
more or lesse as before 2 daies past, to Osekay, p'r mᶦ of
the barke, w'ch dep'rted frõ hence this mornyng.

13.　This mornyng ourecast misty dropping wether, littell
wind N? E'erly, but after a gale most p'rte of the day rany
wether, & lyke p'r night much wind.

70 *tais.*

We paid Jn? Dono seventy *taies* in plate of bars, in full
paym't of the ffee symple of the gadonge over thᵉ way, to
Westward of English howse, wherof one hvndred *taies*
was paid before. Mr. Nealson paid this 70 *taies* out of the
200 *taies* he rec. of China Capt. the other day. Derick de

---

188) Not entered.

December 1615

Invited p'r
Derik de
Friz.

Fries, the m.ʳ of Duch shipp, being ready to dep'rte, envited vs to dyner to morrow. Our bark w'th goodes for Osekay retorned.

14. This monryng a stiff gale wind N.°erly lowring droping wether, but yet sowne after proved dry all rest day & the

Dyned abord
ye Holland
shipp.

lyke p'r night, but littell wind p'r night.

We dyned abord the great Holland shipp & had 3 pec. ordinance shot of at our retorne ashore. Capt. Speck came not to dyner. He is over great in conceate, &c.   [*fol. 63v.*]]

Papist
Christmas.

15. This mornyng overcast wether w'th a small gale, wind at N.° E'erly, but sowne after a stiff gale most p'rte of the day, but littell wind p'r night till breake of day & then storme of much wynd & rayne.

A lettr to
Jo. Durois

I wrot a lettr to Jorge Duros by a China, to send me of all sortes of garden seeds p'r first.

130 pe.
duttes 71 *ta*.
5 *mas*.

And we sould all the remeander of our duttis being 130 peeces severall sortes all monghsteatn rotten staynd & rotteaten, at 5½ *mas* p'r peec. sould vnto Andrea Dittis, the China Capten, amontes *T*. 71 *ta*. 5: 0.

16. This mornyng a stiffe gale wind, Noerly w'th rayne and soe contynewe most p'rte of the day, but littell wind or rayne p'r night, &c.

Frō China
Capt. broth.

Capt. Whaw, the China Capt. brother, sent me a barrell of figges or jar of Japan green figges for a pr'sent. We envited the m'rsters of the Hollander shipps & juncks to dyner to morrow, they being now ready to goe to sea w'th first good wind. And ther was a *tattamy* & a halfe of pinck

1 *tatta*. N.°
85 pink c'llr.

culler brod cloth N.° 85 sould to Andrea Dittis, China Capt., for 10 *taies* p'r *tattamy*, amontes vnto fyfteen *taies*.

Sonday.

17. This mornyng fayre wether littell wind at N.° W. and soe remeaned all day, & forep'rte of night rest more wynd at N.° W'erly.

A lettr to
Mr. Eaton to

I wrot an other lettr to Mr. Eaton p'r the m.ʳ of bark w'ch

December 1615

Osekay.

carid goodes & is now retornd p'r meanes of fowle wether. We envited the Duch to dyner, I say they came to dyner, &

Duch to dyner.

were Derick de Vrize, m.ʳ of a junk, the pilot of the great ship & Mr. Fredrick, the chirurgion. I would haue del'd an open lettr to Dirck to haue carid, but I tould me he thought that Capt. Speck would be content to let hym carry our sealed lettrs, in respect our ship brought his & del'd them. Yf not, that then he would cary both our open & also shut lettrs.   [*fol. 64r.*]⌋

2 lettrs frō Mr. Eaton.

I rec. two lettrs frō Mr. Eaton frō Miaco, 1 of the 23th Novembr in Miaco, & the other of the 30th ditto in Osekay w'th an acc.º of such matters as he hath donne in Edo, Shrong, & Osekay, as also, a note what pr'sentes Capt. Coppendall gaue away aboue.

Damian & Jn.º

Damian retorned frō Langasaque w'th Jn.º de Lieuana, & Damian sent me a barill *morofack* & a dish of peares for a

A lettr frō host Osekay. A l're to Mr. Eaton.

pr'sent. Also our host of Osekay sent me a Japon stameth for a pr'sent w'th a letter. And I wrot in breefe to Mr. Eaton of rec'pt of his lettr & sent it p'r m.ʳ of the bark goodes to ent'r in.

18.   This mornyng littell wind at N.º W., but after a gale most p'rte of day, & the lyke p'r night.

Ther was sould this day to China Cap., as followth:-

15 *cor.* 12 pec. baftas, of 11 Rs., out of pak
 N.º 122 at................................ 8 ma ij pec.
15 *cor.* 00 baftas, of 11 Rs., our of pak
 N.º 123, at................................9 [   ].191)
00 *cor.* 4 pec. baftas, of 11 Rs.,at.................9[   ] pec.
00 *cor.* 3 pec. w't gingams, of   192) Rs., at .... 7 *mas* pec.
00 *cr.* 3 pec. brown gingams, of Rs., at .... 3 *mas* pec.
00 *cor.* 1 pec. byram nill, of 15 Rs., at ....10 *mas* pec.

---

191) This and the following units are illegible.
192) This and the following figures, not entered.

December 1615

00 *cor.* 1 pec. zelas red, of 12 Rs., at ....10 *ma.* pec.

00 *cor.* 4 pec. chader Cambaia, of Rs., at ......10 *mas* pec.

00 *cor.* 2 pec. chader brawdry, of 5 Rs., at .....10 *mas* pec.

00 *cor.* 2 pec. fota longi har er, of 15 Rs, *corg,* gevin.

Som totall   .193)

Also sould Cushcron Dono 1 pe. cha'der Canba, of Rs. for 1: 0: 0; to Gorehon, our *jurebasso,* 1 pec. ditto for 1: 0: 0, to Skidayen Dono 3 pec. chader bradary, of 5 Rs. *corg* for 3: 0: 0.   [*fol. 64v.*]]

19.   This mornyng overcast wether, wind a fresh gale at N? W., rack S. W., fayre wether all day & the lyke night following.

11 pec. borall.   There was 11 pec. boralles of ¹⁹⁴⁾ sould and del'd to the King of Firando, at 1 *tay* p'r peece, is *tais* T. 11: 0: 0.

20.   This mornyng cold wether w'th a stiff gale, wind at N? W., rack, to S'ward of the W., & soe remeaned all day, but not soe much wind p'r night.

Lettrs to Bantam & Syam.   I wrot a lettr to Bantam to Capt. Jourden of what accorrantes haue passed since tharivall of the *Hozeander,* as apereth p'r coppie, as the lyke for Syam, to Mr. Jno Gourney, agent, & a therd to Mr. Adam Denton at Pattania, & 2 others to Capt. Wm. Adames and Ed. Sayer: the first lettr to Bantam sent p'r the ship *Ankewsen,* vnder covert frõ Capt. Jacob Speck, & the other 4 p'r Piter Jn?sons junck for Syam, vndr cavert as aboue said, Capt. Speck offring to send our lettrs the one or other way, in respect

1 frõ Capt. Copendall to Bantam.   we brought their lettrs & del'd them. And 1 lettr enclozed to Bantam frõ Capt. Coppendall.

21.   This mornyng still cold wether littell wind N?erly, but after a fresh gale most p'rte of the day, but not soe much p'r night fayre wether.

---

193) Not entered.
194) Not entered.

350 *ta.*
50 *tais* bar
55 gould.

50 *ta.* bad.

100 *tais.*

629 *catt.*
suger.

5 *pico.*
pepp'r.

And there was 350 *tais* plate bars rec. of Andrea Dittis, China Capt., wherof was 50 *taies* del'd to Skidayen Dono w'th a bar of *oban* gould of 55 *taies*, to goe to buy a mast for our shipp *Hozeander*, but 50 *taies* was bad money & turned back, rest in all 300 *taies*. And I del'd 100 *tais* to Mr. Osterwick for to pay Cosabro[?], this entered rec. p'r Mr. Nealson, & carpenters abort [sic] the *Hozeander*, being in plate bars rec. of Capt. China. Also Tomo Dono bought 6 pico 29 *cattis* course suger, at 2 *tais* p'r *pico*. 12 *ta*. 6 *m*. 0 co. and five *picolles* pepp'r to pay, as rest is sould *T*.   [195)] w'ch pepp'r & suger Ed. Sayer del'd & waid out, but put it not in wastbook, till now Mr. Osterwick put it in.

[*fol. 65r.*]]

22. This mornyng cold calme wether but pr'sently after a gale at N? E'erly all day, but not soe much wind p'r night, still fayre wether.

Duch new
years day.

Junk of
Duch to
Syam.
2 lettrs to
Mr. Wickhā
& Mr. Eaton.

A lettr to
Safian Dono.

About breake of day the Hollanders discharged much ordinance & small shott, it being their new yeares day. The Duch junck that they took priz went out of rode of Firando towardes Syam this day before nowne. And I wrot 2 lettr to Mr. Wickham & Mr. Eaton, dated the 18 & 20th pr'sent, but kept till this day, & sent p'r the servant of Safian Dono, w'th a lettr in Japans to his m?, in answer of recept of his p'r Capt. Adames & seting free of Damian & Jn?.

100 *taies.*
mad. rec.
Mr. Nelson.

6000 fagget
for *Hozean-
der.*

And I del'd one hvndred *taies* plate bars to Mr. Jn? Osterwick to lay out about carpenter, this is made rec. p'r Mr. Nealson, & cawkers wagese for the *Hozeander*. We rec. 6000 small fagges of Cushcron Dono and Tomo Dono for the *Hozeander* at 1 tay p'r 100, is six *taies*.

23. This mornyng fayre calme wether or rather a litell wind

---

195) Not entered.

December 1615

at N? E., but after a gale most p'rte of day, but a stiff gale after midnight.

2 pec. zelas of 8 Rs.

Ther was 2 pec. red zelas more del'd to Bongo Donos sonne, of 8 Rs. p'r *corg*, sould for 1 *taies* peec. It is not Bongo Donos sonne, nor kings brother, but their kinsman,

& had 3 pec. more before, is all 5 pec. This day a boy of 16 years ould was cut in peeces for stealing a littell boate & carying it to an other iland. I sent to the knyng [sic] to beg his lyfe, w'ch he granted me, & in the meane tyme sent a man after the execusoner to stay a lyttell; but he would not, but put hym to death before the p'rdon came, cuting

hym in many mamocks to try their *cattans* vpon hym. I sent Piter Wadden out to Cochi, w'th a barrill wyne, 10 loves of bread, & a baskit of oranges, to Piter Jn?son, m? of the junck w'ch goeth to Syam, w'ch stayeth there to make acc? w'th Japonnars about the reparing of her, the Hollandrs haveing emploid a knave about it w'ch hath deceaved them, as Capt. Adames scrivano hath [*fol. 65v.*]

ta. m. co. 21: 0: 0.

donne vs, and carid 50 *taies* w'th hym w'ch was paid the carpenters vpon acc? of *Hozeander*, & receaved the full paym? of junck besids, del'd Mr. Nealson in bar plate xxj *tail*, is small 24: 1: 5.

24. This mornyng fayre cold wether w'th a stiffe gale, wind N? E'erly, but after vered to W. of N?, & p'r night S'erly, still fayre wether but not so cold.

2 lettrs frō Langa. 2 lettrs to Langasque.

I rec. 2 lettr frō Jorge Durois & Capt. Garrocho, in Langasaque le 24th & 25 currant, new stile, and wrot them answer, at instant p'r conve. of Capt. China.

Our carpenters came & tould me that yf they might not haue the 50 *taies* paid them w'ch Mr. Nealson paid the scrivano of junck, or rather the scrivano deseaved the carpentrs & tould them it was of the junkes acc?, when the truth is it was of shipps. Soe were [sic] are forced to pay this

145

December 1615

50 *tais* againe & keepe it vpon acc? till the junk retorne.

Their came 3 Spaniardes to our English house, w'ch were of the shipp w'ch came frō Aguapulca. They tould me it was true that 7 or 8 shipps were in the S. say, & had donne som hurt one the cost of Peru, so that all was vp in armes; & that the Spaniardes in New Spaine had made pr'clemacon, in payne of death, that all strangrs were to avoid out of New Spaine & never retorne to trade theare any more.

25. This mornyng fayre wether w'th a small gale, wind S'erly, but after much wind w'th rayne & haile mingeld together in the after nowne, but dry p'r night much wind.

Taccamon Dono sent 2 barilles wyne & 2 fishes for a pr'sent; the kyng 2 pec. wale fyshe; the China Capt. a jarr of China wine; & other neighbors other trifles p'r reason of Christmas.   *[fol. 66r.]*

26. This mornyng a stiffe gale wind at N? W'erly overcast cold wether, & soe remeaned all day & night following w'th haile & slite p'r fittes.

I sent our *jurebasso* to thank the king & Takamon Dono for the pr'sent they sent, according to Japon order. The

Hollandrs had a demi cannon of bras cast this day, poz. 5000 wight, a very fayre peece.

27. This mor[n]yng still a stiff gale, wind N?erly, cold wether haile & slite (or small snow), & remend all day, but towardes night wind remoued W'erly, & rayne in som quantety p'r night.

Capt. Speck sent Jacob Swager & Wm. Jn?son for a sow of lead, poz. 230 *cattis*, w'ch was del'd to them vpon acc?, to pay as crest are sould.

And towardes night Soyemon Dono, the kinges steward, came to Eng. howse, taking it in his way (as he said) going to the king, the China Capt. met hym, & his errand was about the money the king oweth the Wor. Company, w'ch as he sayeth, the king will now pay in, & take vp comodeties of vs to pay next yeare at a resonable rate, as the Duch haue geven it hym, whoe haue now sould hym vpon trust for 10000 *tais*. The king (he saieth) taketh this course by littell & littell to bring hym selfe out of debt, w'ch his grandfather left hym to pay, & so, once geting on even hand, will so hould hym. The m'rch'ndiz he taketh vp, he geveth to Japons at Miaco, of whome Foyne Same took vp money in tymes past w'ch still runeth on at intrest, & yf it should so contynew would vndo hym. So I referd this matter ofe till to morrow, because I would take counsell, & in the meane tyme desired hym[196] I was as willing as Capt. Speck to doe the king any service I could, &c. Nicolas Grant, a marener, being drunk, stabd hym selfe thorow the arme, because Mr. Osterwick would not lend him 12 *d.* to goe to a whore. *[fol. 66v.]*

Nota.

28. This monryng overcast lowring wether, wind W'erly and after droping wether, rayne, haile & snow together, but most an end rayne, but dry p'r night, wind vering N°.erly.

Nota.

The China Capt. built or reard a new howse this day, & all the neighbours sent hym pr'sentes, *Nifon cantange*. So I sent hym a barill *morofack*, 2 bottells Spanish wine, a drid salmon, and halfe a Hollandes cheese; & after, went my selfe w'th the nighbours. Where I saw the seremony was vsed, the m.r carpenter of the kinge doing it, & was as followeth:-

First they brought in all the pr'sentes sent & sett them in ranke before the middell post of the howse, & out of eache one took somthing of the best & offred it at the foote of the post, & powred wyne vpon eache severall p'rcell, doing it

---

196) Thompson here adds "to say" with blackets.

in great hvmilletie & silence, not soe much as a word spoaken all the while it was a doing. But, being ended, they took the remeander of the presentes, and soe did eate & drink it w'th much merth & jesting, drinking them selues drunken all or the most p'rte. They tould me they beleeved that a new howse, being hallowed in this sort, could not chuse but be happie to hym w'ch dwelled in it, for soe their law taught them, ordayned by holy men in tymes past.

Nota.

The shipps company came to the Eng'sh howse in a maske, & after plaied Christmas vle games in good sort & meryment.

29. This monryng fayre could wether w'th a stiff gale, wind at N? W'erly, hayle & snow all day & night following much wind, haile & snow, cold wether p'r night.

And ther was sould & del'd to Semi Done p'r Mr. Nealson

4 pec. chaddr Cambaia. To Matiñ.

4 pec. chader Cambaia of   197) for 1 *tay* p'r peece. & I gaue Matinga a pec. satten, cost 5 *taies* & 1 peec. of taffety, cost 1 *tay*, to make her a *kerremon*, & 2 *kerremons* of zelas to Oto

10 *catis* pri. pep'r.

& Fuco. And ther was sould & deliverd 10 *cattis* Priaman pepp'r to the kinges doctor of phisik, rated at 6 *condrins* p'r *catty* or 8 *taies picoll*. & I thought good to note downe how Mr. Hunt, the m?, came in a *fume* 198) ashore & broake Jn? Cocora, the cooks head, at instigation of Jn? shipper, he having first misvsed & beaten hym w'thout reason.

[*fol. 67r.*]

30. This mornyng still a stiff gale wind at N? W'erly, very cold wether, haile & snow, p'r fittes day & night following, but not soe much wind p'r night vering W'erly.

732 bages lyme. 50 *taies*.

And we bought 732 bages white lyme at 3 *condrins* p'r bagg, it being good cheape. And I del'd fyftie *taies* in plate

---

197) Not entered.
198) *Fune* 舟, a boat.

December 1615

bars to Mr. Nealson, to pay for lyme & other matters. And I wrot a lettr to Jorge Durois to look out for *morofack* & cows shewet for shipps vse for chirurgion. God send health, &c.

100 *taies.*

And we rec. one hvndred *taies* plate bars of Andrea Dittis, China Capt., vpon acc? w'ch money Mr. John Osterwick receaved, but Mr. Nealson put it to his accompt. A

Frō a China.

China of Lankyn brought me a pr'sent of a barill of Lankyn wyne & a dozen of China cakes.

Sonday.

31. This mornyng still cold wether wind N? W. or rather more W'erly, haile & sleete p'r fittes all day, but p'r night wind vered W. S'erly, w'th rayne.

30 *taies.*

I paid therty *taies* to   199) for a howse for Matinga, that shee was in being for the Company, & cost as much I paid 20 *taies* 5 *mas* my selfe, & Mr. Nealson paid the rest on my acc?, being 9 *taies* 5 *mas.* Also Taccamon Dono sent me p'r

10 *taies.*

Capt. China or paid the ten *taies* in plate bars sent hym heretofore p'r Company, w'ch money Mr. Nealson receved.

A pr'sent.

And the Japon barber Rappado sent me a pr'sent of a basket of oringese. I forget to note downe how I wrot a

Nota.

few lynes yisterday to Mr. Jn? Hvnt, to haue had hym com ashore about Compa. busynes, to haue had his advice about bras shivers;200) but he retorned me a snapish answer, w'ch letter I del'd to Capt. Coppendall to carry, &c.201)

[fol. 67v.]

---

199) The name, not given.
200) The wheels of pulleys.—Thompson.
201) In a space after this entry is a later remark, reading: "Finis 1615."

[1616][1]

January 1615[6].

1. This mornyng overcast raynie wether, wind at S. W. but after vered N?.erly, rack W'erly, fayre wether most p'rte of day & all night following, &c.

Nota.

Mr. Hunt, the m: of the *Hozeander*, remenyng still in his extreme hvmours (as I haue fownd hym allwais the same man ever since he came into Japon), wrot a letter to Capt. Coppendall, he being sick in bed (as he hath byn most an endever since he retorned frō Miaco), & I verely think that the vnruly company of the shipp to be the cheefe occation —I say he advised Capt. Coppendall he would com ashore to morrow & gaue direction how to cast bras shivars & shot for ordinance, aledging the gvner knew nothing for shot, nor no man else but hym selfe for the rest. Yet, for my p'rte,. I rest dowbtfull whether it be soe or noe, only I wrot hym before in frendly sort to com ashore & assist me in these mattrs, for the service of the Wor. Com., our emploiers,. because the Duch sent away shipp after ship yerly full laden w'th shot, powlder, ordinance, victuells, & munision, & I would in som sort geue a reason or tast to our emploiers of these matters & send them samples w'th price. But, as it should seeme, the m: disenableth all but hym selfe, & others hould back, I know not whether vpon sutteltie to leave the other in lurch, as debasing all but hym selfe. But be it the one or other, the Companies busynes restes vndon,. &c. & the very truth is, here doe I confes before God & the

---

1) Text continues to the entry for December 1615 without changing the leaf. In the original, the name of the year remains as "1615" up to the Easter day.

January 1615[6]

world, I never did see a more vnruly compa. of people, & are far worse then they in the *Cloue*, allthough they were bad enough. & yisternight, very late, came on Jn.⁰ Shippard (a tapster as I vnderstand), & in very deed a shuffling fello, not worthy water for his hier. He is a turbulent fello, a make bate, & setts the mʳ at odds w'th others p'r meanes of his smouth tong, & yet a drunken fello, as most of the rest are the lyke; & came againe into the kitchin to quarrell w'th our cooke at supper tyme, I desyring Mr. Osterwick to put hym out of the howse & send hym abord the shipp; but he fell vpon Mr. Osterwick, & puld his clothes afe his back, & misvsed hym, for w'ch I put hym in the bilboes to cowle his feete till mornyng, &c.   [*fol. 68r.*]⌋

2.   This mornyng fayre wether winde N.⁰erly, rack frō the W., but after heale & sleete p'r fittes most p'rte of day, but much snowe p'r night w'th a stiff gale wind at N.⁰.

A lettr to
Jo. Dorois.
Nota.
Matinga.
Jn.⁰
jurebasso
Gorezano in
Eng. rentes.

I wrot a lettr to Jorge Durois to buy 100 or 200 tallo candelles & bring them w'th hym. And Matinga went into her new howse this day. And Gorezan, our *jurebasso*, removed his howse, & came w'th wife & famely & dwelt in the Companis howse over the way, to keepe the shopp or shew rowme, &c.

3.   This mornyng very cold wether, being a greate snowe, the greatest I saw since our arivall in Japon, w'th a stiffe gale wind N.⁰erly, rack from W. all day, & snow p'r fittes all day, but littell or non p'r night.

Nota.

The King of Firandos host at Osekay came againe & brought a pr'sent of figges, telling me he was to retorne to his howse, the king haveing rewarded hym well, as all the caveleros in his kingdom did the lyke towardes the setting hym vp a new howse, his ould being burned in the wars, w'th all that ever he had. Soe, w'th consent of Capt. Coppendall & the rest, ther was a bar of plate of 4½ *taies*, and

1 bar plate
of 4½ *tais.*

151

1 sack rise of 51 _gantes._ a bag of rise ofe 51 *gantes* geven hym & sent after hym to his lodging. Mr. Nealson paid out the bar of plate.

Nota. Also, ther was del'd to the fownder for formes as foll'th:–

1 bras shiver of the boate,
1 rownd shot of saker,
1 langrell shot of saker, } to make others by.
1 crosbar shot of minion,
5 braz, of severall sortes

And I agreed w'th hym as follweth: to make

5 greate bras shivers of 35 or 36 *cattes* p'r shiver,
5 others of a lesser sise,
3 others of sise of that of boate,
2 others of a bigger sise,
1 qu[i]ntall bras, of severall sortes,

and to pay 12 *taies* p'r *pico.* for all, on w'th an other, ready made, the fownder finding all stuffe.   *[fol. 68v.]*⌋

Also 100 sake shott, ½ rownd & other ½ crosbar; 100 minion shott, ½ rownd & other ½ crosbar; 50 saker langrell shott, all iron;— price made at 14 *mas* p'r *pico.* or 100 wight Japon.

Nota. I was forsed to put out these at hazard p'r ould shott & shivers, the m^r, Jno Hvnt, not coming to geve direction, nether at my request & writing, nor at sending for of Capt. Coppendall, refusing ever to enter againe into the English howse. I could say much of this frantick m^r, Jno Hvnt; but I leve it to other men to tell. Allso the China Capt.,

1 broad cloth. Andrea Dittis, had a littell brod cloth, pinck culler, N° 2) to make his littell doughter a peare of stockinges or boutes this clod wether.

3 sack rise. And there was 3 sackes rise, of 50 *gantes* p'r sack, geven to 3 pore Chinas w'ch lost their junk p'r tempest of the cost of Shashma & came to the China Capt. for releefe, he geveing eche of them a sack rise & a *tay* in plate. & vpon good

---

2) Not entered.

consideration I gaue them, p'r generall consent, each one a sack, as aboue said. Mr. Dorington late at night came to the Eng'sh howse, & tould me the m.ͬ sent hym to tell me the mast was wolled,[3] & ready to bring ship to a caryne.

4. This monryng could wether wind N.ºerly, rack same, but sowne after warme wether w'th a thaw or melting of the snow, wind tornyng W'erly, w'th rayne p'r night.

Nota.

I went to the Duch howse & desird Capt. Speck to send vs his helpe & people to bring our shipp to a caryn, as formerly in frenshipp they had promised vs; w'ch in good sort he assented vnto, & sent for the masters of the great shipp & junck & willed them & the rest to aide vs in what they might. These men came at Capt. Specks first sending for, & did what he ordayned, but Mr. Hvnt sent me word he would never com in the Eng'sh howse, vpon a lunetike hvmour, w'ch each man telleth me is his condition not only heare, but at Pattania & else where hath donne the lyke, &c. Soe I went abord & saw them turne vp the ships keele, but water came in soe fast at port holes & else where that they were forced to right her againe to cawke her bettr. I tould Mr. Hunt I was com to vizet hym abord, althoughe he sent me word he would not com ashore, yet willed hym hereafter to com when I sent [*fol. 69r.*]] for hym or else I would fatch hym. Also I willed hym to send Jn.º Shepp'rd ashore to dresse the Companies meate; w'ch he denied at first, but after sent hym.

Frō Yasimō.

And Zanzabar, *allius* Yasimon Dono, came to vizet me at Eng'sh howse, & brought a pr'sent of oringes & a barrill of wine, & sent 2 men to helpe to bring downe the shipp.

Bundell rattons.
7 *tais* 6 *mas.*

And Capt. Speck sent money for bundells rattons, sould at 7 *ta.* 6 *ma.* p'r bandell, w'ch money Mr. Nealson receaved

---

3) To *would*, to bind ropes about a mast to strengthen it.—Thompson.

in plate bars.

5. This mornyng droping wether wind W'erly, but sowne after broak vp fayre wether all day, and lyke p'r night following, &c.

Ther was sould & del'd to Soyemon Dono, as follow'th:–

1 damaskt peece at 20 *taies* .... *T.* 20: 0: 0

3 pec. whit baftas, of 20 Rs. *corge*, for

15 *mas* pec.   *T.* 04: 5: 0

ta. ma. co.
16: 0: 0

3 pec. boralls, of 4) Rs. *corg* for 1 *tay* peec. ... *T.* 03: 0: 0

_____

T. 16: 0: 0

Retond the
stuffs.

Retornd all but damaskt peec. & was chast.

But pr'sently he retorned the 6 peec. stuffe back both baftas & boralls & the fowling peece was not damaskt but

Zanzabrs.

chast at 16. And Zanzabers littell doughter came to vizet

Frö Yta [*sic*]
Yoquiche
Dono.

me, & brought a pr'sent of wyne, orenges, eggs, & fysh drest. And an ould man of Miaco, now our neighbour, brought me a banketting box for a pr'sent. His name is Yto Yoquiche Dono.

Nota.

Sangero Samme, sonne to Foyne Same, was this day made sure to a doughter of a noble man of Crates. Their was 210 *cattis* ould junk or rops put out to *toose*5) for occom

210 *cantes*
[*sic*] occom.

wherof 50 *cattis* to Domingo, & 160 *cattis* to Vnquan, the China.   [*fol. 69v.*]⌋

6. This mornyng fare wether, wind N? W'erly, & soe vered W'erly, fayre wether all day and the lyke p'r night following.

Nota.

Sugen Dono of Crates sent to borrow a peare of *bubes*, he haveing invited the King of Firando to dyner, in respect he had geven or augmented his yearly stipened frö 500 *gocos* p'r ann? to 1000 p'r ann?. And ther was sould to Taccamon Dono as foll'th, viz.:–

_____

4) Not entered.
5) *Touse,* or *toze,* to unravel.—Thompson.

		ta.	m.	co.
28 pec. chaddr Cambaia, of 6)p'r *corg*, a				
22 pec. chander pintado, of p'r *corg*, at } at 1 *tay* p'r				
05 pec. foota chaꝶ, of p'r *corge*, at	pc..*T*. 55:	0:	0
05 pec. baftas white, of 2 Rs. p'r *corg*,				
at 1½ *tay* pec.	*T*. 07:	5:	0
10 pec. candeque nill of 4 Rs. p'r *corg*				
at 5 *mas* pec.	*T*. 05:	00:	0
Som totall amontes vnto	*T*. 67:	5:	0
And 1 pec. conta chaddr of to Capt. China	01:	0:	0

Nota.

Capt. Speck came to the English howse w'th Derick de Vriz & others to take leave, the great shipp being ready, (as they said) to goe out. They had byn w'th the kyng before they came to vs, &, as it seemed, had drunk hard. It is said they gaue a pr'sent worth 5000 *taies* to the kinge, but I canot beleeve it. Once they haue geven much in respect of the prize they brought in, as also for lycence to carry out munision, victuell, & men for the Molucos.

Sonday.

7.   This mornyng fayre calme wether but after a fresh gale N°erly most p'rte of day, but vered to S. of the W. p'r night w'th rayne.

Ankewsen went out.

The greate Duch shipp, called the *Ankewsen*, went out to Cochi, & I went abord w'th our bark w'th 16 men, to rowe & helpe to toe them out, as the king sent many barks to doe the lyke; & I carid 2 barilles wyne, 3 hense, 2 duckes, 3 fyshes, 20 loves fresh bread, & a baskit of oringes, & dronke to their good voyage; w'ch Capt. Speck took in good p'rte & sent his *jurebasso* w'th complem'to, *Nifon catange*.

N·ta.

Zanzebars wives brothers & her father were abord, & made peace w'th Jn° Gorezano, our *jurebasso*.   [*fol. 70r.*]]

Mr. Nealson gave in vp this wickes charges, is *T*. 14 *ta*.

A lettr to

2 *m*. 7 *co*. and I wrot a lettr to Capt. Jourden & sent it p'r

6) This and the following figures, not entered.

January 1615[6]

Capt.
Jourden.

Derick de Friz, as apereth p'r coppie.

8. This mornyng fayre calme wether, & rather a littell wind
N?erly, but after a stiffe gale most p'rte of the day, but som
rayne p'r night, rack still W'erly.

28 sows
lead.

Ther was sould & del'd to Andrea Dittis, China Capt.,
28 sowes of lead, poz. 65 pec. 19 *catt.* at *taies* great plate p'r
pico.; one sowe wanted 10 *cattis* of that it was wayed before,
& the rest a *catty* peece in respect of a great peare slings it

391: 1: 4
lead.
Nota.

was waid w'th before. The 28 sowes at 6 *tais pico.* amont to
T. .[7] We had made price before w'th Andrea Dittis for
all our lead at 6 *taies* p'r *pico.*; but now a Japon offring vs

29 saws
lead.

6½ *taies* p'r *pico.* he was content to lett vs sell hym the one
halfe. And there was 29 sowes lead sould vnto ,[8] a Japon,
poz. 6742 *cattis* at 6½ *tais* the *pico.* amontes vnto *T.* 438: 2:

100 *tais.*

3. And he paid 100 *taies* in p'rte of payment w'ch money I

3 lettrs frõ
Langasaque.

rec. my selfe. Also I rec. 3 lettrs from Langasaque, 1 frõ
Jorge Durois w'th 16 falling bands at 7 *mas* p'r band.

Frõ a China.

And an ould China brought me a pr'sent of China cakes.

200 *taies.*

Also I rec. two hvndred *taies* of the China Capt. vpon acc?,
and 2 lettr frõ Capt. Goroche & Jeronimo Montauaso.

[*fol. 70v.*]

9. This mornyng lowring wether, littell wind N?erly, rack
W'erly, and [*sic*] but after a fresh gale all day & night
followinge, yet fayre ouer head.

A lettr to
Mr. Eaton.

I wrot a lettr to Mr. Eaton to Osekay, advising how I
had sould the rest of the lead for 6½ *taies* p'r *pico.* & that
Capt. China tould me he could wash the spots or staines
out of the baftas, & therefore he not to sell the worst vnder

2 lettrs to
Langa.

7 *mas* peece. *Y escriuados cartas*[9] to Langasaque, 1 to
Jorge Durois of rec. of his w'th bandes, & an other to Capt.

7) Not entered.
8) The name, not given.
9) "And we (have) written letters (in Spanish)."

January 1615[6]

A lettr frō
Mr. Eaton.

Garrocha in answer of his. I rec. a lettr frō Mr. Eaton, dated in Miaco, the 12th vltimo, w'th a littell chist & 3 scritorios in it for acc⁰ Capt. Adames, cost 24 *mas* peec. w'th 4 *mas* 2 *condrins* for chist & carrying to Osekay, is 7 *ta*. 6 *mas* 2 *condrin*. Also he wrot he hath sould the ganty

Ganty
10 *tais*.
Pep'r
6 tais.
24 *mas*.

for 10 *tais* le *pico*. and the Bantam pepp'r he carid vp for 6 *taies* the *pico*. I paid for 20 mattes for Matinga 24 *mas*, whereof the China Capt. laid out 15 *mas* 4 *condr*., and Yoskey laid or paid out the rest 8 *ma*. 6 *condr*., [som totall is] 24: 0.

Port.
pr'soners
escaped.

This last night, about 10 a clock, 4 Portingale prisoners ran away out of the Duch howse & are scaped & thought got to Langasaque.

A lettr frō
Saflan Dono.

Also I rec. a lettr frō Safian Dono, deted in Sackay aboue a month past, wherin he wrot of the recept of the 10 damaskt fowling peeces, for acc⁰. of the Emperour, & that paym̄t should be made to content w'th other kynde offers

Nota.

of complem'to. Yasimon Dono advised me of a man of his com frō Miaco, whoe repor[t]eth of very fowle wether aboue, and that 70 or 80 barks are cast away p'r meanes therof. God send vs good news of ours sent to Osekay and Tushma, &c.   [*fol. 71r.*]]

10. This mornyng lowring wether w'th a fresh gale, wind N⁰erly, rack same, yet store of rayne all the affore nowne, but dry p'r night.

100 *tais*.
Mr. Nealson
allso is 100
tais.10)
150 *tais*.

And I del'd 100 *taies* to Mr. Osterwick that I rec. in p'rte payme't of the lead of m'rchnt of Miaco, w'ch money is to disburse about the *Hozeander*. Also one hvndred fyftie *taies* to Mr. Nealson to disburse about other matters. Three

Portingals
fownd &
turned back.

of the Portingales w'ch ran away were fownd p'r meanes of men the Kinge of Firando sent out after them, & brought

---

10) This figure seems to be incorrect.

January 1615[6]

back againe to the Hollanders. Gizamon Dono, Zanzabrs

A pr'sent.
Nota.

wives brother, brought me 3 wilduckes for a pr'sent. He tould me that wordes was brought to the kyng that 80 barkes are cast away betwixt this and Shiminaseke now of late, p'r torment most being laden w'th rise. God blesse our bark sent w'th m'rch'ndiz.

11.   This mornyng a stiffe gale wind N°erly, somthing cold, & soe remeaned all day & night following, rack frō N° W.

A pr'sent to
ye king.

The king being ready to goe vp to the Emperour. We laid out a pr'sent & sent hym, I going after accompanid w'th Mr. Nealson & Mr. Osterwick,

2 damaskt fowling peeces, cost .... 11)
5 pec. white baftas, of 20 Rs., *corg* ....
5 pec. blew byrams, of 15 Rs., *corg* ....
5 pec. red zelas, of 12 Rs., *corg* ....
5 pec. boralles or foota chader, of   Rs., *corg* ......
5 pec. chader Cambaia, of   Rs., *corg*   ....
5 pec. buxshaws, of   Rs., *corg*...................
Som totall amontes vnto ....

[*fol. 71v.*]

The king tooke the pr'sent very kindly offring vs any thing we would demand, saying that allthough he went vp to the Emperour yet he had left such order w'th his governor that what we asked should be fulfilled. This pr'sent was sent this day because yisterday Soyemon Dono came to aske what money the king owed vpon bill ffor that yt should be paid forthw'th, wherevpon it was thought fitt to goe w'th this pr'sent before pay'nt were made, otherwais yt might be thought it was sent in respect he paid the money, or else p'rhaps in payinge of it, he might haue expected a greater pr'sent in respect the Hollanders gaue soe much, once how soever he seemed to take it in good

Nota.

---

11) This and the following figures, not entered.

158

January 1615[6]

part & gaue vs a kind welcom w'th 2 colation, serveing vs
w'th his owne handes, ther was sould to a servant of the

2 pec.
baftas.

Kyng of Shashma 2 pec. whit baftas of 11 Rs? *corg* for 12

2 *ta.* 4 *mas.*

mas p'r peec., is 2 *tais* 4 *mas* in bars rec. of hym p'r Mr.
Nealson.

12. This mornyng very cold weth., w'th a fresh gale wind still
N?erly, rack frõ W. N?erly, & so remend most p'rte day &
night foll'g w'th sleete of snow & heale.

1 bag
pepp'r.

Ther was sould & del'd to Andrea Dittis, China Capt.,
1 bag pepp'r N? 103, poz. gros 67½ *cattis,* is net 63 *cattis* tare
related at 4½ *cattis* sould at 6 *tais* p'r *pico.* amontes vnto *T.*
3: 7: 8. Also sould ,[12] our neighbour, being a m'rchnt

30 *cattis*
pepp'r.

of Miaco, 30 *cattis* pep'r Bantam out of bag N? 159 at
6 *taies* p'r *pico.* del'd hym p'r Jn? Gorehon, *jurebasso,*
amontes vnto som of 1 *tay* 8 *mas* bag N? 159, poz. 77 *c.* also

3 *picos* lead.

ther was 3 *piculles* sheet lead del'd vnto Mr. Hvnt for vse
of shipp *Hozeander.*   [*fol. 72r.*]]

13. This mornyng still cold wether, sleete haile & snow, yet
wind to S. of W. a small gale, but after vered northerly, a
stiffe gale, espetially p'r night much snowe.

Skidayen
Dono
retorned.
100 *tais* to
Mr. Nealson.

Skidayen Dono retorned w'th the new mast this mornyng, and I del'd 100 *taies* plate bars more to Mr. Osterwick
to lay out about charges *Hozeander,* made rec. in acc? Mr.
Nealson. And I rec. three hundred therty and eight *taies*
two *mas* and three *condrin* in plate bars for the rest of the
lead sould a m'rchnt of Miaco, poz. 6742 *catt.*, I say *cattis,*

ta. m. co.
338: 2: 3.

at 6½ *ta. pico.* is 438 *ta.* 2 *m.* 3 *co.*, the other hvndred *tais* I
receved before.

Sonday.

14. This mornyng still very cold wether, w'th a stiffe gale
wind N?erly, w'th snow & heale, most p'rte of the day,
but non p'r night yet frostt.

Nota.

Letters came to Capt. Speck that the junk they sent for

---

12) The name, not given.

159

January 1615[6]

Syam is p'r contra[r]y wind put into Shashma in a port (or haven) called Cata ura,[13] soe loose ther voyage.

50 *tais*.

And I paid fyftie *tais* plate bars to the fownder, made rec. p'r Mr. Nealson, advanced vpon acc? for bras shivers & other matters w'th shot for ordinance w'ch he is to cast for to send in the *Hozeander*. The 2 fownders are called Jembio Dono & Scongro Dono.

Nota.

There came certen caueleros Japons from Edo, & came to see the English howse, & looked on such comodeties as we had, but bought non. They report that the Emperour will haue all the kyngs (or *tonos*) in Japon to goe for Edo, & there to remeane for the spare of 7 yeares, & to carry their wives w'th them, & live over one in his howse ap'rte, w'th a servant of the Emperours to be allwais in company w'th them—I meane w'th each one, to heare & soe what passeth. This he doeth to preuent them from insurrections, & will not haue sonns nor kynsmen, but the kinges them selues.   [*fol. 72v.*]⌋

15.   This mornyng still cold wether, littell or noe wind w'th hayle (or sleete), but after turned into rayne wether, not so cold but much wind p'r night at N? W., rack still W'erly.

A letter to Mr. Eaton.

I wrot a letter to Mr. Eaton to Edo, sent p'r Tozamon Dono, a m'rchnt of that place, advising of my other sent 6 dais past, and here w'thall sent, as foll'th, viz.:–

10 *cattis* tobaco to his host, cost 2 *mas* 3 *condr. catty.*
33 egges to his hostice, cost 1 *mas* 9½ *condryns.*
10 *cattis* tobaco to hym selfe, cost as *vt supra.*
02 Faccata gerdells[14] for hym selfe for 3 *mas* peece.

And advised w'thall that Mr. Wickham should make all the hast he could, for that Capt. Coppendall and Mr. Nealson were very sick, &c.

---

13) Kataura 片浦 in Satsuma Province, at Kawabe 川邊 County.
14) Hakata *obi* 博多帶.

16. This mornyng cold wether wind at N? W., rack from W., w'th snow and heale, most p'rte of day, but not soe much p'r night but much winde.

100 *ta.*

Packe N?
126.

Receved of Andrea Dittis, China Capt., one hvndred *tais* in plate bars vpon acc? of m'rchandiz. And we opened pack N? 126 and sould it all to the China Capt., as followeth:–

	taies	m.	co.
Baftas white 9 *cy.* 19 pec., of 9 Rs., *corg*..............			
Baftas white 5: 01 pec., of 12 Rs., *corg*			
Baftas 1 pec. fownd over, is 301 pec. baftas at 8 *mas* p'r peece, one w'th an other..	*T.* 240:	8:	0

Pintado 5 pec., of 5 Rs.,
 corg at 1 *taye* .... *T.* 005: 0: 0

Som totall sould amontes vnto .... *T.* 245: 0: 0	ta.	m.	co.
	245:	8:	0

Nota.

Rowland Thomas, the purcer of the *Hozeandr*, being drunk, did beat Mr. Dorington, m.r mate, Jn? Cocera, the cook, & the servantes in the howse.

17. This mornyng cold wether, sleete or small haile, w'th a stiffe gale wind at N? W'erly, rack from West, & soe remeand all day & night following, now & then snowing & healinge.

357 *ta.*

There was rec. of the kinges plate this day three hvndred fyfty and seaven *taies* in plate of bars vpon acc?, sent frō Oyen Dono p'r Refioen Dono, kinges steward. Toma Dono, or nighbour, had 6 sack rise lent hym of 50½ *gantes* p'r sack, and the China Capt. paid 4 *mas* 8 *condrin* for Quiaco for Matinga. [*fol. 73r.*]]

6 sackes
rise.
m. co.
4: 8.

18. This mornyng still cold wether wind N? W., rack same, and so remeaned all day and night following, w'th spitting

of snow now and then.

We reconed this day w'th Tomo Dono & rest for biskit, and wais out as followeth, viz.:–

To Capt. Adames ....0290 *cattis*.
To Syam voyag ....0556 *cattis*.
To a pr'sent to Duche ....0010 *cattis*.
To *Hozeandr* ....3806 *cattis*.

Som totall rec.   *T*. 4602 *catt*.

A reson of 3 *ta*. ½ p'r *co*. amontes to *T*. 163 *ta*. 1 *ma*. 0 *co*. and ther is paid vpon this acc°., as followth:–

Pro 5 *picos* of pepp'r, at 6 *tais* pc.	030:	0:	0
Pro lead 225 *cattis*, at 6½ *ta*. pc.	014:	6:	2:½
Pro suger 10 *pico*. 65½ *cat*., at 2 *ta*. pc.	021:	3:	2
Som totall paid amontes to	*T*. 065:	9:	4:½
Rest to pay to even this acc°	*T*. 097:	1:	5:½
Som totall is	*T*. 163:	1:	0

And I wrot a lettr to Jorge Durois for candells & other matters, to same effect as my former 9 dais past, and sent it p'r a China.

And w'thin night word was brought me how two of our shipps company were fighting w'th swords one a hill a littell from our Eng'sh howse. Soe I went w'th Mr. Hunt the m.ᵣ & Mr. Osterwick, & fownd them to be Jn° Clough the gvner & Jn° Driver an ordenary marrener, both being drunken, & no hurt donne but that Driver had a scar on his forehead. Soe I put them both in the bilbows till the next mornynge.

19. This mornyng still cold wether, wind at N° W., rack same, and after dyner snow all rest day but littel p'r night, yet cold wether.

Niquan the China retorned from Tushma & brought back all the goods he carid, they offring but 4½ *tais pico*. for pepp'r nether brought he but 120 *tais* plate for the pepp'r formerly sould, but sayeth our hast will be heard shortly & being the rest.*[fol. 73v.]]* And I del'd one hvndred *tais* plate bars to Mr. Osterwick to lay out about *Hozeander.* And the China Capt. paid 105 *ta.* 8 *m.* 7½ *condrin* to Toma Dono & the rest in full paym't of the biskitt.

100 *tais*.
ta. m. co.
105: 8: 7½.

    And our host of Tushma came to Eng'sh howse, & brought a pr'sent of walnvutes & a Corea carpet (or feltro). He tould me he brought m'rch'ndiz to sell to pay me the money the pepp'r was sould for, for that the money of the place he receved for it was not good, as Niquan the China whone [*sic*] I sent to rec. it could witnes, he turnyng back aboue 500 *taies* in receiving 120 *tais*.

Our host of
Tushma.

    Mr. Dorington, the m.ʳ mate of *Hozeandr,* mad showe as though he were lunatick, talking idly; but I thyn[k] he counterfeteth. A strange kind of people they are all of them w'ch came in this shipp. Truly I canot praise any one of them w'ch are seamen. The Hollanders shott ofe 8 or ten pec. ordinance out of the small shipp & out of howse, late w'thin night. The occation we knew not, except the junk went out or that they had hard news that gaue them content.

Nota.

Nota.

20.   This mornyng still cold wether w'th stiff gale, wind at N.º W., rack same, and soe remeaned all day and night following, now & then snow & haile.

    I wrot a lettr to Capt. Jourden to Bantam, how the *Hozeandr* would be ready p'r the end of this moneth & how Mr. Osterwick was to stay heare, w'th other accurant, and sent it p'r conveance of Capt. Speck in the *Ankewsen.* I went to the Duch howse & del'd Capten Speck my lettr. He tells me the occation they shot off the ordinance the last night was for that the King of Firando came to drink a farewell w'th them before he went vp, and that the greate

A lettr to
Capt. Jorden.

Nota.

January 1615[6]

shipp & the junck would be ready to goe towardes Bantam w'thin 7 or 8 daies att ferthest. He also tould me that he receved not letter of the putting of their junk into Shashma, as it was reported vnto me. & the carpentar had 2 sacks rise, & Yoskey & Fashman eache of them 1 sack of 50½ *gantes* p'r sack. Mr. Nealson rec. by Mr. Nealson [*sic*] from Andrea Dittis, China Capt, for Jn? boate hier to Tushma ten *taies* plate bars.   [*fol. 74r.*]

4 sakes rise.
10 *tais*.

Sonday.   21. This mornyng still cold wether w'th a stiff gale, wind att N? W., rack same, but not soe much wind after, yet cold wether both day & night, littell snow or hede.

260 Rs?.   And I del'd two hvndred and three skore Realles of 8 to Andrea Dittis, the China Capt., to change into other plate for China busynes. More, del'd vnto hym at same tyme one bag Rs? of 8, as it came out of England, cont'g one hvndred pownd str., is fyve hvndred Realles of eight for sane[*sic*] purpose. For both w'ch somes he is to bring Refind plate to send in the *Hozeander*. This is donne because the nobles in China should think this plate or Realls, com from the English, rather then to pr'sent them w'th refined plat of this place, &c. The China Capt. sent Niquan, his kinsman, w'th these Rialles to bring plate back fortw'th.

500 Rs. 8.

Nota.   Jn? Osterwick going abroad w'th Mr. Nealson got a littell more drinke then was needfull, & the other was littell better. Yet Jn? Osterwick fell into termes of comparison, disinabling each one but hym selfe. I know not what to say of hym but that he is an overweenyng prowd yowth, I haveing had no experience yet but only by report of Capt. Coppindale. And late in the night, after we were gon to bed, the kinges *bongew* sent to borrow our boate, or *foyfone*,[15] for the king service; w'ch I lent hym.

Nota.

---

15) *Hayafune*. See Note 57) for 1615.

Jonk.

The small junck was retorned to the China Capten, but much out of reprations, w'ch must be amended according to promis, for w'thout her, we could not haue carind our shipp, & soe she had lost her monson this yeare. [*fol. 74v.*]」

22. This mornyng still cold wether, littell or noe wind, rack W. S'erly & a fresh gale wind sowne after some vering S. W., wether not so could, littell rayne towardes day.

ta. m. co.
38: 22: 33.

And I del'd a pap'r of 38 *tais* 2 *m.* 3 *condrns* plate bars to Mr. Nealson, to lay out vpon necessaris, namely to pay 10 *ta.* to Jnº Gorozan, *jurebasso*, vpon accº of his wages.

70 sakes rise.

The China Capt., Andrea Dittis, had 70 sack rise of 50 [?] *gantes* p'r sack, at 6½ *gantes* p'r *mas.*

2 lettrs from Jorge Durois.
183 candls.

I rec. 2 lettrs frō Jorge Durois dated in Langasaque, le 24th & 26th currant, new stile, w'th 2 packetes candells cont'g as he said 185, but there was but 183 candls & the rest he will br'ng to make them vp 225, cost 3 *tais*, so rest

10 *tais.*

42 candelles and Mr. Nelson p'd 10 *tais* plate bars to Goresano vpon accº his wages.

23. This mornyng wynd at S. W. dropping wether, but sowne after cleared vp fayre wether both day & night, wind vering to W. Nºerly.

6 *tais.*

And I gaue 6 *taies* plate bars to Matinga to pr'vide thing[s] against the new yeare. And I paid in bar of plate

2 *ta.* 1 *ma.*

to Domingo my boy, to buy hym ap'rell, poz. 2 *tay* 1 *ma.* and I reconed w'th Jnº Gorezano for 6 *tais* 9 *mas*, viz.:‒

Pro 4 peare sheews & slippers for my selfe ...*T.* 01:	0:	0
Pr. a silver touthpicker for my selfe ....*T.* 02:	1:	0
Pro 2 pere *tabis*16) for Beecho ....*T.* 00:	3:	5
Pro strings for Beechos shews ....*T.* 00:	0:	8
Pro a pere shew for Beecho ....*T.* 00:	0:	4
Pro a lock for Beechoo chist ....*T.* 00:	1:	2

---

16) *Tabi* 足袋, stockings or socks.

Pro 2 peare *tabis* for Jeffrey ....*T.* 00:	3:	2
Pro string for Jeffres shews....................*T.* 00:	0:	8
Pro a pear shews for Jeffrey ....*T.* 00:	0:	4
Pro 2 barrilles wyne I sent to Taccaman		
w'th fish ....*T.* 00:	8:	4
Pr. 1 *mas* paid the shewmak's sonne for roses ..*T.* 00:	1:	0
Pr. 1 *mas* geven the fisherman of Cochi.........*T.* 00:	1:	0
Pro 20 *tattamis*[17] for Matingas howse ....*T.* 02:	4:	0
Pro 20 *cattis* tobaco sent to Miaco, at		
2 *mas* 3 *con.* ....*T.* 04:	6:	0
Pro 02 Faccata gerdell for Mr. Eaton...........*T.* 00:	6:	0
Pro matts to make vp the tobaco ....*T.* 00:	0:	7
	T. 12:	8:	4
	T. 6:	9:	0
	T. 5:	9:	4

Restes 5 ta. 9 m. 4 co. w'ch Mr. Nealson paid vnto hym
& put it vpon my acc°.   [*fol. 75r.*]

To Domingo.
1 pec.
damask.
1 pec.
taffety.

I gaue a pec. blew damaske to Domingo, my boy, to make hym a crate or *kerymon* w'th a pes. Japon taffetie to lyme it, w'th cost 1 *tay* 1 *mas* plate bars, the pec. damaske was geven p'r China Capt.

24. This mornyng fayre wether, littell wind at W. N°erly, but after vered more N°erly, a fresh gale most p'rte of day, but littell or noe wind p'r night.

A lettr to
Jorge Durois.

50 *tais*.

I wrot a lettr to Jorge Durois in answer of his two rec. the other day w'th the 182 candelles, and to buy 3 *tais* candelles more, & 2 jarrs conserues, & 3 barilles *morofack* sent p'r them, w'ch brought the candells. And I paid fyftie *taies* plate bars to Andrea Dittis, China Capt., for reprations his junk lent to carin our ship *Hozeander*, she haveing broken and spoild the junck that the carpenters asked 100 *taies* to haue mended her.

---

17) *Tatami* 疊, mat. See also Note 109) for 1615.

January 1615[6]

Newes was brought to towne that the Emperour is dead; but I beleeve rather it is a fable & geven out of porpose to see how people wold take the mattr. Once the ould man is subtill.

25. This mornyng fayre calme cold wether, but after a small gale W. S'erly, and soe verid S. W., a fresh gale all rest of the day & night following, warme wether p'r night, &c.

ta. m. co.
294: 4: 4½.
100 *tais*.

I receved 294 *ta.* 4 *ma.* 4½ *co.* of Rifioyen Dono, for the kings debt. And I del'd 100 *tais* of it to Mr. Osterwick for to lay out about *Hozeander*. And the China Capt. lent vs the

A mast.

mast of his junck to make a yard for the *Hozeander*, and

42 *cattis*
pepp'r.

I waid the rest of pepp'r in bag N? 159, poz. net 42 *cattis*. Damian Marin fell out w'th Jn? de Lienana ab[o]ut com-

Nota.

parisons betwixt the Eng'sh & Duch, Damian taking p'rte w'th the Duch & Jn? w'th the English, &c. [*fol. 75v.*]

26. This mornyng a small gale, wind S. W., fayre wether, and so remeand all day & night following, &c.

The king sent Soyemon Dono, Skrayamon Dono & another to look vpon our comodeties, to the entent to buy for 2 or 3000 *tais* at tyme. Soe we showed them samples of all & set price; but he took lyking only of pepp'r at 6 *tais pico*, baftas at 10 Rs. p'r pies, buxshews at 9 *mas* pec., boralles at 9 *mas* pec., chint at 8½ *mas* pec., and candē mawy at 4 *mas* pec. and tould the China Capt. he would com & vizet me before he went to Miaco, to morrow or the next day.

27. This mornyng littell wind at N? W., fayre wether, and soe remeand all day & night following.

Nota.

Capt. Speck came & requested that we would looke into our shipp for Bantam as much ebony as we could in not pest'ring our shipp, & he would pay what fraight we thought fitt. And he sent me a barill *morofack* & 4 boxes swetmeate. Also the king sent me word he would com to breckfast to morrow mornyng. So I mad the best pr'vition I could, & the China Capt. sent me 2 powderd storkes, and Soyemon Dono a baskit oranges. And Tome Donos sonne retorned frō Miaco & sent me a pr'sent of Japon figges. He tells me our bark w'th the goods is safely arived at Sackay, but brought no lettr from Mr. Eaton nor Mr. Wickham.   [*fol. 76r.*]

Sonday.

28. This mornyng fayre cold wether w'th a fresh gale of wind N⁰erly, but after a stiffe gale most p'rte of the day & the fore p'rte of the night, rest littell or no wind.

A lettr frō Jorge Durois.

I rec. a lettr frō Jorge Duros in Langasaque, le 4th of February, new stile, to same effect as the former, of the Caffro Bengla called Luis to procure of Capten Speck to send hym to his Mr. Bartolomew de la Rocha. The King of Firando came to dyner to the Eng'sh howse, accompanid w'th 7 or 8 caueleros, & took in good p'rte the entertaynm't he had, & gaue me a *keremon*, & a cloake to our *jurebasso*. He said he was to stay 3 or 4 yeares aboue at Edo; soe I think it is true that the *tonos* (or kings) must stay 7 yeares, as I noted som daies past. There was 3 peeces ordinance shott affe at his entry into the English howse, & 5 at his dep'rture. And Andrea Dittis had 30 sacks rise del'd hym to pay 6½ *gantes* p'r *mas*.

The king to dyner.
4 pec. clad camb to Skyemon Dono at 4 *tais*.
1 pec. ditto to Jn⁰ *jurebasso* for 1 *tay*.

30 bag rise.

29. This mornyng, cold wether, very littell wind N⁰erly, and soe remeaned all day & night following, but som drops of rayne p'r night, espetially towardes mornyng.

Mr. Wickham retornd to Firando.
3 lettrs frō Mr. Eaton.

Mr. Wickham retorned to Firando & brought me 3 lettrs from Mr. Eaton, 1 dated in Miaco, le 29th December & 2 in Osekay, the 2th & 8th January pr'sent, w'th 3 other lettrs, for Capt. Copindall, Mr. Osterwick & Rowland Thomas, w'th certen notes & papers of things bought for Capt. Coppindall, & of matters brought back from Edo to Osakay p'r Mr. Wickham & del'd to Mr. Eaton.

And in the after nowne, Soyemon Dono w'th 3 other[s] came to the Eng'sh howse, to receve the comodeties w'ch the king would buy vpon trust; but they tould me the Hollanders had sould the king pepp'r at 5 *taies* the *pico.*, & therefore thought I would not aske more. I answerd that, yf the Hollandrs set pepp'r at that rate, they sett other comodetis at a hier, w'ch, it might be, cost them nothing but the suting ofe a peece of ordinance as silke at 240 *taies* the *pico.* &c. [*fol. 76v.*]] And, it might be, in pollecie set pepp'r loe, to the entent to cros vs & soe ether to meke vs to sell it better cheape then it cost or else to make vs fall into dislyke of the king, & by this meanes get them selues favour, & vs disgrace. But the truth was, I set it at no hier a rate then I sould to others for ready money, & at such a price as I would promis them to del'r no more at that rate. But for broad cloth, w'ch they set at 14 *taies* p'r *tattamy*, & Syam wood at 3½ *tais* the *pico.*, that I would sell hym at same rate, when our shipps & junck arived. Yet doe I what I could, they said they durst not w'th their honor geue more then the Duch sould for. Soe we concluded to send the pepp'r to Ozekay to Mr. Eaton at kinges charg, & he to sell it, & then to del'r to procead in money the king. & so that matter was ended.

But we del'd comodety to them for acc? of king as foll'th, viz.:–

Baftas, white,	
196 pec., of 11 Rs. *corg.*	
Eidem, lower,	
101 pec., of 20 Rs. *corg.*	
Eidem, lower lodg,	
201 pec., of 11 Rs. *corg.*	
Eidem, lo. lodg,	
120 pec., of 15 Rs. *corg.*	

at 1 *tay* pec.

	ta.	*m.*	*co.*
T.	718:	00:	0

January 1615[6]

> *Eidem*,vp'r lodg,
>   100 pec., of div'rs sorts.
>   Som baftas,
>   718 peces div'rs pr'ses.

Chader Rese Canary, 185 pec. lower, of 4 Rs. *corg.*
Chadr *eidem*, 090 pec., of .... } at 18)
    Som chader, *T.* 275 pec. at. ....

Boralles, 100 pec.
    lodg beloe of .... } at 1 *tay*........*T.* 200: 0: 0.
Buxshaws, 100 pec.
    lodg beloe of ....

4 pec.
chader.
1 pec. ditto.

And ther was sould to Skiaman Dono 4 pec. of chader of Camboia at 1 *tay* p'r peece, and to Jn? *jurebasso* 1 peece of suame19) at 1 *tay*.   [*fol. 77r.*]

30.   This mornyng low[r]ing dropping wether, no wynde, but after brake vp, fayre wether wind N?, rest of day & night following, some dropps of rayne towards day.

To dyner
abord *Hoze.*

The m?, Jn? Hvnt, envited vs abord the *Hozeandr* to dyner. Mr. Wickham & my selfe retorned sowne after a-shore vpon occation of busynes, & had 5 pec. ordinance shot ofe at our dep'rture, & the other 3 peeces when they came ashore. And Gerge Durois came to Firado, & brought 2

2 jar
conser's.

jarrs of conserves, cost both   .20)

Frō Jorge.

And he gaue me in pr'sent, as followth:–

    a box of marme[l]ad.
    a box of craknells.
    a box suger bred.
    a box of chistnvntes.
    a bottell of Spanish wine.

ta. m. co.
44: 4: 4½.

And I deliv'rd a pap'r cont'g 44 *tais* 4 *mas* 4½ *condr.* to Mr. Nealson vpon acc? petty charges.

---

18) This and the following prices, not entered.
19) Perhaps a slip of the pen for "same."
20) Not entered.

January 1615[6]

Holand junk
to Cochi.

The Duch junck went out of rode Firando to Cochi, &
there came to an ankor by the great shipp *Ankewsen*, & Mr.

2 *tais.*

Nealson rec. 2 *tais* plate bars of Cushcron Dono, for 2 pec.
fuka chader sould 8th pr'sent.

31. This mornyng overcast wether w'th a stiffe gale of wind
at N? E'erly all day & lyke night follow'g, but fayre wether
till midnight, & after som rayne.

600 *tais.*

I receved 600 *taies* I say six hvndred *tais*, plat bars of Mr.
Ric'd Wickham, w'ch he brought frō Mr. Eaton, rec. in
p'rte of paym't for lead sould at Osekay at 74 *mas* p'r *pico*.
And in the after nowne Capt. Speck came to the English
howse, & tould me that Gonrok Dono had sent hym a lettr
from Langasaque, advising hym as a frend (as he said) that
he should geue the Hollandrs waynyng[21] before their
shipping went out, as the lyke to the English, that they
should take heed they did not meddell w'th the greate ship
of Amacon, for that the Emperour had much adventure in
her. Yet I say I wish we might take her and then make the
reconying after.   [*fol. 77v.*]

February 1615[6].

01. This mornyng lowring wether w'th a stiffe gale of wind
N?erly, rack from N? W., & soe remeand all day but not
soe much wind p'r night cold wether.

ta. m. co.
28: 7: 0.

And Mr. Nealson paid twenty eight *tais* & seven *mas* to
Jorge Durois vpon clearing his acc?, the 100 *taies* was lent
hym before, being now all paid & his bill retorned. Also he

3 *tais.*
Nota.

paid hym 3 *taies* to lay out in candells. And so he retorned

---

21) Warnyng.

171

to Langasaque. I think to carry newes that our shipp & the Hollanders are ready to goe out. The *bongew* of the rise sent me a pr'sent of orringes. And we opend 2 packes m'rchndiz N⁰ 225 &   , [22] deliverd all the stuffe in them to the kinges *bongew* Soyemon Dono & others vpon acc⁰ for the king hym selfe, but in pak N⁰   their should haue byn   ,[23] but were but   ; w'ch were wropp'rs, and geven to Jorge Durois for his payment taken one pec. baftas w't, of 20 Rs. *corg*, del'd in all to King of Firando in m'rch'ndz, som of 3000: 0: 0.

Frō a bongew.

1 pec. bafta to Jor. Durois.
3000 ta.

02. This mornyng cold wether, littell wind N⁰erly & soe remeand all day, or rather noe wind p'r night.

100 tais.

I del'd one hvndred *tais* plate bars to Mr. Osterwick to pay carpenters or other matters for *Hozeander*. And pr'sently after I del'd hym one hvndred *tais* bars mere to same vse as afforesaid, I gaue a pr'sent to a m'rchnt of Miaco called   ,[24] whoe gaue me a fayre banqueting box before, viz.:–

100 tais.
A pr'sent to m'rchnt.

2 pec. byr.
2 pes. byr.

2 pec. byrams white, of   [25] *corg*, rated at.

2 pec. byrams nill, of 15 Rs. *corg* at.

These are of the Companis goodes.

2 pec. chadr Lullawy of my owne.

He took it in good p'rte & offerd to doe our nation any service he could aboue at Miaco. Mr. Wickham gaue me a *keremon* of them Sada Dono gaue hym at Edo. [*fol. 78r.*]⌡

Mr. Wick.

03. This mornyng fayre wether, littell wind N⁰ W., but sowne after a fresh gale w'th rayne, but not much, nor soe much wind p'r night, &c.

The night past about 11 a clock ther was a house sett on

---

22) This and the next numbers, not entered.
23) Space is left in this sentence.
24) The name, not given.
25) This and the following prices, not entered.

fire p'r necklegence of the people w'ch made it cleane against the great feast of ther new yeare, w'ch is w'thin

this 3 dayis. Soe ther was 7 howses burned downe; & had it not byn for the Eng'sh & Duch, most p'rte of the towne had byn burned. For each one stood gazing one & did nothing, & divers brought their goods into our Eng. howse for sauegard.

Ther was a pr'sent geven to Torasemon Dono, a princepall man in this place, w'ch never had any thing geven vnto hym since our arivall in Japon, w'ch our frendes tould vs of. Soe he had geven

3 pec. byrams, white, of .26)

3 pe., byrams, nitt, of 15 Rs. *corg.*

3 pec. red zelas, of 12 Rs. *corg.*

3 pec. boralles, of 5 Rs. *corg.*

42 *cattis* pepp'r as 27) *pico.*

And the China Capt., Andrea Dittis, went w'th me to viset hym and carid hym a great jar of biskit. And I gaue a

A *kerimon.*

ta. m. co.
2: 1: 9.
ta. m.
1: 1: 0.
6½ *mas.*

kerimon to Matings father, w'ch Mr. Eaton gaue vnto me. And I del'd a bar plate to Jn.º Gorezan pro. 2 *ta.* 1 *ma.* 9 con-*drins.* And he paid to the mer'dr for a peece taffety to lyne Domingos coate 11 *mas* great plate, & 6½ *mas* small plate to the fownder for 2 pans for Matinga. And the kinge sent to haue a gathering throughout Firando towardes the re-leeving the pore people whose howses were burnt; towardes

w'ch we gaue a *tay* in plate, and paid the carpenter, for mending Matings howse.

	t.	*m.*	*co.*
Pr. 26½ dais carpt. work or wagis ....*T.* 3:		7:	2
Pro 30½ days work laborers ....*T.* 1:		5:	2½
Pro neales ....*T.* 1:		0:	9
Pro bord and tymber ....*T.* 1:		9:	8

26) Not entered.
27) Not entered.

February 1615[6]

	Som totall	T. 8:	3:	1½
ta. m. co.	Paid in 2 bars plate, poz. 7 *ta.* 4 *m.*			
7: 4: 0.				
plate bar	0 *co.*, is	T. 8:	5:	0 forw'd
carpenter.	The rest to his serv'nt, is	T. 0:	1:	9½ *cond.*

[fol. 78v.]⌋

25 *taies.* And I del'd 25 *tais* plate bars more vnto the fownders, vpon acc.º of bras shivers w'ch are waid out this day, be-

6 *pc.* 42 *cat.* ing 6 *picos* & 42 *cattis.*

Nota. Mr. Nealson being drunck, (as very often hee is the lyke, to my greefe) fell a brawling w'th the chirurgion, Morris Jones, & cut his hand w'th his daggar. Soyemon Dono

3000 *tais.* came late & brought the kinges bill for three thousand *taies* plate of bars, to be paid w'thin this yeare for m'rch'ndiz

Kinges bill. sould hym. And I del'd hym in the King of Firandos bill for 1000 *taies*, lent at Edo 2 y'res past. I gaue 2 falling bandes

Mr. Wick. w'th lace to Mr. Wickham, cost me 2 *taies.*

Sonday. 04. This mornyng cold wether, w'th a fresh gale, wind Nº W'erly, and soe remeaned all day, but littell or noe wind p'r night.

A lettr to I wrot a lettr to Mr. Eaton of recept of his 3 p'r Mr.
Mr. Eaton. Wickham w'th the 600 *tais* plate bars, and also of the consort or sale of 3000 *tais* in m'rchandz to the king of this place, of w'ch he is to del'r 31 *tatta.* of brod cloth, rated at 13 *tais tattamy*, the rest del'd heare, the price of each thing I wrot of as p'r coppie lettr.

Nota. Capten Copendall came to knowledg that Mr. Nelson had geven it out that he had the pox & that the chirurgion tould hym as much whervpon he brought the chirurgion, Moris Jones, in question whoe vtterly *dexe*[28] it, & took his othe vpon the Bible, that he never spoake any such words, nether did take his disease to be the pox. I del'd one

---

28) *Dixit*(Lat.).

174

February 1615[6]

100 *ta.*

hvndred *tais* more in plate of bars to Mr. Osterwick vpon acc? of the *Hozeander*, &c.

Nota.

Mr. Wickham fell into his ould hvmours of comparisons, misusing me. I thi[n]ck it is because he would goe for Bantam in the *Hozeander*, w'ch I am well contented of. He pr'sumeth the more, because Capt. Jourden wrot hym a

1 *pico.* biskit.

lettr he would geue hym preferment. And I sent a *pico.* biskit to Mr. Eaton p'r the servant of Tome Dono who carid my lettr., & 5 *mas* port on it.   [*fol. 79r.*]⌋

05. This mornyng cold wether, calme, but after a small gale N? W'erly, but vered to N? E. a fresh gale most p'rte of day & the lyke p'r night &c.

Kinges acc̨o.

I made acc? this day w'th Oyen Dono & Shoske Dono for ould debt of the king, w'ch they say is *T.* 950 *ta.* 1 *m.* 0 *co.*, but I find it to be but *T.* 898: 6: 3½. And I del'd fyftie

50 *tais.*

taies to Mr. Nealson for to pay servantes wagis & other ordenary expences and is of the plate w'th Mr. Wickham brought downe.

Cushcron Dono . . . . .a box *muches.*[29)] ⎫
Yasimon Dono . . . . .a barill *morofak.* ⎪
& his father in la[w] . . . . .a *barso* wyne &   ⎬ new years
                            a salmon.   ⎪ giftes.
Jn? Japon .a bundell figges. ⎭

And we waid out the shot for ordinance as foll'th.[30)] And

1 *tay.*

Mr. Nelson rec. I *tay* plate for 1 pec. chader of Cambaia sould 28th vltimo of Jn? *jurebasso.* And Co. Jn? had 1

Per borall.

pec. borall to pay for it 1 *tay.* And I had for my selfe, viz.:-

1 byram white, of 14 Rs. *corg.*
1 byram white, of 16 Rs. *corg.*
2 byrams nill, of 15 Rs. *corg.*
1 pec. borall I gaue Domingo, my boy.

---

29) *Mochi* 餅, rice cake.
30) Details, not entered.

February 1615[6]

And Mr. Nealson made recept for 25 *tais* pad the fownders, and he paid them to ballance 14: 5: 5 *condryn.*

06. This mornyng coled wether w'th a fresh gale wind at N? E., slite (or small) snow, but after brok up fayre wether rest of day & night following, &c.

The fownders reconyng was as followth:–

For: 641 *catties* in bras shwers, at 12

tay p'r *pico.* .... *T.* 76: 9: 2

For: 296 rownd shot sacar & mignion, at

14 *cn.* p'r *catty.* .... *T.* 04: 1: 3

For 230 crosbar & langrell shot, at 25

mas p'r *pico.* .... *T.* 05: 7: 5

Som totall amontes vnto .... *T.* 86: 8: 0

There was a pr'sent of 2 *barsos* wine & 2 fishes sent to Zanzabars father in law, to the China Capt. & to Zanzabr

Fownders.

hym selfe, each of them alyke. And the fownders brought pr'sent 2 iron pans w'th wyne & fysh. [*fol. 79v.*]⅃ And Mr. Osterwick reconed w'th Andrea Dittis, China Capt., for these p'rcelles following put to his acc? for vse *Hozeander*:–

ta. *co.*

5 *pico.*—p'rtes of oyle of China, at 7

ta. p'r *pico.*, is .... *T.* 39: 3: 4

200 sackes lyme at 4 *condr.* p'r sack, cost ..... *T.* 08: 0: 0

47: 3: 4

ta. m.
47: 3: 4.

And made recept of 50 *tais* paid repa'ring junk.

ta. m. co.
76: 3: 0.

And Mr. Nealson rec. 76 *ta.* 3 *m.* 0 *co.* of Keemon Dono, for acc? of Kyng of Crates, wherof 36 *tais* was good & rest Shrongo. More, he rec. of the servant of Semi Dono for accǫ

50 *tais.*

of the King of Crates, fyfty *tais* plate bars, wherof 1 bar Shrongo.

Sunguach.

07. This mornyng fayre wether, wind N? W'erly, a small gale, and soe remeaned all day after, yet som drops of rayne, but calme p'r night fayre wether, till towardes day rayne.

176

February 1615[6]

To *bongew.*

I sent 10 *tt.* pepp'r to *bongew* w'ch vent vp w'th Capt. Coppendale & the lyke to the *bongew* of the kinges rise, they haveing sent pr'sentes before of wine & fish, w'ch was spent in howse. Mr. Jnᵒ Hvnt, mᵣ of the *Hozeander,* del'd me a draught of his voyag from Bantam to this place, w'th all the sownding.

Plot del'd p'r Mr. Hunt.

08. This mornyng droping wether, wind at Nᵒ W., but sowne after broke vp faire wether all day & fore p'rte of the night, but towardes day a stiff gale wind, w'th rayne.

Rec. in plate bars of China Capt., Andrea Dittis, fowre hvndred & fyftie *taies;* and sowne after eight hvndred *taies* in melted plat more of hym.

450 *ta.*
800 *tay.*

And we had a generall covncell this day, wherin it was noted downe that Capt. Raphe Coppindall was, ordayned p'r generall consent to goe vp to the Emperour w'th a pr'sent. Also that Mr. Richard Wickham should haue an alowance of 150 *tais* p'r annᵒ, to fynd hym ap'rell & other necessaries frō our first arivall in Japon vntill the last of August, 1615, we arieving the 12th June 1613. And that Mr. Jnᵒ Osterwick should stay to keepe the bookes, & be alowed 20 1. p'r anᵒ to fynd hym ap'rell & other necessaris, to begyn in Aprill last at his com'g from Bantam. And that Jnᵒ Coker, an Englishman, [*fol. 80r.*]⌋ should stay for cooke in the English house, w'ch is donne p'r his owne consent. And Mr. Wickham to goe vp to lye at Miaco or Osekay, till other occation busynes be to employ hym in, & Mr. Eaton to com to Firando & goe to Tushma, to cleare in that place.

A generall councell.

Soyemon Donos bark was set on fyre p'r neclegence of his servantes, beeing drunk & feasting abord according to Japon fation, this day, but by good helpe was sowne quenched.

Bark on fire.

Capt. Speck came to the English howse & offred to make

Nota.

177

February 1615[6]

> a consort to haue their small shipp & ours to stay to take the Amacon shipp & the great shipp to goe for Bantam; but it was not thought fyt soe to loose our monson.

> 09. This mor'ing lowring rayny wether w'th a stiff gale, wind N°.erly, rack frō W. N°.erly, but after broke vp fayre wether rest day & lyke night following.

A lettr to Jor. Durois.

> I wrot a lettr to Jorge Durois to send stockinges & candelles, & sent it p'r bark sent p'r China Capt. to buy gvnpolder and pitch or rosen, for *Hozeander*. We laded all the bras shwers & shot abord the *Hozeander* this day.

Bras shivers & shot laden.

10 pe. by'am nill 2 pe. by. wt.

> And the China Capt. had 10 pec. byrams nill, of 14 & 15 Rs. *corg*, & two pec. byrames white, of 14 & 16 Rs. *corg* to send to his brother for samples, and the bedell of the ward had 1 sack rise.   *[fol. 80v.]*

1 sak rise.

> 10. This mornyng fayre cold wether, wind N°.erly & soe remeaned all day & night followinge, &c.

14 pec. cop'r.
3 pec. iron.
A pr'sent.

> We laded 14 *picos* copp'r & 3 *picos* iron abord the *Hozeander* this day. Shezque Dono, Sugien Donos father, came to the English howse & brought a pr'sent of *mushos*, wyne, & redish, *Nifon catange*, w'th many wordes of complemento. And the sea *bongews* & others brought pr'sentes, &c.

Sonday.

> 11. This mornyng fayre wether, wind N°.erly but after rayne most p'rte after nowne, as the lyke p'r night towardes mornynge, &c.

> Gonrock sent me money for 155 *cattes* Priaman pepp'r for Emperors accompt, at 7 *tais* p'r *pico.*, is 10 *ta.* 8 *m.* 5 *co.* As also 30 *tais* for chaders Cambias & buxshaws, w'ch one of his men bought on trust. All w'ch money I receaved.

ta. m. co.
10: 8: 5.
30 *tais*.

> 12. This mornyng raynie wether w'th a stiffe gale, wind N°.erly, but after brok vp fare wether & p'r night much wynd w'th haile & snow, cold wether.

A lettr to Mr. Eatam.

> I sent a letter to Mr. Eaton, dated the 4th pr'sent but kept till now, sent p'r the servant of Gonrok Dono, & rec'd

a lettr from Capt. Coppindall w'th an account. I deliverd

A bill of 294 *ta.* to Goresano.

Safian, or Gonrok Donos mans bill of 294 *tais* for 294 pec. buxshawes to Goresano, our *jurebasso*. And Mr. Nelson

ta. m. co. 72: 7: 5.

paid 72 *ta.* 7 m. 5 *co.* to Capt. Coppendall to make vp 200 *taies* of money he is answerable for.

Frō Torasemon Dono.

Torasemon Dono came hym selfe to the English house & brought a pr'sent of a *barso* wyne & 2 faisant cockes.

2 jars oyle.

[*fol. 81r.*]] And there was two jars sweet oyle del'd to the purcer of *Hozeander*, 1 bigg & the other lesser 7 of them,

A pr'sent.

being in a pipe, when it was drowne out; and a pr'sent was geven to   31) for laying *Hozeander* ordinance in his howse, viz.:–

2 pe. byram nill, of 15 Rs. *corg*, amontes .....*T.* 1:	2:	0
2 pe. w't baftas, of 12 Rs. *corg*, amontes.......*T.* 0:	9:	6
2 pe. zelas red, of 12 Rs. *corg*, amontes........*T.* 0:	9:	6
2 pec. borall, of 08 Rs. *corg*, ...*T.* 0:	6:	4

13. This mornyng a stiffe gale, wind N°erly, haile & snow, very cold wether all day & night following, but no snow p'r night, rack frō W. N°erly.

30 *tais.*

Semi Done sent therty *taies* receved p'r Mr. Nelson in plate bars, wherof 10 *taies* was for acc° of the King of Crates, & 20 *taies* for his owne accompt, lent hym in money

1 pec. foota chader. 200 *tais.*

before. & Sangera Samme had 1 peec. foota chader, of   32) Rs. *corg*, to pay 1 *tay*, & Mr. Nelson del'd Mr. Osterwick 200 *tais* plate bars for *Hozr.* acc°. & we owe to Andrea Dit-

47: 3: 4.

tis, China Capt., for oyle & lyme for *Hozeander*, 47: 3: 4.

14. This mornyng still cold wether, wind N°erly, rack frō W. N°erly, a stiff gale most p'rte of the day, and the lyke p'r night followinge.

Kinge of Firando went vp.

The king dep'rted this day to goe to the Emperour, & had 13 pec. ordinance shot out of the *Hozeander* & 5 out of Duch

31) The name, not given.
32) Not entered.

barke, w'th 8 or 10 chambers out of Duch house. I went out w'th a banket of sweet meate, 2 barilles wyne, a jar of bis-kit, & 30 wax candelles; w'ch he took in very good part, and after sent me word p'r a s'rvnt that it had sufficed to haue sent any one in the howse, & not to haue com my selfe.

Mr. Hunt, the m.ʳ of the *Hozeander*, fell into termes w'th Capt. Coppendall ab'ut Rowe and Tomas, the purcer, tell-ing hym he did hym not right about the abuse was for-merly offred, & that the said Tomas should find it when they were at sea. These were bad wordes & were because the said m.ʳ might not keepe the kayes & domenera over the p'rcer in matters of hold. But it is thought [that] the wax was gon out of hold p'r lyke meanes.   [*fol. 81v.*]⌋

15. This mornyng cold wether w'th a stiff gale, wind at N.º, rack frõ N.º W., & soe remeaned all day & night followinge.

ta. m.
10: 5.

Mr. Nealson paid Jn.º Cokora the cooke ten *tais* & a halfe in great plate, vpon acc.º of his wagis, to cleare w'th them he is indebted vnto. And Capt. Speck sent me word

Nota.

he would let vs haue 2 *picos* poulder, yf we stood in neede.

50 sheetes
pap'r.

Of w'ch offer I accepted. And Capt. Speck lent vs 50 sheetes paper. Mr. Hunt desired to haue a councell assembled tuch-

Nota.

ing the abuse offred to hym p'r Rowland Tomas; w'ch was donne. But more falt to be imputed to the m.ʳ, Jn.º Hunt, then the other. Soe we made them frendes, &c.

16. This mornyng cold wether, wind N.ºerly, rack from N.º W., and so remeaned all day & lyke p'r night foll'g, but haile & snow p'r night w'th much wynd.

12 *ta.*

And Moris Jones the chirurgion had 12 *tais* plate bars p'd hym p'r Mr. Nealson, agreed vpon p'r councell for his

11 *tais.*

pains. And Jn.º Corea the cooke, vpon acc.º his wagis, 11 *tais*, all paid p'r Mr. Nealson.

17. This mornyng still cold weth. w'th a stiff gale N.ºerly, rack frõ West, & wind sowne after vered that way, w'th

February 1615[6]

slite & snow, both day & night, but more p'r night then day w'th much winde.

Niquan, the China Capt. kinsman, retorned frõ Langa-saque & brought 370 *cattis* pitch (or rozen), cost *T.* 14 *tais*; and 310 *cattis* gvnpoulder, cost *T.* 64 *tais* 1 *mas*; and for the bark *T.* 02 *tais*. And I del'd 2 bars plate to Jnọ Goresano poz. 6 *ta.* 7 *m.* 5 *co.*, & rec. 1 bar of 3 *tais* 4: 5 *co.* I rec. of Jnọ Cokra fore rest 3: 3: 0 plat bar for me. And he to answer Cokera 3: 4: 5 gret plate. And Capt. Speck sent the 2 baril-les gvnpoulder w'ch he promised, waying   .33) [*fol. 82r.*]]

ta. m
80: 1.

2 bar'll polder.

18. This morn'g still cold wether w'th a stiff gale at Nọ W'er-ly, rack W'erly, haile & snow most p'rte of the day & lyke p'r night.

We waid out the pepp'r to day for the king, & had much a doe w'th the 10 men of ward whoe crinched34) for wight; soe it must be waid over to morrow againe. 77 bages this day did way 49 *pic.* 96 *cattis*, & 80 bages out of China Capt. lodg, 57 *pico.* 35½ *cattis*. And I gaue my case China bottelles of 12 to Capt. Coppendall.

77, poz. pep'r
4996 *cat.*
80 poz.
5735½ *tt.*
To Capt.
Coppendall.

19. This mornyng cold wether, a fresh gale, wind Nọerly rack from Nọ W., yet fayre wether all day & lyke p'r night, but much wind a littell before day.

Del'd thertie *tais* plate bars to Mr. Nealson, of w'ch he is to pay eight *tais* to Jnọ Berry & Mr. Hvnt for 34 fish skins, rated at 10 Rs. 8. This money I del'd not, but paid the 8 *tais* my selfe for Capt. Adames, left p'r hym at Miaco. And I del'd therty *tais* one *mas* plate bars to Rowland Tomas in p'rsonne of Capt. Coppendall for account *Hozeander*, kept p'r Mr. Jnọ Osterwick. We cleard accọ of the 3000 *tais* this day w'th the King of Firandos *bongews*, & del'd them m'rchandiz for 121: 3: 5.

8 *tais.*

ta. m. co.
30: 1: 0.

33) Not entered.
34) Cringe (?), in the sense of to constrain; and so to sticle, or haggle.—Thompson.

181

February 1615[6]

Vnagense Dono sent me a pr'sent of 2 *barsos* wine, 2
Japon cakes (or *muchos*), & 2 mallardes. And we rec. 49
cokes of bras of fownder, poz.   35) *cattis* at 14 *tais*
p'r *catty*. Capt. Speck wrot me a lettr, desyring to haue the
m.r or purcer of *Hozeandr* to make a bill lading of the ebony
sent in *Hozeander* being 927 logges (or stickes), poz., as he
said, 629 *pico*. Soe the purcer, Rowland Tomas, made hym
2 b'lls of the N? of logges, but not of wight, to del'r it to the
Duch, present at Bantam, &c.   [*fol. 82v.*]]

20.   This mornyng a stiff gale of wind N?erly, cold wether,
and soe remeaned all day & lyke p'r night, but much snow
& sleete p'r night, &c.

I wrot a letter to Capt. Speck to will hym send a note
vnder his ferme to pay fraight for the ebony, as shall be
thought fyting betwixt the 2 agentes, English and Duch; as
also to send the prince [*sic*] & wight of the 2 barilles of polder, w'ch Jacob Swager tould me waid 200 *cat.* nett. And
after, Capt. Speck sent word it cost hym 16 *tais* p'r *pico.*, is
32: 0: 0.

The *Hozeander* went out to Cochi, & shot offe 5 pe.
ordinance; and the Duch shot ofe 7 or 8 chambrs at Holland
howse. & I went abord Derick de Frize, & had 3 pe. ordinance shot of at my going away, & at retorne frō *Hozea'dr*
3 more. And Capt. Speck sent Jacob Swager abord the
Hozeandr as we went out, w'th a pr'sent of 3 barilles wyne,
4 greate fishes, and six hense. And I gaue a peec. of
watcht36) damaske to Rowland Tomas, purcer of the
Hozeander, in requitall of a small rough diamond in a ryng
of gould he gaue me the other day, esteemed worth som 4 or
5 *taies*. Also I gaue the chirurgion, Monias Jones, a peece
red damaske & a Rs? of 8 in money for his payns taken in

35) Not entered.
36) *Watchet*, pale blue.—Thompson.

February 1615[6]

howse, & for a bag of synomond & a box of mace he gaue me.[37]   [*fol. 83r.*]

21.   This mornyng cold lowring wether w'th a stiffe gale, wind N°.erly, rack same, to Eastwardes, but fayre wether all day & night following, littell wind p'r night.

Frō the
China Capt.

The China Capt., Andrea Dittis, gaue me a peece of stript & spotted catten grownd black, for a pr'sent. And I gaue

30 *tais.*
15 bagges
rise.

30 *tayis,* I way del'd therty *tais,* more to Capt. Coppendalle vpon acc°. for *Hozeander.* And there was 15 bagges, viz., del'd to China, wherof 10 were of 50 [?] *gantes* & 5 of 50 *gantes* peece. Also I del'd a bages [*sic*] of Rialles of eight, cont'g

500 Rs. 8.
300 *taes.*

500 Rs. of 8 in it, is 400 *tais*; and rec. 300 *tais* in plate of bars of hym. & I watered & new packed vp the ambr greese in 2 leaden potts, same as before, & the musk in an other, m'rked as foll'th:-

		catt.	ta.	ma.		
A	R°. A:	5:	4:	2	is 9 catt. 14 *tay* w't	
B	B:	4:	9:	8	ambr gr., is .... *T.*	38)
C	C:	4:	0:	0	musk in 86 cods, cost.... *T.* 48: 0: 0	

being m'rked w'th the Companis m'rk in the m'rgin. And packed vp all three in one chist vnder same m'rke w'thout N°., & put abord the *Hoze.*

A lettr frō
Jorge Durois.

And I rec. a lettr frō Jorge Durois w'th a baskit cont'g 120 tallo candelles of 6 for a *mas,* w'th 4 pere silke stocking, viz.:-

2 peare at 9 *pezos* or Rs. 8,

2 peare at 7 *tais* plate bars,

and 4 peare cuffs & 1 band, cost 1 *tay.*

And he sent a writing enclozed frō Capt. Garrocho of such mattrs as the China Capt. had geuen hym w'th a cash charg for all mattres in making vp that w'ch is del'd 100

---

37) In a space after this entry is a later remark, reading: "*Hozeander* goes to Cochi."

38) Not entered.

February 1615[6]

tais.

22. This mornyng fayre wether & calme, & soe was most p'rte of the day, wind vering to S. West, a stiff gale all the after p'rte of the night, &c.

To Capt. Copendall.

Capt. Coppendall had a runlet of pery I gaue hym. And I del'd in three billes to Seme Done, viz.:-

1 bill of 70 *tais*, due of ould.

1 bill of 50 *tais*, for m'rch'nds sould.

1 bill of 20 *tas*, for a gvn.

Bill Semi Dono.

And he gaue me a new bill of 250 *tais*, wherof 116: 5: 0 was owing vpon ould acc°, and 133: 5: 0 goodes del'd at Miaco p'r Mr. Eaton, is 250: 0: 0 now owing, to pay at a yeare.

10 *tais.*

And Andrea Dittis, China Capt., sould a boy called Mats to Capt. Coppendall for 10 *taies*, the w'ch plate Capt. Coppendall del'd vnto me. And ther was sould and del'd vnto Andrea Dittis, China Capt., 283 peeces byrams blew, of 14 & 15 *taies* p'r *corg*, for 8½ *mas* peece. And I gaue Capt. Coppindall the 4 peare cuffs & band, w'ch Jorge Durois sent me, cost 1 *tay*. And I gaue 1 pere white silke stocking to Mr. Jn° Osterwick. And the China Capt. had 4 *mas* wight Pr'aman gould at 14 p'r one in plate vpon acc°.

283 pce. byram nill. Nota.

4 *mas* w't gold.

To Mr. Hunt.

And I gaue Mr. Jn° Hvnt, m'r of the *Hozeander*, 2 Japon buckskins & a peare silk stocking. for a pr'sent, in respect he gaue me a case bottell. I wrot 2 lettrs to Mr. Eaton 1 p'r Semi Done and the other by Caquiamon Dono, the kings man, how I had sould for 133 *ta*. 5 *mas* to Semi Done to be del'd in m'rchandiz p'r Mr. Eaton at Miaco, as also he is to del'r 31 *tatt*. broad cloth at 13 *mas tatta*. to the kyngs man, or other m'rch'ndiz to lyke *vallem*,[39] yf the broad

2 lettres to Mr. Eaton.

---

39) *Ad valorem*(Lat.) (?).

An eclipse.

cloth be sould. There was a great eclips of the moone this night, began about 9 a clock. But the wether proued overcast yt we could not observe no star, w'ch we thought to haue donne, to find out the true longetude of this place.

[*fol. 84r.*]]

23. This mornyng a stiffe gale, wind at S. W., overcast darke wether, and after much rayne all day and the lyke p'r night following, wind vering Nᵒ W'erly.

25 *tais.*
Nota.

I del'd twenty and five *tais* plate bars to Capt. Coppendall. The China Capt. sent 2 barilles *morofack*, 2 jarrs biskit, & 2 barilles pickeld tunny for a pr'sent to Capt.

3½ Rs. 8.
1 *tay.*

Jourden for Bantam. I gaue Jnᵒ de Lieuana 2½ Rsᵒ of 8 in Spanish money, & Francisco Carnero one Riall of 8; & passed my word to pay a *tay* in Japon plate to Tome Dono, for Jnᵒ de Lieuanas housrowme.

24. This mornyng rayne wether, littell wind at Nᵒ W'erly, & so remeand most p'rte of day, wind encreasing, but much wind p'r night, yet dry wether.

25 *tais.*

I del'd twenty and five *tais* plate bars to Mr. Osterwick, to pay twenty *tais* to Yayemon Dono & Tayamon Dono,

Holland ship put to sea.

the two carpenters geven ten *tais* a peec. for a pr'sent for payns extraordnary about shipp.

Nota.

The great Holland shipp, called the *Ankewsen*, went out to sea this day, & the junk in compᵃ w'th her. And I went w'th Capt. Cappendall to Hollandes howse to offer Capt. Speck to carry his lettrs to Bantam, as thir shipp did ours, shee being ready to put to sea to morrow; but fownd Capt. Speck was gon out w'th shipp.

Nota.

Jacob Swager brought Capt. Coppendall a bottell of wyne & a cheese for a pr'sent.

Divers Shashmas came to see the English howse, whome I vsed kindly. They said the King of Shashma ment to goe to the Emperour the next moneth. Capt. Speck sent word to desire vs to carry 6 Japon marreners along in our ship for Bantam yt were left behind out of thir junck. I rec. a lettr

A lettr frõ Mr. Eaton.

frõ Mr. Eaton, dated in Miaco, the 6th current, when he adv[i]seth of salle[40] pep'r at 6 *tais* pic.º & wax at 17 *tais* pic.º, &   [41] pec. bad baftas at 6 *mas* p'r pec.

[*fol. 84v.*]]

25. This mornyng a stiff gale, wind at Nº W. W'erly, ouercast lowring wether, but after broke vp fayre wether all day & lyke p'r night, not soe much winde.

I sealed vp my packed lettrs for England, viz.:-

1 to the Wor. Company ⎫
1 to Ser Thomas Smith   ⎪
1 to Mr. Edward James   ⎬ all enclozed to Wor'll Compª,
1 to Capt. Jnº Saris   ⎪ w'th 1 frõ Mr. Eaton.
1 to my brother Walter ⎭

And in that packed the lettrs[42] w'ch went p'r junck p'r way of Syam the last yeare, both to my Lº Treasurer, the Wor'll Compª, Mr. Wilson, Capt. Saris, & others, as also the ballance of the bookes.

More, I wrot lettrs for Bantam as follow'th, viz.:-

𝕬 2 to Capt. Jourden, w'th journall ballance & 4 bookes petty charges, all in a box left open, del'd to Capt. Coppendall; w'th a packet cont'g 2 pere silk stockings, 2 bandes, & 1 per cuffes.

RW 1 to Mr. Ric'd. Wertby, w'th a Japon standish.

IB 1 to Jnº Beamont, w'th a Japon standish & a peare clamps.

𝕿 1 to Piter Turner, w'th a jar biskit.

𝕾 1 to Ffrancis Sewall, w'th a jar biskit.

1 to Harnando Ximenes, w'th a pere silk stockinges.

All w'ch matters I del'd to Capt. Coppindall, & went w'th

---

40) Salty (?).
41) Not entered.
42) I. E., duplicate copies.—Thompson.

hym abord shipp to Cochi & carid as foll'th:-

> To Mr. Jn? Hunt, m.ʳ, a bag bisket, poz. 55 *cattes* & a box
> marmã.
>
> To Mr. Dorington & Mr. Carpenter his mate, 1 bag biskit poz.
> 50 *cat.*
>
> To shipps company 3 barilles wyne & 4 hogges.

The China Capt. accompanid vs abord. We had 1 pec.

Capt. Spek.

ordinance at entry, 6 pec. for healths, & 5 at going away.
Capt. Speck brought a lettr to del'r to Duch pr'sedent at
Bantam.

26. This mornyng fayre calme wether, but after a fresh gale
at W. N?erly, most p'rte of day and the lyke p'r night, but
not soe much wind, &c., till after midnight, littell wind
N?erly.

**A lettr to
Pattania & 1
to Syam.
Ɖ**

I wrot a letter to Pattania to Mr. Adam Denton, & sent it
p'r small Duch yaught, w'th a jar biskit a lettr to Mr.
Gurney, Syam. We receaved back frõ Skidayen Dono 2

**1 bar gold.
2 fowle.**

damaskt fowling pec. and 1 bar *oban* gould. A slaue of the
Admeralls did rvn away & gott secretly abrod our shipp; of

**Hozeandr
staid till
this night.
A lettr to
Mr. Eaton.**

the w'ch I advised Capt. Coppendall. So, when the[y] had
waid ancor & were vnder seale, they came to an ancor
againe & sent hym back p'r shipps boate. Soe, after midnight, wind vering N?erly, the[y] set seale. God send them
a good voyage. *[fol. 85r.]*

To Niquan.

The China Capt. kinsman Niquan being bownd for
China, ther was a pr'sent geven to hym, & an other ould
China w'ch went lyke waies, he having broght first a
pr'sent of banketing stuffe, viz.:-

> 3 pec. dutties of Rs. 43) *corg*, 1 for ould China.
>
> 1 pec. byrams white of   Rs. *corge.*
>
> 1 pec. rangins of 5 Rs? p'r *corge*, all cost   .

Wherof the ould China had only 1 pec. dutties. The chirur-

---

43) This and the following prices, not entered.

Nota.

gion of the *Hozeandr* vsed speeches that Mr. Nealson had not geven hym satisfaction for paines he had taken w'th hym in his sicknes, & to that effort got Capt. Coppindall to write me a letter, & sent a note p'r Mr. Wickham of *dares & tomares*.[44] Soe at the same instant, Mr. Nelson sent all the chirurgions *dares* back to hym, w'th a note of what he had geven hym. The chirurgion is a prating fello, & I think

Hozeandr put to sea.

sett on p'r others, &c. *Hozeand.* put to sea at midnight.[45]

27. This mornyng fayre wether w'th a fresh gale, wind N?erly, and sowne after a stiff gale all day, but not soe much p'r night & after midnight calme, &c.

A lettr to Mr. Eaton 1 to his host. A lettr to Jorge Durois in answer of his Rs. 5 dais past. 1 Rs. 8.

I wrot a lettr to Mr. Eaton & an other to his host; in Mr. Eatons I adviced of the rec. of his of 6th pr'sent w'th answer thervnto; and I wrot an other lettr to Jorge Durois & retorned hym the 4 peare silk stockinges he sent w'th a Rs. 8 enclozed in my lettr for 4 peare cuffes & 1 falling band he sent me before, and wrot hym to send more candelles. Mr. Wickham gaue me a sallinon & I gaue it to China Capten, & he sent hym an other, &c.

Nota.

I had conferrence w'th the carpenters to buld a new gedonge p'r water side, w'ch, according to the note the[y] put in, will cost for tymbr & other stuffe, besides workmanshipp, 681 *tais*. And Oyen Dono & Soyemon Dono sent in plate of bars vpon the kinges acc? *T.* 519: 2: 3½, and vpon acc? of China Capt., Andrea Dittis, *T.* 028: 3: 0; Som total amontes vnto rec. kings acc? *T.* 547: 5: 3½.

ta. m. co. 547: 5: 3½.

[*fol. 85v.*]]

28. This mornyng fayre calme wether, but after a fresh gale most p'rte of the day N?erly, fayre wether, but littell or no wind p'r night w'th som rayne.

---

44) *Andar en dares y tomares* (Span.), to quarrell.—Thompson.

45) In a space after this entry is a later remark, reading: "*Hozeander* puts to sea."

February 1615[6]

The Duch (or Holland) *pataga*[46] went out in the after
nowne toward Pattania.

The China Capt., Andrea Dittis, feasted all the neighb'rs
in respect building his new howse.

I had conferrence againe w'th carpenters about building
the gadong, w'ch, as the[y] noted before,

	ta.	m.	co.
the very tymber & other stuffe would cost .... *T.*	681:	0:	0
and 2530 carp'trs dais work at 1½ *mas* day ... *T.*	379:	5:	0
and 2750 labors daies work at 5 *cond*. day .... *T.*	137:	5:	0
and 0200 plasterrars days work at .... *T.*	040:	0:	0
Som total amontes vnto .... *T.*	1238:	0:	0

Soe, p'r advice & counsell of all, it is thought sit to let the
gedong building rest till the next yeare, & only repare that
on the other side.

29. This mornyng raynie wether, wind N? erly, a stiffe gale all
day, and lyke p'r night, but not soe much rayne p'r night
as p'r day.

I wrot a letter to Mr. Eaton that news is com that wars
is lyke to ensue betwixt the Emperor & his sonne Calsa
Samme, being backt p'r his father in law Massamone Dono,
because the Emperor will not geue his sonne the fortresse
& teretory of Osakay, yf it were gotten, as he promised he
wold doe, &c. I advised hym, yf wars were lyke to ensue,
that he should com away & bring money & put ye rest into
money yf it were possible.

Bongo Samme, *alius* Nobesane, sent me a pr'sent of 10
hense & 2 *barsos* wyne.[47]   [*fol. 86r.*]⌋

---

46) *Patache* (Span.), a tender, or small vessel.—Thompson.

47) Another sentence relating a letter sent to Mr. Eaton to Osekay is entered and
cancelled by the author. The same effect is entered on March 3.

01. This mornyng lowring wether w'th a stiff gale, wind still Northerly and soe remeaned all day & night following yet dry wether, &c.

50 *ta.*

250 *tais.*

Del'd Mr. Nelson 50 *tais* plate bars, paid vnto Capt. China & neighbo'rs for p'rte of 90 *taies* to make ston walles. I del'd also two hvndred and fyftie *taies* plate bars to Andr. Dittis, China Capt., wherof 200 *tais* I adv'nture, viz., 100 *taies* to Liqueas, to buy ambr greese, and the other 100 *tais* into China at his discretion for my best advantage, and the other 50 *tais* I lend hym, to pay at his retorne frõ Langasaque.

10 *tais.*

I del'd the ten *tais* plate bars to Capt. China w'ch Capt. Copendall paid for the boy he sould hym, called Matts. And there was two *tais* small plate paid for a boy called Mon, to serve the Company 15 yeares, fynding hym diet & aper'll, the money paid his mother, whoe gaue a writing in Japons to that effect.

15 years
2 *tais* for
Mon named
Dick.

And I del'd Mr. Osterwick 1 pap'r of 25 *tais* and an other of 19: 2: 3½ *condrins*, is all T. 44 *ta.* 2 *m.* 3½ *co.*, and he paid Skydoyen Dono vpon acc⁰ for these goodes follow, viz.:-

44: 2: 3½.

	ta.	m.	co.
1 great mast for shipp .... *T.* 080:	0:	0
2 yardes for shipp .... *T.* 010:	0:	0
106 barkes lading stones for junck .... *T.* 010:	6:	0
Som totall amontes vnto .... *T.* 100:	6:	0

Nota.
10 *ta.* 8: 6
del'd of
skid[48] for
m'rch'ndz.

The w'ch is paid as followeth:-

	ta.	m.	co.
In plate of bars of yt of Capt. China .... *T.* 060:	0:	0
Pro 131 *cattis* pep'r, at 6 *tais pico*............. *T.* 007:	8:	6
Pro 003 pec. chader bradry .... *T.* 003:	0:	0
	70:	8:	6

---

48) *Scud* (Ital.) (?)

Marche 1615[6]

And now paid in ready money .... *T.* 29: 7: 4

100: 6: 0.

Tonomon Samme, the kinges brother, sent to borrow 50 or 60 *tais* plate for a frend & I sent answer I had no money; yet he sent againe & would haue no nā[*sic*]; but I was still of one minde.   [*fol. 86v.*]

02. This mornyng still a stiffe, gale wind N? E'erly, cold wether, and soe remeaned all day, & the lyke p'r night followinge, cold wether.

I del'd one hvndred *tais* plate bars to Mr. Osterwick to pay for shark oyle bought for building; I say I deliverd hym one hvndred *tais* to lend fiftie *tais* to China Capt., Andrea Dittis, now bownd for Langasaque. And we had 15 trees of a *bose*[49] to sett in our ochard, viz., sypris, spruse, orange, lemon, chistnvt, & other sortes flowres. There was

446⅓ *gantes* shark oyle at 1 *mas* p'r *gante*, amontes to 44 *ta.* 6 [*m.*] 3 *co.* And the China Capt. had 30 pec. duttis of 15 Rs. *corg*, at 1 *tay* peec, is 30 *tais.* Mr. Osterwick lost 2 *ta.* 2 *m.* 1 *condr.* in exchang of 33 *ta.* 9 *cond.* for *Hozeander.* And Mr. Nealson del'd vp his acc. cash to Mr. Osterwick.

03. This mornyng still cold wether, w'th a fresh gale, wind N? E'erly all day, but littell or no wind p'r night w'th som rayne towardes day, rack W'erly.

The China Capt., Andrea Dittis, went to Langasaque, & I wrot a lettr to his brother, Capt. Whaw, & sent hym a Hollandes cheese, a bottell of sallet oyle & a bag of wall-

nvts. I del'd Oyen Dono the King of Fyrandos bill of 680 *tais* for gould, & he gaue me a bill of his owne hand for T. 350 *tais* plate bars, due p'r King of Firando vpon ould acc°, beside the 3000 *tais* last sould for. This bill of 350 *tais* I del'd to Mr. Osterwick. I wrot [*sic*]. And, I wrot a lettr to

---

49) *Bōzu* 坊主, a bonze, or Buddhist priest.—Thompson.

Marche 1615[6]

A lettr to Mr. Eaton.

Mr. Eaton, to buy 10 or 15 *cakis* & rest in *shishero*[50] tables for the halfe our howst oweth of that was burned in Osekay.

1000 *ta*.51)
A lettr fro Mr. Eaton.

And sowne after I rec. a lettr from Mr. Eaton, dated in Osakey, le 20th vltimo, w'th 1000 *tais* in plate barres & a pap'r of 13 *tais* 2 *condrin* for Jnᵒ Japon that came w'th Capt. Coppedall. I say I rec. a thousand *tais* in plate bars &

ta. con. 13: 2.

thertyn *tais* two *condrins, vt supra*, in w'ch letter Mr. Eaton advised me that Sada Dono was dead, & that Osakay was on fyre when he wrot the lettr, & aboue 500 howses burned & the fyre not quenched. And ther was lent to

1 *tay*.
10 *cat*. pep'r 7 *tais*.

Piters father that went in *Hozeandr* 1 *ta*. small plate vpon accᵒ of his wagis. And Miguell, *jurebasso*, had 10 *cattis* pepp'r Pattania at 7 *tais* pec.   [*fol. 87r.*]⌋

04. This mornyng overcast raynie w'ther, littell wind Nᵒerly, but after a fresh gale all day, & much wind p'r night w'th quantety of rayne, &c.

5 carp'rs.
2 labo'rs.
5 labo'rs, bos.
14 other lab'rs.

This day 5 carpenters to make orchard walle on the back side of gedonge, & 2 lab'rs. And we planted the trees geven p'r the *bose* of Cushensh,52) being 17 trees, for doing where-of we had 5 of the *boses* men, whome we paid 6 *d*. or 1 *mas* p'r peece, w'th 14 other laborers at 5 *condrins* p'r peec., to carry and plant the same trees.

Frō Chinas.
2 pe. duttis
1 ta.: 5: 6½.

And 2 Chinas came from Langasaque & brought me a barill wine & 2 hense for a present. And Mr. Osterwick rec. of Mr. Wickham 16 *mas* small plate for 2 pec. duttis of 10 Rs. p'r *corg*, sould in August last, is in greate plate, 1: 5: 6½ *condryn*; & a *bose* came to vizet me w'th a pr'sent of

A lettr to Jorge Durois
1 to China

fans, & I wrot a lettr to Jorge Durois, & an other to China Capt. p'r the Japon *twerto*.

---

50) *Shishiro* ししろ, barked logs or square timber to saw in planks.
51) This marginal note must be put after the next one.
52) Perhaps **Jishoji** 慈正寺 of the Lotus Sect located once at Tasuke 田助.

Marche 1615[6]

Capten.

05. This mornyng a stiffe gale, wind N°erly, lowring wether, but after pr'ved dry both night & day, yet much wind both p'r day & night.

6 carp'trs.
2 labo'rs.
10 labo'rs.
40 bordes.
30 bundels cane.
10 rownd postes.

This day 6 carpenters & 2 labo'rs for them, w'th 10 labors to temper & make clay. And 40 bordes of 5 p'r a *mas*, 30 bundelles canes at 5 p'r *mas*, 10 rownd postes at p'r post.

6. This mornyng still cold wether w'th much wind N° E'erly all day, but littell or no wind p'r night, ffayre wether, &c.

6 carp'trs.
25 labors.

This day 6 carp'rs & 2 labo'rs to them w'th 12 labo'rs to tempp'r clay & 11 lab'rs to playne way for orchard walles.

50 *tais*.
A pr'sent to a *bose*.

And I del'd fyftie *tais* plate bars to Mr. Osterwick to lay out in Building & other occations. And we sent a pr'sent the *bose* that gaue vs the trees, viz.:-

1 barill wyne of 50 *gantes*.
10 *cattis* pepp'r w'th 2 small bars plate, poz.   .53)

[*fol. 87v.*]]

7. This mornynge fayre calme wether, & sowne after a fresh gale, wind [*sic*] most p'rt of the day, & the lyke p'r night till towardes day & then the wind wakened vp, & overcast wether.

6 carp'trs.
33 labo'rs.

This day 6 carpenters w'th 2 labo'rs for them 12 labors about orchard walles, and 19 labo'rs to carry and temper clay.

A lettr to China Capt.

And I wrot a lettr to Andrea Dittis, China Capt., that I del'd 5 bordes of plankes to the China w'ch carrieth the junck & lent hym a boat mast & a seale, all w'ch he may geue them, yf they be frendes of his, w'ch I leave to his

3 trees.
Gonsoluo.

discretion. The *bose* sent 3 trees (or plantes more) & came to thank me for the pr'sent sent. A Portingall called Gonsolua came to the English howse w'th complementall

---

53) Not entered.

wordes. I esteemed he came to spie (or learne out) whether our shipp & the Duch yaught staid for to take the Amacon shipp.

8. This mornyng a stiffe gale, wind at N̥. E'erly, w'th hayle & rayne mingeld together most p'rte before nowne, but dry wether after nowne & not soe much winde.

I del'd a note to Mr. Wickham of tymbr & neales to be bought at Osekay & Tomo.

This day 7 carpenters & 7 labo'res.

9. This mornyng fayre calme wether or rather a littell wind S. W'erly, but after vered N̥erly, a fresh gale most p'rte of the day, yet littell or no winde p'r night, &c.

This day 6½ carpenters & 33 labo'rs all sortes.

I wrot a letter to Mr. Eaton w'th the coppie of the note of tymbr bordes & neles to be bought aboue the princepall, wherof is del'd to Mr. Wickham w'th the forme or sample of the neles made in wood, &c. And I del'd 400 tais to Mr.

Osterwick, wherof he del'd 100 tais to Mr. Wickham, to carry to Osakay to buy tymbr & neles I say I del'd foure

hvndred tais to Mr. Osterwick. And I lent my book of St. Augustyn, Citty of God, to Mr. Wickham, & the Turkish History & a book of forme of debitor & creditor to Mr. Nealson.   [fol. 88r.]⌋

And I gaue a fyne chint I bought of Water Carwarden to

woman Mr. Wickhams gerle.

10. This mornyng calme wether but sowne after a fresh gale, wind at N̥erly most p'rte of the day, but rather calme p'r night, wind vering W. S'erly.

Mr. Nealson went to the bathes at Jshew, fynding hym selfe ill at ease. And Mr. Wickham went for Miaco, to take acc̥ of Mr. Eaton, & he to retorne for Firando, as apereth

p'r coppies. And I wrot a lettr to Jor. Durois to buy som frute trees & send me, yf he conveniently can; & sent this

Marche 1615[6]

lettr p'r. Nic? Martyn.

Also we sent pr'sentes to Tonomon Same, Nobesne, Oyen Dono, Sugian Dono, & his father, Soyemon Dono, Gonosco Dono, Vnagense Dono w'th the two sea *bongews*, is all 10 p'rsons, each of them 2 *barsos* wyne, 4 fishes, and a quantety of pepp'r. Also I wrot a letter to Capt. China. There was 4 carpenters & 1 laborer to day.

11. This mornyng fayre calme wether, & but littell wind after N?erly most p'rte of the day & night, calme fayre wether still.

This day 4 carp'trs & 36 labo'rs in all.

Mr. Wickham dep'rted not till this mornyng towardes Miaco, & left woman his gerle behind hym, w'ch he sayeth he bought of yow[54] & that he advised hym, in a lettr of the 20th vltimo, how her mother did think to bring yow in trowble for seling her. W'ch is the occation I write yow now she is at Fi'ndo.

And I del'd the thrteen *tais* two *condrins* to Jn? Japon, w'ch Mr. Eaton sent for hym & took a receapt of his hand for it. And we had 21 *cakis* or square postes of Yasimon Dono, at 1 *mas* pec., & 30 bundelles straw of Synemon Dono, cost 1½ *mas*.

And I sent a verneson pastie to Mr. Eaton & an other, the China Capten.   [*fol. 88v.*]]

12. This mornyng fayre calme wether, & after but littell wind variable, but the later p'rte of night much wind at S. W. w'th som drops of rayne.

This day 6 carp'rs & 36 labo'rs in all.

The night past Andrea Dittis retonred frõ Langasaque, and brought me a lettr from Capt. Whaw, his brother, whoe sent me a jarr of oranges, w'th a littell fyshpond (or jarr)

---

54) The author has here retained the words of his own letter to Mr. Eaton, as suggested in the margin.

Marche 1615[6]

Capt. Whaw.

w'th live fish in it, & bought 15 pigions for me, cost 1 *tay* 5 *condrins*.

The China Capt. telles me ther is much adoe about *fybuck*, & Jorge Durois tells me the lyke, I say, writes me the lyke, & sent me som hard wax to seale letters & the 2

2 per. stok.
7 *tais* pd.
A lettr frõ
Jorge Dutois.
M.ʳ. plastr
came.

peare si[l]ke stocking, w'ch I reto.ʳ at 7 *taies* the 2 peare w'ch 7 *tais* the China Capt. paid & brought back the stockinges.

Also the m.ʳ workman plasterrer came along w'th hym to repare our new bought gadong.

And vpon hope of trade into China I lent Capt. Whaw,

500 *tais*.

the China Capt., at Langasaque, 500 *tais*, I say five hvndred *tais*, in plate of bars.

A lettr to
Mr.
Wickham.

And I wrot a lettr to Mr. Wickham, & sent hym the halfe of sealing wax w'ch Jorge Durois sent me, & advised hym my mynd it had byn better he had carid his gerle woman along w'th hym.

And we made prise for tymber w'th Skidayen Dono, and paid hym 50 *taies* plate bars in hand, as foll'th:-

	ta.	m.	co.
0450 *cakis* of 2 *tatta.* long at 1 *mas* peec.......T. 045:	0:	0	
0550 *nvkis* of 2 *tatta. isonuque*[55]) 3 p'r a *mas* ..T. 018:	3:	1	
0040 *ficamons* of 1½ *tatta.*, of 1½ *mas* pec.......T. 006:	0:	0	
1000 ordinary bordes, of 1 *tatta.* of 6 p'r a *mas* ....T. 016:	6:	4	
0070 other boardes, of 1½ *tatta.* at 1 *mas* pe....T. 007:	0:	0	
0035 *isonuque*, of 2 *tatta.* at 2 *mas* pec........T. 007:	0:	0	
0040 *nandange*, of 1½ *tatta.* of 4½ p'r *mas* .....T. 000:	9:	0	
0150 *marroque*, of 2 *tatta.*, at 3 p'r a *ma.* ......T. 005:	0:	0	
0003 *monfashta*, of 1½ *tatta.*, cost all 3 ....T. 001:	0:	0	
0015 *Tambu*, of 2 *tatt.*, at cost all 15 ....T. 003:	0:	0	

55) This and the following names in Japanese are evidently various sorts of timber, including *nedagi* 根太木, *maruki* 丸木, *monbashira* 門柱, *hikaehashira* 控柱, &c.

196

Marche 1615[6]

0002 *ficaye fashta*, of 2 *tatta.*, cost both .... *T.* 000: 5: 0
0020 *cakina ita*, of 4 *tatta.*, at 9 *mas* pec. ...... *T.* 018: 0: 0

Som totall amontes vnto .... *T.* 128: 3: 5.

The tymber to be all deliverd in Firando the next moone.

[*fol. 89r.*] ⌋

2 pr'sentes.

And ther were 2 pr'sentes geven to Joco Conde Dono and Vshanusque Dono, each 2 *barsos* wyne & 4 fishes, w'th a littell pepp'r, viz.,[56]

A man executed

And the China Capt. envited hym selfe to our *ffro.* And I forgot to note downe that this day a man was cut in peeces, whoe had layne in prison 3 yeares, for rvning away w'th his wife & 2 doughters to Faccatay, they being slaues to the king of this place (of Firando), he writing to the King of Ffaccata to retorne them, w'ch he did. It is said the begy[n]ing proceaded for that the king of this place would haue had the vse of his oldest doughter. They being Christians rather choose to rvn away, w'ch cost the father his lyfe, & yet the doughter, &c. & yt is said the wife, hearing her hvsband is executed, is secretly fled, or, as som think, hath made her selfe away. Word was sent to me to the Eng'sh howse that, yf such a woman were com to me, I should retorne her back, &c.

13. This mornyng a stiffe gale, wind at S? W., droping wether, but sowne after brake vp fayre wether & not soe much wind, nether p'r day nor night.

10 carp'ts
31 labo'rs.

This day 10 carp'trs & 31 laborers.

6 *tais.*
50: 6: cordes.

18 bordes.

There was lent p'r Mr. Osterwick to Andrea Dittis, the China Capt., six *taies* in small plate, and we had 50 bundelles straw cordes of king, cost 1 *ta.* 3 *m.* 5. And there was 18 bordes boght at 3 p'r a *mas*, is 6 *ma.*

The mans wife, whose hvsband was executed yesterday,

---

56) Not entered.

197

Marche 1615[6]

[fol. 89v.]]

A woman hanged her selfe.
2 sackes rise.

& shee fled, was fownd dead this mornyng, she haveing hanged her selfe vpon a tree. The China Capt., Andrea Dittis, had 2 sackes rise as the[y] cost.

14. This mornyng fayre calme wether, but sowne after a fresh gale at N? W., vering N?erly but verly littell wind or rather calme p'r night.

14 carp'trs.
35½ labo'rs.
Nota.

This day 14 carp'trs & 45½ labo'rs in all.

I gaue Andrea Dittis, the China Capt., 2 letters testimoniall (or of favor) in the names of Capt. Gotad & Roquan, to goe into China, yf in case they met w'th Eng'sh shiping.

25 *tais*.

And the China Capt., Andrea Dittis, had twenty & five *tais* lent hym in plate bars paid p'r Mr. Osterwick.

378½ *cattis* seaweed.

There was 378½ *cattis* sea weed bought this day, at 7½ *mas* p'r *pico.*, amontes vnto ;[57] also 14 bundelles great canes of Capt. China.

A pr'sant.

And Joco Condo Dono sent me a pr'sent of 3 hanches salt veneson, w'th certen shelfish called *woby*.[58] Matinga had

5 bales rise.

5 bales rise of [59] *gantes* p'r sack & 6 *gantes* p'r *mas*, for w'ch I answered.

15. This mornyng still fayre calme wether, but after a fresh gale at S. W., but vered to S., a stiff gale most p'rte of day & night following, w'th rayne after midnight.

15 carp'trs.
50 labo'rs.
50 *tt.* pepp'r.
A lettr to Capt. Whaw.

This day 15 carp'trs and 50 labo'rs in all.

I wrot a lettr to Capt. Whow & sent hym 50 *tt.* Pattania pep'r for a pr'sent. And Gentaro Same, the kinges youngest

To kinges brother Genta Samme.

brother, the adopted sonne of Bongo Samme, sent to buy 3 or 4 peeces stuffes, he being bownd to lye at the Emperours Court, viz.:-

2 peec. odony pister of 5 in a peec., at 3 Rs.,

---

57) Not entered.
58) *Awabi* 鮑, an ear-shell.
59) Not entered.

Marche 1615[6]

p'r *corg* amontes vnto .... *T.T.*   . 60)

1 pec. allecas of Rs. p'r *corge* .... *T.*   .

1 pec. borall or, of Rs.° p'r *corg* .... *T.*   .

Som totall amontes to & cost .... *T.*   .

W'ch, in respect ther was never nothing geven vnto hym before & he going to lye at Cort, was geven hym for a pr'sent. And Bongo Sama e[n]vited Mr. Osterwick & my selfe to dyner to morrow, as he hath donne the lyke to the Hollanders. [*fol.* 90*r.*]⌋

Invited to dyner.

There was 28 rownd poles rec. of Skidayen Dono of 3 & 4½ p'r *mas*. And ther was 16 rownd poles bought of a neighbour at 5 p'r a *mas*; and 26 bundelles straw for 2 *mas*. There went divers pilgrams to Tencha *dire*61) w'th an *ammabush*62) for their gide, the pilgrams haveinge letters written on the backs of their *keremons* (or coates).

28 rowndes poles.
16 rownd poles.
26 bundels straw.
Nota.

16. This mornyng a stiffe gale wind S'erly, w'th rayne in great aboundances all the affore nowne, but after drye wind slaking, & calme all night.

This day 15 carp'trs & labo'rs 7 in all.

15 carp'trs.
7 labo'rs.
Nota.

We went to dyner to Bongo Sammes, Mr. Osterwick & my selfe, where we met Capt. Speck w'th an other Duchman & a *boz*. We had very good cheare. And Genta Samme, the kinges youngest brother, came in at later end, & thanked me for the pr'sent geven hym the day before, & tould me he was going vp to the Court (after his brother) to the Emperour, vnto whome I desired hym to offer my service & that I made acc° to vizet them before it were longe, God sending our shipping to arive in saffetie.

17. This mornyng fayre calme wether, but sowne after a stiff gale N°erly most p'rte of day, but not soe much wind

Sonday.

---

60) This and the following figures, not entered.
61) *Tera* 寺, in composition *dera*, a [Buddhist] temple.—Thompson.
62) *Yamabushi* 山伏, an order of travelling priests.—Thompson.

Marche 1615[6]

<table>
<tr><td>13 carp'trs.
15 labo'rs.</td><td>p'r night, w'th fayre towardes day.</td></tr>
</table>

13 carp'trs.
15 labo'rs.
Capt. China
to Lan-
gasaque.
50 *cattis*
pepp'r to
Capt.
Whaw.63)
A lettr to
Jor. Durois.
2 *cakis*
30 boa[r]des.

p'r night, w'th fayre towardes day.

This day 13 carp'trs & 15 labo'rs in all.

I wrot a lettr to Jorge Durois p'r Andrea Dittis, the China Capt., who went this day to Langasaque & I lent hym our *foyfone* or bark, & wrot a lettr to his brother, Capt. Whow, and sent hym 50 *cattis* Pattania pepp'r for a present. This 50 *cattis* was nomenated before le 15 present. We bought 2 *cakis*, cost 2 *mas* & 30 boardes at 4 for a *mas*. [*fol. 90v.*]]

18. This mornyng rayny wether w'th wind N?erly but brock vp sowne after, w'th droping wether now & then som p'rte of the day, but dry p'r night & windie.

11½ carp'trs.
24 labo'rs.
4 trees.
1 *tay.*
5 trees.

This day 11½ carp'trs & 24 labo'rs in all.

We bought two fig trees, an orrenge tree, & a peche tree, cost all 1 *tay*, & 2 other oring trees, cost ;64) & had an oring tree, a quince tree, & a pere tree geven.

19. This mornyng a stiff gale, wind N?erly, cold wether, & soe remeaned all day, & the lyke p'r night.

11 carp'trs.
46 labo'rs.

This day 11 carp'trs and 46 labo'rs.

20. This mornyng still cold wether w'th a stiffe gale wind N?erly most p'rte of day, but not soe much p'r night, fayre cold wether.

9 carp'trs.
51 labo'rs.
9 pols.
2 fig trees.

This day 9 carp'trs & 51 labo'rs in all. And we bought 9 Rs. wud poles at 6 for a *mas*. And Capt. Speck sent me 2 Portingale figg trees.

21. This mornyng still cold wether, wind N?erly a fresh gale encreasing all day, & the lyke p'r night following, much wind dry cold wether.

2 tilers.
7 carp.
44 labo'rs.
1000 tiles

This day 7 carp'trs & 44 labo'rs.

And we receved 1000 tiles of all sortes to tile the new porche w'th 2 head tiles & we bought 9 rownd poles at 3½

2 hed tiles
9 pols.

p'r *mas*. [*fol. 91r.*]]

63) This marginal note must be put after the next one.
64) Not entered.

200

22. This mornyng still cold wether, wind N.º W'erly a fresh gale all day, but littell or no wind p'r night, still cold wether, &c.

7 carp'trs.
47 labo'rs.

This day 7 carp'trs & 47 labo'rs in all.

2 a [sic] lettrs to Mr. Nealson

I sent a letter to Mr. Nealson, p'r Jacob Swager, for the bathes at Ishew, he goeing to buy cattell of Bungo Samme, the king having geven them at iland to seed them on. Alson [sic] an other letter to Mr. Nealson p'r Vshenusque Dono to buy hense, pork & a beefe yf he fynd any good. And I

A lettr frõ Mr. Nealson.

receved a letter frõ Mr. Nealson, dated in Ishew at the bathe the 20th current, &c.

23. This mornyng still cold wether, yet calme or rather a small gale at S.W. most p'rte of the day.

6 carp'trs.
51 labo'rs.

This day 6 carp'trs & 51 laborers in all.

4 lettr.

And I sent away 4 letters, viz.:–

1 to Jorge Durois ⎱ p'r s'rvant of Skyamon Dono.
1 to Capt. China ⎰

1 to Mr. Nealson p'r conveance of Yasimon Dono.

1 to Mr. Wickham p'r servant of Tome Dono.

China Capt frõ Langasaque.

The China Capt. came back frõ Langasaque & brought me 2 China stooles for a pr'sent, w'th a baskit of great orranges.

A lettr frõ Jorge Durois.

And I rec. a lettr from Jorge Durois w'th 3 quince trees, 5 fogg slipps, an orange tree, & a peare tree, w'th some garden seeds. His letter was dated in Langasaque, le 25th

A lettr frõ Capt. Garrocho.

of M'rch, new stile. Also I rec. an other. He rec. frõ Capt. Garrocho, w'th certen rowles of ruske. The great shipp of

Amacan ship pvt to sea.

Amacan put to sea on Sonday last.   [fol. 91v.]⟧

Sonday.
Papist Ester.

24. This monryng fayre calme milde wether & not much wind after S. W'erly both day and night followinge, &c.

3½ carp'trs.
11 labo'rs.

This day 3½ carp'trs & 11 labo'rs in all.

I sent a bark to Sugian Donos grang (or farme) to fetch

6 trees

6 frute tres, viz.:–[65]

---

65) Detail, not entered.

Marche 1615[6]

Niquan, the China Capt. kynsman, dep'rted towardes China 7 daies past from Langasaque; from whence he sent me a peec. of rofesate red velvet for a pr'sent, & desird me to lend his wife 20 *taies* in his abcense to buy her pr'vition, for w'ch he would be accomptable at his retorne, & Andrea Dittis his shewrty for repañt.

1616.

25. This mornyng fayre mild wether w'th littell wind at S. W., but after a stiff gale w'th rayne towardes night, & in great quantety p'r night, w'th much wind S'erly.

4 carp'trs.
38 labo'rs.
Canes.

This day 38 laborers & 4 carpenters.

And we had greate canes of the China Capt. to make an arbor or shed for a vyne. And 6 rownd poles bought at 1 *mas* & 6 rayles or *nuquis* at 12 *condrins*. And a *bose*, frend to Capt. China, sent me 3 or 4 trees, 1 of peches & the rest of flowres.

6 poles.
6 rayls.
Frō *bos.*

26. This mornyng lowring wether, wind at S. W., yet re-meaned dry all day, & lyke night following, warme wether.

31 labo'rs.
A vine tree.

This day 31 labo'rs.

Vshenusque Dono gaue me a greate vine treee, w'ch I planted in our new orchard on the West side our gadong. And there was lent one bar of *oban* gould, to Andrea Dittis of 55 *tais* w'th 50 *tais* more, in plate of bars, is all one hvndred and fyve *taies* to be repaid at demand. And twenty *taies* in small plate to Niquans wife, for w'ch the China Capt. is surety, w'ch 20 *ta*. Mr. Osterwick paid & my selfe the 105 *tais*. And a caualero of Tabilo,[66] sent the China Capt. an oring tree, a pear tree, & 2 peche trees, w'th other flowrs, w'ch he gaue all to me, to plant in our new orchard.

105 *tais.*

20 *tais.*

6 trees.

News.

News came to Firando that the King of Shashma would passe this way som 3 or 4 dais hence.   [*fol. 92r.*]]

27. This mornyng overcast wether, wind S'erly, but re-

---

66) Tabira 田平, located on Kyushu coast facing Firando.

meaned dry wether all day, wind verying N°erly, a shift gale in thafter nowne, but no soe much p'r night.

48 labo'rs.
This day 48 labo'rs.

A lettr to Jor. Durois.
I wrot a lettr to Jorge Durois, sent p'r the Admiral his conveances, but after del'd the China Capt.

28. This mornyng fayre mild wether w'th a fresh gale, wind at N° W. all day, but littell or no wind p'r night, &c.

4 carp'trs.
44 labo'rs.
A lettr to Capt. Garo.
All keys lost.
This day 4 carp'trs & 44 labo'rs.

And I wrot answer to Capt. Garrocho of his of the 25th pr'sent.

All the keyes of our howse dores, being 6, were stolne, & one of them sent in truck of rise, w'ch coming to my knowledg, I laid hould on hym w'ch bought it to bring forth the p'rtie w'ch sould it, & kept hym prisoner in our Eng'sh howse all night, but could get nothing of hym. Soe, vpon the word of the China Capt. w'th 2 other neighbours, I let hym goe free vpon his promis to looke out for the p'rtie w'ch sould it. & soe we sett vp a bill in wryting, that I would geue a bar of plate to hym w'ch brought the kayes.

3 trees.
We had but 3 oryng trees frõ Sugien Dono, the[y] being so great the bark could bring no more.

A lettr frõ Mr. Nealson.
I rec. a lettr frõ Mr. Nealson, dated in Ishew, le 26th current.

29. This mornyng fayre mild wether, wind S. W'erly, a very stiffe gale most p'rte of day & night followth, w'th som rayne towardes day.

5 carp'trs.
30 labo'rs.
15 *cakis*.
King of Shashma.
To King Shashma.
This day 5 carp'trs & 30[67] labo'rs.

And we borowed 15 *cakis* or squar postes of the China *jurebasso*. And about nowne the King of Shashma passed by Firando & came to an ancor a league from Firando; whither I went to vizet hym, being accompanied w'th Mr.

---

67) This number is written upon cancellation of "46."

Osterwick, and carid a pr'sent of 2 barilles wyne, cost *T.*

,[68] 2 bundelles fysh, cost *T.* , & 2 damaskt

fowling peeces, cost *T.* . [*fol. 92v.*]]

And at our coming to the roade where he staid at an ancor, we fownd Tonomon Samme, the kinges brother, w'th Bongo Samme his vncle, ready to present the King of Shashma w'th a pr'sent, as also Capt. Speck was ready to do the lyke for the Hollandrs, having 3 other m'rchantes to accompanie hym. But Tonomon Samme willed vs both to stay till they had byn first w'th hym, & sent me word I should com next after; yet the Duch pressed forward p'r meanes of Zanzabars brother in law, & stept into the bark

Nota. before me. But at his retorne I tould hym, that all might heare me, that he knew well my place & ranke was to haue gon before hym, & caused our *jurebasso* to signefie as much to the King of Shashma, & that the King of England had vassales much greater then the prince (or county) w'ch governed the Hollanders, and that their state or government was vnder the comand of the King of England, he haveing garrisons of English souldiers in their cheefest fortes or places of strengh they had. In fine, the King of Shashma took notis of my speeches, & sowne after sent a greate load vnto me to thank me both for this pr'sent (as also for the other) the yeare past, & w'thall sent me 10

43 *taes.* bars of silver waying 43 *tais*, & the lyk som, as I vnderstand, was sent from hym to the Duch, after they had byn w'th vs.

Frõ Duch. But I forgot to note dowing [*sic*] the pr'sent geven p'r the Duch, viz.:–

1 greate gilded looking glasse.

1 or 2. *tattamis* stamet cloth } very good cullers.
1 or 2. *tattamis* stamet kersies }

---

68) This and the following prices, not entered.

I know not well whether the cloth as I sayed was 2 *tattamis* in a peec. or 1 *tattamy*. They pr'sented allso divers peeces of China stuffs, but I think they were for his followers, for the[y] put vp a petission to the king (as I think) to have trade into his cvntrey, but, as I vnderstand, were put offe till his retorne. As also I deliverd hym the Emperours letter, pr'cured formerly, to haue trad into all his dominions; but he gaue me no answer, but sent [*fol. 93r.*]] sent [*sic*] me word p'r hym w'ch brought the pr'sent that, at his retorne from the Emperours Court, he would com and vizet our English howse & geue me answer to content.

There was 5 *taies* of the plate geven to Goresano, our *jurebasso*, the rest was put to Comp.ª accompt.

A frend of the China Capt. sent me 2 orange trees and a peach tree frõ Tabola, I sending a bark & men to fetch them. Pedro the porter entertaynd at a *tay* p'r month. And I wrot a letter to Mr. Nealson & sent hym a bottell skarbear, an other of syder, & 6 loves bread; & Capt. China sent hym 2 boxes ma'lad, all sent p'r Yasimon Dono.

30. This mornyng rayny wether, wind S'erly, but pr'sently vered N.º W'erly, & soe N.º E., but dry in thafter nowne, & littell or no rayne p'r night.

I sent Goresano, our *jurebasso*, to a cavelero w'ch accompanid the Lord of Shashma yisterday, when he came to the English howse w'th the pr'sent, to thank hym for his paynes, & that I did not expect any pr'sent at all, yet, it being sent from so greate a prince as the King of Shashma was, I could not refuse the receaving therof. He retorned me answer that it was not for the vallu of the mony that the king sent it, but only as a token of good will, according to the Japon custom, & that I might be ashewred, yf we had a mind to trade into Shashma, that we should be welcom & fynd that gret man ready to further vs in what he might

Marche 1616

for the good entertay'm't he had at our English howse yisterday.

This day 4 carp'trs and 3 labo'rs.

And there was a barr more of *oban* gould of fifty five *taies* lent to Andrea Dittis, the China Capt., to send to his brother Whaw, to geue to the sonne of Twan Dono. I wrot

a lettr to Jorge Durois p'r conueance of China Capt., to buy garden seedes & candelles. Our nighbours enuited them selues to dyner to morow, it being our Easterday, I meane the 10 of two wardes & princepall men. 　　*[fol. 93v.]*⌋

31. This mornyng lowring wether, w'th a stiff gale, wind at N. E'erly, but after much rayne most p'rte of the day, yet not soe much p'r night, &c.

Our neighbours came to dyner, 24 persons.

There was reportes [*sic*] geuen out the Emperour is dead, and that Frushma (or Tushma) Tay, a great lord or prince in the North, is slayne p'r the Emperours people, coming from Edo to Mi'co; but I esteem this ordenary Japon newes, w'ch proue lyes. Also they report the King of Shashma taketh this voyag to reueng Frushma Tais death.

Aprill 1616.

01. This mornyng lowring wether, wind N⁰.erly, but after brok vp fayre wether all day & night following, cold wether, &c.

This day 5 carp'trs, & 35 labo'rs.

I receued a lettr frõ Mr. Wickham, dated in Osakay, the 22th vltimo, wherin he aduiseth me the tymbr & neales is pr'uided, & that the tymbr will be put abord a bark of Fingo to morow, fraight 10 *taies*. Also he reportes of news, but so variable yt it was not worth writing of. And I wrot an other

April 1616

lettr to Jorge Durois to buy 2 or 3 jarrs conserve, all that was left being geven to the King of Shashma, & Tonomon Samme, Sangero Samme, & Soyemon Dono sending after to me to haue had som for the said king, &c.

02. This mornyng faire cold wether, wind N°erly, and soe remeaned all day, but littell or no wind most p'rte of the night, still fayre wether.

5 carp't.
40 labr's.
A letr to
J°. Dorois.

3 great
cakis.

This day 5 carp'trs & 40 labo'rs.

I wrot an other lettr to Jorge Durois p'r conveance of China Capt., to same effect as former, to call to the Caffro for thother, yf he del'd it not. We bought 3 greate square postes or *cakis* for portall, cost, all three, one *tay*.

[fol. 94r.]]

03. This mornying fayre calme cold wether, rack W'erly, & after a small gale variable every way, but littell or no wind p'r night.

8 carp'tes.
42 labo'rs.
A lettr to
Mr.
Wickham.

A lettr to
Mr. Nelson.

A lettr frõ
Mr. Nelson.

This day 8 carp'rs & 42 laborers.

I sent a lettr to Mr. Wickham, dated the 30th vltimo, but kept till now, sent vnder cõvart [*sic*] of Capt. Speck. Also I sent an other letter to Mr. Wm. Nealson of same date, but kept till now; advsing also of recept of a letter of his, dated the 29th vltimo, rec. at this instant of Migaell *jurebassos* report, tuching Mr. Wickhams leand behavior at Edo, &c.

And we borowd 8 peec. tymbr of Capt. Speck, and ther was sould & del'd vnto Capt. Spakes *jurebasso*, Symon, for

Capt. Spek 20 *cattis* tynne at 4 *mas* p'r *catty*. And Mr. Osterwick paid 25 *tais* in plate of bars to Skydian Dono, vpon acc° tymbr.

The King of Shashma went our [*sic*] of harbo'r at Fyrando this mornyng. And Sugian an [*sic*] Dono sent me a fyne tree of flowers to plant in our garden.

04. This mornyng dark overcast calme wether, somthing cold, rack frõ W., w'th som drops of rayne in the after

nowne, but dry wether & littell wind p'r night.

7 carp'trs.
30 labo'rs.

This day 7 carp'trs and 30 labo'rs.

10 bu'dles.
straw.
20 bundles.
Nota.

69) Dono a caualero on thother syde sent me 10 bundells of rise straw towardes building walles, and we bought 20 bundelles of Synemon Dono.

The wife of a fellow, w'ch hath stolne 17 *mas* of themperous plate & is run away, is seazed vpon w'th her sonne & servantes & all she hath, & were to haue byn put into pr'son. Soe her frendes came to me & Andrea Dittis to speake to the justis for her, w'ch we did. Soe they staid her frō going into pr'son, & take councell what is to be donne

70 tiles

therein. And we had 70 end tilles to repare roofe gadong.

[*fol. 94v.*]]

05. This mornyng fayre mild calme wether, but sowne after a stiff gale Nºerly most p'rte of the day, but littell or no wind p'r night, rack W'erly.

9 carp'ts.
21 lab'rs.
A lettr. to
Jor. Durois

This day 9 carp'rs & 21 labo'rs.

I wrot a letter to Jorge Durois to same effect as my 2 former, p'r Caffro, & conved of Capt. China, and sent this lettr p'r Goresanos wife; and in it the lettr, I thought, had

caffro
Antony.

byn carid p'r the Caffro, but he was sent for back, & Soyemon Dono desired he might be kept at English howse as Jnº, the other Caffro, was at the Duch. So he brought me back my letter, telling me he was sent for back, when he was onward towardes Langasaque halfe the way.

Mr. Nelson
fō Jshew.
A lettr
from Jⁿ
Durs.

Mr. Nealson retorned to Firando frō Jshew and I rec. a lettr frō Jorge Durois, dated in Langasaque, le 13th of Aprill, new stile, w'th 84 tallo candelles & a littell hard wax; also an other lettr frō Capt. Garrocho, dated in

A lettr
frō Cap.
Garocho.

Langasaque, le 12th ditto, w'th a lettr for Andrea Dittis, the China Capt., w'ch I del'd hym.

---

69) The name, not given.

April 1616

06. This mornyng faire calme wether, but after a fresh gale, wind most of day N̊erly, rack from West, w'th rayne som 2 howers before day.

10 carp'trs.
15 labo'rs.
This day 10 carp'ts & 15 labo'rs.

100 *tais.* And I del'd one hvndred *tais* plate bars to Mr. Osterwick, to chang for small plate & to pay 25 *tais* to Skydayen Dono, he retornyng the former 25 *tais* back, not being to his lyk-

8 postes. ing. We rec. 8 rownd plates small sort of Skydayne Dono.

Sonday. 07. This mornyng rayny wether, wind N̊erly, and soe re-meaned all day, small slitie rayne & like p'r night follow-ing, but littell or no wind p'r night.

10 carp'trs.
01 labo'r.
This day 10 carp'trs & 1 labo'r.

Tonomon
Samme.
Tonomon Samme, vnderstanding of my golden fish, sent to desire to haue it; so I gaue it hym, & he gaue me a great black dogg. He desired to haue a littell pepp'r & som cloues,

2 *cat.* clovs. w'ch was also sent hym, som 2 *cattis* pepp'r & a few cloues.

[*fol. 95r.*]

Japon feast
*Sanguach
Sanch.*
08. This mornyng lowring mistie wether, littell wind N̊erly, but after a fresh gale, drislinge wether all day not to be accompted rayne, & lyke p'r night but more winde. I sent

1 barill wine. Matin a barill wyne, cost .70)

09. This mornyng a fresh gale wind N̊erly, overcast lowring wether, w'th sleete or mist before nowne, but dry after nowne, as the lyke p'r night w'th wynde.

10 carp'rs.
06 labo'rs.
This day 10 carp'trs and 6 labo'rs.

A lettr to
J̊ Durois &
1 to Garro.
And I sent 2 letters to Jorge Durois & Capt. Garrocho, dated yisterday but kept till this day; & sent J̊ som salue for green wownd w'th Jurryelana71) seedes, cost 2 *ma.* 2½ *co.* & the baskit, w'ch brought the candelles, & answer of his lettr & Garrochos, dated in Langasaque, le 12th & 13th ditto, new stile; & sent then p'r the *Tuerto* Debrire to

---

70) Not entered.
71) Juliana(Span.), galliflower.

209

April 1616

Andrea Dittis, China Capt., three *mas* wight Priaman gould, to pay 14 p'r one in plate bars gould 22 peeces. And

we borowed 40 boardes *sugie*[72] thyn of China Capt.

10. This mornyng lowring wether w'th a stiffe gale, wind N? E'rly, yet remeaned dry all day, wind slackyng & the lyke p'r night following.

This day 10 carp'trs & 21 laborers.

I had a peece of byrams nill for my owne vse, being roteaten, of 14 Rs? p'r *corg*, rated at 6 *mas*. And the China Capt.,

Andrea Dittis, gaue me a peece crisped white silke, lyke sipers.[73] Mr. Osterwick said he bought the lyke at Bantam for 2 Rs? of 8.

And we had 2 barkes of gravill to day.   *[fol. 95v.]*⌋

11. This mornyng, lowring wether littell wind N?erly, but sowne after broke vp fayre son shine wether all day, & the lyke fayre wether night following.

This day 10 carp'trs & 13 labo'rs, & Tomo to cawke.

The China Capt., Andrea Dittis, went on pilgremage to a pagod neare Goto, for a voy [*sic*] he made for recovering of his brother Whaws health, &c.

Oyen Dono envited vs to dyner to morrow. We had 320 tilles flat for gadong walles.

12. This mornyng fayre calme wether or rater a littell wind N?erly, but after a stiff gale all day & the lyke all night following, dry wether.

4½ carp'ts.
13 labo'rs.
A lettr frõ
J? Durois.
36 candls.

This day 4½ carp'trs & 13 labo'rs.

And I rec. a lettr frõ Jorge Durois w'th 36 tallo candls, p'r our *jurebassos* wife, but she retorned w'thout geting her father set at liberty, Twan not being willing to despence w'th hym.

Mr. Nealson, Mr. Osterwick, & my selfe went to dyner to

---

72) *Sugi* 杉, Japanese cedar.

73) *Sipres*, or *cipress*, a kind of gauze or crape.—Thompson.

April 1616

Oyen Donos this day, & were well entertayned, and amongst other speeches we had conferrence of the Hollanders presumynge to haue entrance to the King of Shashma before vs, & of my reprouing Capt. Speck for it, &c. But all took it rather for a reproofe to the Duch then otherwais, in respeck, the King of Eng'd keepeth garnison in the princepall fortresses they haue, at his charge. They

News.
Pasqual de Banais.
Anto. Dies.

Hollanders can not deny yt. There came 2 Spainardes[74] from Edo this day, and tould me it is comonly reported aboue that the Emperour is dead, & that they met the King of Figen going to Shronge w'th greate forcese. So they esteem their will be warrs aboue. They said the[y] thought Mr. Wickham & Mr. Eaton were providing to com to Firando w'th such matters as they haue resting, standing in dowbt what might ensue.

China. Capt. retound.

The China Capt., Andrea Dittis, retorned from his pilgremage he took in hand for recovering of his brothers

8 canes.

health, &c. We had 8 greate bambous or canes of the China Capt. this day.   [*fol. 96r.*]]

13. This mornyng fayre wether w'th a stiffe gale of wind N?erly all day, but rayne towardes night, & so remeaned all night, but not soe much wind, &c.

10 carp'trs.
11½ labo'rs.
Nota.
90 great neales for tyles.

70 bandls strow for 5 *mas*.

This day 10 carpenters, & 11½ laborers.

Pasquall the Spaniard made enquiry w'ch of the English in Firando was Mr. Wickhams kinsman, & in the end it proued to be Mr. Osterwick, vnto whome he sent *recoudo*[75] that he had sould 2½, I say two *cattis* & a halfe, of excellent white amber greece at one hvndred *taies* the *catty*, & gaue Mr. Osterwick order to receve the payment; as also he sent an other *catty* of the lyke to Capt. Jourden to Bantam p'r Mr. Copindall, refusing to sell it heare to me for the Com-

---

74) The names of these Spaniards are put in the margin.
75) *Recado* (Span.), message.

211

panies vse at twenty *taies*, haveing secretly emploid others before to haue sould it for a greater price, but could not. Thus now am I not deceaved in hym, that I imagened he had made an India voyage in the Liqueas, having fingered 4 or 5 *cattis* of excellent amber greece, w'ch made hym to stand vpon his puntos to haue gon away in som Japan junck or Holland ship for Pattania or Bantam. Yet let both hym & the world judg of me yf I dealt frendly w'th hym (I meane Mr. Wickham), when I let hym put to acc° for his

For his wagis.

wagis[76)] what he would, & yet, over & aboue, lent hym one hvndred and fiftie Rialls of eight to make benefite of, & gaue hym as much w'th it of my owne to doe as a frend, yf occation were offred. But he retorned me my money as I del'd it, & emploid all his owne, *vt supra*, &c.

Capt. Speck camt to vizet me, & amongst other matters I tould hym I marveled he thrust hym selfe forward to haue entrance to the King of Shashma before my selfe. His

Nota.

answer was, he knew no reason to the contra[r]y, & that in these p'rts he tooke the Graue Moris & the Estates of Holland to be as much as the King of England, yf not more, &c.

To supp'r to China Capten.

The China Capt. envited Mr. Nelson, Mr. Osterwick, & my selfe to supp'r amongst many Japans, &c.   [*fol. 96v.*]]

Sonday.

14. This mornyng raynie wether wind N°erly, & soe remeaned all day little wind & small misty rayne, but dry wether all night w'th much winde, *vt supra*.

8 carpts.

This day 8 carp'trs, & 3 labo'rs.

3 labo'rs.
A lettr frō
Mr. Eaton.
Tymbr.

I receved a lettr from Mr. Eaton, dated in Osakay, le 24th of Marche, sent p'r a bark of Figen w'th tymber, viz.:–

Buanuqo,[77)] (or) boades, 1200, in 100

---

76) These three words are taken from the margin after a guide mark.
77) These are evidently the names of Japanese various kinds of timber, perhaps including *bōnuki* 棒貫, *sugi-geta* 杉桁, *takanuki* 高貫, &c.

bundelles of 12, cost......................	*T.* 03:	0:	0
Sugingeta, (or) rayles, 0500, at 27			
mas p'r. 100, is	*T.* 13:	5:	0
Beauff, (or) rayles, 0300, at 2½			
condrin p'r peece	*T.* 07:	5:	0
Shishiro, (or) boardes 0040, at 58			
condr. peece, is	*T.* 23:	2:	0
Tacca nvca, (or) sqr. p°[78] 0015, at			
6 *mas* peec., is	*T.* 09:	0:	0
Sugeta, (or) boardes, 0100, at 73			
condr. 10 boardes	*T.* 07:	3:	0
Som totall bordes & tymbr, cost...........	*T.* 63:	5:	0
More for boate hier carrying all aboard	*T.* 00:	5:	0
	64:	0:	0.

A lettr to Jor. Durois. And I sent a lettr to Jorge Durois in answer of his, rec. p'r Goresanos wife, & sent this lettr p'r Pasqual de Banais.

5 *tais*. 4 *tais*. Mr. Osterwick paid the 5 *taies* to Kisky Don. for rest fraight of the tymbr brought downe, 4 *tais* being paid p'r Mr. Eaton before. And Andrea Dittis the China Capt. had of our tymbr, as foll'th, to pay for it, as it cost, viz.:–

Shishero, (or) boardes, 3.

Sugeta, (or) bordes, 30.

Tacca nuca, (or) suqr. [*sic*] 02, heretofore.

Frō Tº Samme. 2 knives. 4 Holl. cheese. Tonoman Samme sent me 2 hanches venison for a pr'sent, & I sent hym 2 Eng'sh knyves & a quarter of a Hollands cheese, he sending after to buy som.

15. This mornyng overcast wether w'th a stiff gale wind Nº-erly, but remeaned dry wether all day, but not soe much wind p'r night, &c.

14 carrp'trs. 17 lab'r. Frō boz. This day 14 carp'trs & 17 labo'rs.

The *boz* or pagon prist aboue sent me a tree of white flowers for a present.

---

[78] Thompson read these two words as "spars."

April 1616

And I sent a lettr to Jorge Durois kept till to morrow sent p'r bark that went for boardes. *[fol. 97r.]*

16. This mornyng cold wether, wind Nºerly but remeaned fayre all day, & lyke p'r night, but calme.

This day 15 carp'trs and 22 labo'rs.

We sent a boate to Langasaque, to buy 400 Shashma boardes to cover the endes of our gadong; & Mr. Oster-

wick del'd vpon accº to a China w'ch went to buy them, 15 *tais* small plate, wherof one *tay* was for boate hier.

Our new wall of the North side, made p'r our neighbours, shronk soe it was this day broaken vp agane, or rather puld downe.

This mornyng fayre calme wether, and after a littell wind Nºerly most p'te of the day, but calme p'r night or rather a littell wind Sºerly.

17. This day 14 carp'trs & 23 labo'rs.

And news was sent me p'r Oyen Donos sonne that the Emperour had geven the King of Firando leave to retorne to his contrey, & that they thought he would be heare w'th-in this 10 dayes.

And at same tyme the King of Crates man came to vizet me, & said it was reported that the Emperour was very sick w'th a fall he had frõ his horce in going a hawlking, so that no man might speake w'th hym. Yet, notw'tstanding, Shun-go Samma[79] had geven leave to the King of Ffaccata & the King of Figen to retorne for their cuntries, but comended all the rest to stay his ferther plesure.

And I rec. a lettr frõ Jº Durois the Portingale w'th a jarr of conservs, cost foure *taies* & a halfe, as p'r lettr, rec. p'r one Leon Dono.

And towardes night a cavelero sent me word how it was

---

79) *Shōgun Sama*. See Note 27) for 1915.

214

trew that the Emperour was alive, and had spoaken to the King of Firando & two other princes only, of purpose to stop the mowthes of these w'ch reported hym to be dead; only it seemed to them he was not halfe well, &c. We rec.

2 *cakis.*

2 *cakis* of Skidayen Dono. [*fol. 97v.*]]

18. This mornyng lawring wether w'th littell wind S⁰erly, but after variable N⁰erly w'th rayne & thvnder in the after nowne, much wind p'r night S'erly w'th rayne.

15 carp'trs.
25 labo'rs.
660 tiles.

This day 15 carp'trs and 25 labo'rs.

We receved 660 tiles, viz., 360 for gadong walle and 300 tiling flat tiles.

A lettr frõ
J⁰ Durois.

And I receved an other letter frõ J⁰ Durois, dated in Nangasacque, le 24th of Aprill, new stile, wherin he advized me how the speeche went that Shashma Dono was building the fortres at Osakay and Frushma Tay w'th hym, &c.

Soyemon
Dono.
Nota.

Also Soyemon Dono sent me a lettr how they could not sell the m'rch'ndiz, viz., the white baftas they tooke for the King of Firando. Soe he willed me to take them back againe. Vnto w'ch lettr I retorned answer, I could not doe it in respeckt I had advized the Company into Eng'd of the sale thereof, as also the lyke to the agent at Bantam, &c.

From
Gonosque
Dono.
35 rond
postes.
Frõ Sky.
Dono.

Gonosque Dono sent me 2 hanches of venison for present. We rec. 34 rownd postes of Skidayen, called *yofen nuquy*[80] Skiamon Dono came frõ Langasaque & sent me a present of confittes & craknills.

19. This mornyng overcast droping wether w'th a stiffe gale, wind S⁰erly, & soe remeaned droping p'r fittes all day, but not soe much wynde, yet a gale N⁰erly p'r night.

15 carp'trs.
13 labo'rs.
Nota.

This day 15 carp'trs & 13 labores.

The 2 sea *bongews* came to vizet me, & amongst other matters we had speeches tuching Capt. Specks goinge

---

80) *Yosenuki* (?).

before me to salute the King of Shashma, & of my reproue-
ing hym for it, wherin they said I had reason & that they
knew it not till now.   *[fol. 98r.]*⌡

20. This mornyng lowring wether, wind Nºerly, but sowne
after broke vp fayre wether, & so remeaned all day and
night followinge.

17 carp'trs.
24 labo'rs.
Mr. Eaton
fō Osakay.

2 lettr frō
Mr. Wikham.

This day 17 carp'trs & 24 labo'rs.

Mr. Eaton arived frō Osakay w'th a Spaniard in his company, called   ,81) pilot of the ship w'ch came from
Nova Spania. Mr. Eaton brought me 2 lettrs frō Mr. Wickham, dated in Miaco, the 4th & 6 currant, in w'ch he wrot
me somthing humerously, both about busynes as also about
my misvsing of his gerle woman, w'ch is vntrew, &c.

3 lettrs.

2 basons.
10 dishes.

Also I rec. a letter frō Ricd. Hudson, w'th 2 others, 1 from
Capt. Adames sonne, & the other from our hostes at Miaco
& Osakay, he of Miaco sending me 2 pewter basons for a
pr'sent, & the other of Osakay 10 pewter pottage dishes.

And we rec. tymber of Skidayen Dono, viz.:–

79 *cakis, mates nuque*, of 2 *tattamy* long.

20 *cakis, tabu nuque*, of 2 *tattamis* long.

45 *nendangi*, or rownd poles, of 2 *tatt.*

Nota.

Mr. Nealson in a pot hvmor fell out w'th Antony the
kinges Caffro, & struck hym in my sight, &c.

Sonday.

21. This morng fayre calme wether, but after a fresh gale
at S. W., vering to Nº W., but calme p'r night very faire
wether.

17 labo'rs.
18 carp'trs.
213 [sic]
bordes.

13½ Rs. 8.

This day 18 carp'trs, 17 labo'rs.

We rec. 113 small boardes, q'tr, 6 p'r *mas* of Skydaen
Dono. I bought a duble silver & gilt salt, poz. 13 Rs. ⅛ Rsº
of 8 for same wight Spanish money.

A lettr to

The 2 Spaniardes went to Langasaque, & I wrot a lettr

---

81) The name, not given.

April 1616

to Jor. Douris p'r the pilot. *[fol. 98v.]*]

22. This mornyng fayre calme wether, but after a fresh gale S. W'erly most p'rte of day, but littel or no wind p'r night.

23 carp'trs.
28 labo'rs.
15 railes.

This day 23 carp'trs & 28 labo'rs.

We had 15 rayles of the China Capten, and I del'd 5 ould gould ringes of Matingas to the gouldsmith, to make new

Gould.

poz. 2 *mas* 0 *co*. 5c. w'th other gould w'ch poz. 2: 0: 8, [som totall is] 4: 1: 3, is 4 m. 1 *condrin* 3 cashes. And Mr. Eaton gaue me, 5 Japon beakers, 4 pottage dishes, 8 other Japon dishes, & a wassell bole.

ta. mo.
565: 2.

And I rec. 565 *tais* 2 *mas* plate bars of Mr. Eaton at his retorne, wherof 400 *tais* for his owne acc⁰, and 165 *tais* 2 *mas* of Mr. Wickhams acc⁰, viz.:–

400: 2: 0: of Mr. Eaton acc⁰.

100: 0: 0: from Mr. Wickham, sealed vp.

065: 2: 0: for goodes sould Spanish pilot on Mr. Wick. acc⁰.

I say rec. in all five hvndred sixtie & five *tais* two [*sic*] *mas*.

400 bordes.

We receved 400 boardes frõ Langasaque p'r the China

A lettr frõ
Jorge Durois.
1 jar
conserves.

w'ch we sent & cost all   .⁸²⁾ Also I rec. a lettr frõ J⁰ Durois, dated le 29th currant, new stile, w'th an other jarr conserves, cost 4 *tais*, &c.

23. This mornyng fayre calme wether, or rather a littell wind S⁰ W'erly, but after overcast clowdy wether all day, yet dry but som dropes of rayne p'r night.

33 carp'trs.
41 labo'rs.
Tymbr.

This day 33 carp'trs and 41 laborers.

And we rec. tymbr of Skidayen Dono, viz.:–

297: *nuquis* (or rayles).

017: *fashack*, or rownd poles.

070: inche bordes *fashock json*.

030: *cakis* or square post of 2 *tatta*.

A lettr to J⁰.

And I wrot a lettr to Jor. Durois of rec. of his, dated 29th

---

82) Not entered.

217

April 1616

currant, new stile, w'th jar conserves; *Tuerto*[83] re. more of Skidayen Dono, tymber, viz., 19, 2 inche planckes, [and] 40 *cakis*; and in 1 boate 700 howse tiles, & in an other 700 tiles more, viz., 450 howse, tiles 250 flat for gedong.

700 tils.
700 tils.

[fol. 99r.]⌋

24. This mornyng overcast lowring calme wether, but after nowne rayne w'th a stiffe gale, wind S'erly, but calme p'r night, & dry.

33 carp'ts.
43 labo'rs.
40 poles.

This day 33 carp'trs & 43 labo'rs.

And we bought 40 rownd poles, cost 2 *mas*, littell ons to cover carpenters shed. Tome Dono lent vs 20 mates or *tomas*,[84] and the China Capt. lent vs 6 bundells of small canes to cover carp't[ers] shed. And 40 matts bought of 2 others p'r Gorezan.

20 mats.
6 bundells
s. canes.

25. This mornyng overcast lowring wether w'th littell wind S'erly, but after broke vp and remeaned fayre wether all day, & lyke p'r night.

29 carp'trs.
33 labo'rs.
200 mattes.

This day 29 carp'trs and 33 labo'rs.

And we borowed 200 *tomas*, or straw mattes, of Sifian Dono, of 20 p'r *mas*.

26. This mornyng fayre wether wind S. W'erly, and so remeaned all day, & the lyke p'r night, but more wynd *vt supra*, hot wether.

30 carp'trs.
43 labo'rs.
3 tilers.
750 tiles.
A lettr to
King of
Firando.

Carpenters 30, and 43 labo'rs, & 3 tilors. And we rec. 750 tiles this day, howse tiles.

I wrot a letter to Figean a Camme, King of Firando, complementally, that I was glad to vnderstand of his safe arivall at Shrongo & kind entertaynm't of themperour; and that yf any shiping arived heare frõ England or our junck frõ Syam, that I would adviz hym thereof. This letter I sent p'r conveance of Oyen Dono.   *[fol. 99v.]*⌋

83) Perhaps *tuerto* (Span.), one-eyed. See the entry for April 9, 1616.
84) *Toma* 苫..

And I reconed w'th Gorezano our *jurebasso* for monies he disburced for me as foll'th, viz.:-

Gozeman.

	ta.	m.	co.
Pro a kettell or furnes for Matinga 0:	6:	5
Pr. a peec. taffety to lyne Domingos *kerymon* 1:	2:	6½
Pr. a barill wyne for Matinga 1:	1:	2
Pro gerdell for Mat. 2 frvntes 1:	0:	0
Pr. cotten woll for Jeffres kerremon 0:	1:	5
Pro a pere shews for Carnero, port'r 0:	3:	0
Pro fishing lyne for my selfe ....*T*. 0:	1:	0
Pro a blindman yt songe 85)..................*T*. 0:	1:	0
Pro dressing me 2 ould hattes...................0:	4:	0
Pro a *kitesoll*86) for my selfe 0:	2:	0
Pro a *cattan* for Domingo 0:	8:	0
	6:	0:	8½

6: 0: 8½ .

And he had of myne in his handes, viz.:-

ta.

in bar ....2: 1: 9 }
more in a bar ...3: 3: 0 } 5: 4: 9; is small *T*. 6: 3: 1½

So he rest indebted to me 2 *mas* 3 *condrin*.

27. This mornyng still fayre wether, wind S. W'erly, and so remeaned all day' hott wether, & the lyke p'r night w'th more wind then p'r day.

32 carp'trs.
51 labo'rs.
2 tylors.
100 *tas*.

Carp'trs 32 and 51 labores, & 2 tylors.

And I del'd one hvndred *tais* plate bars to Mr. Osterwick, vpon acc⁰ building, because the plate he hath (as he saith)

50 *tais*.

will yild no exchange, and 50 *tais* plate bars to Mr. Nealson, to chang for R. of 8 money for money w'th Yasimon Dono.

Tymbr.
750 tils.

And we rec. 14 plankes for bridg of 2 fathom and 08 *cakis*, all of Skidayen Dono. Also we rec. 750 howse tiles. [*fol. 100r.*]⌋

---

85) *Biwa hōshi* 琵琶法師 (?).
86) From *quita-sol* (Port.) An umbrella made of bamboo and paper.—Thompson.

April 1616

Sondy.

28. This mornyng overcast wether, wind S. W'erly, yet proved fayre all day & lyke p'r night following, &c.

35 carp't.
34 labo'rs.
2 tylors.

This day 35 carp'trs, 34 labo'rs & tylors.

And we rec. 3 square post for the water gate, 1 plank for the bridg, & 7 small *ficamons* servisable, all of Skidayen Dono. And we had 6 bundelles canes frõ Synemon Dono,

6 bundls
canes.
1070 tils.
Frõ Capt.
China.

gret canes, also we rec. 1070 tiles this day. The China Capt. gaue me 2 pe. China lynen, for 1 he willed me to geue to Mr. Eaton.

29. This mornyng close calme wether, but sowne after a stiffe gale at Nº W'erly w'th rayne most p'rte of the day, & the lyke p'r night, windy.

33 carp'trs.
34 labo'rs.
50 *tais.*

Cap'rs 33 and 34 labo'rs.

I rec. back the fyftie *tais* I del'd to Mr. Nealson to chang into Rº of 8, the p'rte being over curious in chowsing his money. And I reconed w'th Yoskey for monies laid out for me, viz.:-

To shewmaker for making buskins & 2 per. shews
    for my selfe 00:   4:   0
To Matinga, 1 peare *tabis* 00:   2:   6
To pint tugger 00:   5:   0
    Som totall is . . . . .01:   1:   6.

t. m. co.
1: 1: 6.

And I del'd hym a bar plate to change into small money poz. 2 *ta.* 9 *m.* 8 *co.* The China Capt., Andrea Dittis, had one *tay*

ta. m. co.
 2: 9: 8.
1 *tay* wight
Pri. gould.
P'd 1 *ta.*
1 *m.* 6 *co.*
R'd 2 *ta.*
2 *m.* 7 *co.*
A letter to
Jº Durois.
1 m'rk tile.

wight Priaman gould for his brother at 14 *tais* in silver vpon accº. And Yoskey changed the bar at 15 p'r c'nto, is in small plate 3 *ta.* 4 *m.* 3 *co.*, soe he paid hym selfe 2 *ta.* 2 *m.* 6 *co.*, and retorned vnto me 2 *ta.* 2 *m.* 7 *co.* I wrot a lettr to Jº Durois to same effect as my former p'r conveance of Capt. China, and we had I head tile w'th Companies mark.

[*fol. 100v.*]]

7 *fikamon.*

We bought 7 rownd postes (or *fikemons*), cost 1 *tay*, and we had 10 bundelles small canes from the China Capt.

220

April 1616

30. This mornyng overcast lowring wether, wind at N? W., a stiff gale, but after broke vp fayre all day, wind vering to S. W., & p'r night to N? W., faire weth'r.

34½ carp'trs.
24½ labo'rs.

Carp'trs 34½ and 24½ laborers.

2: *flcā*.
1: 1 pole.

And we receved postes or *ficamons* of Skiden Don and a long pole to make a laddr of, of Yayemon Dono.

A lettr
from Mr.
Wickham.

Also I rec. a lettr frō Mr. Wickham, dated in Miaco, le 13th currant, w'th an other from our host at Osekay, w'th a *barso* of *morofack* for a pr'sent. Mr. Wickham writ he del'd 25 *tat*. broadcloth to the King of Firandos man, of the 31 *tattamis*. We were to del'r Mr. Eaton, having sould the other 6 *tattamis* black before.

News.

Also of the lying news of Fidaia Sammas being alive, & that 200 Japons are put to death at Osakay for selling peo-ple after the wars, & that Micawna Camme Samme,[87] the Emperours sonns sonne, bought a *caboke,*[88] or player (a

240 tiles.

whore), cost hym *10000 taies*, is 2500 *ld.* str. We rec. 240 tilles of the tylores & lent 280 to Zanzabers wyves brother.

May   1616.

01. This mornyng fayre wether littell wind at N? E., after variable to S. W., yet dry all day, & the lyke p'r night fol-lowing, &c.

36 carp't.
53 labos.
Varnish.

Carp'trs 36 and 55 laborers.

We had varnish (or *orish*)[89] of Skidamon Dono for one

A carp'tr
set on work.

mas. And Torazomon Donos steward brought a carpenter desyring he might be sett on work & paid as I paid others.

[*fol. 101r.*]⌋

---

87) Matsudaira Tadanao, *Mikawa-no-kami* 松平三河守忠直, Ieyasu's grandson.
88) *Kabuki* 傾き or 歌舞伎, an actress.
89) *Urushi* 漆, lacquer.

May 1616

02. This mornyng fayre calme wether, & littell or no wind after at S. W., but calme p'r night very fayre wether.

38 carp'trs.
53 labo'rs.

Carp'trs 38 and 53 labors.

We reared the frame vnder the N? sidet [sic] of our howse this day.

Envited to dyner.
26 *ficamon.*

Zanzabar, *allius* Yasimon Dono, envited vs all to dyner this day & vsed vs kyndly, &c. We rec. 26 *ficamons* of Skidayen Dono.

03. This mornyng fayre calme milde wether, and after but littell wind S. W'erly most p'rte of the day, but night calme.

36 carp'trs.
57 labo'rs.
90 bordes.
32 bordes.
25 *tais.*

Carp. 36 and 57 labo'rs.

We receved 90 small bordes of Skydayen Dono of 6 p'r *mas*, and 32 more of same. And Mr. Osterwick paid Skidayen Dono vpon acc? tymber twenty five *tais* plate bars.

4600 tils.
4 *mas*
straw.
10 *cakis.*

And we receved in 2 barkes foure thousand six hvndred tils wherof 50 were for gadong walle, & ther was 4 *mas* in straw bought. Also we had 10 *cakis* of Sky Don.

04. This mornyng overcast calme wether, but after a stiffe gale, wind S. W'erly most p'rte of the day, but calme p'r night, fayre wether.

37 carp'rs.
48 labo's.
Tymbr.
1 pole for laddr.
40 bordes.
A lettr fr Jor. Durois.
1 bark ston.

This day 37 carp'trs & 48 labo'rs.

And we rec. 3 plankes for bridg & 10 *cakis* and 1 rownd tree to make a ladder of Yayemon Dono. And we had 40 more small bordes of hym of 6 p'r *mas*. And I rec. a lettr from Jor. Durois, dated in Langasaque, 12th May, new stile, complem'tall lettr. And we rec. a bark lading ston [of] Cushcron Dono.   [*fol. 101v.*]]

Sonday

05. This mornyng fayre calme wether, sultery hott, but after a small gale at N? W'erly most p'rte of day, and calme againe p'r night following, hot wether.

38 carp'rs.
33 labo'rs.
1 b'k ston.
950 tils.

Carp'trs 38 and 33 labo'rs.

We rec. a bark lading stones of Cushcron Dono. And we rec. 950 titles in one bark yisterday.

News.

The sonne of Tuan Dono of Langasacque[90] dep'rted to sea w'th 13 barkes laden w'th souldiers to take the iland Taccasange, called p'r them soe, but by vs Isla Fermosa. & it is reported he is at Goto, staying for more succors w'ch are to com from Miaco, & thought they meane to goe for Lequea, to look for Fidaia Samme.

Piter & Migell put away.

Peter, our new porter, and Miguell, Corean *jurebasso*, went about to haue gotten a Japon servant to the Jesuites to haue served in our English howse, w'ch I refuced to doe, but Peter let hym lodg one night in the howse, w'ch Gore-sano tould me of, w'ch both the other took soe in snuffe that they thretned to kill Gorezano. Soe I turned Piter out a dores. W'ch Miguell, in his vsuall drunken hvmor, stom-ocked & entered into termes w'th me that I had no reason to doe it; soe I turned hym out lykewais to beare the other company, &c.

06. This mornyng fayre hot calme wether, but after a stiff gale, wind S'erly most p'rte of day w'th rayne towardes night, but littell wind & much rayne p'r night.

35 carp'trs.
62 labo'rs.
35 bordes.
17 *cakis.*
20 *cakis.*

Carp'ters 35 and 62 labo'rs.

We rec. 35 small boardes of Skidayen Dono, of 6 p'r a *mas*, w'th 17 *cakis* or square postes. And also we rec. more 20 *cakis* or square postes.   *[fol. 102r.]*

07. This mornyng calme rany wether, but sowne after broke vp fayre wether, wynd variable from S. to W., but littell wind p'r night.

36 carp'rs.
labr's.[91]
60 bordes.
1 bark ston.

Carp'trs 36 and 15 labo'rs.

We rec. 60 bordes of 6 p'r *mas* of Skidayen Dono. Also we had a bark, lading stone from Cushcron Dono.

08. This mornyng fayre wether, wind at N? W'erly, and so

---

90) Murayama Joan 村山如安, son of Tōan.
91) Not entered.

May 1616

remeaned all day, but rather calme p'r night, fayre wether still.

28 carp'trs.
72 labo'rs.
5 tylors.
100 *tais.*

Carp'trs 28, labo'rs 72, w'th   92) tylors. And I del'd one hundred *tais* plate bars to Mr. Osterwick, wherof he del'd 50 *tais* lyke to Mr. Eaton to goe to Ikenoura to buy tymbr, because Skidayen Dono deceaveth vs.

The p'rticul'rs of tymbr is as foll'th, viz.:–

250 *cakis*, or squar post.
250 *nvkis*, or rayles.
800 small boardes, of   .93)
004 *mombashra*, or dore postes.
100 rownd postes.

50 *tay.*
20 *tais.*
800 tiles.
2 m'rk tils.
10 *cakis.*
105 bordes.
70 rayles.
Capt. Spek.

Mr. Eaton had 50 *tais* to geve the *dico*, Sobio Dono, and 20 *tais* to lay out or bring back, and we rec. 800 ordinary tiles & 2 mark tiles. And we rec. 10 *cakis* of Skidayen Dono, w'th 105 small boards, went lent 70 short rayles (or   )94) to Capt. Speck.

09.   This mornyng still fayre calme wether, but after a fresh gale wind S'erly most p'rte of day, but calme againe p'r night, dry wether.

36 carp'trs.
65 labo'rs.
3 tylo'rs.
100 *tais.*
45 *tais.*

Carp'ters 36 w'th 65 labores and 3 tilors.

I del'd one hvndred *tais* more in plate of bars to Mr. Osterwick, wherof he paid 45 *tais* same money to our nighbours for rest of ston walles 50 *tais* being advanced before

1400 tiles.
2 botes
gravill.

we rec. 1400 ordenary tiles to day, w'th 2 boates lading of gravill.   [*fol. 102v.*]⌡

10.   This mornyng fayre calme ryny wether, but after a small gale wind N°erly most p'rte of day w'th rayne towardes night, & soe contynewed all night followinge.

36 carp'ts.

Carp'trs 36, Labo'rs 71, and 2 tilo'rs.

---

92) Not entered.
93) Not entered.
94) The Japanese equivalent, not given.

224

May 1616

71 labo'rs.
2 tylo'rs.
Tymbr.

We receved tymbr of Skidoyen Dono, viz.:–

57 *cakis*, or squar postes.

32 *marraquy*, or rownd postes.

40 *nuquis*, or rayles.

2 barkes
stones.
4 of gravill.
2 sand.
820 tiles.
3 h'd tils.
To Synemon
Dono.

Also we had 2 barkes lading flat stones of Tome Dono, and Cushcron Dono, to pave yord, w'th 2 of gravill, & 2 more of gravill from China Capt. & 2 of sand. And we rec. 820 ordinary tiles & 3 head tiles. We lent 15 short rayles (or   )⁹⁵⁾ to Synemon Dono w'th 5 *ficamons*.

11. This mornyng rayny wether, very littell wind N̊.erly, but after variable on all p'rtes, rayne all the afore nowne, and some p'r night following, not much wind.

40 carp'trs.
11 labo'rs.
6 barkes
gravill.

Carpenters 40 and 11 labo'rs.

And we had 6 boates lading gravill this day, viz., 4 of China Capt., and 2 of Toma Dono & Cushcron Dono.

5 jars.
5 *barsos*.
A lettr frō
Mr. Wikham.
Sonday.

We lent 5 empty shark oyle jarrs to Tome Dono, and 5 *barsos* lyke ro China Capten. I rec. a lettr from Mr. Wickham, dated in Miaco, le 28th vltimo.

12. This mornyng fayre calme wether, or rather a littell wind N̊. W'erly, but after variable as day before, but a stiff gale S. W'erly, fayre wether.

38½ carp'trs.
13 lab'rs.
Chi. Capt.
to Langa.
A lettr to
J̊. Dur.
A lettr to
Mr. Ea.

Carp'trs 38½ and 13 labo'rs.

The China Capt. went to Langasaque p'r whome I wrot a letter to Jor. Durois, and an other to Mr. Eaton, to bring 3 or 400 bayes lyme a *pico*. of baskit, & an other of flower w'th a jarr of pork shewet, & sent J̊. Durois 10 sheetes pap'r.   *[fol. 103r.]*⌋

1 bark
gravill.
250 *tais*.

We had 1 bark gravill of China Capt. Mr. Wickham wrot in his lettr he had sould 50 pec. baftas at a *tay* p'r peece & receved 200 *taies* in p'rte paym't for wax.

13. This mornyng fayre wether w'th a stiffe gale, wind at S.

---

95) The Japanese equivalent, not given.

225

W., but after variable, & littell wind p'r night.

38 carp'trs.
51 labo'rs.
1 bark gra.
1660 tiles.
Tymbr.

Carp'ters 38 and 51 labo'rs.

And we had 1 bark gravill of China Capt'n. We receved 1660 tiles in 2 boates. And ther was rec. of Skidayen Dono, viz.:–

016 ordenary *cakis*.

004 *cakis* of 3 *tattamis* p'r peece.

270 small boards.

2 barkes
ston.
3 *ma*. straw.

And 2 barkes lading paving stones of Tomo Dono & Cushcron Dono; & 3 *mas* in straw.

14. This mornyng fayre wether, lyttell wind N? W'erly, & so remeaned all day, but calme p'r night, &c.

41 carp'trs.
65 labo'rs.
5 tylo'rs.
1896 tils.
3 *mas* in straw.
900 tiles.
Tymbr.

Carp'trs 41 and 65 labo'rs w'th 5 tylors.

And we rec. a bark tyles cont'g 1740, & out of towne 156, is all 1896 tyles. And 3 *mas* in straw. Also we had 900 tiles in an other bark, and we rec, tymbr frõ Skidayen Dono, viz.:–

051 ordenary *cakis*, (or squar postes).

160 *nvkis* (or rayles).

017 *marraquis*, or (rownd postes).

2 barks
ston.
Frõ Vna-
gense
Do.

And we had 2 barks lading paveing ston of Tome Dono & Cushcron Dono.

Vnagense Dono sent me a pr' sent of halfe a wild bore. [*fol. 103v.*]⌋

15. This mornyng fayre calme wether, & after a small gale variable frõ S. to N? p'r W., but calme p'r night, &c.

43 carp'trs.
59 labo'rs.
3 lettrs to
Langa.

This day 43 carp'ts, 59 labo'rs.

I wrot 3 lettrs to Mr. Eaton, China Capt. and Jor. Durois, advising Mr. Eaton to com away w'th what tymbr he had bought & buy no more, but bring 3 or 400 bags lyme. And sent these letters p'r Skeyo yt was our skullion.

120 bordes.
8 bordes.
24 bordes.

We rec. 120 small boardes to day of Yaymon Dono as I think for acc? of Skidayen Dono of 6 p'r *mas* w'th 8 inch

May 1616

bardes of 2 *tatta.* & 24 inch bord of 1½ *tattamy* of Yaymon Donos acc?, w'th the 4 bordes before of same of 1½ *tatt.*, is 28 in all of them. And we had 2 barkes lading tiles cont'g 1720 tiles, and our bark retorned w'th 18 *cakis* lent vs p'r the kynges *bungew.*

1720 tils. 18 *cakis.*

16. This mornyng fayre calme wether, but after a small gale N?erly, vering W'ward, & calme most p'rte of night following, &c.

42 carp'trs. 19 labo'rs.

Carp'trs 42, w'th 19 laborous.

And I rec. three hvndred & fyftie *taies* plate of bars of Oyen Dono, in full payment for the ould debt due p'r King of Firando, besids or aboue the 3000 *taies* due p'r hym last. I say the King of Firando oweth 3000 *tais* over & aboue this 350 *tais* now paid; w'ch three hvndred & fyftie *taies* Mr. Osterwick receaved.

350 *tay* of king. Nota. Mr. Eaton.

Also Mr. Eaton fell out w'th a Japon of Figen, whoe misvsed & struck hym w'th a staff & knockt hym downe, thinking to haue kild hym, for spite he bought tymbr at a hier rate then he. But Mr. Eaton, in defence of hym selfe, hath dangerously wownded the other.[96] But the Vmbrians had murthered hym. Soe he standes on his gard till I send to cleare hym the Vmbrians protecting hym.   [*fol. 104r.*]⅃

China Capt. frō Langasacque.

The China Capt. retorned frō Langasaque, & brought me word how Mr. Eaton was abused by them of Fingo, & that it was a marvell he escaped w'th life. So, p'r his councell, I sent a bark w'th 4 ores to cary a lettr to Mr. Eaton & w'thall sent an other in Japons to the *dico* of Ykanaura, desyring hym to haue a care that no violence were offred to the scrivano, *allius* Mr. Eaton, for that to morrow I ment to send a letter to the King of Umbra, his master, to haue hym set at liberty & retorned to me, as our pr'veleges

96) Murakami refers the reader to 2 letters of Eaton about this incident in *Calender* of *State Papers.*

227

May 1616

A lettr to K. Vmbra.

geven p'r the Emperour spesefied, as the King of Firandos man could testefie, whoe I ment to send Mr. Nealson along w'th in the mornyng about same matter. And so I gott Jubio Dono of Crates to write me a lettr to the King of Vmbra, *vt supra*.

Frō Capt. Whaw.

Capt. Whaw, the China Capt. brother, did sent me a pr'-sent of vallance for a bed, being of embradered. We rec. frō Skidayen Dono 25 *cakis*, and frō Mr. Eaton as followeth, viz.:–

25 *kakis*.
Frō Mr. Eaton.

119 *cakis*.
800 small board.
400 sakes white lyme.

12 *kakis*.
3 beanes.
2500 ord. tiles.
4 m͏ꞏk tiles.

Also we had rec. before but p'r kings *bongew*, 12 *cakis*, & 3 other greate beanes. And we rec. 2 bark lading of tyles, wherin were 2500 w'th 4 mark tiles.   [*fol. 104v.*]]

17. This mornyng fayre calme wether, but after a stiffe gale, wind S.ºerly espesially in thafter nowne, but littell wind p'r night w'th score of rayne.

42 carp'trs.
53 lab'rs.
4 tylo'rs.
10 caks.
40 bordes.
Mr. Nelson Vmbra.
60 *tais*.

Carp'trs 42, labo'rs 53 w'th 4 tylors.

We lent 10 *cakis* & 40 bordes called   97) w'ch came frō Langasaque to Soyemon Dono.

And I sent Mr. Nelson to Vmbra w'th the lettr written to the king & he carid 50 *tais* in plate bars & 10 *tais* in small plate w'th hym, paid hym p'r Mr. Osterwick. Also I wrot a lettr to Mr. Eaton p'r Mr. Nealson. We rec. in one boate 860 tiles, & in an other 210 tils, is all 1070 tils ordenary, w'th 4 head tiles.

A lettr to Mr. Eaton.
1070 tils.
4 head tils.

Leafe gould.

And the China Capt. lent vs leafe gould to gild one mark & 2 head tiles.

18. This mornyng raynie wether w'th littell wind S'erly, good store of raynge before nowne, & drisling wether in the after, as the lyke p'r night, not much rayne.

97) The Japanese equivalent, not given.

May 1616

Carp'trs 43 w'th 13 labo'rs. There came a man from Vmbra about the quarell of the Fingonians w'th Mr. Eaton,

saying they swagered mightely because they thought the man would dye.

This mornyng lowing wether littell wind W. E. but after variable, tornyng against to S., yet fayre wether all day, & lyke p'r night much wind S'erly.

43 carp'trs.
18 labo'rs.
A lettr frõ
Mr Nealson.

A lettr frõ
Mr. Eaton.

Carp'trs 43, w'th 18 labo'rs.

I rec. a lettr frõ Mr. Nealson at Fooky[98] 3 leage hence, being staid p'r contrary wind, but dep'rted frõ thence this mornyng before day. Also the small bark I sent to Mr. Eaton w'th a lettr retorned, & tells me the man w'ch he hurt is in no danger of death; yet not w't'standing they of Vmbra will suffer no man to speake to hym, not so much as hym w'ch carid hym my letter, nor a Spaniard w'ch came to hym frõ Langasaque w'th a pr'sent. I think it is the saturne-call hvmor of the ould kyng, because he is a Christian, he being a mortall enemy to that name for hatred of ye Jesuistes. [fol. 105r.]] And, after we were gon to bed, Tonomon Samme, the kinges brother, sent me word that he ment to send an expres to the King of Fingo[99] I say Fingo, & that yf I would write he should carry my lettr. I retorned hym word that I know not what to write to Fingo till I knew the certenty of what passed in Vmbra, w'ch will be when Mr. Eaton and Mr. Nealson (w'ch went for hym) retorned.

Capt. Speck lent vs 2 greate plankes of 5 inch thick & 2 tattamis long p'r peece.

20. This mornyng a stiffe gale, wind S'erly, fayre wether, & soe remeaned all day, and the lyke p'r night following, &c.

Carp'trs 42 w'th 34 labo'rs.

---

98) Haiki 早岐.
99) Cocks cancelled the Word "Fige."

May 1616

Nota.

I went to Soyemon Dono to tell hym I marveled them of Vmbra vsed the scrivano (*alius* Mr. Wm. Eaton) soe hardly that they would suffer no man to speake w'th hym nor let hym haue victuelles for money. He answered me that the Vmbrians kept such ward about hym for his good, because the Fingonians, being aboue 150 p'rsons, had mad bragges they would kill hym, &, Ikanoura being a littell towne (or village), were afeard of the worst, & so kept ward; but that they skanted hym of victuells he marveled, but he was assured it was not of mallice, but knew the place was bare of pr'vition, & that I might rest assured that, when the *bungew* w'th Mr. Nealson were arived, that Mr. Eaton should pr'sently be set at liberty; & in the meane tyme I must haue pasience, for their trowble was much more then ours. He also tould me that yf I would write Mr. Eaton or Mr. Nealson, that he ment to send a man expres to Vmbra this day. Soe I wrot them both, & sent them p'r a man sent frō Firando of purpose p'r kinges brother.

2 lettrs to Mr. Eaton & Mr. Nelson.

[fol. 105v.]

1700 tils. Rearing.

We had 2 barkes tiles to day of 850 in eache one, is 1700 in both barkes. We reared the building to the S'ward of our howse in Firando this day.

21. This mornyng a stiff gale wind still S'erly, but sowne after vered Nºerly, yet fayre wether all day, & lyke p'r night following w'th much wynde.

44 carp'trs. 62½ lab'rs. 2 tils. 850 tils. A lett to Jor. Durois.

Carp'ters 44, labo'rs 62½, w'th 2 tylors. And we rec. 850 tils more in 1 bark.

I wrot a lettr to Jº Dorois, & therinclozed the other I thought to haue sent p'r Skezo, kept till now p'r meane of contrary wynds, in w'ch lettr I advized hym of the trowbls of Mr. Eaton at Jkanaura in Vmbra; sent p'r servant Bugo Same.

And after, we rec. in 2 barkes, viz., in 1 530 tils & in the other 870 tiles, is all 1400 tils. Also we had 3 barkes lading ston, viz., 1. of Tome Dono, 1. of Cushcron Dono, [and] 1. of Synemon Dono. And we had 35 bundelles canes of the China Capt.

And towardes night I rec. a lettr from Mr. Nealson dated in the gulfe of Vmbra le 20th currant, & sent p'r the *bongew* w'ch went along w'th hym, whoe now retorned back, w'th many compl'entes from them of Vmbra, but deternen [*sic*] not to set Mr. Eaton at liberty till they had enformed the *Tono* of Fingo therof.

Mr. Nelson went to Jkanora to vizet Mr. Eaton & furnish hym w'th such matters as he stood in need of, vnderstanding the Vmbrians kept hym soe short. And we paid 15 *cakis* to China *jurebasso* borowd of hym. Yosky the butler, being sick, asked lycense to goe to his howse to take phisick.

[*fol. 106r.*]

22. This mornyng still a stiff gale, wind N⁰erly, and soe remeaned all day and night following, yet overcast lowring wether most in end, &c, & cold.

Carpters 46, & 62 labo'rs w'th 2 tilors.

And we rec. one barke of tils cont'g 650 tils, and 20 bundelles canes of China Capten.

23. This mornyng still a stiffe N⁰erly wind, lowring wether, but after proved fayre all day & lyke p'r night, but not so much wind p'r night.

Carp'trs 44, labo'rs 64, w'th 2 tilors.

And we rec. one bark lading of tiles cont'g 730 tils, & after 120 tils in Firando, w'th 600 in an other bark frõ Tabila, ys all 1450 tils. And we paid the China Capt. 40 bordes w'ch we borowd of hym called   , and lent Capt. Speck 10 more of some sort. Capt. Speck sent me a littell pot of butter of som 2 *ld*. Migell, our *jurebasso*, desired lycense to goe take phisick being very ill at ease, & as I think of the pox.

1400 tils.
3 barkes ston.
35 bu'des canes.

A let. frõ Mr. Nelson.

15 *cakis.*
Yosky sick.

46 carp'trs.
62 labo'rs.
2 tilors.
650 tils.

44 carp'trs.
64 labo'rs.
02 tylors.
1450 tils.
40 bordes p'd Capt. China.
10 same lent Cap̄.
Spek.
Frõ Cap̄ Speck.
Nota.

231

24. This mornyng fayre mild wether, littell wind N°erly, & soe remeaned all day, or rather vering to N°. W., littell or no wind p'r night.

Carp'trs 40 w'th 46 labo'rs.

We had fliing news how our ship the *Hozeander* w'th the Hollanders haue met w'th the great Portingall ship of Amacan & fought w'th her neare to the Liqueas & som escaping out of her ashore retorned p'r way of Xaxma to Langasaque w'th news, but know not the end of fight whether the[y] escaped or no. Of the w'ch I advised Jor. Durois p'r Skezo or his *cafero* in a lettr, but I esteem it ordenary Japon news w'ch are lyes, [*fol. 106v.*]⏌ dowbting (according to the English proverb) that it is to good to be true, yet accoding to an other, I wish that there never com worse news to the towne.

Migell our *jurebassos* wife came & brought me a small jarr of *achar*[100] for a pr'sent, desyring me to exskews her hvsband in that he abcented hym selfe to take phisik in this tyme of busynes. And after I was gon to bed, Soyemon Dono sent to haue a *jurebasso* to com to hym about news they had from Jkanoura. Soe I went my selfe vnto hym, & he tould me that the King of Fingo had sent a lettr to Vmbra, wherin he advised that allthough the English had kild a man of his, he made no reconyng of it, only he was advised that som of Firango that was in comp'ny of the English had stolne somthing wherby this quarrell grew. This was the matter he sent to tell me of, & that to morrow they ment to send a man expres to Jkanoura about this matter. So I desyrd hym he might carry me a lettr to Mr. Nealson, &c.

25. This mornyng still fayre mild wether, calme, & verly littell wind after variable frō S. to N°. p'r W., but rather

---

100) Hindustani, pickles.–Thompson.

calme p'r night, &c.

Carp'trs 35 w'th 28 laborers.

Mr. Nealson retorned frō Jkanaura, but Mr. Eaton staid behind till the *bongew* retornd from Fingo. The man Mr. Eaton hvrt dyed the other night, wherevpon they sent for

Co. John, Mr. Eatons boy, & cut afe his head, for that he began the brute; & thought to haue donne the lyke p'r Skite, because he took Mr. Eatons part when they misvsed hym, and the lyk of Tome, his *jurebasso*. All was about a peece of straw cord not worth a farthing.   *[fol. 107r.]*⌋

And I rec. 3 lettrs and a note frō Mr. Eaton p'r Mr. Nealson, dated the 23th & 24th curant, the note manifesting the tymbr, boardes, & lyme he had bought, viz.:-

	ta.	*m.*	*co.*
250 *cakis*, at 13 *tais* p'r c'nto, is ....*T.* 32:	5:	0
100 rownd postes, or *marakis*, 3 p'r *mas* .....*T.* 03:	3:	0
250 *nukis*, at 5 p'r *mas* ....*T.* 05:	0:	0
004 *mombashta*, or dore postes ....*T.* 04:	3:	0
This paid to *bongew* at Ika...............*T.* 45:	1:	0
Also 400 saks lyme at 3½ *condrin* 14:	0:	0
800 boardes at 7 p'r *mas* ....*T.* 11:	4:	0
	70:	5:	0

Also he write he rec. 100 tallow candelles of Georg Durois at Langasaque, wherof he burned 23 in pr'son & Mr. Nealson 5 p'r way. So Mr. Nelson brought 72 to Firando. And Mr. Nealson del'd [*sic*] Mr. Eaton, viz.:-

	ta.	*m.*	*c.*
In plate of bars ....*T.* 37:	6:	5
& in small plate ....*T.* 12:	1:	3
Som totall ....*T.* 49:	7:	8

And we rec. 2 barkes lading of tiles in eache of them,

900 tiles, is 1800 tils.

26.   This mornyng fayre calme mild wether, but sown after a fresh gale of wind S'erly, most p'rt of day, but vered

W'erly towardes night, calme p'r night.

38 carp'trs.
62 labo'rs.
4 tyls.
A lettr
frō Jor.
Durois.
Tymbr.

Carp'trs 38 w'th 62 labo'rs & 4 tylors.

I rec. a lettr fro Jor. Durois, dated in Langasaque, the 2th of June, new stile, in answer of myne sent p'r the serv'nt of Bongo Samme. We receaved a barkes lading of tymbr frō Jkanaura of the p'rcell bought p'r Mr. Eaton, viz.:–

   69 *cakis,* of 13 *tais* p'r c'nto.

   04 dore postes, or *mumbashta,* at 4*ta* 3 *mas* all.

   102 *nukis,* or rayles, of 3 p'r *mas.*

Also a bark lading of tyles, cont'g 900 tiles, and 7 *condrins* in canes to make a malt hvrdell.   *[fol. 107v.]*⌡

I wrot a lettr to Mr. Eaton to buy 3 or 400 small boardes w'th 150 inch bordes of 2 fathō long, & to bring or send them & the 100 *marakis* first. Also I wrot an other lettr to the *dico* of Jkanoura to desyre hym to geue me boardes for the *cakis* & *nukis* not sent away. And we rec. 22 inche boardes of 2 *tatta.,* vpon acc? of Yayemon Dono.

Also towardes night the bark Mr. Eaton went in retorned from Jkanoura & brought me a lettr from hym, dated the 25th current, wherin he make mention of these tymb'rs following w'ch are com in her, viz.:–

   58 *cakis*

   51 *nvkis*   } frō Jkanaura.

   31 *marakis*

27.   This mornyng fayre calme wether, but after a small gale, wind N? W'erly most p'rte of the day, but calme p'r night, very hot wether.

A lettr to
Mr. Eaton.
38 carp'trs.
36 labo'rs.
27 bordes.
12 bordes.
8 con. canes.

I wrot answer to Mr. Eaton of recept of his dated 2 dais past, and sent it p'r bark man that carid the other.

Carpenters 38 w'th 36 labo'rs.

Also we rec. 27 inche boardes of 2 *tattames* w'th 12 small board of 1 *tattamy* long vpon acc? of Yamemon Dō, and 8 *condrins* in canes for an other melt hvrdell.

28. This mornyng still fayre calme hot wether, and after but littell wind variable, enclying S'erly but calme p'r night, &c.

41 carp'trs.
40 labo'rs.
1 tylors.
21 sbordes.
7 bordes.
A lettr to
Jor. Durois.

358 tils.
330 tiles.

Carp'trs 41 w'th 40 labo'rs & 1 tylors.

We [re]ceved 21 inch bord of 2 fatham vpon acc? of Yayemon Dono, w'th 7 small boardes of 6 p'r *mas*. And I wrot answer to Jor. Durois of the recept of his lettr of 2th June, new stile. Also we rec. in 1 barke from Tabola 330 tiles w'th 28, other tils from a boy, is all 358 tils. But we retorned the 28 tils bark to the boy, so restes 330 tiles. *[fol. 108r.]*⌋

29. This mornyng still fayre calme hott wether, but after a fresh gale variable frõ S. to Nº W., but calme p'r night, &c.

45 carp'rs.
17 labo'rs.
Mr. Nelson
to Jka.

Carp'rs 45 w'th 17 labo'rs.

I entred into cowncell w'th Mr. Nealson & Mr. Osterwick, whether it were best to send Mr. Nealson back to Mr. Eaton w'th a bark to bring hym away, yf he be set at lyberty at the retorne of the *bongew* from Fingo, as they pr'mised he should. So it was concluded vpon, &, because I had ernest occation to vse Gorezano in howse, I got lycense of Capt. Speck to haue a *jurebasso* w'ch s'rvd the Duch, w'ch he granted me. But when they were ready to dep'rt, there came a Japon & whispered our Duch *jurebasso* in the eare, whoe pr'sently refuced to goe on our pr'tended affares. So I was forced to send Gorezano agane w'th hym & a soaldier of the kinges, whome Tonomon Same, the kings brother, sent w'th them at my request. The pointes of busynes tuching Mr. Nealsons proceading apeareth in a memoriall of

A lettr to
Mr. Eaton.
A lettr frõ
Jor. Durois.

this dapte [*sic*], the coppie wherof I kept, &c. I wrot a lettr p'r hym to Mr. Eaton and rec. a lettr frõ Jor. Durois, dated in Langasaque, le 5th of July, wherin he wrot me the news of the meeting of our Eng'sh shipp w'th that of Amacan was a lye, only the great ship toed a boate after her, wherin were 2 horses w'th provision of meate for them & 4 or 5 p'rsons to look vnto them, but, p'r stormy wether, were broaken frõ the shipp & cast on the cost of Xaxma, having passed much danger, the bark being sunke, &, 4 got vpon a peece of tymbr, living 5 days w'thout meate or drink.

6 laskaras.
2 Caffros.

I say 8 gott on it at first, wherof 4 dyed before they got aland at Liquea. *[fol. 108v.]*

30. This mornyng fayre calme wether, but after a fresh gale of wind most p'rte of the day S. W'erly, & calme p'r night, &c.

43 carp'rs.
21 labs.
3 [sic] sakes barly.
8 bordes.
7 plantes.
24 bordes.

9 *marky.*

Carp'ters 43 w'th 21 labo'rs.

Jubio Dono of Crates lent vs 5 sackes new barly, of 51 small *gantes* p'r sack, till we could get other to malt. And we receved 8, 2 fatham inch bordes w'th 7 plankes of 1½ fathom, 2 inch such as Skidayen Dono del'd to make the bridg, w'th 24 small bordes all vpon acc? of Yayemon Dono. And Tayemon Dono, our carpentr, lent vs 09 *marrakis* (or rownd tymbers).

31. This mornyng still fayre calme wether, but sowne after a fresh gale, wind N?erly most p'rte of day, but calme p'r night, &c.

46 carp'rs.
31 lab'rs.

7 *ta.* 8 *m.*
for cutel.

Carp'trs 46 w'th 31 labo'rs.

And we sould 10 fardelles rotten cuttelfish to our fishmonger for 7 *tais* 8 *mas* to tak fish for howse in payment. This cuttellfish was bought for first voyag of our funck to Syam, &, she loosing for voyage, new put in place.

June 1616.

01. This mornyng still fayre calme wether, but after a fresh gale S'erly most p'rte of day, but calme p'r night, very hott wether.

37 carp'trs.

Carp'trs 37 w'th 32 labo'rs.

32 labs.
23 *markes*.
We bought 23 *marrakis* at 2½ p'r *mas* our carp'trs wanting tymbr to work vpon.

Sonday. 02. This mornyng still fayre calme wether, but sowne after a stiff gale, wind S'erly, yet drye wether all day, but rayne most p'rt of the night.

35 carp'trs.
22 lab'rs.
A lettr frō
Mr. Nealson.

Carp'trs 35 w'th 22 lab'rs.

I rec. a lettr frō Mr. Nealson, dated in Jkanoura, le last of May, signefying he staid the retorne of the *bongew* frō Fingo, & that Mr. Eaton was better vsed [*fol. 109r.*]⏟ now then heretofore, & that the *bongew* w'ch vsed Mr. Eaton soe strictly is put of of his place & lyke to loose his head for dutting affe our servantes head.

2 lettrs to
Mr. Eaton.
Tymbr.

Also I rec. 2 lettrs frō Mr. Eaton, dated in Jkanaura, le 29th & 31th of May, w'th a bark, lading of tymbr, viz., 05 *kakis*, 66 *marakis*, 97 *nukis*, all of ould accompt, and 50 *marakis* of a new acc? of 4 p'r *mas*. And sowne after arived an other bark from Langasaque w'ch tuched at Jkanowra,

420 bodes.
A lettr to
Mr. Eaton &
Mr. Nelson.

& brought 420 small boardes, cost all 6 *taies* & 6 *mas* for fraight. And I wrot a lettr to Mr. Eaton & Mr. Nealson p'r bark of Jkanoura, advising of rec. tymbr w'th 418 boardes frō Langasaque. As also I thought best to buy the 100 bordes of 4 *tatta*. at 3½ *mas* pees., & the 200 of 2 *tatta*. at 73 *mas* p'r 100 bodes according as he wrot me the[y] prised

40 bordes.

them. And we bought 40 boardes at 5 p'r *mas* greate plate, w'ch bordes came frō Jkanoura.

Tymbr.

Also we rec. tymbr of Yayemon Donos accompt as foll'th, viz.:–

13 jnch bordes of 2 *tatta*.
10 plackes of 1½ fathom 2 jnch thick.
25 small boardes.

Nota.

The Hollanders reared a new gadong this day, as bigg as their other, & made an other thatcht one a mile ofe, to buld shiping & put tymbr in, & haue mad other much

237

building this yeare, planted 2 orchardes, & made a new key
out of the sea. *[fol. 109v.]*⌋

03. This mornyng lawring rayny wether w'th a stiffe gale,
wind S'erly, but after nowne vered N⁰ W. but rayned all
day, & lyke p'r night, but not much wind.

36 carp'trs.

Carp'ters 36 w'th 07 labo'rs.

07 lab'rs.
A lettr
to Mr.
Nēlson.

I wrot a lettr to Mr. Nealson, p'r the man w'ch carid the
other, how I thought best he retorned, for that it is nothing
but delayes of the Vmbrians who haue sent to the Emperours Court about the mattr, as I think, or, yf he stay vpon
good occation, then to send back Gorezano, &c. I reconed

5 *tais.*

w'th the teliers, and paid the fat tealor 5 *tais* in small plate

2 *tais.*

for making me 5 new garmentes and sowing two ould gown-

1 *tay* 4 *ma.*

es & a satten dublet. And he paid me 2 *tais* greate plate out
of it for 2 peeces duttis sould hym.

Also I paid the China button maker 1 *tay* 4 *mas* for but-
tons, in small plate.

And I reconed w'th the leane telor, and paid hym

	ta.	*m.*	*co.*
for dyvers gaumentes & mending ould			
as apereth p'r p'rticlrs 7:		6:	0
& for making 3 sutes for Caffro 1:		8:	0
& for sowing the flagg or making 0:		2:	0.

m. co.[*sic*]
9: 6.

Also we reconed w'th our plasterrer of Langasaque &
Mr. Osterwick paid hym for his work, viz.,[102]

10: bund.
canes

We had 10 bundelles small canes of China Capt.
[fol. 110r.]⌋

04. This mornyng lowring droping wether, wind at N⁰ W.,
but after nowne brake vp fayre wether, & lyke all night

25/carp'rs.

littell wind.

06 lab'rs.
A lettr to
Mr. Eaton.

Carp'trs 25 w'th 6 labo'rs.

I wrot an other joynt lettr to Mr. Eaton & Mr. Nealson

---

102) The detail, not entered.

June 1616

Want
boardes.

to same effect as former & sent it p'r same conveance he
staying p'r meanes of fowle wether. We put most of our carpenters away for want of boardes to set them a work.

05. This mornyng fayre mild calme wether, or rather a littell
wynd S. W'erly, & soe remeaned all day, but rayne later
and of night wind verying to N? W., a small gale.

05 carp'rs.
20 labo'rs.

Carp'trs 5 w'th 20 labo'rs.

A lettr frō
King of
Firando.

I rec. a lettr frō Figen a Came, King of Firando, dated in
Shrongo, 18 dais past, w'th 3 salmons for a present. Also he
writes me of the good entertaym't the Emperour gaue hym,
w'th lycense to retorne to Firando when he pleaseth, & that
the Emp'r gaue hym 18 *keremons* or gowns, w'th 18 storkes
or salted fowles, for a pr'sent, a matter much esteemed in

1 frō
Torayemō
Dono.

these partes. Also I received a compl'entall lettr frō Torayemon Dono, w'th an other inclozed for the China Capt.
w'ch I del'd pr'sently. Torayemon Dono advized of pr'sentes
geven the king.

Mr. Nealson
& Mr. Eaton
retorned.

And after dyner Mr. Nealson retorned from Ikanaura
w'th Mr. Eaton, & the *bongew* of Firando w'ch went to Fingo, & Mr. Eatons host of Langasaque called   103) who
went to vizet hym at Ikanoura so sowne as he heard he was
in trowble, & hath kept hym company ever since, conveas-
yng a musket & other armes into pr'son to defend hym a-
gainst [*fol. 110v.*]] them of Fingo, yf they went about to
offer violence, offring his p'rson for his defence till the
death, yf need required.

Nota.

The *bongew* w'ch went for Fingo retorned w'th answer to
them of Vmbra that they should sett the English man at liberty, for that he would not medell w'th them, being vnder
the Emperour his pr'tection; & that them of Fingo w'ch
began this brute, went vpon their affares w'thout knowl-

---

103) The name, not given.

edg to hym, & therefore he would not defend them in the action. Yet, not w'thstanding all this, they of Vmbra would not deliver Mr. Eaton in 2 daies after the news came, siting still in *dancos* (or councell) about it, making delayes, keeping hym barecaded till the last hower. And, although the other *bongew* vsed Mr. Eaton kindlie at first, & let Mr. Nealson goe & vizet hym, yet after he restrayned hym & would not let hym speake w'th hym in 2 daies. Their hatred against vs (I meane them of Vmbra) is p'r meanes of the pa[d]rese or pristes, who stered them vp against vs to make vs odious to the Japons, for they are all, or the most part, papisticall Christians in Vmbra, & attribute a great (or cheefe) occation of banishm't of them out of Japon p'r meanes of the English, many pristes & Jesuistes lying secretly lurking in most p'rts of Japon till this hower. Yet I hope in tyme to vse the lyke frenship to them as they haue donne now to vs. And it is serten them of Vmbra are enemies to them of Firando, for that Foyne Samme recovered from them much land w'ch they had taken from Doca Samma[104] his father, and ad[d]ed much of Vmbra vnto it, w'ch they of Firando p[o]cesse till this day.   [*fol. 111r.*]

6.   This mornyng rayny wether, wind at N? W. pr'vinge a stiffe gale most p'rte of the day, & the lyke p'r night, rayne p'r fitts & wind variable.

A coop'r to mend bucketes & other vessell, w'th 3 lab'rs.

I rec. 2 lettr frō Mr. Wickham, dated in Miaco, le 22th vltimo, w'th an other from Co. Jn? *jurebasso*, both p'r the *keremon* sellar, or mercer, w'th 2 barrill wyne, cost both 13 *mas*, w'th 2 *catabras* for Matinga, 2 for his woman Femega, and 1 for Mr. Eatons woman. He writes that the King of

---

104) Dōka Sama 道可樣, the name of the cloistered Lord of Firando Matsura Takanobu, *Hizen-no-kami* 松浦肥前守隆信 (1529–1599), grandfather of the present lord of the same name.

June 1616

Xaxma w'th Frushma Tay[105] & other *tonos* were com to Miaco, & all other p'rmitted to retorne for their cvntres.

I wrot an other lettr to Jor. Durois, of Mr. Eatons retorne to Firando, & sent the other lettr, of le 31th vltimo herinclozed, advising hym of news Mr. Wickham wrot me.

I gaue 1 salmon to Capt. China of them the king sent me.

07. This mornynge lowring droping wether w'th a stiff gale wind Nọ W'erly, but sowne after broke vp fayre, & so remeaned all day, & the lyke p'r night following, calme after midnight.

The coop'r agane.

I receved a lettr frō Albaro Munois p'r Mr. Eaton, dated in Langasaque, the 22th May, new stile, & wrot hym an answer this day p'r Mr. Eatons hostes, who retorned this day; we gaue hym a pr'sent as followeth, viz.:–

1 pec. whit bafta, of [106] Rs. p'r *corge.*

1 pec. blew byram, of 15 Rs. p'r *corg.*

1 pec. red zela, of 12 Rs. p'r *corg.*

This man enformed me how he was in Cochinchina when Mr. Peacock was kild, & that the King of Cochinchina knew nothing thereof, & that he thought, yf we sought, we might haue restitusion of all. He sayeth they were 5 men w'ch murthered both the Eng. & Duch, whereof 2 were of Cochinchina, 2 Japons, & the other a China [*fol. 111v.*]] there names being as followeth:–Mangosa Dono, Sanzo Dono, Japons; Mangosa, Mr. Peacockes host; Hongo, a China; Vncam, *bongew* of junk, Amy, *bongew* of barkes, of Cochinchina.

I offred hym that, yf he would put me in suffitient sureties at Langasaque to be answerable that he should render the Wor. Company a just accompt of all he recovered or

---

105) Fukushima Masanori, *Saemon-no-Tayu* 福島左衞門大夫正則.
106) Not entered.

receaved, that then I would geue hym power to follow the matter, & be bownd to geve hym satisfaction for doing thereof to his owne content, & procure the Emperours letter to the King of Conchinchina, yf need so required. So he gaue me answer he was content to put me in sureties to content. The present was geven hym, as well in respect of the paines he hath taken w'th Mr. Eaton, as also for hope we haue to employ hym vpon Cochinchina busines. The China Capt.

42 rayles.   lent vs, 42 rayls or coop'r tymbrs called *case.*

08. This mornyng fayre calme wether somthing overcast, but after fayre sonshine wether all day, littell wind N?erly, & rather calme p'r night.

Japon feast.   This day was a Japan feast, being the 5th day of ther 5th

China Capt.   month called by them *Gunguach Ioriore.*[107] The China Capt. sent me 2 small *barsos* of wine & 2 fishes for a pr'-

China teler.   sent this Japon feast & the fatt China telior & buton mak-

To China   e[r] sent me 1 *barso* & 2 fyshes. And I sent the China Capt. a
Capt.
salmon & a phan. I was enformed that the King of Firando spake not w'th the Emperour, but only was p'rmitted to enter into a chambr, where they said he la sick in a littell cabbin coverd w'th pap'r, Codgkin Dono the secretary going into it & telling hym that the *Tono* of Firando was theare to v[i]zet hym, & came out againe telling hym, the Emperour thanked hym & haue hym lycense to retorne to his cvntrey. But they verely beleeve he is dead & that they keepe it secret, yet it may be a pollecie to see whether any

An elle   will rise against hym in armes. Mr. Osterwick paid 9 *mas*
speare.   for a eile speare.   *[fol. 112r]*

Sonday.   09. This mornyng fayre mild calme wether, but after a fresh gale variable frõ S. to W. N?erly, but littell or no wind p'r night.

---

107) *Tango* 端午. *Gogatsu Itsuka* 五月五日. "Goguat itçuca"—*Vocabulario da Liugua de Iapam*, Nagasaki, 1603.

June 1616

2 coop'rs. We had two coop'rs to make *barsos.*

Nota. We trid our elle speare afore oure howse & took 65

4 boates gravill. fresh elles. We had 4 boates lading of gravill of Capt. China.

Mr. Eaton gaue his boy Co Jnᵒs aparell & *wakydash* to

10 *mas.* his father, w'th 5 *mas* in plate & I gaue hym 5 *mas* more, w'ch 5 *mas* Yoskey paid for me & 5 *mas* more to my boy Domingo, is for me 10 *mas.*

10. This mornyng fayre mild calme wether, & after littell wind most p'rte of day W. Nᵒerly, & calme p'r night.

2 coop'rs.
10 labo'rs.
9 *markis.* Coop'rs two, w'th 10 labo'rs.

We paid (or retorned) 9 *marrakis* or rownd tymbers to Tayamon Dono, w'ch he lent to as before. Tome, our *jure-*

2 hense. *bassos* father, brought a pr'sent of 2 hense.

11. This mornyng fayre calme wether, but after a stiff gale S. W'erly, rayne in the after nowne and the lyke all night,

2 cop'rs.
1 *tatt.*
10 lab'rs.
2 boates stones. much wind *vt supra.*

Coop'rs two, 1 *tattamy* maker & 10 labo'rs.

We had 2 boattes lading paveing stoones of Cushcron Dono & Tome Dono; but the Duch grud[g]ed to let vs haue them, saying the king had geven them the iland & p'r con-

100 *tas.* sequence the stoanes. And I del'd one hvndred *tais* plate bars to Mr. Osterwick vpon and to pay carp'trs & smith &

100 *tais.* labo'rs, also one hvndred *tais* plate bars after to pay for boardes & other matt'rs. [*fol. 112v.*]] Also I had 2 pec. more of w't byrams of 14 Rs. *corg* spotten, as the other two were & not vendable, yet I took them to mak me shertes of at 8

4 pec.
w't byrs.
Nota. *mas* p'r peece, is for the 4 pec., 3 *tais* 6 *mas.* Mr. Nealson fell out w'th me extremly this day, misvsing me as he hath donne the lyke many tymes before, w'ch I haue put vp &

100 bordes. still borne w'th his contynewall drunken hvmors. We rec. 100 boardes this day of our host of Ikanaura of inch thick

4 boates gravill. & 4 fatham long at 3 *mas* pec. Also we had 4 boates lad- ing gravill of the China Capt.

June 1616

12. This mornyng raynie wether w'th a stiff gale at S. W'erly, but not so much rayne after nowne, yet greate quantety p'r night w'th much wind *vt s'pra.*

1 *tatta.*
9 cap'rs.
2 coop'rs.
2 lab'rs.
2 lettr frō
Jor. Durois.

Carp'rs 9 w'th 2 coop'rs & 2 labo'rs, 1 *tatt.* maker.

I rec. a lettr frō J? Durois dated the 12th currant, new stile, w'ch is 10 dayes past, w'th a note in it, dated the 18th ditto, new stile, in both w'ch he writes how it is certenly reported the Emperor is dead, w'th other news of Japon; as also to send back his negro or slave, yf I can procure it.

Tymbr.

We rec. tymbr frō Yayemon Dono as followeth:-

10 inch bordes of 4 *tatt.* long.
08 inch (& littell more) bordes of 2½ *tatt.* long.
06 inch (& littell more) boardes 2 *tatt.* long
14 small boardes.

20 bordes.

Also we rec. 20 inch boardes of China Capt. father in law, of 2 *tatta.* long, is 2½ fathom long.

China.

2 Chinas came & vizeted me & brought me a pr'sent of a jarr China wine. And we had one bundell of 10 small tymbrs or rayles called *bous*108) of Skiamon Dono. [*fol. 113r.*]

10 rayes.

13. This mornyng still rayny wether, w'th a stiffe gale of wind S'erly, vering to W., much rayne all day, but littell or non p'r night, nether soe much wind.

10 carp't.
01 coop'r.
01 *tat.*
4 labo'rs.
Newes.

Carp'rs 10, coop'r 1 *tattamy* maker 1 & 4 labo'rs.

Heare is reportes geven out that Fidaye Same is alive & in keeping of the Dayre,109) & that the Emperour being dead, it is now mad knowne, & that he shall be Empe'r & his fortresse at Osakay built againe. But I doe verely think this is a lye.

14. This mornyng fayre wether, littell wind at S. W., but after a fresh gale all day, but not soe much or rather calme p'r night, &c.

108) Bō 棒 (?).
109) *Dairi*. See Note 107) for 1615.

244

June 1616

11 carp'trs.
11 lab'rs.
Newes.

Carp'rs 11 w'th 11 labo'rs.

The night past came an expres from the king, how he was at Anushma,[110] a port of Faccata, som 30 leagues hence, & that he ment to be at Firando to night or to morrow. So Soyemon Dono & other caueleros went out to meete hym, or rather to goe to hym to the place where he is, the wind being contrary.

149 bages
lyme.

We had 149 bagges white lyme frō Langasaque w'ch should have byn 150, but one was left by the way, the cost all   ,[111] w'th   for fraight, is all   .

2 barkes
gravill.

Also we had 2 barkes lading gravill of the China Capt.

15. This mornyng fayre calme mild wether, but after a small gale, wind N°erly most p'rte of the day, but rayne in greate quantety after midnight.

11 carp'ts.
5½ lab'rs.
A
lettr to Jor.
Durois.
2 ba'k gr'ill.

Carp'rs 11 w'th 5½ labo'rs.

I sent a lettr to Jᵉ Durois dated the 12th pr'sent & kept till this day, & sent p'r the man w'ch brought the white lyme. We had 2 barkes landing gravill of China Capt.   [*fol. 113v.*]]

16. This mornyng calme rayny wether, & so remeaned all day & night following, much rayne & som wind p'r day S. W'erly, but littell or non p'r night.

11 carp trs.
2½ lab'rs.
King of
Firando
arived.

Carp'trs 11 w'th 2½ labo'rs.

The King of Firando arived at Firando about midnight, & the Duch shott off certen chambrs at his passing by their howse. I sent our *jurebasso* to Oyen Dono to desyre hym to tell the king that I was glad of his Highnes health & safe retorne, & that I would com & kis his handes, yf he weare at leasure, &, whiles he was speaking w'th Oyen Dono, the kyng p'r fortune or else of purpose passed by & gaue our *jurebasso* very kind wordes & said I should be

110) Ainoshima 藍島, now called Aishima, an islet off Kokura.
111) This and the following prices, not entered.

245

welcom when soever I came.

To dyner.

Tayamon Dono envited vs to dyner, I meane all the English, he being our m.ͬ carpenter, and our work all most ended.

Nota.

I sent our *jurebasso* also to Semi Dono, and Taccaman Dono to bid them welcom home, & to tell them I would com & vizet them when they were at leasure. Semi Dono sent me word, it was certen that the ould Emperour was dead 26 daies past, & that he saw the place where he was baryed; & that Shongo Samme did it of purpose, that they might see he was dead.[112] And the pr'sentes w'ch were geven to eache *tono* were the legasie of the dead Emperour, being great matters both in bars of gould & vestmentes. & that Shongo Samme gaue them leave to stay 3 yeares w'thout retornyng to vizet hym, to take theire ease for the paynes they had taken in tym past. But I do verely beleeve he will sowne rise againe, yf any wars be moved against his sonne w'thin these 3 yeares.

Gonrock Dono passed by yisternight to Langasaque to be governor; w'ch doth rather conferme me in my opinion.

[*fol. 114r.*]

17. This mornyng still rayny wether, very littell wind S. W'erly, but after vered to N.ᵒ W'erly much rayne p'r night as well as p'r day, calme.

5½ lab'rs.

Labo'rs 5½ to take away the falne walles.

Nota.

The grownd on the W. side our new gadong did shrink w'th the extreme rayne, & 3 panes of our orchard wall fell downe & spoild divers frute trees, & all the rest of the wall much shaken & lyke to fall, the grownd geving way.

Present to ye king.

We went and vizetted the king, all of vs together, viz., Mr. Eaton, Mr. Nealson, Mr. Osterwick & my selfe, and

---

112) A later remark, reading "Emp'rs death," is written in the margin for this line.

carid a present of 2 barrilles wyne, & 20 cordes of drid fysh of cuttell, & shell fysh, of eather 10 cordes, w'th a small pott of conservs of oreng flowers. He was accompanied w'th Bongo Same his vncle, & the father of Sugen Dono of Vmbra, & 2 *bosses* or pagon pristes, w'th the agent of Crates. He took our vizetasion & pr'sent in kind p'rte, offring vs any thinge we stood in need of, & soe I craved p'rdon, telling hym I would retorne som few dayes hence to his his [*sic*] Highnesse handes, after he had rested hym selfe of his journey, to make knowne som matters vnto hym to haue his Highnesse councell therin.

Nota

The king had a flat galle pot in his handes & his vncle an other, w'ch som body had presented vnto them. So he asked me whether we had such in our cuntrey, & I answered we had. So he desyred, yf any came in our shiping, that they might be kept for hym. &, retornyng to the English howse, by chance Mr. Nealson had such a one as the others were, but paynted after an other fation. So I sent it to the king, w'ch he took in good part. [*fol. 114v.*]]

18. This mornyng still calme rayny wether, but after a small gale, wind at W. S'erly store of rayne all day, but more p'r night, wind a gale variable w'th lightnyng & thonder.

carp'rs.
labo'rs.
Nota.

Carp'trs 113) and labo'rs .

I del'd Seme Donos accǫ & bill to Mr. Osterwick, wherin it apearth he oweth due p'r bill 250 *ta*. rest w'th 2 *mas* 5 *condrins* p'r his steward. Also I del'r[d] hym two other bills, viz., 1 of Tonoman Same for 20 *tt*. wax [and] 1 of Matasabr Same for 5 pec. zelas of 8 Rs. at 1 *tay* pec.

1615 Octobr
12.

To Semi
Dŏ &
Taccamon
Doñ.

I went & vizeted Semy Dono & Taccaman Dono, & carid each of them 2 small *barsos* wyne w'th 10 cordes drid fysh, 5 of a sort to each one. They tould me the ould Emperour

---

113) This and the following figures, not entered.

died 28 daies past, & that all is now in quiet to Xongo Samē his sonne, in respect of the death of Fidaia Samme. I del'd a bill Japons of Kinges Crates man for 60 pec. w't baftas, & 5 tapis Suras sould le 17th of Decembr 1615 to Jubio Dono for the king his mr, the baftes at 1½ *tais* pece & Suras at 1 *tay* in all 95 *tais*.

Bill del'd
to Mr. Ostr.

After I was in bed, Yesimon Dono sent me word he vnderstood of a ship or junck that was on the cost of Firando, neare an iland 3 leags hence, & that he had advised the Hollandrs the lyke.

News.
junk.

19. This mornyng extreme rayny wether w'th light'ing and thunder, wind at S. W'erly, & so remeaned all day & lyke p'r night following, extreme fowle wether contynewall lightnyng & thunder all night.

Carp'trs 4 w'th 1 lab'rs.

4 c'rp'rs.
1 lab'rs.
Nota.

The China Capt. tould me how he vnderstood by som w'ch came this night past from Langasaque, how the[y] heard 2 pec. of ordinance ship affe p'r som shipp or junck, of the w'ch I advised Capt. Speck in a lettr sent p'r our *jurebasso* Gorezan. He retorned me answer that he had the lyke reportes brought vnto hym, & had sent out men to heare yf it were true, but could heare [*fol. 115r.*] of no such mattr. And, sowne after, others brought news how they heard 3 peeces ordinance shot affe. So I sent out a boate, w'th 6 ores, to look yf they could see any shipping on the cost; but they retorned sowne after, the wether being dark & much rayne, & could see nothing.

Capt. Speck said he desired to talke w'th me about the state of Japon, for that he dowbted their might be som alteration by meanes of these reports of the death of the Emperour.

A China
junck.

The junck proued to be a China, & went along for Faccata not tuching at Firando. Yt was a small *soma* or junck.

June 1616

To king.
The King of Firando sent to begg my 2 golden fishes w'ch the China Capt. brother sent me, w'ch much against my will, I gaue hym, haveing geven his brother the other

Nota.
before. I coming to recon w'th Cushcron Dono for 50 *tais* plate, I lent hym & the other of the ward 3 years past. He putes 27 bagges rise to my acc?, I knowing but of 22

12½ *tais*, China Captain.
& had paid them in acc? to the king before, & 12 *ta*. & a halfe they put vpon China Capt. his accompt.

20. This mornyng still extreme stormy fowle raynie wether, w'th lightning & thunder wind at S., but not so much rayne after nowne, & dry calme wether p'r night.

1 labo'r. Frō ye king.
We had one laborer to make cleane bridg & the King of Firando sent his chamberlen to me w'th a pr'sent of 2 Japon *catabras*, w'th much wordes complementall for that he did not com to vizet me sin[c]e his retorne frō the Emperos Cort, aledging the fowle wether to be cheefe occation. The chambrlen also gaue me a *chaw*[114] cup of

Nota.
tynne. [*fol. 115v.*]] I sent our *jurebasso* to thank the king for the pr'sent he sent me, & to tell hym I did not exteeme my selfe worthie of such honor as his Highnesse did vnto me in sending me such a pr'sent. He retorned answer, he esteemed me worthie of much more, & was ashamed it was no bettr, yet desird me to take it in good p'rte, such as it was.

21. This mornyng fayre calme mild wether, & littell wind after S'erly vering to W., & fayre calme wether all night followinge.

3 cap'trs. 3 lab'rs.
Carp'rs 3 w'th 3 labo'rs.

A lettr to Jor. Durois.
I wrot a lettr to Jor. Durois, of one effect of retorned King of Firando & death of Emperour a month past. One

2 lettrs.
of letrs sent p'r his slaue w'ch retorneth to serve hym,

---

114) *Cha* 茶, tea.

June 1616

& the other p'r Cuemon Dono of Langasaque our plastarer.

A junk or ship. Towardes night came news that a junk or ship was seene vpon the cost of Firando, 4 or 5 leages offe. So the China Capt. went out in a boate, & Jnọ Cocora, our cooke,

4 bagg rise. w'th hym. I had 4 sackes of rise w'ch I gaue to Matinga out of howse, for w'ch I am answerable.

And about midnight came an Englishman w'th a lettr from Mr. Jnọ Baylie, mŗchnt, & an other frõ Mr. Richard News.
Thomas
ariued. Row, mŗ of the *Thomas* who is arived w'thin 5 leages of Firando, & com p'r way of Molucos, & came frõ Bantam the 20th of January last.[115)] *[fol. 116r.]*⌋

22. This mornyng fayre calme mild wether, but after a fresh gale, wind most p'rt of day S'erly & calme p'r night.

5 carp'rs.
3 lab'rs.

Thomas
entrd
rode of
Firando. Carp'trs 5 w'th 3 labo'rs.

I went abord the *Thomas*, & pr'cured boates frõ Firando to toe her in. So she entred the harbo'r about nowne, & shot of 3 pec. as we passed p'r the Duch house & 11 for the towne, coming to an ancor. Jacob Speck, the Duch Capt., Capt. Speck. came abord before she came in, & brought a pr'sent of 2 barilles wyne, 2 hogges, & a salmon, & had 3 pec. ordynance at dep'rture. And the Duch answerd w'th chambars, both as we passed as also at his dep'rture.

Lettrs. I rec. 2 lettrs frõ Wor. Compª w'th div'rs coppies of others sent before, thervnto accepted the one lettr p'r the *Cloue* & the other p'r the *Defence* w'th div'rs other lettrs frõ friendes, &c.

A letr frõ
Mr.
Wickham. Also I rec. a lettr frõ Mr. Wickham, dated in Osakey, 10th of June, &c. And sent hym these lettrs following;–

2 dated 25th of Aprill ⎫
1 of first May ⎮

---

115) In a space after this entry are written the later remarks, reading "Nota," and "News of the *Thomas*."

1 of 11th May	all kept till 23th or to
1 of 8 June	morow, & sent p'r Skeete.
1 of 22th June	

Sonday. **23.** This mornyng fayre calme wether, but sowne after a fresh gale, wind N°erly most p'rte day, but calme wether all night, hot wether.

2½ carp'rs. Carp'rs 2½ and 4 labo'rs, at 3 *condrins* peec.
lab'rs.
Nota. The king sent to haue a note of what comodeties was com in our ship, to thentent to send it to the new Emperour. So I gaue it hym. [*fol. 116v.*]]

Nota. Also we procurd orders from king to set vp in the ship that no Japon should com abord w'thout leave, to pr'vent stayling & cozenyng the marreners, w'ch the Japon are adicted vnto.

Femega & Woman w'th her mother dep'rted towardes Miaco this mornyng. Skite accompanyng them, p'r whome
50 *ta*. I sent 50 *ta*. in plate of bars to buy neales of our hostice of Bingen a Tomo, w'ch 50 *tais* I del'd Mr. Osterwick & he
A lettr. del'd it to Skeete w'th a lettr in Japon to our hostis to mak ready these neals, following, viz.:–

> 4 *picos* of Spikes.
> 2000, 2 sh. neales.
> 2000, 20d. neales.
> 2000, 6 d. neales.
> 2000, 4 d. neales.
> 20000, shething neales.
> 06000, 6 d. shething neales.

8 gvns The King of Firando retr. 8 fowling pec. w'ch the Empro.̅
retornd. should haue had; but now he is dead Safian Dono retor's them.

24. This mornyng still calme whot [*sic*] wether, & also remeaned all day & the lyke p'r night foll'g.
A lettr I sent an other lettr to Mr. Wickham to same effect as

to Mr.
Weckham.

that of 22th sent p'r Skeete. This lettr was sent p'r King Firandos man, whoe goeth to the new Emperour w'th a note of tharivall of our shipp, & what she bringe in her.

3 chistes.

5 chistes.

And we rec, goodes ashore, as foll'th:– 3 chistes N? 4, N? 6, & N? 13, w'th gallie pottes in a bark, 4 chistes N? 2, 3, 5, & 14, galle potes, & N? 4, w'th picktures in 1: bark, 2 fardes N? 72, 91, clo. Gozerat, 2 trusse pold'd, 1 fard Russa hides [?], 2 rundletes cont'g 2 globes, all in ships boate, N? 1, no 2, hol[   ].

Pr'sentes.

Sugen Dono sent a pr'sent 6 fyshes, his father 2 *barsos* wyne & a drid fish, Taccamon Dono a *catabra* & a hankercheffe.

1½ carp.
15 lab'rs.
4 botes
stoanes.

We had 1½ carp'rs & 15 labo'rs. And 4 boates lading of stoanes of Capt. China.   [*fol. 117r.*]⌋

25.   This mornyng still whot calme wether, but after a small gale N?erly most p'rte of the day, but calme p'r night.

1 carp'tr.
26 lab'rs.
12 ship.

Carp'rs 1, labo'rs 26, w'th 12 labo'rs abord the ship.

Mr. Osterwick paid the tylors yisterday for all the tiles & work they did this yeare, viz.:–

Ffor 116)

Ffor

And we receved goodes ashore in 2 boates, viz., in first N? 117)&, 2 balls cloth, N? B, a trunck, N? 7. 1 chist glasses; & in the other 4 bales, viz., N? 6, 93, 70 & 95; & N? 5, cont'g Ffra Drakes voyages; more in an other bark, 6 balles & 2 chistes, viz., N? 20, 8, 19, 4, 20; balles, N? 07, 10; chistes.

Frō Vna-
gense.

We rec. more, but confusedly, & not set doone. Vnagense Dono sent me a pr'sent of 2 *barsos* of wyne, & 6 fishes.

News.

And Semi Dono, w'th others, came from the king to look on our gally pots, and carid som of them, w'th jugges & pottage dishes to shew the king.

---

116) This and the following figures, not entered.
117) This number, not given.

A China
j'nck.

This after nowne came in a small junck of China, w'ch came frō Osakay & came into Japon the last yeare.

26. This mornyng still calme hot wether, & soe remeaned all day & the lyke p'r night following.

6½ carp't.
23½ lab'rs.
12 ship.
3 barkes
for goodes.
3 barkes
ston.
Galle pottes,
&c.

Galy pot.

1 fagot
stels.

6½ carp'trs, 23½ w'th [*sic*] labo'rs & 12 lab'rs abord ship.

We had 3 boates of Cash To & China Capt. to land good this day. Also we had 3 boates lading of greate ston frō China Capt. And, the king had divers sortes gally potes, posset potes, & jugges more sent hym this day, as also Semy Dono had 2 galle potes & 10 gren podingers. [*fol. 117v.*]] And Skiamon Dono had 2 or 3 broaken gally pottes & 1 whole geven hym, he comying to fetch the other for the kyng. Ther was a faggot of steele let fall over board p'r neclegence of handing in. Mr. Rowe sent me a pr'sent of a case bottell w'th wyne.

27. This mornyng still calme hot wether, & soe remeaned all day and the lyke p'r night following.

5 c'rp't.
38 labo's.
12 ship.

Carp'trs 5, labo'rs ashore 38 w'th 12 labo'rs abord.

We had 2 boates for shipps vse to vnlade goodes, I meane the shipps pr'vition this day.

Nota.

Alvaro Munois, Alferis Tuerto, & Pasqual Benois came this day to Firando frō Langasaque, & came to the Eng. howse to vizet me. I think their coming is to learne what news is at Molucos & Surat, the w'ch I did not want to tell them the truth. Albaro sent me a pr'sent of 2 bandes & cuffes, w'th 3 roles of rusk, & Alferis Tuerto a jar of conserves, &c.

Pr'sentes.

To Duch
capten.

We lent the Duch capt. a barill gvnpolder & a peece of a cable, for w'ch he will del'r the lyke before ship goes.

28. This mornyng still hot calme wether, & littell wind after variable w'th a good shower of rayne towardes night, but dry calme wether all night.

6 carp'rs.
38 lab'rs.

Carp'trs 6 w'th 38 laborers.

5 barkes grª
04 ba. ston.

We had 5 barkes lading gravill of Capt. China & 4 barkes more of hym greate stones. I made bargen w'th Tome Dono & Cushcron Dono for plank & tymbr as in the wastbook apereth, and bought 300 inch plank of Yayemon Dono to be del'd w'thin a mᵒ as 3 *m.* 2 *co.* p'r pec. of 4 fathom long, & 200 same sort of China Capt. father in law of same sort & price. There was 2 men of Fingo & of of [*sic*] Firando cutt this day for quarreling on w'th an other.   [*fol. 118r.*]

Tymbr.
500 inch.
plank.

2 men cut.

29.   This mornyng hot calme wether, but sowne after a fresh gale, wind all day S'erly, & the lyke all night following, fayre wether.

06 carp't.
48 lab'rs.
07 ship.

Carp'ters 6 w'th 48 la'ors aland and 7 labo'rs abord.

I am enformed how the King of Fingo hath sent to Ikanaura, and caused the man to be cut w'ch began the brute w'th Mr. Eaton.

Sugen Dono sent a pr'sent of frute & came & vizeted the Eng. howse, &c. Also Capt. Speck sent to borrow 8 or 10 fathom of ould rope or cable, w'ch was lent hym. And Yayamon Dono, kinges shipwrite, hat 4 blockes or pulleis lent hym to make others by.

10 fath.
rope.
4 blockes.

Sonday.

30.   This mornyng fayre wether w'th a fresh gale, wind S'erly, and so remeaned all day, but rayne towardes night, & soe p'r fittes all night w'th much wind.

3 carp'trs.
58 labo'rs.
Nobleman
of Xaxā.

Carp'trs 3 w'th 58 labo'rs.

The king sent me word that a nobleman of Xaxma was com to Firando and desired to vizet our Eng'sh howse & to goe abord our shipp, & that he was a man of accᵒ, & therefore wished me to vse hym respectively; w'ch I did in shewing hym the howse & making hym a colation, as he had the lyke abord & 5 pec. ordinance for a farewell.

8 barkes
ston.

We had 8 boates lading, viz., 4 gravill & 4 ston of Capt. China.

Pr'sentes.

I send Albaro Munois & Gil'mo de la Barreda, the Al-

pheris, each of them a gallon bottell oyle & a quart bottell
Spa. wyne, glasse bottells & all for a pr'sent.

Nota.

The noblemen of Xaxma sent to haue a sample of gallie
pottes, jugges, tvns, podingers, lookinglasses, table bookes,
chint bramport & combarbands[118) w'th the prices, but it
was resser[v]ed till ñ.   [*fol. 118v.*]」

July 1616.

01. This mornyng overcast droping wether, wind S'erly,
rayne p'r fittes all day, but not soe much p'r night, yet a
stiffe gale wynd.

6 carp'trs.
8 labr's.

Carp'trs 6 w'th 8 labo'rs.

Pr'sent.

Soe vpon good consideration we sent these thinges
following for a presente to the 2 noblemen of Xaxma,
vnderstanding they are kyn to the king & greate men
in these partes, viz.:–

2 looking glasses, 1 square & 1, 8 square.
2 pere tablebookes, N? 4.
2 gallepottes, fflat, of 6 *tt.*
2 gallepotes, fflat, of 4 *tt.*
2 gale pottes, fflat, of 1 *tt.*
2 gall pottes, high, of 6 *tt.*
2 gale pottes, high, of 4 *tt.*
2 gale pottes high of 2 *tt.*
2 green jugges.
2 green posset pottes.
2 gren tvnns.
4 single combrbandes harer.
2 sing. peeces chint bramport.

W'ch pr'sent they took in good part, & retornd me answer

118) Cummerbands.—Thompson.

July 1616

p'r Mr. Eaton that, yf we would haue any busynes w'th the King of Xaxma, we should fynd they were men that could doe somthing & would not be forgetfull both of their entertaynm't at Eng. howse as also abord the shipes; & yt w'ch bownd them the more, the[y] sending these pr'-sentes vnto them of thinges they had neauer seene the lyke before, & therfore would not want to signefie so much

Nota.

to the king their master. And sowne after they sent me thankes p'r 2 of their men, & eather of them sent me a

Pr'snt.

present of a banketing box w'th furneture of trenchars, dishes, & other mattrs, for 5 men to eate w'th, after Japon fation.

Pr'sent.

Mr. Rowe went to Duch howse w'th a pr'sent of a run-let wyne, a jarre conservd nvntmeg & som conservd ginger, & was frendly entertaynd.

Domingo bownd prentis.

Domingo was bownd to serue me 5 years, where I will out of England, & to fynd hym meat & drinke & clo., & the rest at my leasure.   [*fol. 119r.*]⌋

C2. This mornyng overcast drowing wether, wind S'erly, much rayne before nowne, but dry after, & the lyke p'r night, or very littell rayne.

7 carp'rs.
2 ship ca'r.
14 labo'rs.
6 lab'rs ship.
Nota.

Carp'trs aland 7, & 2 for ship, w'th 14 labo'rs land & 6 abord the shipp.

The cavaleros of Shaxma sent to buy 20 green tvns & 20 green porringers, w'ch I set at 6 *mas* p'r peece. But they would not geue the price, but retorned them.

Pr'sent.

And a cavelero kinges man sent a calfe for a pr'sent.

Nota.

Albaro Munos, the Alferis & Mr. Eaton w'th them, went abord the *Tho.* & had 3 pec. of ordinance shot afe

A lettr frõ
J? Durois.

at their retorne. I rec. a lettr frõ J? Durois of 6th currant, new stile.

03. This mornyng overcast lowring wether, littell wind S'erly & not much more neather p'r day nor night foll'g,

July 1616

still fayre weth.

5 carpts.
15 lab'rs.
A lettr
to Jor.
Durois.

Carp'trs laid 3 w'th 2 for ship & 13 lab'rs laid 2 ships..

I wrot a lettr to J? Durois, dated le 27th past but kept till this day & sent p'r Sangro Dono, Skidayen Donos brother, advising hym of rec. of 2 of his w'th 3 pere silk stockinges, a pere milstons, and a *nerremon*.119) I gaue Albaro Mvnois child 2 pec. sing. chint bramport of120)

2 pec. chint.

Rs. *corg*, for a pr'sent & will pay for them as rest are sould.

News.

We had news how the junck of Vilango Luis is arived at Nangasaque frõ the Manillas, & Miguell de Salinas in her. They bring news that Don Jn? de Silva is dead before Malicca, & his fleete retorned to Manilla, but first he droue away the Mores of Achin, & the Duch forcesse frõ Malacco, as they say.

A lettr
to Capt.
Garrocho.
Junck
Manilla.

I wrot a lettr to Garrocho & sent hym a case bottells p'r Pasquall, price 10 *tais*. We hat news of an other Japon jn? [*sic*] arived frõ Manillas at Langasaque, m? Yasemon Dono [*fol. 119v.*].] We went to the King of Firando w'th a pr'sent as followeth, viz.:–121)   [*fol. 120r.*].]

04. This mornyng fayre mild wether, littell wind S'erly, and so remeaned all day, & lyke p'r night foll'g, still fayre wether very hott.

7 carp'rs.
19 lab'rs.
Pr'sent.

Carp'trs 2 ashore, & 5 abord; lab'rs 17 ashore & 2 abord.

By generall consent there was a pr'sent sent to Capt. Whaw, the China Capt. brother, viz.:–

1½ *tatt.* stamet cloth, N?   .122)

1½ *tatt.* staw color baces, N?

1 pec. Sleze land, N? G.

---

119) *Nerimono* 煉物, artificial jewels (?). Also, *norimon* 乗物, the best sort of palanquin. See Note 177) below.
120) Not entered.
121) Details of the presents are not entered, but a space is left on the rest of the page.
122) This and the following numbers, not given.

257

July 1616

1 flat 4 *tt.* gallepot.

1 flat 1 *tt.* galle pot.

2 table bookes, N.⁰ 4.

20 ambr. beades, best sort.

20 ambr. beades, second sort.

2 table bokes, N.⁰ 4.

Pr'sent.

And Torazemon Dono sent me a gerdell & a p're *tabis* for a wo[man]. Also ther was a pr'sent sent to Tonomon Same, viz.:–

1 *tatt.* brod. cloth stamet, N.⁰   .123)

1 *tatt.* bayes black, N.⁰   .

1 *tatt.* bayes strawcullr N.⁰   .

5 pec. chint bramport, of   124) Rs., *corg.*

5 pec. candeque abalupta, of   Rs., *corg.*

5 handkercheffs chint bramport.

5 handker. rumall cottony.

5 combarbandes.

20 ambr. beades, best sort.

20 ambr. beades, worst sort.

02 writ. table bookes, N.⁰ 4, N.⁰ 1.

01 looking glastes [*sic*] ovall.

[fol. 120v.]⌋

05.   This mornyng calme hott wether, but after a fresh gale wind S'erly most p'rte of day, but calme p'r night.

carp'rs.
lab'rs.
30 tils.

Carp'trs for howse 2½, for ship 4; labo'rs howse & for ship 13.

We lent 30 tils to the tyler. And we sent these pr'sentes foll'g, viz.:–

To Bongo Same,125)

[fol. 120r.]⌋

06.   This mornyng calme hott wether, but after a fresh gale

---

123) This and the following numbers, not given.

124) This and the following prices, not entered.

125) Details of the presents are not entered, but a space is left on the rest of the page.

July 1616

most p'rte day S'erly, w'th a shower rayne towardes night, but after dry.

6 carp't.
16 lab'rs.
ta. m. co.
4: 9: 3.
To Matt.
more 7 *cond.*
100 *tais.*

Carp'trs 2 for howse & 4 for ship. w'th 8 labo'rs howse & 8 for ship.

I gaue Matinga a bar plate p'r 4 *ta.* 9 *m.* 3 *co.*, w'th 7 *condrins* in *fibuck*, is all 5 *taies* bars. And I del'd 100 *tais* plate bars to Mr. Osterwick.

And ther was a pr'sent geven Andrea Dittis, the China Capt., as hereafter followeth:–

To China
Capt.

1 *tatt.* broad clo. stamet, N°   .126)

2 *tatta.* black bayes, N°   .

1 pec. Sleze land N° D.

20 ambr beades, best sort.

20 ambr beades, second sort.

02 pere table bookes, N° 4.

01, 4 *tt.* gallepot, flat.

1 Duch jugg.

1 green tvn.

1 green podinger.

Pr'sentes.

And there was geven two pr'sent to Soyemon Dono, and Torazemon Dono, as foll'th, viz.:-

1 *tatt.* brod clo., blak, N°   .127)

1 pec. Sleze land N° D.

1, 4 *tt.* galle pot, flat.

1, 4 *tt.* galle pot, high.

1, 2 *tt.* ditto, flat.

1, 2 *tt.* ditto, highe.

1, 1 *tt.* ditto, flat.

1 green tome.

I say each of them had a pr'sent as afforesaid.

4 barkes
gravill.

And we had 4 barkes gravill of China Capt. The gentle-man of Firando, w'ch came fro Xaxma, I meane Fony

---

126) This and the following numbers, not given.
127) The number, not given.

July 1616

Sames[128] kynsman, came to the Eng. howse, & sent me 2 bar[ri]ls wyne & 2 fyshes for a pr'sent. He tould me the King of Xaxma had rezolued in counsell to let vs haue free trade into the Liqueas & all other p'rtes of his dominions, but that the 2 noble men, w'ch were here the other day, durst not tell me so much w'thout order from the king, yet assured hym it was true. [fol. 121v.]]

Sonday.   07. This mornyng fayre calme hott wether, but after a stiffe gale, wind most p'rte of day S'erly, overcast wether after nowne, but much rayne w'th light'ing & thvnder all night.

1 carp'tr.   Carp'rs 1 w'th 4 labo'rs all ashore.
4 lab'rs.
A lr. frō   I rec. a lettr frō Capt. Whaw for Langasaque, wherin
Cap. Whaw.   he writes thankes for the pr'sent sent hym, as also advising
News.   me how 3 of Twans barkes are retorned, w'ch should haue gon for Tacca Sange, or the Iland Fermosa, but went not thither, but rather a boothaling on the cost of China, where they haue taken 11 boates or junkes, & put all the people to death because they stood out & fought w'th them.

Nota.   He also wrot his brother to advize me not to goe towardes Miaco this 10 or 12 daies, & that when I went, to goe well provided, for that it was reported there were pilferyng knaues abroad on the cost of Arima, & speeches geuen out that the *Tono*, or King, of Xaxma meaneth to make wars against the new Emperour in right of Fidaia Same, whom they report to be alive, & that he meaneth to begyn w'th Langasaque. This is now the common report, &c.

Nota.   Yt is said that one boate of Twans men put into a creek at Iland Fermosa, thinking to haue discoverd ferther into the cvntrey; but, before they were aware, were set on p'r the cuntrey people, &, seeing they could not escape, cut their owne bellies because they would not fall into the

---

128) Hōin Sama. See Note 55) for 1615.

July 1616

enemies hands.

A lettr
frō Mr.
Wickham.

I rec. a lettr from Mr. Wickham yisterday, dated in Miaco the 24th vltimo, wherin he wrot of but ease sales aboue, & the rather p'r meanes of his bad, ill sorted comodeties, yet that all was in quiet aboue & so hoped it would remeane.   [*fol. 122r.*]]

08.   This mornyng littell wind S. W'erly w'th much rayne, all the fore nowne, but not so much after and dry lowring wether all night.

2 lettrs
frō J?
Durois
& Albaro
Munois.
Pr'sent.

I rec. 2 lettrs, 1 frō Jor. Durois of the 16th of July, new stile, & the other frō Albaro Munois of the 17th ditto, w'th a peare blew silk stockinges & a jarr of *nipa* sent me for a pr'sent, & Mr. Eaton & Mr. Rowe each of them a jarr of *nipa*. They wrot me how the Portingals had 4 gallions at Mallaca, w'ch came from Goa, one wherof the King of Achin burned w'th his gallies, & the other 3 the Hollandrs

Nota.

burned after, yet before Don Jn? de Silua arived at Mallaca, & were gon towardes Molucas before he came, he dying for greefe that he did not com in tyme, as the Spa. & Port. report.

3 carp'trs.
3½ lab'rs.

Carp'rs 3 w'th 3½ lab'rs all ashore.

09.   This mornyng overcast lowring calme wether, or rather a littell wind S'erly, and so remeand all day & lyke p'r night following.

16 c'rp'trs.
5 lab'rs.
A lettr to
J? Durois.

Carp'rs ab'rd 16 w'th labo'rs abord 4 1 & in the howse.

I sent Jor. Durois a lettr & retorned hym the milstones being to littell. And I sent hym 2 *tt.* cloues a littell mace w'th a few nutmegges & a peec. of cheese & the China Capt. sent hym halfe a cheese. And we had 6 barkes gravill of

6 barkes
gravill.
16 men.

China Capt. and 16 of the marrenars labor'd all day about baling vp clo. & bayes & waying lead. I meane 16 of Japon men yt are to goe w'th it to Miaco. The king sent a melch

Goate.

goate & a kid to Mr. Baylie for a pr'sent, to make vse of the

261

Frõ ye
Chi. Capt.

milk, he being sick. The China Capt. sent me a peec. black taffety, or rather slight grogren for a pr'sent. [*fol. 122v.*]

10. This mornyng droping overcast wether, littell wind S'erly, or rather calme, but after a small gale S'erly most p'rte day, & much lighting & thvndr w'th rayne p'r night, a stiffe gale vering N? W'erly.

Nota

I sent Mr. Eaton w'th our *jurebasso* to desyre the king to let vs haue a great bark to carry vp our goodes, & our ould *bongew* to accompany me, for that I was desyrous to keep our ould, as the Duch did, & not to chang every yeare a new, as hetherto we had donne. He retorned me answer that he had pr'sent vse of his greatest barkes, meanyng to go to the Emperour hym selfe w'thin few daies, yet, not w'thstanding, he would provide me of a good bark, & not of the least; & for our ould *bongew*, he could not spare hym, having put an office into his hands, but for any other I might make choise & keepe my selfe to hym ever hereaftr yf I pleased. Mr. Eaton said he fownd the king accompanid w'th all his cheefe men, surveing of armor; soe I dowbt there will be som broyles in Japan before long. God grant all may fall out for the best.

5 carp'rs.
12 labo'rs.
Pasqual.

Carp'trs 5 abord, w'th 6 labo'rs ashore & 6 aboard. Pasquall the Spaniard retornd frõ Langasaque, & Christophell the Alman w'th hym, & an ould souldier called   129) Reales. They said yt 2 junckes of China were arived frõ Caggalion in Phillippinas, & 2 other China junckes from Camboia, laden p'r Portingalls. And late in the night the

Pilot.

pilot   130) arived w'th an other Spaniard called   131) in company w'th hym. Pasquall retorned back the case bottell

Pr'sent.

from Capt. Garrocho, & gaue me a present of Portingale

---

129) The first name, not given.
130) The name, not given.
131) The name, not given.

July 1616

phigges conserved a small gar, & an other to Mr. Rowe the
m.^r of the *Thomas*, &c. Mr. Ric'd Rowe gaue me a pr'sent
of 1 *tt.* mase.   [*fol. 123r.*]⌋

11. This mornyng still droping overcast wether, wind at
N.^o W., & soe contynewd rayny wether w'th lightnyng &
thvnder most p'rte of day, but dry wethe[r] most p'rt or
all night followinge.

5 carp'trs.
2 lab'rs.
1 pere
stocking.
A lettr
frō Albaro
Munois.

Carp'trs 5 abord, & 2 labo'rs ashore.

Georg Durois sent me a peare silk stockinges p'r a
Japon woman, stockinges of cullor green. Also I rec. a lettr
from Albaro Munois, dated in Langasaque, le 20th of July,
new stile, wherin he writes yt the + [*sic*] was deare at 20
ld str., he having showd it to dyv'rs that would not geue so
much for it. Also that he had bespoke candelles to com p'r

the first, &c. I gaue Mr. Row. 2 peare new silke stockinges,
cost me 7 *tais*, one skye culler, & thother blew.

And we sould to the Spanish pilot & his consorts, Pasquall, & Antony Peris for ready money:-

320 pec. red zelas, at 7½ *mas* p'r peec., is   .... *T.*[132)

110 chintes amad, at 9 *mas* p'r peec., is   .... *T.*

074 candequy nill, at 4 *mas* p'r peec., is   .... *T.*

009 pec. candeque abalupt, at 9 *mas* peec.......... *T.*

002 pec. candeque abalupt, at 8½ *mas* pec.......... *T.*

In p'rte of paym̄t wherof he paid 11 bars *coban* gold at 62
mas p'r bar, w'th condition that yf the[y] vallued more,
at his coming to Miaco, then Mr. Wickham is to pay it to
hym, but yf the value lesse, then they are to alow so much
to Mr. Wickham, of the w'ch I advized hym in a lettr sent
p'r the pilot.

And I waid out my 2 chapet sword & dagger to the gouldsmith, w'ch poz. iron & all together, 2 *ta.* 3 *ma.* 2 *condrins*,
& silver alone, 7 *mas* 8 *condrins*.   [*fol. 123v.*]⌋

---

132) This and the following prices, not entered.

12. This mornyng overcast lowring wether, littell wind S'erly, rayne a littell towardes night, but much more in the night, yet littell or no wind.

14 carp'trs. 3½ labo'rs.

Carp'ts 2 ashore, w'th 3½ labo'rs for ship to saw; w'th 12 abord ship, viz., 6 ashore all day, 12 abord ½ day.

A lettr to Mr. Wickhā.

I wrot a lettr to Mr. Wickham of sale good sould Spaniardes yisterday, as also of recept of his of 24th vltimo, and that I am ready to com vp w'th a cargezon goodes, w'thin 3 or 4 dais, yf Capt. Adames arive not in junck to com w'th me. As also of news Duch burnyng 4 gallions of Portugeyes at Malacca, & of the death of Don Jnº de Silva before Malacca, & his armado retorned to Manillia w'ch letter I sent p'r ¹³³⁾ the Spanish pilot.

Ship *Aduiss* ariued in Cochi yⁱ- night.

And towardes night Zanzabar, (*allis* Yasimon Dono) sent me word that an English or Duch shipp was com to an ancor in Cochi roade, a league frō Firando. Soe I sent out a boate to look who they weare, & it proued to be the *Adviz*, an Eng'sh ship, the mʳ called Jnº Totton.¹³⁴⁾ I sent a hogg & a barrill wyne to company. And the purcer or m'rchnt, Mr. Ed. Willmot, came ashore, and brought me divrs lettrs, viz.:–

1 frō Wor'll Compa., a joynt lettr to rest.

1 frō Capt. Jnº Jourden a duble lettr, viz., copie of that sent p'r *Tho.*, dated at Jaccatra, le 12th January, 1615, w'th an other p'r *Advice*, dated in Bantam, le 29th May, 1616.

1 other frō Capt. Jor[den], a duble lettr, viz., copie of 1 sent in *Hozeander*, w'th 1, 10th August, 1615, sent p'r ditto *Adviz* frō Bantā, who lost her monson, & retorned to Bantam, &c.

1 frō Capt. Copp'dall, dated in Bantā, le 25th May, 1616.

1 frō Diego Fernandas in Bantam, le 13th May, ditto accọ

ta. m. co. 3: 5: 8.

I del'd 3 *tais* 5 *ma.* 8 *condrin* fyne plate to gouldsmith to

---

133) The name, not given.

134) In the margin is written a later remark, reading "Sp. *Advice* at Cochi."

July 1616

make buckles for my sword hangers & chape,[135] sword &

ta. m. co.
1: 5: 2.

dagger, & I waid the buckels & clasps my ould gerdell poz. 1 *ta.* 5 *m.* 2 *co.*

A lettr
Albaro
Monis.

I sent a lettr to Albaro Munois, to buy 15 or 20 *pico.* rozen & som candell.

9 *mas*
1 *condr*

And the gouldsmith brought the 2 chapes of my sword & dagger, being silver, & poz. 9 *mas* 1 *condrin.* [*fol. 124r.*]]

13. This mornyng raynie calme wether, and after wind variable w'th contynewall rayne all day, & lyke most an end p'r night, littell or no wynde.

crp'rs.

Carp'trs.   [136]

lab'rs.
Advis
entred the
roade
Firando.

I went abord the ship *Advice* to Cochi, and saw her safely brought into the roade of Firando. We shott of 7 pec. to salute the towne, & 3 when the *bongews* went away, & 5 at our going ashore, as also 3 were shot afe at our first coming aboard. And the *Thomas* welcomed them w'th 3 peeces frō ashore, her ordinance being landed.

I rec. these lettrs foll'g, viz.:–

2. frō Sr. Tho. Smith, 1 of Novmbr 24th, 1614, & other of 26th Aprill, 1615.

1 frō Wor. Company, div'rs coppies, w'th 1 inclozed to all vs.

1 frō Capt. Jnọ Saris, 24th Novmbr, 1614.

1 frō Mr. Georg Saris, 20th January, 1614.

1 frō Mr. Franc Sadlar, of 25th Novmbr, 1614.

1 frō Mr. Tho. Fferris, of 18 February, 1613.

5 frō my brother, Walter Cockes.

All the abouesaid lettrs from London.

1 frō Mr. Jnọ Gourney, 30th of May, 1616.

1 frō Mr. Jnọ Hvnt, 27th of May, ditto.

1 frō Jnọ de Lievana, 5th June, ditto.

1 frō Capt. Brower, of 21 August, 1615.

All the abousaid other lettrs frō Bantam.

---

135) The metal piece protecting the end of the scabbard.—Thompson.
136) The figures, not given either in the text or in the margin.

July 1616

1. frõ Jnọ Fferris abord th *Adviz* at Syam River, le 24th of Novembr, 1615.

[*fol. 124v.*]]

Sonday.

14. This mornyng overcast droping wether, calme, yet fare most p'rte of the day, wind variable, but rayne p'r night in som quantetie.

5 carp't.
0 labo'rs.
Jaccatra
arived.

Carpe'rs 5, wherof 4 abord, but no labo'r.

The bark *Jaccatra* arived at Cochi this mornyng, & bringeth news of an other greate shipp of Holland, w'ch came out 4 daies before her frõ Pattania.

A lettr
to Mr.
Wickham.

I wrot a lettr to Mr. Wickham of arivall of the *Adviz*, & sent it p'r Spanish pilot.

Nota.

Here came reportes of the arivall of the bark *Jaccatra* & an other greate Hollands shipp; but as yet non com in.

15. This mornyng overcast wether, littell wind S'erly, som drops rayne now & then all day, but dry p'r night littell or no wynd.

carp'rs.
labo'rs.
A lettr
to Mr.
Wickam.
Goodes
ashore.

Carp'ts .[137]

I wrot an other lettr to Mr. Wickham p'r Antony Peris, how no Duch shipp was arived & how the report went.

Rec. aland the 7 packes broad cloth, w'th the rest m'r-ch'ndz, viz., Russia hides, 4 balles; gild leather, 1 case; 3 chistes gallipot; 1 chist jugges; 2 chistes glass botts; 8 case botts, 1 w'th whot waters; 2 casses furs; 1 box callico, &c; 1 box corall; 1 bag ambr; 1 tronk falconaria,[138] w'th a box rootes frõ Cape, but are rotten & not worth any thinge.

Nota.

2 ships.

News were brought that 2 Duch shipps are entred harbr at Cochi, a league frõ Firando.

Envited to
dyner.

The kyng envited vs to dyner to morrow, w'ch I gladly would haue put ofe, but could not. The kinges brother

Nota.

---

137) The figures, not given either in the text or in the margin.
138) Perhaps implements and fittings for hawking.—Thompson.

came to Eng'sh howse to viset me.   *[fol. 125r.]*⌋

16. This mornyng overcast rayny wethr, calme, & so remeaned all the afore nowne.

16 carp'ts.   Carp'trs all for shipp 16.

I cleard w'th Yoskey for these mattrs foll'g:–

	ta.	*m.*	*co.*
Pid to gouldsmith	0:	1:	2
P'd for dying an ould gowne	0:	1:	3
P'd Domingo, my boy	0:	5:	0
P'd for a straw hat for Dom'go	0:	0:	2
P'd Mr. Eatons boyes father	0:	5:	0
P'd for tryming my hat	0:	2:	0
P'd for a *catabra* for Domingo	0:	9:	5
P'd making cleane my *cattans*	0:	2:	5
	2:	6:	7
More paid for a *kitesoll*	0:	2:	0
More for 2 pec. shews for Dick King	0:	3:	0
	3:	1:	7

And I del'd hym a bar plate poz. 3 *ta.* 1 *m.* 8, is small plate
3: 6: 5½, wherof deducting 3: 1: 7, so rest, due to me *T.* 4:
8½.

To dyner   We were ynvited to dyner p'r the king, & well entertayn-
to king.   ed, & the China Capt. w'th vs. Mr. Rowe, Mr. Totton, Mr.
Wilmot & the purcer of *Tho.*, w'th Mr. Eaton, Mr. Nealson
& my selfe.

Duch   And after nowne the 2 Duch shipps entred the haven of
shipps
entred.   Firando, viz., the one called the *Black Lyon*,[139] a shipp of
Nota.   7 or 800 tonns, & the other the bark *Jaccatra*. The Hollanders report that all the Hance townes[140] in Germany, w'th
the Kyngs of Denmark & Sweaden, are entred into confe-
dracy w'th the States.   *[fol. 125v.]*⌋

17. This mornyng droping wether, but sowne brake vp, &

139) De *Swarten Leeuw*, Dutch ship.
140) The Hanseatic towns.

July 1616

so remeaned fayre all day & lyke p'r night following, littell
wynd S'erly p'r day, buy calme p'r night.

20 carp'trs.
3 lab'rs.

Carp'trs 20, to say 18 for ship & 2 for howse, & 3 lab. for
shipp.

A man ran away.

There was a man of the *Advice* ran away, called Tho.
Heath, being gvner, but was staid by the offecers of the
King of Firando, & word sent to me thereof.

A lettr frō Jor. Durs.

I rec. 2 lettrs frō Langasaque, 1 frō Jro. Durois of 25th
July, new stile, w'th a p'rer ashculler sak stocking, 140
tallo candelles, w'th a botell rose water and a p'rcell

A lettr frō Alb. Munos. Pr'sent.

cardinvm, for Mr. Bailie; rose wa. & card, and an other
letr frō Mr. Albaro Mvnois w'th 69 tallo candelles.

We carid the king a pr'sent as foll'th, viz.:–

4 *tatta.* brod cloth, N? ,141) tawny.

1 great sheet gilt leather.

1 pec. callice, fyne, N? 11, cost .142)

Conyskins black.

10 knyves at 11*d* p'r knyfe.

1 case bottelles.

1 comb case & glasse.

Ffalconaria.

25 *cattis* gad stile.

1 make [*sic*], monarky Br'ttan.

1 map, king in p'r liament.

1 genelogy all kyng[s] frō Brute.

3 Duch juggs, w'th covers.

And I had conferrence about our abuse offred p'r them of
Vmbra, w'ch the king tould me he would assist me in it,
in what he might, taking the pr'sent in kynd part, &c.

I went to Duch howse, where they vsed vs very frendly,

A lettr from Pattania.

and Wm. Jn?son, m? of bark *Jaccatra*, del'd me a lettr frō
Mr. Jn? Browne, dated in Pattania, the 14th of June, but

141) The number, not given.
142) Not entered.

July 1616

it had byn opend by som other before it came to my hands. He advized in it of the *Sea Adventurs* arivall at Syam. Jn:

Jn: Yossen.   Yossen arived at Firando from Edo.   [*fol. 126r.*]⌋

18. This mornyng calme hot wether, but after a stiff gale wind S'erly most p'r day, and rayne in the later p'rte of night, calme wethr.

A mane died.

5 carp'rs.
3 lab'rs.

Fals a larom.

For ye Hollanders.

Pr'sent of Mr. Baylie.
To China Capt. wife.

A man died out of the *Advise* called   .[143]

Carp'trs 5 & 3 labo'rs all abord, or for *Thomas*.

Yasimon Dono came rvning, & brought me word that our junk *Sea Adventure* was arived, but it proved a falce larom. The Hollandes mʳ, capt., & Capt. Speck came to English howse, & brought me a pr'sent of a bar'll Spa. wyne, a great glasse bottell aquavite, 2 Hollandes cheeses, and a small pot buttr. Mr. Jn: Baylie gaue me a beza ston[144] for a pr'sent—a reasonable bigg one; China Capt. brothers wife a pere ambr beades, geven her cont'g 55 beades, poz. 3 *tay* 7 *mas* 2 *condrins* of best ambr.

19. This mornyng overcast droping wether, & so remeaned p'r fittes most p'rte of day, w'th a stiffe gale, wind S'erly, but not so much p'r night, yet more rayne.

4 carp'rs.
0 lab'rs.
Present China.

Carp'rs 4, wherof 3 for ship *Thomas*.

The China Capt. brother at Langasaque sent me a peece corse wroght velvett, yello, red & black, to make cushins of.

3 pec. kersies.

Mr. Jnọ Totton sould 3 pec. Devonshir kersies, viz., 1 stamet, 1 black, & 1 sad blew for four skore *taies* alltogether, to Andrea Dittis, China Cap., to pay before ship dep'rte frō hence.

Frō Sug̃ Dono.
Currall.

Sugen Dono sent me a barell salt raspas[145] for a pr'sent. I waid out a box currall of Mr. Totton, viz.:-

---

143) The name, not given.
144) *Iseki* 胃石. A bezoar, formerly thought an antidote.—Thompson
145) Raspberries.—Thompson

269

July 1616

cat. ta. ma. co.

N? 4 & 5, best sort, poz. ....0: 15: 2: 4 ⎫
more ditt sort, poz............0: 14: 3: 0 ⎪
N? 2 & 3, an othr sort, poz. ....1: 01: 4: 0 ⎬ in a box to goe vp.
more ditto sort, poz...........0: 04: 8: 0 ⎪
N? 1, an othr sort, poz. ....0: 11: 7: 0 ⎪
N? 6: 1: branch, poz. ....0: 01: 6: 4 ⎭

  som totall, all poz. 4: 1: 0: 8

More del'd the China Capt. to mak poz. of, viz.:–

  No 6, 1 branche, poz. 0: 1: 8: 0
  No 1, 5 branches, poz. 0: 1: 4: 2

  som totall of this, poz........0: 3: 2: 2 ⎤ *cat. ta. ma. co.*
         4: 1: 0: 8 ⎦ 4: 4: 3: 0

                 [fol. 126v.]]

20. This mornyng still lowring droping wether, littell wynd S'erly, but after much rayne all the afore nowne, but fayre wether aftr & lyke p'r night following.

   Carp'trs .[146)]

300 *tas.* I deliverd three hvndred *tais* plate bars to Mr. Osterwick, to pay botemen, & to del'r som to Mr. Eaton to defray charges vp, & rest to remeane for other occations.

   And the China Capt., Andrea Dittis, came & bought currall, wherein the other he rec. yisterday was wayed, viz.:–

                   ta. ma. co.

 2 branches of N? 6, both poz. 3: 4: 4
 11 littell branches, N? 1, 4, & 5, poz. 6: 6: 0

                 10: 0: 4

   At 10 *tays* plate for 1 *tay* wight currall.

   I rec. of the gouldsmith 2 hookes & 12 buckles for my

3 *tais.* sword hanger, w'th a littell pec. silver poz. just 3 *tais.*

Sonday. 21. This mornyng lowring calme wether, but after proued

---

146) Not entered.

fayre all day & the lyke p'r night following, yet a fresh gale, wind S. most p'rte day.

Frō Mr. Totton. To Mr. Totton. Mr. Totton, mr of the *Advice*, gaue me a target & a peare Pattania pikes for a pr'sent. And I gaue hym 2 pere silke stocking, viz., I peare red of my owne & an other peare greene, sent frō Jor. Durois the other day.

Allowais. And I waid out 2 whole pottes allowaies, viz., N° 2, poz. 6½ *cattis* pot and all; an other poz. 6 *cattis* pot & all; an other rest, poz. 3 *cattis*, 12 *tay* wight pot & all; w'ch 3 p'rcelles I carry vp w'th me for Edo.

Nota. A Dduch marener, being drunk, stabd a woman, because she would not let hym enter into her howse.

News of our junckes ariuall at Si. About 10 a clock at night, Harnando Ximines came to the Eng. howse & brough[t] word how Capt. Adames was arived in our junck from Syam, & that we had goodes com in 2 junkes more besids her. [*fol. 127r.*]⌡

22. This mornyng fayre mild wether, littell wynd S'erly, but proved more afterward w'th a littell rayne after nowne, but dry & calme p'r night.

Junk ye *Sea Adventur* ariued at Firando. I went to Cochi, & there met Capt. Adams in our junck, and carid boates to tow her into the roade, w'ch they did. And I rec. a packet lettrs frō Mr. Beniamyn Ffary, wherein was contayned, viz.:–

1 a note all chrges vpon the junkes voyage.

2 Invoiz goodes sent in *Sea Adventure*.

3 Invoiz goodes reladed in her.

4 Invoiz goodes laden in Capt. Shobick junck.

5 Invoiz goodes sent in Capt. Geequans junck, wherin Ed. Sayer goeth.

6 Mr. Farys lettr to me, dated at Judea,147) in the river of Syam, le 3th June past.

7 Invoiz of goodes retorned to Andrea Dittis, China Capt.,

---

147) Yuthia.—Thompson.

for his sulfer or brimston.

23. This mornyng fayre mild wether, no winde yet after variable frō S. to N̊., vering back W'erly, but calme p'r night, som drops beginyng night.

1 c'rp'rs.

A lettr
to Ed.
Sayer.
A letr
to Albaro
Munois.

Carp'rs 1.

I wrot a lettr to Ed. Sayer to Langasaque yf he should chance to arive theare, as also the othe[r] junck. And I wrot an other to Albaro Munois to look out for pitch. As also in answer of his of 29th carrant, the lettr for Ed. Sayer went p'r conveance of China Capt. & the other p'r fello w'ch brought candelles frō Albaro Munois.

We had a generall councell this day of divers mattrs, viz.:–   [*fol. 127v.*]⌋

1. Yt was thought fyting to buy or fraight a small China junk.

2. To sell our junck w'ch came frō Syam, yf we can.

3. To send Mr. Willmot to Nangasaque to attend coming junkes.

4. To land our goodes at Langasaque, & put it in a sure gadong, rather then bring it to Firando, it being a bettr place of sale then Firando.

5. To procure a *bongew* of king to remeane abord to see the Japons haue their due, & no more for avoyding of scandaloz tonges, &c.

Capt. Adames del'd me 4 lettrs w'ch came out of England in the new years gift, viz.:–

1 from Mr. Tho. Syth, dated le 18th Feb'y, 1613, cop'y.

1 frō Mr. Tho. Willson, 16th Februay, ditto.

1 frō my brother Walter, ditto, 16th, 1613.

1 frō Mr. Ed. Dodysworth in Surat, 20th Novbr, 1614.

24. This mornyng fayre mild wether, calme, but after a fresh gale all day at N̊. E., veryng N̊.erly, but calme p'r night; fayre hott wether, &c.

July 1616

Carp'trs 23, all for shipp *Tho.*

Capt. Adames went w'th me to viz. the kyng, he being comen frō Syam, I meane Capt. Adames. And we carid a pr'sent as foll'th, viz.:–

2 barelles *morefack.* ⎱
2 salmons. ⎰ frō my selfe.

5 China plattars porselon. ⎱
1 parrakita. ⎰ frō Capt. Adames.

But he was sick, & kept his bed; so we could not speake w'th hym.

Late towardes night came news how the Duch junck is arived at Nangasaque many men being dead, & the rest so weake & sick that they weare forced to put in theare for want of men to bring her to Firando. I meane the Duch junck w'ch comes from Syam.

Sangero Samme fownd a woman of his yisterday playing falce w'th another Japon, for w'ch he presently cut her in peeces w'th his owne handes, &, after the man was brought to the place of execution & cutt in peeces; & his brother had the lock of haire on his head cut affe p'r the hangman w'th the same *cattan* w'ch cut his brother in peecese. [*fol. 128r.*]⌋

25. This mornyng fayre calme wether, but sowne after a fresh gale all day, at N.º E'erly, and the lyke p'r night following, yet not much wind.

Carp'trs 19 for shipp *Tho.* all.

Our host of Osakay (or Sakay) sent his barke to seek fraight & to carry me vp, yf I came. Mr. Wickham wrot a letter to our *jurebasso*: how he sent her to bring me vp, yf I weare not provided for before; but he wrot me no word at all.

Our hostis at Bingana Tomo sent her sonne w'th the neles we wrot for p'r skite only 2 *pico.* of the greate want,

273

w'ch are to com after her.

110 *tais*
2 bar goldes.
18 *tay* w't
gould.

And I del'd two bars *oban* gould to Mr. Eaton w'th 18 *tay* wight Priaman gould. I say I del'd it to Mr. Osterwick to geue to Mr. Eaton, & put it into the invoyz goodes carid vp; the bars *oban* gould at 55 *tais* p'r barr.

Willmot.
Ed. Sayer.

I del'd a memoriall to Mr. Willmot of mattrs to be donne at Langasaque, as apereth p'r coppie, & wrot a lettr to Ed. Sayer.

26. This mornyng fayre wether, wynd N:°erly, but after proved variable on all partes of ye compasse, w'th som rayne, lightnyng & thvnder towardes night, but sowne ended, & after fayre weth'r.

16 carp'trs.
148) lab'rs.

Carp'trs 16 labo'rs all for howse to v[p]lade goodes and 15 of the carpentrs were for shipp.

Goodes.

Ed. Sa.

We rec. all the sappan that was out of hould ashore w'th 44 bundelles of skins, all for the Company. Allso 11 bundell skins, 1 tiger skyn, & 12 jarrs black varnish for Ed: Sayer.

Nota.

And the king sent 2 *bongews* abord to see the marreners haue their owne, they being brabling knaues, espetially the boteswayne.

Harnando
Ximines.

Farnando Ximines gaue me a new hatt w'th a bang [*sic*] gouldsmiths work, a peare silk garters, w'th gould fring, & shewstring same, ruch.149)   [*fol. 128v.*]]

27. This mornyng fayre calme wether, but after wynd variable frõ N:° to S., yet dry all day but much rayne p'r night, a stiffe gale S'erly.

[ ] c'rp'tr.
[ ] lab'rs.
Nota.
Nelson.

Carp'trs 16 w'th labo'rs.

I gaue an other memoriall to Mr. Nealson & Mr. Osterwick of my opinion of thinges fit to be donne in my abcense at Emperors Court, as apeareth p'r coppie. The Hollandes

Holand junk.

junck frõ Syam arived at Firando this day in the after

---

148) Not entered.
149) Rich.—Thompson.

nowne. Duch shot affe much gvns.

The King of Firando was very sick this day, so that his brother & all the nobilletie went post hast to vizet hym. And sowne after the king sent word he was very ill, & that showting of ordinance disturbed hym much; wherefore he desired both English & Hollanders not to shoute affe any more till he fownd hym selfe better.

We put all matters abord to goe towardes the Emperours Court to morrow, God p'rmiting wynd & wether.[150]

I del'd an other remembrance to Mr. Osterwick & Mr. Nealson of mattrs to be donne at Firando in my abcense, as apeareth p'r coppie.

28. This mornyng rayny wether, much wind S'erly, and soe remeaned all or most p'rte of the day, and the lyk p'r night following, conty'all rayne.

29. This mornyng still contynewall rayne, littell wind S'erly and so remened rayny wether all the fore nowne, but dry after, yet much wynd & som rayne p'r night.

We rec.   [151]bundelles skins more out of junk w'ch is the full complement to make vp the skins for acc⁰ of Honorable Company.   [*fol. 129r.*]

30. This mornyng rayny lowring wether w'th a stiffe gale, wynd S'erly, but proved fay[r]e most p'rte day & night following, &c.

I rec. a lettr frõ Albaro Monois, dated le 6th August, new stile, & sent p'rt his man p'r whome I ret'rned answer & sent hym a Hollandes cheese for a pr'sent. I rec. a lettr frõ Mr. Wickham p'r Skitte, dated in Miaco le 14th currant, w'th 3 others, viz., 1 for Mr. Osterwick, 1 for Mr. Baylie, 1 for Mr. Rowe & 1 for Mr. Wilson, w'ch I del'd them, but had no tyme to read my lettr over, being ready to dep'rte

---

150) A later remark in the margin reads "Visit to Emperour."
151) Not entered.

for Edo, & Capt. Adames abord before me.[152] Soe we sett forward in the after nowne, & having a good gale wynd, & got to Langowne[153] that night, where we came to an ancor, it being calme.

31. This mornyng calme wether, all afore no wind but a fresh gale after W'erly most p'rte of day, but night calme.

About midnight we wayed ancor, the tide serveing, & rowed it vp all the affore nowne; but, after, had a fresh gale W'erly, so that late at night we got to the streate of Ximina Seke, where we came to an ancor.

August 1616.

01. This mornyng calme wether, but after wind variable frõ S. E. to W., but calme most p'rte of the night.

We wayed ancor this mornyng an hower before day, but we[re] forced to stop the tide for want of wynd; but, a gale coming vp after at W., we got after midnight neare vnto Camina Seke,[154] & there came to an anker till mornynge.

[fol. 129v.]

2. This mornyng fayre calme wether or rather a littell wind S. E'erly, but after proved a fresh gale most p'rte of the day & for p'rte night, rest calme.

Tacca Sacky.

After daylight we waid ancor & passed the strantes [sic] of Camina Seke, and, the wind being good, we gott to a pl'ce called Tacca Sackey,[155] in a bay, to an ancor, haveing made 32 leag., & watedd in the way at a place called Camangare,[156] where our host of that place brought me a

---

152) A later remark in the margin reads "Iovrnal of Voyage."
153) Nagoya 名護屋.
154) Kaminoseki 上ノ關.
155) Takasaki 高崎.
156) Kamakari 蒲刈.

pr'sent of dry fysh, & I sent hym a *barso* of wyne.

3. This mornyng fayre calme wether, but after a fresh gale, wind most p'rt of day at S. E'erly, but calme all night. After daylight we waid ancor frō Taccasackey, &, having calme, rowed it vp till the gale came; & soe, late at night, got to an ancor at Woshmado,[157] haveing made 30 leagues.

Sonday.   04. This mornyng calme hot wether, & so remeaned till 10 a clock, & then a fresh gale at S. E'erly mos p'rte of the day, and a stiff gale towardes night, but after calme. Before day we dep'rted frō Woshmado, rowing it vp till the wynd came; & late in the night got it vp neare the bar foote of Osakay, where we rode at an ancor till mornyng.

05. This mornyng a littell wind E'erly, but sowne after vered W. S'erly all rest of day, but night calme, fayre hott wether.

We arived   We put in over the bar of Osackay, rowing against the
at Osakay.   wind, meeting aboue 300 barkes going out; but it was past 10 a clock before we got vp to the towne, where Mr. Wickham, w'th our hostes, came out & met vs w'th a banket, *Nifon catange*.[158]

A lettr   I wrot a lettr to Mr. Nealson & Mr. Osterwick, how I
to Mr.   was advized p'r many that it was dangros to send about our
Nealson &   small junck to Edo, yf she were not com away befor this
Mr.   lettr came to his handes, & then my opinion was to send
Osterwik.   her for Osackay. Also, not to sell lead vnder 7 *taies* p'r *pico*. This lettr I sent p'r coñ Mr. Albartus.   [*fol. 130r.*]⌡

Sr. Albartus came to vizet me, accompanid w'th his host & others w'th a banket, *Nifon cantange*, as many others did the lyke, & late towardes night our host of Sackay did the lyke, & brought me a silk coate or *catabra*, & an other of lynen to Capt. Adames, w'th comendacons frō Safian

---

157) Ushimado 牛窓.

158) A later remark in the margin reads "I. of V. ends," and another in the text, "Osacca."

August 1616

Dono, whose man he was, as also from Chubio Dono, his brother, w'th offer of much frenship.

Nota. Also our ould host of Miaco came to vizet me, & brought 2 barilles wyne for a pr'sent. He fownd hym selfe agreeved the Eng'sh were gon frō his howse, & would needes know the occation, w'ch proved to be hys bad vsag of Mr. Wickham, who lodged aboue 3 months in his howse, in all w'ch tyme he never would so much as eate nor drink w'th hym, but gaue out bad wordes against all our nation. Soe I sent him away w'th goodes [*sic*] wordes, telling hym I knew by report he was a ruch man, & needed not to care for any for the Eng'sh (as he reported), nether would the Eng. be vndon whether they lodged at his howse or in an other, &c.

06. This mornyng fayre calme wether, or rather a littell wynd at S. W., hot wether all day & the lyke p'r the night following, still dry wether.

Pr'sentes rec.

Pr'sentes geven. *ta. m. co.* 4: 3: 8.

Our ould host of Sackay, w'th our boateman & Domingos mother, came to vizet me, & brought me pr'sentes of frute, hense, & wyne. And I gaue eache of them a singell peec. chint bramport, and a bar plate, poz. 4 *ta.* 3 *ma.* 8 *co.* to Mr. Eatons child, Hellena, to carry her mother, & a *catabra* to the wench w'ch brought her, cost   .[159)]

07. This mornyng overcast wether, calme, & sowne after rayne in greate aboundance all day & the lyke p'r night foll'g, wynd variable N°erly, a small gale.

A lettr to Mr. Nealsn. I wrot an other lettr to Mr. Nealson & Mr. Osterwick, as apereth p'r coppie; & sent it p'r Syusa, or boateman.

A lettr to Safion Dono. Also yisterday I wrot a lettr to Safian Dono, in complem'-tall sort, & rec. answer frō hym p'r our *bongew*, w'th many good wordes.

Enuited to dyner. Our ould host of Osakay, where Mr. Wickham yet lieth,

---

159) Not entered.

August 1616

called   160) envited vs all to dyner this day, where
we had extraordenary & kynd entertayment. [*fol. 130v.*]⌋
08. This mornyng rayny wether, wynd N°erly, not much
wynd nether p'r day nor night, yet variable, w'th much
rayne all day & lyke p'r night.

   We paid to the kinges bark men & owr owne, as foll'-
th:–

		ta.	m.	co.
To the m.ʳ of kynges bark, 1 bar plat, poz. ....T.		3:	0:	0
To pilot & stersman of same, lyk plate, 1 b'r ..T.		3:	0:	0
To 42 men marin'rs, same bark, 1 bar ....T.		2:	2:	0
To mariners, our bark, same plate ....T.		1:	4:	0
Som totall all amontes vnto ....T.		9:	6:	0

ta. m. co.
9: 6: 0.

Paid out p'r Mr. Wickham, & is for demoragese in staying
at Firando 10 or 12 daies after they were laden.

   Allso ther was lent vnto Ishon Dono, the Kynge of

ta. m. co.
5: 0: 0.

Firandos chirurgion, 5 *tais* plate bars to be paid in Firando
to Mr. Osterwick at demand, w'ch money was lykwais paid
p'r Mr. Wickham. And   ,161) the China Capt. man,
w'ch goeth vp w'th me for a servant had nothing paid till

ta. m. co.
2: 0: 0.
A lettr to
Inga Dono.

now, so he had 2 *tais* advan[c]ed pad p'r Mr. Eaton.

   I wrot a lettr to Inga Dono, Lord Cheefe Justice of
Japon, to exskewse me I went not to Miaco to kisse his
Lordships handes, w'ch at my retorne frõ the Emperours
Court [I ment to doe].

2 lettrs.

   Also I wrot 2 other lettrs, one to the King of Firando and
the other to Andrea Dittis, the China Capt., & sent them
p'r the kinges bark now retorning to Firando. In the kinges
lettr, I recomended our Eng'sh howse & our affares to the
tuition of his Highnes in my absence, desiring hym to haue
a fatherly care therof, & to assist them w'ch I left in all

---

160) The name, not given.
161) The name, not given.

279

August 1616

occations they stood in need of.   [*fol. 131r.*]⌋

09. This mornyng lowring wether, & calme, but after som wynd variable, varing W. S'erly, yet dry wether both day & night following.

Lettr. I kept the lettr to Mr. Nealson & Mr. Osterwick dated the 6th pr'sent till now, & sent it w'th that to the China Capt. by Synze of boateman, & an other lettr, yt was to King of Firando, p'r his owne boate man. The chirurgion sent his

Nota. bill for the 5 *tais* but it was after my lettrs were gon.

I sent our *jurebasso*, accompanid w'th our host, to vizet the Governor (who is the Emperous kynsman) to exskewse me that I went not to kisse his Lordshipps handes, by reason of the fowle weather & the hast I made to go to the Emperour, but that at my retorne I ment to doe it, God willing. He took it in good p'rte, & sent me word I should be welcom, & that I should fynd him ready to doe ether me or our nation any good he could.

Mr. Eaton. Mr. Eaton went this mornyng for Miaco to put mat'rs in order, & to retorne to Sakay to morrow.

10. This mornyng, fayre calme wether, & littell wind after W'erly most p'rte of day, but calme p'r night w'th som drops of rayne, but not much.

Goodes sent. We laden all our m'rch'ndz & other matters for Edo in in [*sic*] 2 barkes, & sent it for Fushemi[162) by water to saue

Jnọ Hawtery. chargis, Jnọ Cook & Jnọ. Hawtery going along w'th it. Jnọ Hawtery went out of our lodging to a whorehouse, & pawnd a shert & a pere silk stocking.

Lettrs. I wrot 4 lettrs to Firando, viz.:–

1 to Mr. Nealson & Mr. Osterwick.

1 to Mr. Jnọ Bayly.

1 to Mr. Ri'd Rowe.

1 to Mr. Jnọ Totton.

---

162) Fushimi 伏見.

August 1616

The King of Firandos man retornd frō Court, & bringes word the Emperour will haue all our lead & tynne, of w'ch I advised Mr. Nealson & Mr. Osterwick, & sent the chirurgion of the kyngs bill for 5 *tais* therinclozed.

Mr. Wikham. Also I del'd a rem'brnce to Mr. Wickham of such matters as I thought fyting, as apereth p'r coppie.

Ther was a *bose*, or pagon prist, murthered in his howse, but murtherers canot yet be fownd out. The justis haue set out   163) gould cont'g   *tais* each bar for hym that will disclose or bring to light the morthers. [*fol. 131v.*]]

Sonday. 11. This mornyng fayre calme wether, & very littell wynd after yet dry wether both day & night following.

Nota. Mr. Eaton not retornyng frō Miaco, we were forced to stay heare this day.

A lettr to Mr. Nelson. I wrot a word to Mr. Nealson & Mr. Osterwick how the King of Firandos man retorned frō themperour, & brought word yf the Emperour would take all our lead & tynne, so I advized them to keepe it yf it were not should before. Also **Bill.** therinclozed I sent the bill for the 5 *tais* lent the King of Firandos chirurgion. This lettr I sent p'r conveance of our *bongew*.

12. This mornyng fayre wether, littell wynd variable, but fayre wether most p'rte of the [day], w'th som drops of rayne towardes night, but fayre all night after, calme.

Mr. Eaton retornyng to Osakay before day, wee set fowardes on our voyage towardes Edo, & dyned at Fraggata,164) our charges costing *T*.,   165) & horsehier **ta.** that day to Fushema, cost *T*.   . Soe we lodged this **7: 8: 0.** **1: 0: 0.** night at Fueshmay, the charges of the howse amonting vnto

---

163) This name and the following price, not entered.
164) Hirakata 枚方.
165) This and the following prices are not entered but they are given in the margin.

281

August 1616

1 pe. chint. *T.* 8: 8: 0, w'th 1 *tay* to servantes & 1 pec. chint to hostice.

Nota. I thought good to note downe that, as we passed along the river side before we came to Fushima, we saw a dead man cast vpon the shore, whome had byn mvrthered p'r som villans; yet the cuntry people let hym lye, & not geveing hym buriall. And on the other side was a man cursefied vpon a crosse for mvrthering a m'rchntes servant. And in an other place (as we passed) I saw som 8 or 10 malefactors heades set vpon tymbrs by the hie way side. Yf it were not for this strict justice, it were no liveing Nota. amongst them, they are so villanouse desperate. And I thought good to note downe that, coming to Fushima, w'ch is but 3 leagues frō Miaco, we were enformed, that, som villanous people sett vpon the gard w'ch kept the 30 bars *oban*, w'ch was ofred for sallary to hym that would d'scovre the murtherer of the *bose* (& could be no other but the mvrtherers them selues , yet carid away the gould at nowne dayes. This is the report, but whethr it be true or no I know not. It is said this crue[l] [men] haue vowed to kill many men. *[fol. 132r.]*⏌

13. This mornyng fayre mild calme wether, and so remeand till towardes night & then som few drops of rayne, yet fayre all rest night; littell wynd som p'rte of day E'erly.

Nota.
Hautery. Jn.º Hawtery, being sent afore w'th our goods p'r water to Fushami frō Osakay, & haveing 4 *tais* del'd to hym to defray charges, in two dais space idly spent the one halfe in whorehowses & drunkennesse, I fynding hym so drunken he could skarse stand on his feete; &, when he is drunk, [he] is mad furious.

200 *tais.*
100 *tais.* We passed p'r a towne called Otes,[166] where Mr. Wickham met vs, & brought 300 *tais* in plate of bars w'th hym,

---

166) Ōtsu 大津.

282

August 1616

wherof he paid 200 *tais* to Mr. Eaton & 100 *tais* to Capt.
Adames p'r Mr. Order vpon acc.°, I say three hvndred *tais*
vnto them both, w'th 6000 cash to Mr. Eaton, wherof 3000
were del'd to Jakese, to lay out for horshire p'r way. And

Cosa'tes. at night we arived at a towne called Cosantes,[167] where
we la all night, & our charges cost in all   . Jaquese,
w'th Mr. Sweetland & 3 others, went before vs w'th all
our m'rch'ndz to avoid trowble to be ½ a day before vs, &c.

Nota.
Billes. And I rec. of Mr. Wickham, viz.:–

1. bill Mickmos,[168] for 1 black cloth & 2 pe. bafta.
1. bill Migmoy, for 4 *cattis* allowais.
1. bill Migmois, for gould rec. at a hie rate.
1. rec'pt of Migmois for 4 brod clothes & other comodetis rec. of Jn.° Phebie.
1. rec'pt of Migmois & his sonns for goods left at Edo.
2. bill Andres Capt. Adams brothr in law for 554 *mas* 1 *condrin*.
1. rec'pt for pott allowais del'd to Shibio Dono.

All w'ch billes I or [sic] receptes I del'd to Mr. Eaton at Cosates.

Nota. Here our host tould vs that Jn.° Yosson passed by to goe
for Edo yisterday.   [*fol. 132v.*]⌋

14. This mornyng fayre calme mild wether, but towardes
nowne a fresh gale, wynd at N.° E. w'th much rayne in the
after nowne, & lyke p'r night.

Minna
Cochi. We dyned at a place called Mina Cochi,[169] & charges
cost as followeth:–

	ta.	m.	co.
To the goodman for all our dietes ....*T.*	3:	0:	2
To the servantes 100 of *gins* ....*T.*	0:	1:	0

Tuch'ama. So we went to an other place to supp'r, called Tuchiama,[170]

---

167) Kusatsu 草津. The charge, not entered.
168) Or. Mickmoy. Mikumoya 三雲屋, a Japanese trader.
169) Minakuchi 水口.
170) Tsuchiyama 土山.

283

August 1616

Tablebok. where we were forced to stay all night by meanes of the rayny wether. I had a peare table bookes of Mr. Eaton, yt were
of Mr. Willmotes. Our charges at Tuchiama was, viz.:—

	ta.	m.	co.
To goodman of howse for all our dietes .... T.	5:	0:	0
To servantes of howse 300 *gins*, is .... T.			. 171)

15.   This mornyng fayre calme wether, all the afore nowne,
but som rayne about 3 a clock till towardes night, and so
remeaned dry wether all night foll'g.

We dyned at Camiama,172) and cost to howse *T*. 2 *ta*. 0 *m*. 0
co., and to servantes of howse 100 *gins*, is *T*.   .173) And

Shrok. we went to bed to Shrock174) & spent *T*.   .And, the wether
seemyng to be good, we hired 2 bark to carry our goodes

Nota. in; & about 10 a clock at night did embark our selues to
haue passed an arme of the sea of som 21 leages, to haue
shortend our journey as also to save charges. But about
midnight the sea began to rise w'th a stiffe gale, wind E'-
erly, soe that we altered our determenation & put downe

Meea. into the cod of the bay to a place called Meea, where we
arived the morrow after nowne, not w'thout much danger,
haveing had an extreme gust of wynd, w'th much lightnyng
& thvnder, accompanid w'th rayne, so that it might be

Toffon. accompted a tuffon. One of our barkes w'ch carid the
goodes lagged behind, & so got not in the mornyng tide, as
we did, soe that she ran a greate risga175) to haue byn cast
away by laysynesse of the bark men. But our *bongew*, w'th
Goresano *jurebasso*, behaved them selues so that they got
the bark into a creeke (not w'thout much danger, runing
ouer sholes), being assisted w'th the men & marreners of

---

171) Not entered.
172) Kameyama 龜山.
173) This and the following prices, not entered.
174) Shiroko 白子; and the opposit town Meea is Miya 宮.
175) Riego (Span.), risk.

August 1616

one of the Emperours barkes, w'ch la endocked in the same creeke.

This night began the feast of the dead,[176] & candels hanged out all night. *[fol. 133r.]]*

16. This mornyng close, overcast wether, w'th a stiff gale, wynd E'erly, veryng more S'erly, w'th greate store rayne sowne after most p'rte of the day, but espetially in the after nowne; & towardes night proued a tuffon, very extreme wether, yet dry wether all night followinges, & not much wynd.

We could not know this night whether our goodes be much wet or no, the villanous barkmen are occation that we got not all ashore (before the tuffon came), as we did out of our barke.

17. This mornyng fayre wether, wynd S'erly, enclynyng W'erly, yet dry all day, & the lyke p'r night following.

We fownd our goodes not so bad wett as we thought, soe haveing opened the fardelles, & new packt them, we got to bed this night to a place called Ocasaqui,[177] it being 7½ leagues. We gaue the host at Mia for our dietes a bar *oban*, w'th 200 *jins* to the howse, & spent 400 *gins* p'r way.

Nota. The ould Emperour was borne in this towne of Ocasaque, in w'ch place their is a very great castell.

Sonday. 18. This mornyng fayre calme wether, but after a fresh gale variable frõ S. to E., yet dry wether all day, but rayne p'r fittes all night.

Yosenda. We dyned this day at Yosenda,[178] & p'd howse 3: 0: 0, and the servantes 100 *gins*. And we went to bed to Aray,[179]

---

176) The first day of the *urabon-e* 盂蘭盆會, the 13th day of the 7th month in Japanese lunar calendar.
177) Okazaki 岡崎.
178) Yoshida 吉田.
179) Arai 新居.

August 1616

& pid w'th   180) *gins* to servantes.

Here we had news how Calsa Samme hath cut his belly, being attaynted of treason against his father & brother, to haue destroid them & set vp Fidaia Samme, his enemie. It is thought it will goe hard w'th Masamone Dono, his father in law; & speeches are geuen out that the Jesuites & other padrese are the fyre brades & setters on of all this, in pr'voking children against parentes & subiectes against their naturall princes, &c.

This night ended the feast of the d[ea]d.   [*fol. 133v.*]]

19. This mornyng droping wether, wynd at S. E., & soe remeaned rayny wether all the forenowne, but was dry wether after w'th night following.

We came to dyner to Fame Mach,181) & paid 3 *ta.* 5 *m.* 8 *co.*, and to the servantes of the howse 200 *gins.* And we la all night at Mitsque,182) & p'd,   183) and to the servantes of howse.

Here we had news how Calsa Same was to passe this way to morrow to goe to a church neare Miaco, called Coye,184) som say to cut his bellie, others say to be shaued a prist & to remeane theare the rest of his daies. All his owne men are taken frō hym, & he sent w'th a gard of themperour his brothers men. His wife he hath sent to Massa Monede Dono, her father. All [he] hath for his alowance in the pagon church, 1 *mangoca*185) p'r annᵒ. He lodgeth this night at an vncles howse som 4 leagues hence, called

---

180) Not entered.
181) Hamamatsu 濱松.
182) Mitsuke 見附.
183) This and the following prices, not entered.
184) Kōya 高野. More precisely, Kazusa was banished to Asama 朝熊 in Ise 伊勢 province, on the 6th day of the 7th month, that is, August 8, 1617, old style.
185) An income of ten thousand *koku* 石 of rice. A *koku* equals 5.13 bushels.— Thompson.

August 1616

Cacken Gowa.[186]

20. This mornyng fayre calme wether, but sowne after store of rayne p'r fittes all day, yet dry all night, wynd littell at S. E'erly.

Cakinggaua.
Nota.

We dyned at Cackingawa, the towne where the castill is where Calsa Samme la all night. We met hym & others on the way in 3 or 4 troups, but could not well vnderstand in w'ch of them he went, because he kept hym selfe close

News.

in a *neremen*.[187] It is said there goe divers other w'th hym to that church (or pagod), where it is thought they shall all cut their bellies, som of them being men of 40 & 50 *mangocas* p'r ann°., w'ch is 8 or 10 tymes more then the King of Firando hath. Also their is speeches that the Emperour is making ready forcese to goe against Massamono Dono.

Nishew
Sacka.

We came to supp'r to Nishew Sacka,[188] so we made but 6 leagues this day, & there overtook our goods sent before. So we were forced to stay theare all night for want of horsese, all being taken vp for the Emperourse service to carry alonge these noble men. We paid for our dyner at Cakingaua 1500 *gins*, w'th more to the servantes 0100 *gins*, and for supp'r at Nisi Zaca 1500 *gins*, and to the the [*sic*] servantes 0100 gins.   [*fol. 134r.*]」

21. This mornyng overcast calme wether, but after a littell wynd at W. S'erly, yet dry wether all day, but a great shower of rayne in ye beginyng night, rest dry. We dyned at Fugi Eda,[189] & gaue to howse 1000 *gins*, & to servantes 0100 *gins*.

Newes.

And so we came to Shrongo to bed to Stibios, where we

---

186) Kakegawa 掛川.
187) *Norimono*. See Note 114) above.
188) Nissaka 日坂.
189) Fujieda 藤枝.

287

August 1616

vnderstood that the ould Emperour had left order w'th Shongo Samme (now Emperor) not to kill his brother Calsa Samme, but to confine hym into the pagod aforsaid for 10 yeares, and in the end, fynding hym conformable, to use his discretion.

A lettr to Mr. Wickha.

I wrot a lettr to Mr. Wickham, of our arivall heare, & how Jn? Cook, & Jn? Hawtery had staved me 5 bottell wyne, 2 pottes conserve, a barill of Zant oyle, & let falle my bag biskit into a river. This lettr sent p'r conveance of our host Stibio.

22. This mornyng overcast calme lowring wether, but after littell wynd S'erly, & fayre wether all day, but rayne after midnight.

A lettr to Mr. Nelson.

I wrot an other lettr to Mr. Nealson & Mr. Osterwick to same effect as yt to Mr. Wickham, & that all the horses were taken vp to cary plate to Edo, soe yt we stay here for horses, viz., 100 horse to cary plat.

About 10 a clock we dep'rted frō Shrongo, and paid our host for the howse a bar of *coban* gould, vallued at 5 *tais* 4 *mas*, and to the servantes of howse 200 *gins*.

Canbar.

So we went to bed this night to Cambr,[191] is 7 leaguis frō Shrongo, & spent p'r way 0600 *gins*, and we paid to howse 2000 *gins*, and to servantes in 2 howses 0400 *gins*.

23. This mornyng raynie wether, wynd S., yet after pr'ved fayre all day, & lyke night following, not much wynd, *vt supra*, &c.

Barra.
Mishma.

We dyned at Barra,[192] & paid 0400 *gins*, and went to bed to Mishima[193] 2500 *gins*, and to servantes 0200 *gins*, & might haue gon ferther but could get noe horses p'r reason

---

190) A later remark in the margin reads "Sorongo."
191) Kambara 蒲原.
192) Hara 原.
193) Mishima 三嶋.

August 1616

all were taken vp before for the Emperour.   [*fol. 134v.*]」

24. This mornyng fayre wether, or rather a littell wind S'erly, fayre wether all day, but much wynd p'r night E'erly, w'th greate store of rayne.

Hacone.

And we went to Haconey[194] on the top of the montayne, where the great pond w'th the devill is, as they report, and

Odowar.

spent in the howse 0300 *gins,* and after went Odawar,[195] where we la all night; but night haue gon ferther, but coud not for want of horses.

2lettrs.

I wrot two letters, 1 to Mr. Wickham, & an other to the pilot of the Spanish ship, yt to Mr. Wickham sent p'r   ,[196] a m'rchnt of Fushama, and the other p'r an expresse sent frō Mr. Eaton.

Sonday.

25. This mornyng raynie wether w'th a stiff gale, wynd E'erly, contynewall rayne all day, wind veryng W'erly, dry wether all night.

The wether pr'ving extreme fowle, we were constraind to stay at this place called Odowar.

Nota.

I thought good to note downe how in the tyme of Ticus Samme,[197] there was a strong castill in this place, kept by one Wigen a Dono[198] (whoe marid the doughter of Ogcsho Samme, the deseased Emperour). This stood our against all the forcesse of Ticus Samme having 100000 men w'th hym in the castell, w'ch Ticus seeing he could not bring hym vnder, sent Ogosho to parly w'th hym & bring hym to reason, or else to cut his owne belly. So, vpon the p'rsawsion is [*sic*][199] Ogosho, he rendred vp his castell,

---

194) Hakone 箱根.
195) Odawara 小田原.
196) The name, not given.
197) Taikō Sama 太閤様, Toyotomi Hideyoshi 豊臣秀吉 (1536–1598).
198) Hōjō Ujinao 北條氏直 (1562–1592).
199) This should be "of."

vpon condition that he & all the rest might live peaceably w'thout punishm't. Yet Ticus Samme, having hym in his power, made Wigen a Dono to cut his belly, contrary to pr'mis. [*fol. 135r.*]⌋

Wigen a Dono.

26. This mornyng fayre wether, wynd W'erly, and soe contynewed all day, & the lyke p'r night followinge.

Odowar.

We haueing remeaned at Odowar 2 daies dep'rted from it this mornyng, & paid to the howse a bar *coban*, 6 *ta*. 4 *m*. 0 *co*., and to the servantes in the howse 0300 *gins*, and for passage, 2 places, 0520 *gins*, and at Oyesa[200] for wyne & meate & to s'rvantes 1200 *gins*, and at Fugisau[201] for dyner 1000 *gins*.

Oyesa.

Fugesaw.

At this place two of Capt. Adames tenantes of Febys[202] met vs, and brought a pr'sent of 10 loves white bread, and a dish of boiled beefe w'th 2 bottelles wyne.

Tozuka.

And soe we went to bed to Tozuka,[203] 10 leagues short of Edo, from whence Capt. Adames went before to make ready his howse to receave vs, & to com & meete vs in the mornyng before wee enter the city.

A Rs. of 8.

I gaue our hostes doughter at Oyesa a R. of 8 w'ch I had of Mr. Wilson.

27. The mornyng still fayre wether, wind at W. S'erly, a fresh gale all day, and the lyke p'r night.[204]

We paid the howse at Tozekay,   [205] and to the serv- antes, and dep'rted from thence & paid at   for meate, 0500 *gins*, and at   for dyner 1500 *gins*.

We arived at Edo.

And soe we arived at Edo this day about 3 a clok in the

---

100) Ōiso 大磯.
201) Fujisawa 藤澤.
202) Hemmi 逸見.
203) Tozuka 戸塚.
204) A later remark in the margin reads "EDO."
205) This and the following prices, not entered.

August 1616

after nowne, & lodged at Capt. Adames howse, he meeting vs at the entry of the cittie w'th our men w'ch went afore w'th the goods, who arived heare also this mornyng.

Nota.

  Capt. Adames doth now vnderstand that his brother in law Andrea playeth the k[naue] w'th hym, w'ch he would hardly beleeve before.

  The King of Firandos brother sent his man vnto me to bid me welcom to Edo. The Spanish pilot & an other Castillano came to my lodging to bid me wellcom.

28. This mornyng still a stiff gale, wynd at S. W., & so contynewed all day, yet fayre wether, & the lyke the night following, but not much wynde.

Pr'sentes.

  The King of Firandos brother sent me a pr'sent of 2 barill wyne & 2 piggs, & 1 bar'll [wyne] & 1 pig to Mr. Eaton. & Codgskin Dono sent me a chist figges, 10 b'ndell of *wobi*, & a dish musk millians, & a m'rchnt brought me a dish grapes. I sent our *jurebasso* to thank them all, *Nifon catange.*

2 lettrs.

  And I wrot 2 lettrs to Mr. Wickham & Mr. Nealson p'r King Firands man, advising of our arival at this place & to look out for sales m'rch'ndz.

           [fol. 135v.]⌋

29. This mornyng fayre calme wether, & very littell wynd after ᴐathe[r] p'r night or day, & that N⁚erly, w'th rayne p'r fyttes most p'rte of the night, &c.

Andrea.

  Andrea, Capt. Adames brother in law, arived heare frō Orengaua[206] late the night past. He brought a pr'sent of fresh bread w'th a littell sallet oyle & som poulderd beefe. He is a craftie k., &c. I noted downe this pr'sent wrong, for Ca[p]t. Adames sonne sent it & not Andrea.

30. This mornyng lowring droping wether, wind N⁚erly, &

---

206) Uraga 浦賀.

rayne p'r fittes all day, but much more p'r night following, yet not much wynd nether p'r day nor night, &c.

Nota.

Codgkin Dono sent this mornyng betymes for Capt. Adames, and tould hym he had spoaken w'th the Emperour, & tould hym of our being heare, & that we might com w'th our pr'sent when we would. Yet they thought it best to stay till the first day of the new mowne, w'ch they accompted a happie day.

Earthquake.

About 3 a clock in the after nowne there hapned an exceading earthquake in this citty of Edo in Japon, w'ch contynewed, from the begyning to the end, about the eight p'rte of an hower; but about the halfe tyme it was soe extreame that I thought the howse would haue falne downe on our heades, & so was glad to rvn out of doares w'thout hat or shewes, the tymbers of the howse making such a nois & cracking that it was fearefull to heare. It began by littell & littell, & so encreased till the middell, & in lyke sort went away againe, &c.

About som 22 yeares past their hapned an earthquake in the pr'vince (or kyngdom) of Bongo, in w'ch there was a towne (or rather a cittie) of 4000 howseholdes sunck into the sea, not any living creature being saved.[207] And at same tyme a mowntayne neare adioynyng was cloue in the middell. And it rayned long haire lyke vnto that of mens heades. This hapned som two yeares before Ticus Samme died. And, amongst Japons, earthquaks are held for prodigious things; yet they say this pr'vince of Quanto is more subiect to them, then any other part of Japon.

Nota.

We opened our m'rch'ndiz to lay out a pr'sent for the the Emp'ror, & fownd wanting a treble peece of chint

---

207) On the 13 th day of the intercalary 7th month, the 1st year of Keichō 慶長元年閏七月十三日, 1596, Uryu-jima 瓜生嶋, an island with about 1000 houses and 5000 inhabitants, disappeared under the sea.—Murakami.

292

bramport, w'th aboue a *catty* wight of ambr, & 9 writing
table bookes; and most p'rte of our gally pottes broaken
p'r the rude handling of our hackny men & falt of them
should haue looked to it. Also 2 bars of tyn stolne p'r the
way, & 1 treble peec. chint stolne heare, after they were
opened, &c. [*fol. 136r.*]]

31. This mornyng calme raynie wether, & after littell wynd
N°erly most p'rte of day, w'th much rayne, but not so
much p'r night, &c., most p'rte dry wether.

Migmoy. Migmoy brought me a pr'sent of wyne, grapes, and
waffar caks, & tould me that for any difference of acc°,
ether betwixt Mr. Wickham or Mr. Eaton & hym, he was
content to remit it to my discretion. He is a crastie fello
& very such. Amongst the rest, he tould me he lyked our
religion so well that he ment to turne Christian, &c.

A lettr to I wrot a lettr to China Capt. & put it into that of Mr.
China Capt. Nealson & Mr. Osterwick of the 28th current & kept till
this day, sent p'r King of Firandos man, vnto whome was
500 *gins*. geuen 500 *gins*, to spend p'r the way.

Jn° Yossen. Jn° Yossen came yesterday to vizet me & envite me to
dyner w'th Capt. Adames & the rest. I answerd hym I
would vizet hym before I retorned, &c. The King of Fi-
Pr'sent. randos brother sent me a pr'sent of peares.

Earthquakes. There was a feeling of an earthquake 2 or 3 tymes againe
this day, espetially about 5 a clock in the after nowne. It
shaked the howse mightely, but nothing so forsably as the
other day, nor of so long contyewance. And about midnight
following ther was an other earthquak much lyke vnto
this.

September 1616.

01. This mornyng fayre calme wether, & so remeaned the afore nowne, but after rayne wynd S'erly rest of day as lyke p'r night, a stiffe gale w'th rayne, &c.

This day we carid the pr'sent to the Emperour Shongo Samme, whoe rec. it in kind p'rte, Codgscon Dono & Shongo Dono assisting vs in the matter. But it was long before we could be dispached, by reason all the nobles went w'th pr'sent to the Emp'r, it being the first day of the new moone. Amo[ng]st the rest was the King of Faccata, who as yet is not p'rmitted to retorne into his contrey; the reason I canot learne. I think there were not so few as 10000 persons at castill this day. It is a place very strong, duble diched & ston walled about, & a league over each way. The Emperours pallas is a hvge thing, all the rums being gilded w'th gould, both over head & vpon the walls, except som mixture of paynting amongst of lyons, tigers, onces, panthers, eagles, & other beastes & fowles, very lyvely drawne & more esteemed [then] the gilding. Non were admitted to see the Emperour but my selfe, Mr. Eaton, & Mr. Wilson. He sat alone vpon a place somthing rising w'th 1 step, & had a silk *catabra* of a bright blew on his backe.[*fol. 136v.*]⌋ He sat vpon the mattes cros-legged lyke a telier, & som 3 or 4 *bozes*, or pagon pristes, on his right hand in a rum somthing lower. Non, no not Codgskn Dono, nor his secretery, might not enter into the rowme where he sat. Yet he called me once or twise to haue com in, w'ch I refused, w'ch as I vnderstood afterward, was well esteemed of. I staid but littell in the place, but was willed to retorne; and both at my entrance & retorne, he bowed his head. I forget to note downe that all the rowmes in his pallas vnder foote are coverd w'th mattes edged w'th damask or cloth of gould, & lye so closse joyned on to

294

September 1616

an other that yew canot put the point of a knife betwixt them. The pr'sent geven was as followeth, viz.:-

1½ blak cloth N? 52, cont'g   208) y'rdes.

1½ stañet, N?   ,209)   y'rdes.

1½ strawcullr, N?   ,   y'rdes.

1½ black bay, N?   .

1½ stã bay, N?   .

1½ straw bay N?   .

3   Russia hides.

3   pec. diaper.

3   looking glasses; 1 blak, 1 gilt cover, 1 w'th comb & sozers.

2   pee. Holland cloth.

2   pec. Sleze land.

10   single peec. chint bramport, 3 in a peec.

2   branches currall, poz.   .

10   polisht amber beades.

2   cheanes white (or corse) ambr beades, poz.   •

2   chins better amber bead, all vnpolisht, poz.   •

3   dozen cony skins, silver heard, black & gray.

1   faggot of steele.

     cattis gad stile.

     Ffalconaria.

6   gallie pottes, sundry sortes.

2   green gvggs.

2   gren tonns.

1   possit pot.

1   great gilt India hide cont'g hides or peeces.

50   *cattis* tynne in bars.

5   *picos* lead p'r tickit.

I sent our *jurebasso* & *bongew* to Codgskin Dono & Shonga Dono to thank them for the paines they took about our busynes, & know of them when it pleased them I should

---

208) This and the following figures, not entered.
209) This and the following figures, not entered.

September 1616

com & vizet them to kisse ther handes, but they were not com from the Emperours castell. So they left word w'th ther servantes.   [*fol. 137r.*]⌋

02. This mornyng overcast lowring wether, much wynd at S. W'erly, & rayne p'r fittes both day & night follo'g, w'th a stiff gale wynd.

Nota.

I sent of *jurebasso* Gorezano in the mornyng to Codgskin Dono, & Shongo Donos howses, to see yf they were at leasure, that I might com & vizet them; but he plaid the k[naue], & I think went not at all, but tould me they were gon to the castell. But, after Capt. Adames went, they &[*sic*] sent me word they were at home. So I made what hast I could; yet, before I could com, the Emperour had sent for them, so I lost my labo'r, & retorned to my loding w'th the pr'sentes, refering it till to morrow.

Migmoy.

And sent the acc.̊ to Mickmoy to p'rvse over, for that I would make an end before I retorned.

03. This mornyng rany wether, much wynd at S. W'erly, but sowne after broke vp fayre wether, all rest of day & lyke p'r night following, littell or no wind p'r night.

We carid 3 pr'sentes, all alike, to Codgskin Dono, Oyen Dono, and Wotto Dono,[210] 3 cheefe men next to the Em-

Pr'sentes.

perour, to each of them alyke, viz.:–

1¼ *tatta.* black cloth, N.̊ 48.
1¼ *tatta.* stamet clo., N.̊ 20.
1¼ *tatt.* straw clo., N.̊ 01.
1¼ *tatt.* blak bay, N.̊ 46.
1¼ *tatt.* stam bay, N.̊ 30.
1¼ *tatt.* straw bay, N.̊ 4.
1   pec. Holland cloth, N.̊ D.
1   pec. Sle[z]land N.̊. G.

---

210) Doi Toshikatsu, *Ōi-no-kami* 土井大炊頭利勝 and Sakai Tadayo, *Uta-no-kami* 酒井雅樂頭忠世, councillors of the Shōgun.

296

September 1616
                 1 looking glasse, lardg.
                 1 looking glasse w'th comb.
                10 blak conyskins.
                 9 *cattis* gad steele.
                    galli pottes 1 each sort.

Also I went & viseted King Firandos brother & carid hym
a pr'sent, as followeth, viz.:–
                1¼ *tatt.* black cloth, N? 48.
                 3 pec. chint bramport, of   .211)
                 5 single handke'ch & rumall chint branport.
                 1 looking glasse.
                 3 table bookes.
                 1 pec. Sleze land, N? E.

                                              [*fol. 137v.*]⌋

04. This mornyng fayre calme mild wether, but after a small
     gale, wynd at N? W., or rather more W'erly most p'rt of the
     day, & calme p'r night, still fayre wether.

Nota.   We were enformed of an other noble man neare the
        Emp'r, called Ando Tushma Dono,212) vnto whome it was
        thought fitt to geue a pr'sent as to the former, this Em-
        perour being newly com to the crowne, & the Spaniard
        haveing geven out ill reportes of vs that we rob & stayle
        from all we meete at sea, w'ch was tould to vs by greate
        men in the Emperours pallas, w'ch is because Capt. Keel-
        ing took 3 of their shipps (I meane Portingals) coming
        from Surat. But Capt. Adames did enforme them the
        trew occation thereof, how they Portingals did still molest
        our shiping at Surat, so that now we had wars against them
        & comition to take either Spa. or Port., where we met
        them, in regard they took vs. Yt seemeth there is many
        papistes in these partes, w'ch would doe vs a mischeefe yf
        they could; yet the best is, the Emperour & them about

211) Not entered.
212) Andō Shigenobu, *Tsushima-no-kami* 安藤對馬守重信.

297

hym are no frendes of Portingals nor Spa., & the rather for extreme hate they beare to Jesuites & pristes, whome they canot abide, & gaue vs warnyng that we should com in their company, but rather to reveale them, to the entent they might be punished, &c.

Jacob, the Duch man, w'ch came into Japon w'th Capt. Adames, came to vizet me, & offerd his servis to the English. He is a cawker, a pore fello. The Duch offerd hym 3 *l*. 10 *s*. p'r month the last yeare; but he refused it, & after would haue taken it, but then they would not geue it. & I put hym afe w'th fayre wordes, telling hym we wanted no people, but had more then our trade did afford. I gaue his wife & her sister each of them a single pece chint bramport, &c.

2 pec. chint bramport. Pr'sntes.

Also we gaue 2 pec. grogren, 3 pec. chint bramport, & 6 table bookes to the secretaris of Codgkin Dono & Oyen Dono.

Earth quake.

This day in the after nowne, about 4 a clock, was an other earthquake, but of small contynewance, & gaue but one greate shake.

Lettr.

Mr[s]. Adames & her sonne sent me a lettr frō Oringaua, w'th a peec. pouldren beefe, exkewsing their not coming to Edo, in respeck of the Spaniardes w'ch did lie at their howse. [*fol. 138r.*]⌡

05. This mornyng still fayre calme wether, & very littell wynd after N°erly, but calme p'r night, still fayre wether both day and night.

Pr'sentes.

We went to Ando Tushma Dono, w'th a pr'sent as the other, wanting a small looking glase & som sortes gally potes, w'th 2 maps of London & 88 [*sic*]. This man was not w'thin, yet we left the pr'sent behind, & tould his man I would com & vizet hym when I knew he was at home.

Yoosen.

I sent our *jurebasso* to Jn° Yossen to tell hym I would

298

September 1616

vizet hym to morrow at dyner tyme.

Present.   A ruch m'rchnt called   213)came to vizet me and brought me a fatt hoog for a pr'sent. Codgskin Dono sent me peares, grapes, & wallnvts for a pr'sent.

06. This mornyng still fayre calme wether, & soe remeaned all day & night following, fayre wether littell or no wynd Nº.erly.

Dyned at Jnº Yosen.   We dyned all [sic] Jnº Yoosen the Hollandrs, where we had good entertaynm't. And, in regard of the kyndnesse he allwais hath shewed to Mr. Eaton & Mr. Wickham, to goe to the Court to speake for them in the abcense of Mr. Adames, it was thought food to geue a pr'sent to his wife

Pr'sent.   and doughter as foll'th, viz.:–

1 whole pec. chint bramport cont'g 3 pec. of R. *corg.*

1 peec. black silk grogren, cost   .214)

07. This mornyng still fayre calme wether, & litt'll wynd after at Nº W. all day, but a stiff gale p'r night, yet dry over heat.

Nota.   I went & vizeted Wotto Dono & Tushma Donno, & thanked them for the paynes taken in our affares, offring them to procure for them out of England anything they pleased to geue me notis of. They took my visetation kindly, & said they would get our privilegis renewed, & *goshons*215) or passes sealed this day, yf it were possibly.

And frõ thence we went rowndabout the kyngs castell or fortresse, w'ch I do hould to be much more in compas then the citty of Coventry.216) It will cont'n in it aboue 200000 souldiers in tyme of wars.   [*fol. 138v.*]⌋

---

213) The name, not given.
214) Not entered.
215) *Go-shuin* 御朱印, a written license on which the Shōgun's official cinnabar seal was affixed.
216) A city in Warwickshire, attributed to the author's birthplace.

September 1616

We dyned at the Kynge of Firandos brother, where we were well entertaynede. And towardes night the secretary of Oyen Dono came & vizeted me at my lodging & brought me a pr'sent of hense; & amongst other speeches he began to talke of the padres, & that it were good we had no conversation w'th them. Wherevpon I took occation to answer hym that he needed no[t] to dowbt of vs, for that they were enemies to vs, & to the state of England, & would destroy vs all yf they could. But that it were good he advized the Emperour to take heed of them, lest they did not goe about to serve hym as they had donne the Kinges of England, in going about to kill & poizen them or to blow them vp w'th gunpoulder, & sturing vp the subiectes to rebell against their naturall prince, for w'ch they were all banished out of England, &c.

08. This mornyng fayre wether, w'th a stiff gale of wynd at W. S'erly, and so contynewed all day, but littell or no wynde p'r night, fayre wether, &c.

We dyned, or rather supp'red, at a m'rchntes howse called Neyem Dono, where he provided *caboques*, or women plears, who danced & songe; & when we retorned home, he sent eavery one of them to lye w'th them yt would haue them all night. I had a bar of *coban* gould of Mr. Eaton cont'g 6 *tais* 4 *mas* w ch I gaue them.

09. This mornyng fayre calem wether most p'rte of the forenowne, but after a fresh gale wind at S. W., rest of the day, & most p'rte of the night, yet dry wether.

Mr. Eaton sould 6 or 7 broaken galle pottes the peeces of them at two *tais*. Jacob the Hollanders wife brought me a pr'sent of *muchos* & other stuff, *Nifon catange*, she being ready to dep'rte towardes her howse.

Capt. Adames this day, as the lyke every day, staid at the Cort to solicet of dispach to get our pr'velegis & passes,

September 1616

but still put afe; & amongst the rest the secretary tould hym yt it was reported how there were semenary pristes in his howse at Orengaua. So Capt. Adames sent away an express [*fol. 139r.*]⌋ with a lettr to his wife to look to it that there were no such matter. Ther is new edicts[217] sent out into all p'rtes of Japon, as namely to Langasaque, Arima, Vmbra, & Bongo, w'ch are most of them Xxristians, to see to it, that no padres be fownd amongst them, & them in whose howse they are fownd shall be put to death w'th all their generation. This must be foll'd w'th extremetie.

10. This mornyng overcast lowring wether, w'th a fresh gale, wynd N°.erly, drifting rayne all day, & the lyke p'r night following, &c.

Codgskin Dono sent for Capt. Adames, w'ch we hoped was to haue geuen vs our dispach; but it proved to be nothing but to enquire ferther about the padres. So he retorned w'thout doing any thing, they willing hym to retorne on the morrow, as they haue donne the lyke any tyme this 9 or 10 daies, w'ch maketh me to marvell, as I doe the lyke of the long stay of the Hollanders. God grant all be well in the South partes, & that they rise not in armes there.

11. This mornyng still rayny wether, but after brok vp fayre wether rest of the day, & som rayne p'r night, yet not much, nether any wynd p'r day or night.

Capt. Adames was all day at Cort againe to attend for our dispach, but retorne w'thout any thing; only they willed hym to haue patience & to com againe in the mornyng. Oyen Donos secretary came to vizet me, & tould me he suspected that our dalay grew p'r meanes of the

Nota. (margin)

Nota. (margin)

---

217) An edict banning Catholic religion was issued in Edo on the 8th day of the 8th month of the 2nd year of Genna 元和二年八月八日, or September 8, 1616, old style.

September 1616

looking out for padres, w'ch weare much sought after by the Emperour, & reportes geuen out that som were at Capt. Adames howses at Orengaua & Phebe. So Capt. Adames wrot againe to his folkes, to look out that no such matter were proued against them, as they tendered their lives.

Yt is thought that the Emperour hath a meanyng to bunish all Christiens out of Japon. God grant all may fall out for the best, for our so long detaynyng maketh me much to marvill, & the Emperours hate against the Jesuistes & fryres very greate, &c. [*fol. 139v.*]]

2 lettrs from Firad.

I rec. 2 lettrs frō Mr. Nealson & Mr. Osterwick, dated in Firando, le 5th & 6th vltimo, & sent by Gonosque Dono, who is com vp to vizet Codgsquin Dono, in respect of his fathers death, & bringes hym a pr'sent of 30 bars silver from the King of Firando. In these lettrs they adviz me of the trowble they had w'th the covetos mareners of the junck w'ch came frō Syam, &c; & that, as then no news of the other 2 junkes arivall at Langasaque, w'th Ed. Sayer. Also that the news is that the Amacan shipp will not com to Langasaque this yeare, she being arested p'r a marchant of Goa for money the Amacan m'rchntes owe hym. This news is came p'r a gallie & a galliot w'ch are arived at Langasaque, & came frō the Manillias.

12. This mornyng close calme wether, and after but littell wynd N°erly nether p'r day nor night, yet proued dry wether both night and day.

Nota.

In respect we are put affe from day to day & canot haue our dispach, I got Capt. Adames to goe to Oyen Dono, the Emperours secrettary, accompanid w'th our *bongew*, & Goresano our *jurebasso*, to geue hym to vnderstand, yf he make any dowbt of the matter, that we are no frendes of the Jesuites nor fryres, nether suffer any of their sect to remeane in England, but punish all them w'ch are fownd w'th death; this course haveing byn kept in England for aboue the space of 60 yeares, so that the Emperour needed not feare our conversation w'th that sect, for that their hatred against vs & our religion was more then against any other whatsoever, &c.

Oyen Dono, the secretary, vsed Capt. Adames kyndly, & tould hym & the other 2 how the Emperour was much offended against the padres, & therefore advized vs not to haue conversation w'th them nor to let them Christen any children of ours, yf we chanced to haue any, for then they might presume we were of their sect, whome the Emperour ment vtterly to extinguish out of Japon. He willed Capt. Adames not to think it long we were not dispached, the Emperours busynes being such that as yet it could not be donne, but w'thin a day or 2 he hoped to end it to our content. [*fol. 140r.*]]

13. This mornyng fayre calme wether, or rather a littell wynd N?erly, yet som drops of rayne towardes nowne and the lyke p'r fittes p'r night, littell or no wynde.

Empr'rs.

The Emperour went a hawking this mornyng, w'th a troupe (as it was thought) of 10000 men. It is said he will retorne this night, &c.

2 lettr
to Miaco
& Firando.

I wrot 2 lettres to Mr. Wickham & Mr. Nealson & Oster-wick, as apereth p'r coppie, & sent them away p'r expres p'r one of our people, because we stay here so longe. These lettrs were kept till to morrow after nowne.

14. This mornyng close calme wether, & after som rayne but much more p'r night, w'th a stiff gale, wynd N?erly.

Nota.

Capt. Adames & our *jurebasso* went to the Cout to get our dispach, but could not be ended to day, but referred till morrow. The councell tould them that the Emperour would not write any letter to the King of Cochinchina, nor meddell in other mens matters.

September 1616

Earthquak. This night past about 2 a clock hapned an earthquake;
but of no greate contynewance. Som say they felt it 3 severall tymes, but I felt it but once.

We haue much ado w'th Nic? Machievell *allius* Migmoy,
about clearing acc? w'th hym; but as yet not donne. Mr.

ta. m. co. Eaton paid Singero, the expres, 1½ tais to spend p'r the
1: 5: 0. way.

Sonday. 15. This mornyng raynie wether, wynd N?erly, & soe remeaned all day & lyke p'r night following, much rayne.

Capt. Adames went this day againe to the Court for to
procure our dispach, but could not be ended, but refered
till to morrow & then he to com w'th Codgskin Dono, & so
an end to be made.

16. This mornyng still raynie wether, littell wynd N?erly,
and so remeaned all day, but littell or no wynd p'r night.

Nota. We could not com to acc? w'th Nic? Machiavell, *allis*
Migmoy; so we are forced to go to Lan. w'th hym.

Capt. Adames went againe to the Cort to haue had our
dispach, but by meanes of the fowle wether the Councell
went not to the Court, so that he retorned back w'thout
doing of any thing. Capt. Adames envited the m'rch'ntes
to supp'r to morrow that envited vs the other day.

[*fol. 140r.*]]

17. This mornyng overcast lowring wether, wynd N?erly,
yet remeaned dry wether most p'rte of the day, and the
lyke p'r night following, &c.

2 bar *coban.* I rec. two bars *coban* gould w'th ten *ichibos*, of 4 to a
10 *ichibos.* *coban*218) all gould, of Mr. Eaton to be acc? for as I should
haue occation to vse them in gestes or otherwais.

Sup'r. We envited them to supp'r w'ch envited vs the other day,

218) The *koban* of 1 *ryō* 兩, was a standard unit of gold coin, equal to 4 *bu* 分
(*ichibu*) or 16 *shu* 朱, although the fineness differed over the course of
time.

304

September 1616

& had the *cabickes* as they had. I gaue 4 bars, called *ichi-bos* to one of them.

18. This mornyng somthing lowring wether, very littell wynd N?erly, yet remeaned dry wether all day, but much rayne p'r night, littell or no wynd.

Nota.

Capt. Adames went againe to the Cort to procure our dispach, & fownd all the Councell busyed about matters of justice of lyfe & death; & amongst the rest, one man was brought in question about Fidaia Samme, as being in the castell w'th hym to the last hower. This man was racked & tormented very much, to make hym confes where his m.r was, or whether he were alive or dead, but I canot heare whether he confessed any thing or no. Also the Admeralls sonne (our great frend), called Shonga Dono,[219] came to towne, having byn sent out by the Emperour before about busynesses. He had much talke w'th Capt. Adames about sea matters, and other greate men in company w'th them. And, amongst other mattrs, they tould Capt. Adames that they vnderstood their were certen islands to the Northward, very ruch in mynes of gould and silver, w'ch the Emperour ment to conquer, & asked hym wher (vpon good tearmes) he would be pilot. He made answer, he was not now at his owne dispose, being servant to the English nation, & therefore could not serve two masters. They asked hym whether he had heard tell of any ilands called les Ladrones, or of the theeves. He answered yis, but that his opinion was that they were of no moment, in respect the Spaniards had not taken them, they lying in his way as they passed frō New Spaine to the Phillippinas. They also spoake of an other iland, called p'r the Spaniard Hermosa

219) Mukai Tadakatsu, *Shōgen* 向井將監忠勝, admiral or *0-fune-bugyō* 御船奉行, son of Hungo Dono, or Mukai Masatsuna, *Hyōgo-no-kami* 向井兵庫頭正綱.

305

September 1616

(or *Rico en oro y plata*).[220] He answered he had heard of such a place in conferrence w'th Spaniardes. In fine, the Councell tould Capt. Adames all our dispach was ready, only they wanted Codgkins Donos hand, he being sick. So he was referred to com to morrow & bring Codgskin

3 *ichabs.*   Donos letter. Paid out to *cabokes* 3 bars *ichabo* gould.

[*fol. 141r.*]]

19. This mornyng raynie wether, wynd N?erly, but after nowne dry wether, & the lyke all night following.

We went to the Admerall yonger, Shonge Dono, & carid

Pr'sent.   hym a pr'sent, as followeth, viz.:–

1¼ *tatta.* black cloth, N?   .[221]

1¼ stamet cloth, N?   .

1 pec. Sleze lande, N?   .

1 looking glas 8 square dy, N?   .

& Capt. Adames gaue hym 3 gilt Syam skins, & a tigers skyn. He took our visitation kyndly, & offerd vs to do for

Nota.   our nation what he could. This man & his father are the trustiest frendes we haue in these p'rtes, &c. And I thought good to note downe how this man entred into speeches about the ilandes Ladrones, taking them to be ruch in myne of gould and siluer. My answer was, that I knew no such matter, but to the contrary esteemed that yf the[y] had byn such, that the Spaniard would haue had them before now, they lying in the way frõ Agua Pulca to the Phillippinas. But my opinion was that yf the Emperour pr'tended to make a conquest of any, that the Phillippinas them selues were of more emportance, & the Spaniardes weake & ill beloved of the cvntrey people, & that herein

---

220) Span., meaning "rich in gold and silver." It was a fictitious islet, although some contemporary European maps indicated its location and some expeditions were actually dispatched by the Spaniards and the Dutch, in the early 17th century.

221) This and the following numbers, not given.

September 1616

his Ma^t.^{is} needed not to dowbte the assistance both of the Eng'sh & Duch, as occation should serve. At w'ch speeches he seemed to make a pawse, & in the end said that they wanted such shipps as ours were. Vnto w'ch I answered I marveled the Emperour did not make such haveing both men (I meane workmen), tymber, and all thinges else necessary. Yt seemed to me that he tooke notis hereof, &c.

A lettr frō Mr. Wickham.

Towardes night I receved a lettr fro Mr. Wickham, dated in Miaco, the 27th vltimo, wherin he wrot that as yet he heard no newes nether of our small junck nor bark that should com w'th wood & skins frō Firando; w'ch maketh me to marvell very much.

Nota.

Capt. Adames went to the Court againe for our dispach, but was put affe till to morow. [fol. 141v.]]

20. This mornyng fayre calme wether, but sowne after a fresh gale of wynd N?erly all rest of the day & the lyke all night following, could dry wether.

Nota

Gonosque Dono retorned to Firando, & viseted me at my lodging, offring to carry my lettr, yf I would write, for the w'ch I gaue hym thanks, telling hym I hoped to follow after to morrow, &c.

Capt. Adames went againe to the Court (w'th our *jurebasso*) to procure our dispach, but could not dispach till to morow.

Migmoy. 25 bar coban.

Shonge Dono the Admerall made an end w'th Migmoy for our difference. So he gaue twenty fyve bars *coban* gould for ballance of all acc?, w'ch Mr. Eaton receaved.

1 bar coban. m. co. 6: 6.0 corall.

Also I rec. one bar *coban* gould of Mr. Eaton for a littell peec. of curall, poz. 6 *mas* 6 *condrins*, sould to a cauelero for that price.

Hawtery.

Jn? Hawtery plaid the lewd fello againe, & stole 2 peeces chint bramport w'th 2 handkerchefs Rumall cottony, & a peare tablebookes to geue to whores. Thus much we fownd

307

& was retorned back. But we lack many other things, as of same chintes, amber beades, table bookes, bars of tynne, w'ch out of dowbt he hath taken, but forswearth it, as he did the other till we brought the partis before his face. And that w'ch was much worse, he went & cut his haire after the pagon fation, thinking to turne pagon; w'ch he could not do heare, allthough he would. Yet there wanted no good will in hym. And, besides, he is a comon drumord, yf he may com by drink, & when he is drunk is as a mad man, as ban [sic] a humor as any o' the rest; for then he will fall out w'th all men, & kill & slay, &c.

21.　This mornyng fayre wether, wynd a fresh gale N.?erly, and so contynewed all day, but no so much p'r night, yet fayre could wether both day and night, &c.

Nota.

Migmoy came this mornyng & brought a pr'sent, *Nifon ca[ta]nge,* & w'th hym came a servant of Shonge Dono the Admerall, to make frendship. So we drunk together & p'rted frendes, but I would wish no man to trust hym any more.

Nota.

Capt. Adames & our *jurebasso* went againe to Court to procure our dispach, but could not. And Chubio Dono came to towne. Yocotta Kaqueamon Dono,[222] Oyen Donos

Pr'sent.

secretary, secretary [sic] brought me a pr'sent of 2 *catabras,* 1 silk, & the other lynnen.　　　　　　　　　　*[fol. 142r.]*⌋

22.　This mornyng fayre calme wether, & so remeand all rest of day & the lyke p'r night foll'g.

I forgot to sett downe pr'sentes geven yisterday, viz.:—

To a *box* [sic] I gaue a hogg, viz.,

1 pec. alleias, of 30 R. p'r *corg.*

1 pec. iasanyharer [?], of 15 R. p'r *corg.*

& to 3 Capt. Adames tenantes yt broght pr'sent, viz.,

3 pec. can'equi abalupta, of 16 R. p'r *corg.*

1 handkerchefe, chint bramport, to a gerle.

---

222) Yokota Kakuzaemon 横田角左衞門.

September 1616

A lettr
to Mr.
Wickham.

I wrot a lettr to Mr. Wickham, but the p'rte, w'ch should haue carid it, went away w'thout it.

23. This mornyng fayre calme wether, & so remeand till towardes night & then we had rayne, but after midnight fayre.

Empr'rs
pr'sentes.
& other.

The Emperour sent me 10 *kerimons* & an armor for a pr'sent, 2 *kerimons* to Mr. Eaton, & 2 to Mr. Wilson. And Oyen Dono sent me 5 *kerimons*, & 1 & 2 *catabras* to Mr. Eaton, & the lyke to Mr. Wilson, & our *jurebasso*. And we rec. of privilegis & *goshons* frō Emperour.

Also I sent a pr'sent to Chubio Dono, viz.:—

1¼ *tat*. brods cloth black, N.º   .223)
1 *tat*. samet, N.º   .
1 Russia hide.
1 lookinglas, N.º   .
1 pec. Sleze land, N.º   .

Pr'sentes
Chubio.

And towardes night he sent me thankes w'th letters for the King of Firando, & sent me a *wakadash* for a pr'sent, & 2 pec. taffate to Mr. Eaton.

We could not by any meanes procure the Emperours lettr to King of Cochinchina, he saying he would not meddell in other mens matters.

Nota.

Goresano plaid the babling fello against Capt. Adames, whereby Oyen Dono, the Emp'r secretary, had lyke to haue falne out w'th hym. Yt is this fellos foolish triks w'ch hath gotten hym many enemies, & put me to much trowble heretofore to save his lyfe.   [*fol. 142v*.]]

24. This mornyng lowring warme wether, yet remeaned fayre all day, and the like p'r night following, calme or rather a littell wynd, variable.

Pr'sntes.

Otto Dono sent me 5 *catabras* for a pr'sent, w'th wordes comple'ntall. And I sent our *jurebasso* to geue hym thank,

223) This and the following numbers, not given.

309

September 1616

as the lyke, to Chubio Dono, & sent Jnọ Yossen word we
were ready to dep'rte to morrow mornyng toward Firando.

I gaue the *cabukis* 1 bar *coban* & two *ichibos* of gould.
Shezero the *caboke* sent me a Japon cap, & I gaue her that
brought it 5 *mas* 4 *condrin*, paid p'r Goresano.

We carid a pr'sent to Safian Dono, viz.:-

1¼ *tatt.* black brodcloth, Nọ   .224)
1¼ *tatt.* strawcullr cloth, Nọ   .
1   Russia hide.
1   peec. Sleze land, Nọ   .
1   looking glasse Nọ   .

And sowne after he sent me thanks for it, w'th a box or
packet of letters for the King of Firando. And Jno Yoosen

sent me a lettr to carry to Capt. Speck. And Shonge Dono,
the Admerall, sent me a saddell for a pr'sent. Also Otto
Dono & Tushma Dono sent me each of them 5 *kerremons*
for a pr'sent, & Tushma Dono sent 3 *catabrs* to Mr. Eaton,
2 to Mr. Wilson, & 3 to our *jurebasso* Goresano.

Migmoy got the Admerall to entreate me to com to his
howse, & to drink w'th hym to make frendship, as well as
he had donne w'th me. But I desire his Lordshipp to p'rdon
me, for that tyme did not now p'rmit me, nether could I
goe to Migmois howse in such sort w'thout disparidgment
vnto me, &c.

And so this night we packed vp all matters to retorne for
Firando to morrow, God p'rmitting.

25.   This mornyng raynie calme wether, & so remeaned most
p'rte of the day, but dry wether p'r night, littell or no
wynd at all, &c.

I sent Goresano before day to the clark of the Privie
Seale, to fetch our our [*sic*]225) *goshon* (or prevelegis), & to

---

224) This and the following numbers, not given.
225) A modern retouch makes this word read as "ould."

September 1616

carry hym a pr'sent of a peece of black silke grogran. He del'd the pr'sent but retorned w'thout the writing, willing hym to retorne anon.

1 tay.

I gaue a Englishmans child called Tho. Flood, a *tay* in *tagemon*226) plate, paid p'r Goresano.

We could not get our ould pr'veleges againe, & soe we [were] forced to dep'rte w'thout them. *[fol. 143r.]*⏌

26. This mornyng fayre calme wether, but after nowne a stiff gale, wynd at N? E'erly, rest of the day, but night calme.

1 ichobe.
1 catabra.
1 bar coban.
We dep'rted
frō Edo.

I gaue the *caboque* Shezero an *ichobe* & a silk *catabra*, and sent the m.ʳ of them a bar *coban*. We dep'rted towardes Orengava this mornyng about 10 a clock, & arived at Febe som 2 howrs before night, where we staid all that night, for that Capt. Adames wife and his two children met vs theare. This Phebe is a Lordshipp geven to Capt. Adames p'r the ould Emperour, to hym & his for eaver, & confermed to his sonne, called Joseph. There is aboue 100 farmes or howseholds vpon it, bisids others vnder them, all w'ch are his vassals, & he hath power of life & death over them, they being his slaues, & he as absolute authorete over them as any *tono* (or king) in Japon hath over his vassales. Divers of his tenantes brought me pr'sent of frute, as oringes, figgs, peares, chistnuttes, & grapes, whereof there is aboundance in that place. The *cabokes* came out to sea after vs in a boate & brought a banket. So I gaue them a

1 bar coban.

bar of *coban* to make a banket at their retorne to Edo, &

1 ichibo.

gaue the boate men w'ch rowed them an *ichibo*, both w'ch soms Mr. Eaton paid out.227)

27. This mornyng fayre calme wether, & not much wynd

---

226) *Teijimon* 丁字紋, a silver bar with a die of the character *tei*.
227) In a space after this entry is written a later, remark reading "1st Dep̄ture frō Edo."

September 1616

after, & that at N°. E., rayne wether all day but a greate
showre of rayne about midnight, &c.

1 bar *coban.* We gaue the tenantes of Phebe a bar of *coban* to make a
banket after our dep'rture from thence, w'th 500 *gins* to
1000 *gins.* the servantes of howses, & 500 *gins* to the horsmen (or
hankney men) w'ch carid vs frõ thence to Orengaua; the
cheefe of the towne accompanyng vs out of ther pr'sincts
& sent many servantes to accompanie vs to Orengaua,
w'ch is about 8 or 9 English miles, all rvning before vs on
foote, as homegers to Capt. Adames. I sent a lettr to the
Admerall that I ment to vizet hym to morrow; but he hearing of our coming hither, had sent me a lettr before to
envite me to com to hym, w'th many kynd offers of frend-
shipp. After our arivall at Orengaua, most of the neighbors
came to viset met [*sic*] & brought frute & fysh & reioiced
(as it should seeme) of Capt. Adames retorne.

[*fol. 143v.*]]

28. This mornyng fayre wether, littell wynd, but after
proved a fresh gale N°. E'erly most p'rte of the day, but
not so much p'r night, yet store of rayne p'r night, &c.

We went p'r water to a towne called Misackey,[228] 5
leagues frõ Orengaua, to vizet Fungo Dono, the ould Ad-
Pr'sente. merall,[229] & carid hym a pr'sent as followeth, &c.

1¼ *tatta.* black cloth, N°.   .[230]
1¼ *tatt.* stamet cloth, N°.   .
1 peec. Sleze land, N°.   .
I lookinglas, N°.   .
1 peec. chint amad, borowd of Capt. Adams.

Nota. And Capt. Adames gaue hym a leopardes skin & 5 handkes
chint bram, and Mr. Eaton gaue hym 2 single pec. chint bram-

---

228) Misaki 三崎.
229) *Hyōgo-no-kami.* See Note 207) above.
230) This and the following number, not given.

312

port. He entertayned vs kyndly at dyner & sent vs meate for supp'r, & gaue me a *wacadash* (or short *cattan*) from his side; & sent his men to shew vs his sonns howse newly built, being a very fayre place. This man is one of the best frendes we haue in Japan.

Sonday. 29. This mornyng raynie wether w'th a siffe gale wynd N⁰.erly, and so remeaned all day, w'th rayne p'r fittes, but much more rayne & wynd espetially p'r night ver[i]ng to S. E'erly.

We retorned p'r water to Oringaua, not w'thout much diffeculty. And the Admerall Fongo Dono dep'rted p'r water towardes Edo, to vizet the Emperour the first day of the new moone; but the sea being greate, & wynd contrary, he went ashore & so went overland p'r horse.

We gaue our hostis at Misakay 2 *ichibos* for howsrowme, & dyet, & 1 *ichebo* to her eldest dowghter, being wife to a Hollander, & 500 *gins* to her yongest doughter, & 200 *gins* to servantes in the howse, & 300 *gins* to the howse where Mr. Eaton did lye. And Capt. Adames gaue pr'sentes, viz.:–

1 handkerchefe & an *ichebo* to Adrian the Holl. wife.
1 handker. & 500 *gins* to the mother.
1 handkerchefe & 100 *gins* to yongest doughter.
1 handkerchefe to Mr. Eatons hostis.
And 100 *gins* to servantes of the howse.

[fol. 144r.]⌋

30. This mornyng lowring droping wether w'th a stiffe gale, wynd (or rather a storme) at S. E'erly, but more rayne wind p'r night, then p'r day wynd vering N⁰.erly.

Pr'sentes. I gaue Capt. Adames 2 *keremons*, & Andrea his brother in law, one of them the Emperour gaue me. And there was geuen out in pr'sentes, as followeth, viz.:–

To Capt. Adames wife,

313

September 1616

1 pec. blak grogren.

1 pec. Sleze land, N? .231)

1 cheane ambr beades, poz. .

And to Josephe her sonns, viz.,

1¼ *tatt.* black cloth, N? .

And to Suzanna, her daughter, viz.,

1 whole peec. chint bramport, of R. *corg.*

And to Andreas wife,

1 pec. black grogren.

And to Capt. Adams wives mother, & an other doughter, viz.,

2 single pec. chint bramport.

And 1 single pec. chint bramport to Adrians doughter.

Lettrs from Mr. Wickham & others. And towardes night arived a man of Capt. Adames expres, sent frō Mr. Wickham w'th lettrs & others frō Firando, Mr. Wickham advising that p'r proclemation at Miaco, Osakay, & Sackay, it was defended that no Japon should buy any m'rch'ndiz of strangers. Where vpon he could make no sales of our comodeties, & therefore did wish me, yf I met the expres on the way, to retorne to Edo to redrese it, yf I could.

4 lettrs frō Mr. Nealson, of 9th, 16th, 17th, & 20th August.

2 lettr frō Mr. Osterwick, of 8, 16, ditto.

1 lettr frō Mr. Wickham, of 19th Septembr.

1 ould lettr frō Mr. Wickham.

2 lettr from Mr. Rowe, of 10th, & 17th August.

1 lettr frō Mr. Totton, of 20th August.

1 lettr frō Mr. Ed. Willmot, of 11th August frō Langa.232)

[fol. 144v.]]

---

231) This and the following numbers and figures, not given.
232) In a space after this entry and again at the top of the following page are written a later remark reading "Return to Edo."

October 1616.

1. This mornyng stormy raynie wether, much wynd N?erly, but about nowne it broake vp, & remeaned dry rest of day & night foll'g, littell or no wynd, &c.

2 lettrs.

I wrot 2 letters, one to Mr. Wickham & an other to Mr. Nealson & Mr. Osterwick, & retornd them p'r same expres, vnto whome Mr. Eaton del'd 3 *ichebos*; & he said Mr. Wickham del'd hym 60 *mas*, wherof he spent 43 *mas* p'r the way. And Mr. Wilson, Jn? Cook, Wm. Sweetland, Jn? Hawtry, our *bongew*, & others, to the halfe of our company, I sent away directly towardes Miaco. & Capt. Adames, Mr. Eaton, & my selfe retorned againe towardes Edo, & lodged at Phebe. We gaue 1000 *gins* to the servantes at Orengaua, for Capt. Adames nor his wife would let vs pay nothing for diet.

Mr. Eaton deliverd to Mr. Wilson to be acc? p'r way, viz., 8 bars of *coban* gould, 233) *ichebos*, & 2000 *gins*, and 10 *ichebos* to my selfe.

2. This mornyng fayre calme wether, or rather a littell wind E'erly till about nowne, & then the wind vered N?erly, a great gust all the rest of the day, but no so much p'r night.

By meanes of this storme (we being onward on our way towardes Edo p'r water) we were forced to run over the sholes right ashore, not w'thout danger; so that it was dark night before we got our thinges on land, & went to a towne in the way 4 leagues short of Edo, called Cowa Saky;234) where we had bad lodging & worse fare, &c.

We paid for our diet at Phebie, w'th our hors hier from Oringaua & geven in the howse, viz., 2 *ichebos* in gould, & 1000 *gins* paid out p'r Mr. Eaton. And for our boate hier to Cowa Sackey 1 *ichebo*, & 400 *gins* geven to a pilot to

233) Not entered.
234) Kawasaki 川崎.

315

helpe vs ashore in a place to land our goodes.

Nota.

I forgot to note downe how Mrs. Adames sent powderd beefe, fysh, & bread, w'th rise, after vs to Phebie.

3. This mornyng raynie wether, wynd N? E'erly & soe remeaned all day & night following, &c.

We went to the secretary Oyen Donos howse to haue spoaken w'th hym about our occation of retorne, but were p'rswaded p'r his men to attend his coming to the howse of justice, & there might speake to hym & the rest as they entred; w'ch we did, but were referred of for answer till the next mornyng. [fol. 145r.]] So from thence we went to Codgskin Donos, but fownd Inga Dono, the cheefe justis of Japon, arived frō Miaco & com to vizet hym. So we could not speake w'th hym, &c.

Also we met theare a Spaniard, com from an iland neare Langasaque, where he was arived in a small shipp by contrary wyndes going to Manilla, & might not be sufferd to goe out againe w'thout lycence from the Emp'ror.

Nota.

Jn? Yoosen came to vizet me, & tould me he howrly expected the Hollandrs, & that, tuching the cortalling of our prevelegesse, it was not to be suffered, it being wrought p'r Safian Dono & other his assosiates to haue vs pend vp at Firando, to the entent to work vpon vs as they did on the Portingals & Spaniardes at Langasaque; but (said he) the Hollanders will forsake Japon, before they will be bownd to do it, &c.

4. This mornyng raynie wether wind N?erly, and so contynewed droping all day & night following.

Pr'sent.

1 *tay*.

A Duchmans sonne came to vizet me, & brought me a pr'sent of powndgranetes & oringes; vnto whome I gaue a *tay* in plate fyne, paid p'r Gorezano.

I got Capt. Adames to goe to Codgskin Dono w'th our *jurebasso*, to make the occation of our retorne knowne

vnto hym, & to aske his councell (as our cheefe frend)
what course we should take. He spoake w'th hym & the rest
of the councell and, as it seemeth, they will enlarge our
previlegese.

Supp'r.

A m'rchnt, our frend, called ²³⁵⁾ envited Capt. Adames,
Mr. Eaton, & my selfe to supp'r, & sent for the *cabokis,
Nifon catange.*

5. This mornyng still droping wether, wynd N°erly, & so
remeaned all day & the like p'r night following.

A lettr to
Mr. Wikham
& rest.

I wrot a lettr to Mr. Wickham, & so to send it for Firando, advizing how I hoped to dispach our matters to content very shortly; & sent this letter p'r a yong man of
Firando, neighbour to Yasimon Dono.

We could haue no answer this day tuching our busy-
ness. [*fol. 145v.*]⌡

Sonday.

6. This mornyng still droping wether, wynd N°erly, and so
remeaned most p'rte of the day, but not so much rayne p'r
night & very littell wynde, &c.

We went to haue spoaken w'th Oyen Dono & rest about
our busynes, but could not com to speech of them, they
were so busye about other matters.

A lettr to
Oreng.

I wrot a lettr to the *seniora*²³⁶⁾ at Orengaua to thank her
for our kynd entertaynm't.

7. This mornyng overcast lowring wether, wynd N°erly,
more p'r night then p'r day, w'th rayne p'r fittes p'r both,
&c.

We carid a pr'sent to Inga Dono as followeth, viz.:–
1¼ *tatta.* black cloth, N° .²³⁷⁾
1¼ *tatta.* stamet cloth, N° .
1¼ *tatta.* black bayes, N° .

---

235) The name, not given.
236) *Señora* (Span.), Mrs. Adames.
237) This and the following numbers, not given.

1¼ *tatta*. stamet bayes, N° .
1 peec. Sleze land, N° A.
1 red Russia hide.

This man is Lord Cheefe Justice of Japon, & now newly com from Miaco. I made knowne vnto hym the occation of my retorne, p'r meanes of the proclemation at Miaco that we should sell non of our goodes in those p'rtes. He tould me it was true that the Emperour had sent downe such order, that we should haue no other place of sales but Firando. I answerd hym that the Emperour might as well banish vs right out of Japon as bynd vs to such an order, for that we could make no sals at that place, as I had fownd p'r experi. of 3 yeares space & vpwardes. He answerd me he could not w'thstand the Emperours pleasure, & that at pr'sent all matters were in other manner in Japon then in tyme of the ould Emperour, & that he could do vs small pleasure in the matter, it being in the secretaries power to doe most; yet, as tyme should serue, he would doe his best.

Lettr.

The lettr I sent to Mr. Wickham was kept till this day, & sent p'r a man of Firando, neighbour to Yasimon Dono; wherin I advized hym I dowbted I should not make an end so sowne as I thought, & therefore wished hym to send away Mr. Wilson & the rest to Firando, but, for the *bongew*, he might stay my coming yf he would. We went also

Nota.

to the howses of Codgskin Dono & the rest, but could not com to speech of any, they, as it seemed to me, playing least in fight, w'ch caused me to write 2 letter to Cawkesayemon Dono, secretary to Oyen Dono, willing hym to stand our frend to solicet his m.r for our dispach; w'ch he answered me he both had donne & still would doe, but verely thought we could haue no dispach till after the hollidaies or feast, w'ch begineth the 9th currant & lasteth 3 or 4 daies. *[fol. 146r.]*

8. This mornyng still lowring wether, wynd N?erly, but after vered S'erly, w'th much rayne in the after nowne, & the lyke all night following, yet littell wynd.

Nota. We went to vizet the councellars againe, to haue our dispach in remembrance. & first to Oyen Dono the secretary, whoe tould vs that we should speake to Codgskin Dono, for that he could do nothing of hym selfe. Vnto w'ch I answerd that the rest did refer vs to hym, & therefore I besought his Lordship to procure our dispach; for I stood in dowbt my long staying & want of sales of our goodes (p'r meanes of this edict) would be an occation I should not send away our 2 shipps & junck this yeare, w'ch would be a borthen to hevie for vs to beare or to answer to our employers. He said he would doe what he could & take councell w'th the rest what might be donne. So from thence we went to Codgskin Dono, whome the servantes tould vs was in the house. Yet could I not com to speech of hym, but lost my errant w'th his cheefe man.

Nota. I forgot to note downe that Safian Dono was at the secretaries howse, siting in a darke corner, I being cald in & apointed to syt on the better hand of him, not knowing whoe he was till Capt. Adames tould me, w'ch then I went on the other side & craved p'rdon as not knowing hym. In fyne, every one complayneth that matters are worse then in the ould mans daies, & that this man doth nothing but change offecers & displace *tonos*, sending & changing one into an others contrey; so that much grudging is at it & all in law & plitos on w'th an other, so that what will com of it God knoweth, for, as the comon report is, no man dare speake to the Emperour of any matter they think is to his discontent, he is so furious, & no meanes but death or distruction. So that what will com of vs or our sute I know not, for I tell them it were as good for the Emperour to banish vs all out of Japon as to shut vs vp in Firando, it being a place of no sales.

9. This mornyng still raynie wether, littell wynd at E. S'erly, but pr'sently vered N°erly much rayne all day, but littell or non p'r night, yet much wynd & very cold wether.

Sheco.   This day was a greate feast of Japon called *sheco*²³⁸⁾ being the 9th day of the 9th month. Soe we could do nothing this day about our busynes at Court. But all day afternewne yesterday Capt. Adames & our *jurebasso* staid wayting at Court gate to speake w'th the councellers, who still geue good words.   [*fol. 146v.*]⌡

Nota.   Jn° Yoosen sent me word his man was com from Miaco, & that the Hollanders would be heare w'thin a day or two.

And Cacozayemon Dono wrot me 2 lettr that he had soliceted Oyen Dono his mr about our affares, & that they were not vnmindfull of it, but would shortly dispach vs; only their busynes was much at pr'sent by meanes of the caueleros w'ch came to vizet the new Emperour, as also for the sending away of the widdo of Fidaia Samme, doughter to the Emperour that now is, whoe is geuen in second marriadg to a *tono* called   ²³⁹⁾ whoe fought very valiently in defence of the Emperour at the overthrow of Fidaia Samme.

Mrs. Adams   Mrs. Adames & her 2 children arived heare yesterday
2 ichebs.   from Orengaua. And I gaue Shezeros child an *ichebo* & Mr. Eaton del'd an other to the *twerto*²⁴⁰⁾ that plaid on the

---

238) *Sekku* 節句. The 9th day of the 9th month is called Chōyō 重陽.
239) The name is not given, but the man to whome Senhime was given in second marriage was evidently Honda Tadatoki, *Nakatsukasa-no-Daiyū* 本多中務 大輔忠刻, the son and heir of the Lord of Kuwana, Honda Tadamasa, *Mino-no-kami* 美濃守忠政. See Note 27) for 1615.
240) *Tuerto* (Span.), one-eyed.

October 1616

10. This mornyng cold dry wether w'th a stiff gale, wynd N̊.-erly, & so remeaned most p'rte of the day, but littell wind p'r night.

An vprowr.

This man did not kill his sonne, nether will ye Empror let him nor the other haue ye land, for yt ye sonne of so vnworthie a father is not fit to inherit as he saieth.

Late towardes night was an vprower in the cittie of Edo, for that a cauelero, called Deo Dono,242) gaue it out that he would take the Emperours doughter as she went to morrow towardes her new hvsband, for that the ould Emperowr in his life tyme had promised her to hym, in respect of his service donne at Osekay against Fidaie Samme. But the Emperour now would not concent theirvnto, but sent hym word to cut his bellie, w'ch he refuced to doe, in taking of his howse w'th 1000 men his followers, whoe all shaved them selues, w'th 50 women of his, lykewais protesting to stand out till the death; wherevpon the Emperour caused his howse to be beset w'th aboue 10000 men armed, & ofred to leave his land to his eldest sonne of som 19 years ould, yf his servantes would deliver vp the m.r in quiet; w'ch coming to the fathers knowledg, he kild the said sonne w'th his owne handes; yet after, his servantes kild their m.r & deliverd his head to the men w'thout, vpon condition to haue their lives saved, & the lands to remeane to the other sonne; w'ch as it is said, the Emperour hath condecended vnto.243)

11. This mornyng cold warme wether, yet dry all day & the like p'r night following, very littell wynd & that N̊.erly.

A pr'sent.

I went & viseted the King of Firandos brother, & carid hym a pr'sent of 2 barills wyne & a dish of figges, w'ch he tooke in good p'rte & offred to send to the Emperours Coun-

---

241) *Shamisen* 三味線, a guitar of three strings.
242) Sakazaki Naomori, *Dewa-no-kami* 坂崎出羽守直盛.
243) Thompson suggests in his footnote that the marginal note is "in contradiction of some of the details."

cell to desire our dispach in his brothers name, w'ch I thanked hym for.

I went to Jn? Yossen to vizet hym & see what newes he heard of the Hollanders. But, as it seemed, they were not com to Osakay when Albartus wrot hym his lettr to 23th vltimo; so God knoweth when they will hither. Ther was

2 tatt. cloth.

2 *tatta*. black cloth, fyne, N? 42, sould to Oyen Dono secretary for 7 bars *coban* gould. [*fol. 147r.*]]

12. This mornyng still fayre cold calme wether, but towards night a stiff gale, wynd N?erly, but not much wynd the later p'rte of the night, yet both day & night fayre wether.

Nota.

We went to vizet (or rather solicet) the Emp'rs Councell for our dispach, but could not com to spech of any of them. We fownd our Castillano at Codgskin Donos, but could haue no audience no more then we. And after nowne Capt. Adames & our *jurebasso* went agane to the Cort & sawe all the Councell together, whoe gaue them fayre wordes as before, biding them com agane to morow.

And towardes night an expres of the Hollandrs arived at this place, whoe came for a *goshon* for their junck to goe

Mr. Baylie dead.

for Syam. He geveth it out that Mr. Baylie is dead, but I haue no lettrs of any such matter.

Sonday.

13. This mornyng still cold fayre wether, littell wynd N?erly, and so remeaned all day & night following, yet more wynd p'r day then night, espetially in the after nowne.

Nota.

We went this mornyng betyme to Codgskin Donos, before son rysinge, because we would be sure to find hym w'thin; but had answer he was sick, & therefore willed vs to com agane at nowne, for that he would not goe out all this day. & so we retorned to Oyen Dono the secretary, & met his secretary by the way (w'th the Spaniard man), whoe tould vs he was gon out, & that he want after hym to procure that mans dispach, w'ch it may be will be at later Lammas, &c. But afterward we went againe to Codgskin Dono, and in the end speake w'th hym & made our case knowne vnto hym, w'ch he seemed to pittie, & tould vs he was not the man now that he was in the ould Emperours tyme, only he was of this mans Councell, & in his opinion yt was not tyme now to seeke to alter that w'ch the Emperour had so lately ordayned, but that in tyme it might be amended, our case being better considered of; & then we should fynd hym ready to assist vs in what he might. Jnº Yoosen was theare at same tyme when we speake vnto hym, & heard what past, and at same tyme pr'sented hym a lettr frõ the Hollandes Capt. telling hym he was on the way to com vizet the Emperor, but held back p'r fowle wether, yet in the meane tyme desired to haue out a *goshon* to send their junck for Syam. But Codgskin Dono answered he might stay for it till the Hollandes Capt. came. So now I determen to put vp a petition to haue lycence to sell such goodes as we haue at Miaco & those p'rtes, & so to retor[n]e w'th their answer, good or bad, desiring in my petition that their honors will bettr consider of our first privilegese hereafter.   [*fol. 147v.*]]

14. This mornyng still cold overcast wether, wynd a fresh gale Nºerly, & so remeaned most p'rte of the day w'th som drops of rayne towardes night, but dry all night littell or no wynd.

2 lettrs. I wrot two lettrs, dated yisterday but kept till this day, the one to Mr. Wickham to Miaco & the other to Firando to Mr. Nealson & Mr. Osterwick, advising them of what is past, as also sending two *goshons* to Firando, one for Co-chinchina & the other for Syam, to be a meanes to helpe to sell our junck, as apeareth p'r coppis of lettrs extant. Also I wrot a lettr in Japons to the China Capt., Andrea Dittis, **2 lettrs.** & an other to Matinga; and sent all these letters expres p'r

October 1616

Jaquise.

Cacayemon Dono, the Emperors secretary,[244] sent me word late yisternight how he had spoaken w'th his m.ͬ, & gaue me concell to send Capt. Adames & Gorezano our *jurebasso* betymes this mornyng to speake w'th his m.ͬ, w'ch they did before son rising; but he was gon out to the Admerall of the Sea, Shongo Dono, before they came. So they retorned w'thout doing any thinge. And after, the said secretary, Cakeamon Dono, came to me & gaue me councell to make a petition to them all, & goe and watch them as they came from the Admeralls howse & del'd it vnto them. He tought me to indite it, desyring them that yf their affares were so emportunate at pr'sent that they could not speake to the Emperour for enlard[g]ing our privelegese, that then it would please them to geue me a letter of pasification to the Justice of Miaco & those partes, for the selling of such goods as we had theare, & the next spring I would retorne to renew my sute about our privelegese. This petition I deliverd to to [sic] Oyen Donos handes, w'ch he receaved w'th a frownyng countenance, calling Capt. Adames to hym & gaue it hym back, asking hym whie he let on com to hym that could not speake, & bad hym bring our petition hom to his howse. Soe sowne after, Capt. Adames went to his howse, w'th our *jurebasso*, but could not com to speach of hym, & soe retorned. It is said that the m'rchntes of Miaco are com to this place to sue to the Emperour that we may sell no goodes in this place of Edo nether, w'ch as yet is not denid vs. I am still of the opinion that the Councell, haveing put it into the Emperours head that it is fitt we should be restrayned to Firando, dare not now speake vnto hym to the contrary, he being

244) This must be Oyen Dono's secretary Yokota Kakuzaemon. See Note 222) above.

324

such a furiose man. So I dowbt we shall not now get any
good answer, to my no small greefe, &c.   [*fol. 148r.*]]

15. This mornyng fayre wether, very littell wind N°erly,
yet fayre wether all day, & the lyke p'r night following.

Nota.   Capt. Adames & our *jurebasso* went againe betimes this
mornyng to Oyen Dono w'th our petition, & he bad them
bring it to the castill, w'ch they did, & in the end had for a
finall answer that the Emperou[r]s pleasure was that we
should keepe factors at no other place but at Firando, &
for our goodes w'ch we had in any other place, to put it into
the custody of any Japon we would for this tyme to make
sales for vs, but not to leaue any factor English, nor to send
any goodes hereafter from Firando, but to sell all theare.
Wherevpon Mr. Eaton & I thought good to leave all our
goodes in this place vnder the custody of Capt. Adames,
for this tyme; & he to leve order what other he thought
fyt to make sales in his abcense, because he goeth downe
w'th vs now to cleare all reconynges & to receave his
sallary, due to hym p'r Wor. Company acc? to consort,
he not haveing receved any thing till now, &c.

Newes.   Here is reportes geven out that the Emperour doth determen to put Massamone Dono & the Kyng of Faccata to
death, w'th an other *tono* or kyng. And it is said Fidaia
Samme is alive; but what will com hereof I know not.

16. This mornyng fayre cold wether littell wynd N°erly, and
so continewed all day & lyke night following, &c.

Nota.   Andrea, Capt. Adams brother in law, came frō Orengaua
to Edo, & he got (I meane Capt. Adames) his writing of
his howse at Edo out of his handes & paid hym 35 bars
coban, w'ch is 5 more then he was to pay; & so made an
end w'th hym to the content of his *senora*. And Cauke-
sayemon Dono, the secretary to Oyen Dono came to vizet
me, & to take his leave, we being to dep'rt to morrow, &

willed me to take patience for a while tuching our privelegese, for a matter of state being once concleuded could
not in a day nor 2 be revoked. Yet he dowbted not but the
next yeare it would be amended, when the Emperour &
his Councell had well considered of the matter, as now
they began to enter into it; for all this is donne to banish
padrese out of the cuntrey, & that, for his mr & Codgskin
Dono, we might be assurd of them, as he had heard frō his
mrs owne mouth; and that it were not amis, yf I met the
King of Firando p'r the way coming vp to the Emperour,
to put hym in mynd to solicet the matter, &c. We gaue this

A cloake
geuen.

Cakeyamon Dono a cloth cloke of Mr. Eatons, in respect
of the paines he took since our coming, &c.

[*fol. 148v.*]

And I sent to the King of Firandos brother & to Jnọ Yoosen to adviz them how we were to dep'rte to morow mornyng
towardes Firando, yf they ment to write any letters. Mr.

15 bars
coban.

Eaton lent Capt. Adames 15 bars *coban* gould.

An earth-
quake.

And there was an earthquake at 5 a clock in thafter
nowne.

17. This mornyng fayre calme wether, or rather a littell
wynd Nọerly, but after vered to S. E., yet faye wether all
day & night foll'g.

From Edo.

Hollanders
4 lettrs.

We dep'rted from Edo at 9 clock & lodged at Caningaua[245] all night, where we met the Hollandrs going vp,
who brought me 4 lettrs, viz., 3 frō Firando, & 1 from Osakay, viz.:–

1 frō Mr. Wickham in Osakay, le 2th Octobr.

1 frō Mr. Baylie in Firando, 28th August.

1 frō Mr. Osterwick in Firando, le 23th August kept till 1th
Septembr.

1 frō Mr. Nealson in Firando, 28th A'gust kept till 4th Septmbr.

---

245) Kanagawa 神奈川.

October   1616

Wherin they advized me of Mr. Baylies deth, w'th many other mattrs.

Pr⸱sentes.

I forgot we gaue pr'sentes as foll'th, viz.:–

To Mrs. Adames:–

1 looking glasse, N?   .246)

1 picture of Soloman.

2 blew tuns.

2 handkerchefs chant bramport.

And I gaue *cabukes* 6 handkerchefes & 2 bundells pap'r; & 2 handkerch'es to Capt. Adams hostis. Also ther was 1000 *gins* geven to howse; 1 single peec. chint bram. to Capt. Adams father in law, and 1 whole pec. chint bramp't. to Mattem Dono, a m'rchnt, our frend. We gaue to host at Caningaua 2160, and to s'rvantes in howse 0200.

Nota.

The Hollandrs tould me ther junk, w'ch came frõ Syam & arived in Shashma, was cast away coming about for Firando, goods & all, only men saved. Also they reported that the great Spanish shipp in Shashma is cast away, coming frõ thence to goe to Langasaque.247)

18.   This mornyng fayre cold wether, wind N?erly encreasing, a stiffe gale w'th som drops rayne in the after nowne, yet dry rest day & lyke p'r night, but extremene wynde all night.

Camacora.
Nota.

We dyned this at a towne called Camacra,248) w'ch in tymes past (500 yeares since) was the greatest cittie in Japon, & (as it is said) 4 tymes bigger then Miaco or Edo is at pr'sent, and the *tono* or kyng of that place called   249) was cheefe comander or Emperour in Japon, & the c[h]eefe

---

246) The number, not given.

247) In a space after this entry is written a later remark reading "IInd Depture from Edo."

248) Kamakura 鎌倉.

249) The name is not given, but the author evidently refers to Minamoto-no Yoritomo 源頼朝.

327

(or first) that took the authoretie royall from the *Daire*[250) who was suckcessor to Shacke.[251) But now at pr'sent it is no cittie, but scattared howses seated heare & theare in pleasant valles betwixt divers mountaines, wherin are divers pagods very sumptuose & a nvnry (or rather a stews) of shaven women. I did never see such pleasant walkes amongest pyne & spruce trees as [*fol. 149r.*]] as [*sic*] are about these pagodes, espetially 5 of them are more renown-ed then the rest. But that w'ch I did more admire then all the rest was a might[y] idoll of bras, called by them *Dibotes*,[253) & standeth in a vallie betwixt 2 movntaynes, the howse being quite rotten away, it being set vp 480 years past. This idoll it [*sic*] made siting cros legged (telor lyke) & yet in my opinion it is aboue 20 yardes hie & aboue 12 yardes from knee to knee. I doe think there may aboue 30 men stand w'thin the compas of the head. I was w'thin the hollownes of it & it is as large as a greate howse. I doe esteem it to be bigger then that at Roads, w'ch was taken for 1 of the 7 wonders of the world, &, as report goeth, did lade 900 camells w'th the ruens therof. But for this, it is thought 3000 horses would nothing neare carry away the copp'r of this. In fine, it is a wonderfull thinge. Som report this cittie to be destroid w'th fire & brimston; but I enquir-ed of the enhabetantes, & they say they never heard of any such matter, but only that it was burned and ruenated p'r war, &c.

The littell doughter of Fidaia Samma[252) is shorne non in this monestary, only to saue her life, for it is a sanctuary & no justis may take her out.

---

250) *Dairi.* See Note 107) for 1615. Yoritomo, like Ieyasu did not necessarily usurped the *Dairi*'s sovereign but was sanctioned to assume the office of the Shōgun.

251) Shaka 釋迦, Gautama.

252) Tenshu-ni 天秀尼 entered Tōkeiji 東慶寺 at Kamakura.

253) Daibutsu 大佛, the great image of Buddha, erected in 1252; its height is 11.36 m. Thompson suggests that the breadth from knee to knee is 36 *shaku*, or 12 yards.

October 1616

Frõ Camacora we went to Fugesaw[254] to bed; & paid for diet, night & mornyng, 2 *ichibgins*,[255] and to servantes in the howse *T*. 0200 *gins*.

19. This mornyng overcast wether, much wynd N?erly and so remeaned all the affore nowne, som drops of rayne, but fayre wether rest of day, littell or no wynd & the lyke p'r night following.

Woyso.

2 handker-
chfes chint
bramp't.

Odouar.

We dyned at Woyso; and paid to howse 1500 *gins;* and to the s'rvantes 0200 *gins*. And I gaue his littell doughter 2 handkerchefs of chint bramport smallr sort, borowied of Capt. Adames. And so from thence we came to Odouar to bed. And paid for dyet, night & mornyng, 2000 *gins*, and to servantes of howse 0200 *gins*.

Sonday.

20. This mornyng fayre calme wether, yet sowne after a stiffe gale wynd at W. S'erly, & so remeaned all the rest of day & p'rte of night, rest calme.

Faconiama.

We dyned at Faconiama[256] on the hill & paid 1000 *gins*, & to servantes in howse 0100 *gins*. And at Mishma, at hill foote, for colation 0300 *gins*. And so we went to supp'r to

Sammabash.

Sammabash,[257] and paid for dyet, night & mornyng, 2000 *gins*, and to servants of howse 0300 *gins*.

Nota.

We met an expres p'r way, sent p'r Duch for Edo, but vpon what occation I could not learne.   [*fol. 149v.*]」

21. This mornyng fayre calme wether, but after a small gale, wynd S'erly, varing to N?ward of W., a stif gale the later p'rte of the night.

Cambra.

Vuy.

We went to dyner to Cambara; & paid *T*. 1200 *gins*, and to servantes *T*. 0100 *gins*. And at Vuy,[258] where Capt. Adams

---

254) Fujisawa 藤澤.
255) The latter half of this word (*-gins*) seems to have been cancelled by the author.
256) Hakoneyama 箱根山.
257) San'maibashi 三枚橋, what is presently Numazu 沼津.
258) Yui 由比.

October   1616

Nota.   fell afe horse, *T.* 0500 *gins*, viz., 300 *gins* to a bonsetter &
A mishap.   200 *gins* to the howse. For it is to be vnderstood that a burd
flying out of a hedg caused Capt. Adames howse to start,
so that he fell backward & put his right shoulder bone out
of the joynt, & 1000 to one that he had not broake his neck.

Yezery.   And we went to bed to Yezeri,[259] and paid for dyet, night
& mornyng, *T.* 3000 *gins*, and to the servantes *T.* 0200 *gins*.

22.   This mornyng fayre wether, wynd at W. N?erly, very
littell all day, & losse p'r night.

Capt. Adames fynding hym selfe somthing better, we
Shrongo.   went this day to Shrongo to dyner, to our host Stibio,
where we paid for dyner *T.* 2000 *gins*, and to the folkes of
howse *T.* 0200 *gins*.

Pr'sent.   And we gaue for a pr'sent to Stibie and his wife, viz.:–
ta. co.
1 : 1.   1 pec. black silk grogren, cost *T.*   .[260]
            1 single pec. chint bramport, cost *T.*   .

And I gaue his yongest sonne in plat, p'd p'r Goreza, 2 *ta.*

And in respect Capt. Adames feared his arme would
goe out of joynt againe, he thought it best to stay 4 or 5
daies at Shrongo, and we to goe befor. So we went to bed
Fugida.   to Fugida; & p'd ho[w]se 2000 *gins*, and to the servantes *T.*
0200 *gins*, and to Capt. Adams hostes sonne brought pr'sent
T. 0300 *gins*.

23.   This mornynge fayre calme wether, or rather a littell
wynd at W. S'erly, & so remeaned all day & night following, yet more wynd p'r day then p'r night, &c.

Cagingaua.   We dyned at Cagingaua; & paid the howse *T.* 1500 *ginis*,
Jor. Duros.   and to the servantes *T.* 0200 *gins*. We met Georg Durois a
league before we came to this towne, going to the Court to
4 pere   seeke justis against Safian Dono. He gaue me a box of
stocking.   marmelad, and del'd me 2 peare silk stockinges, 1 silver

---

259) Ejiri 江尻.
260) This and the following prices, not entered.

330

Newes.

culler & other black, w'th 2 peare white wollen stockinges, but set no price till he retorne to Firando. He tould
me that it was the littell Spanish [*fol. 150r.*]⌡ shipp that is
cast away neare Shashma, & not the greate. Also he said
that the great shipp w'ch is in Shashma bringeth newes
that the Kyng of Spaine hath mad proclemation that all the
English & Duch pirattes that rob at sea, that he will take
them vnder his protection, & geaue them freely all such
goods & shipps as they shall take, w'thout reserving any
part to hym selfe.

We went to bed this night to Mitsque, & pad to the
howse, for night & mornyng, *T*. 2000 *gins*, more to the servantes of the howse *T*. 0200 *gins*.

11 leags.

24.   This mornyng overcast wether, wynd W. S'erly, but after,
rayne all the afore nowne, but dry wether after, w'th much
wynd at W. N°erly, that it blew downe howses & vncoco-
verd [*sic*] others; but dry wether p'r night & not soe much
wynde.

Araye.
12 leags.
Yosenda.

We dyned at Araye, and paid 1300 *gins*. And we went to
bed to Yosenda, p'd 3500 *gins*, and to the servantes *T*. 0300
gins, and to the children *T*. 0200 *gins*. This extraordenary
charg was for that we had extraordenary good cheare,
being brought thether p'r a m'rchnt of Edo, our frend,
called Neyemon Dono and every one a wench sent to hym

1 *ichebo.*

that would haue her. I gaue one of them an *ichebo* but
would not haue her company, &c.

25.   This mornyng fayr wether, wynd at W. N°erly, a fresh
gale most p'rte of the day, but rather calme p'r night.

Fugicaua.
13 leages.
Naromy.

We dyned at Fugicaua,[261] & paid to ye howse 1200 [*gins*],
and to the servantes *T*. 0100. And we went to bed to Naromy;[262] p'd 2000, and to the servantes *T*. 0200.

---

261) Fujikawa 藤川.
262) Narumi 鳴海.

26. This mornyng fayre calme wether, or rather a littell wynd at N? E'erly som p'rte of day, but calme p'r night, &c.

Mia.
Quanno.

We broake fast at Mia, & took boate frõ thence for Quanno,[263] 7 leages. And paid at Mia *T*. 0500 *gins*, and at Quanno for night & mornyng *T*. 2300 *gi*., and to the servants *T*. 0200 *gi*. For we could get no horses to goe from thence, although we arived theare at nowne, for that all were taken vp p'r them w'ch came to vizit the princes. [*fol. 150v*.]⏌ Our host at Quanno tould me that it was strange to see the pr'sentes w'ch came daylie to this noble man & his wife (she being the Emperours doughter), for that all the noble men in Japon came to vizet hym w'th pr'sentes, som w'th 100 bars *oban*, & as man garm't. (I say *keremons*), each one according to his degree. So that there was no day passed w'thout playes, I meane comodies or tragedies. So that the rezort of people to that place was such that we could get no horse, &c.

8½ leagues.

Sonday.

27. This mornyng fayre could wether, calme w'th 2 hor frost & remeaned dry wether all day till night, & then blew vp stiff gale W'erly w'th a shower of rayne, rest night dry w'th much wynd.

Shono.

We went to dyner to Shono;[264] & paid to howse *T*. 1200 *gins*, and to the servantes *T*. 0100 *gins*, & I gaue the children 2 *mas* in money Spanish. And we spent at a howse in the way call[ed] Sacke[265] *T*. 0200 *gins*. So we went to bed to Sacca,[266] & paid host *T*. 2000 *gins*, and the servantes *T*. 0300 *gins*. I lent a bar of *coban* gould to Mr. Eaton.

2 *mas*.
Saccay.
11½ leags.
1 bar of
coban.

28. This mornyng a cold hor frost w'th a stiff gale, wynd

---

263) Kuwana 桑名.
264) Shōno 庄野.
265) Ishiyakushi 石薬師 (?).
266) Seki 關.

October 1616

W'erly; wynd encreasing all day, so that it might be accompted a tuffon, but not so much wynd p'r night, &c.

Ishbe.

We dyned at Ishbe[267] and paid the host *T.* 1300 *gins*,
and to the s'rvantes *T.* 0100 *gins*, and gaue the *ropshakes*[268]
to drynk *T.* 0100 *gins*. And we went to bed to Otes, & paid
host *T.* 5 *tais* plate, and servantes *T.* 0300 *gins*, and for

13 leags.
Nota.

passage over water *T.* 0300 *gins*. We met som trayne of the
Kyng of Figen going towardes Edo, but he hym selfe went
an other way, because he would not vizet the princes at
Quanno, as we were enformed. There went aboue 20 wom-
en (in the trayne we met) w'th the wife of the Prince of
Figen, who went to her hvsband w'ch lyeth pledg at Edo,
as all the rest of the kinges sonns of Japon do the lyke, &
those w'ch are married bring their wives w'th them.

[*fol. 151r.*]

29.   This mornyng still cold wether w'th a hor frest [*sic*] a
fresh gale N°erly, vering W'ward, but not so much wynd
p'r night, very cold wether, &c.

Miaco.

We went to Miaco to dyner, where we fownd Mr. Wickham, & so I wrot for our host of Sackay to com to som end
of our busynes, & sent an other lettr to Cuiaman Dono, our
bongew, how I was arived heare. And sowne after I was
arived, an ould *boze*, a vserer, came to vizet me w'th our

To supp'r.

host of Osakay; & he envited me to supp'r, & the *boze*
to dynner, to morrow.

3 lettrs.

And Mr. Wickham del'd me 3 lettrs frō Firando, viz.:–

1 frō Mr. Nealson, dated the 23th Septembr.

1 frō Mr. Osterwick, dated le 15th ditto kept till 21th.

1 frō Mr. Rowe dated, le   ,&c.[269]

w'th 2 enclozed 1 for Mr. Eaton, & 1 for Sweetland.

---

267) Ishibe 石部.

268) *Rokushaku* 陸尺 or 六尺, a sedan chair-bearer.

269) Date, not given.

333

October 1616

30. This mornyng still could wether w'th frost, little wynd
N^o W., & soe remeaned all day, & the lyke p'r night following, but calme, &c.

I wrot a lettr to Capt. Adames, & sent it p'r Jenkese, his
man, advising of the base vsage of our host of Otes, willing
hym to go to an other lodging, yet to tell hym fo his kna-
very as he passed, & to buy me 8 or 10 salt salmons, yf they
be to be had.

We went to the *bozes* howse to dyner, called Sosa Dono,
where we had entertaynm't for a prince w'th all them w'ch
followed vs. I meane Mr. Wickham, Mr. Eaton, our host,
w'th 2 others, our *jurebasso* & my selfe, & all servantes, &c.
This man is a greate vserer, & the King of Firando oweth
hym much money at intrest, &, as he said, for his sake in
whose domynions we were recedent, & p'r letters frõ hym
was comanded to shew vs what service he could, was ready
to p'rforme it to his power, accompting it a great honor yt

I would com vnder his rowfe, &c. I sould this day a littell
peece of currall of the 2 I had out in the box, cont'g 3 *mas*
7 *condrin* wight, for the som of five *tais* plate of bars, yet not
receved. Our host of Fushamy came to vizet me w'th a pr'-
sent of orengis, being glad, as he said of my selfe retorne.

We haue much goodes at his howse, w'ch they of Miaco
would not suffer to enter into the towne, standing vpon
their puntos p'r meanes of the Emperours inhebitions, &c.

[*fol. 151v.*]⌡

31. This mornyng still cold frosty wether, but calme, no
wynd to be accompted of nether p'r day nor night following.

I sent Goresano, our *jurebasso*, to thank the *boz* for our
kynd entertaynm't yisterday, & to tell hym I thought
it best to goe & vizet the Justis of Miaco w'th a pr'sent
had geuen me to sett my busynes in order & to leave the

October 1616

rest w'th whome I thought good. The *boz* came vnto me & councelled me not to cary any thing to the Justice howse, for that neather he nor his deputie were not at home, but, yf either of them came while I remeaned heare, he would adviz me thereof.

4 lettrs.

I rec. 4 lettrs to day p'r a Hollands bark, w'ch came from Firando, viz.:–

1 frō Ed. Sayer, dated at Conugeshma[270] in Shashma, of his arivall there in our junck in greate misery, the capt. & many others being dead, he vndr God saveing her, &c.

1 frō Jnº Ferres, in Syam le 25th of May, sent p'r Ed.

1 from Mr. Edmond Willmot in Farando, le 23th Septembr.

1 frō Mr. Nealson in Firando, le 6th of Octobr *1616*.

Mr. Nealson advising me the King of Firando showed them but a sower countenance in their affares, & denyed them a lettr of fauour to the King of Shashma, apointing his brother after long attendance to doe it.

Tozayemon Dono.

Our host of Sackay called Tozayemon Dono, arived hear yisternight. He is the man w'ch hath most helpen Mr. Wickham in our affares. I bought 8 puppetes to send Capt.

ma. co.
1 : 2.

Adams children, cost 1 *ma.* 2 *co.*, paid p'r Gorezano.

November 1616.

01. This mornyng fayre calme wether, & not so cold as before and very littell wynd, W'erly or rather non at all nether p'r day nor night following, &c.

Nota

Tozayemon Dono, our host at Sackay, tould me that Chubio Dono had advized hym to shew vs all the favour he could. & to furnish vs w'th 10000 *taies* in plate or m'rch'ndiz, yf we wanted it. Also he said, for the copp'r we

270) Kagoshima 鹿兒嶋.

wanted, that he would furnish vs w'th it for 3 *mas* p'r *pico.* better cheape then the Hollanders had bought of other. God grant all proue trew. Yet I haue a good opinion of this man. *[fol. 152r.]*⌡

02. This mornyng fayre calme mild wether, but sowne after wynd Nᵒerly, w'th store of rayne in the after nowne, and the lyke p'r night following, &c.

Monum'nte.

I went to se the mouvmentes of the towne, viz., the temple of *Dibottes*,²⁷¹⁾ w'th the hudge collosso or bras imadg (or rather idoll) in it, it being of a wonderfull bignes, the head of it reaching to the top of the temple, allthough he sat croselegged, it being all gilded over w'th gould, & a great wall or plate behind the back of it the lyke, whereon was carved the pickture of the son. The temple of it selfe is the hvgest peec. of building that eaver I saw, it not haveing any other thing in it but the idoll, w'ch standeth in a cercle or chappell just in the midell therof, w'th 4 rowes of pillars of wood, 2 on eather side, frõ the on end of the temple to the other, each one reaching to the top of it; the compose of each pillar being 3 fathom & all dyed over w'th red occar, as all the temple w'thin is the lyke. And a littell from the North end of the temple is a tower w'th a bell hanging in it, the bigest that ever I saw. And from the Easter dore of the temple stand two rowes of ston pillars, of som dozen in a rowe, a pretty distance on from the other, going downe to a mightie hvge gatehowse, on eather side of w'ch w'thin stands a mightie gilded lyon, & w'thout the gate on lack side (as portars) a hvdge giant, mad after a furious fation. The truth is, all of it is to be admired.

And not far from this temple is an other, of very neare 10 skore yardes in lenghe, I say ten skore; but it is narow.

---

271) *Daibutsu* of Hōkōji 方廣寺 in Kyoto. The figure was dedicated in 1612 but melted down and coined into "cash" in 1625.

And in the midest thereof is placed greate bras *Dibotes* (or idoll), but nothing neare the greatenes of the former. & out of the sids of it proceed many armes w'th hands, & in each hand on thing or other, as speares, sword, dagges, spades, arrowes, knyves, frutes, fyshes, fowles, beastes, corne, & many other matters & formes; & out of the head procead many littell heades, & over the great head proceadeth a glory of long bras rayes made lyke to the son beames, as the papostes paynt over the saintes. & on both sids, to the end of the howse, are set 3333 other bras images, standing on foote vpon steps, on behind an others back, all apart on from an other, w'th glories over their heades, armed out of their sids, [*fol. 152v.*]] and littell heades out of the great, as the *Dibotes* had. I enquired what those handes, & heads did signefie; and it was answered that they signefied the good and charetable deeds that those saintes (or holy men) had donne while they were liveing. And it is to be noted that both the *Dibotes* & all the other 3333 idols were made after an excellent forme neare to the life, & clothed w'th a gowne (or loose garment) over them, and all gilded over w'th pure gould, very fresh and glorious to behould. And just before the *Dibotes* below were sent [*sic*] 3 or 4 roes of other idolls, most of them made after a furious forme, rather lyke divells then men; & behind them all stood two deformed ons, one carring a sack of wynd on his shoulders, & the other a cerkled wreath or hoope w'th many knotes in it, the one resembling the wyndes, & the other the thvnder. In fyne this temple is the most admerablest thing that ever I saw, & may well be reconed before any of the noted 7 wonders of the world.

And som distance Westward frō these 2 temples stands the sepulcre of Ticus Samme, *allis* Quambecon Dono,[272)

272) *Kampaku Dono* 關白殿. The person who bore the title *Kampaku*, Imperial

a thinge to be wondred at, & rather by me admired then to be discribed, it is a hudge big howse, of an admerable workmanshipp both w'thin and w'thout far excelling either of the other temples, and w'thin it may pillars covered w'th bras nameled & gilded ou[e]r w'th gould, & the flowre of plankes very black, shynyng lyke ebony. But we could not be sufferd to enter, but only to look in a wyndos or grates. And to the place where the corps (or ashes) are set, yow must assend vp 8 or 9 steps or degrees, very lardg, made p'rte of gilded bras & p'rte of black wood or ebony. & by the corps borneth a contynewall lampe, watched by a *boz*, or pagan prist. And for the workmanshipp about that place, it exceedeth my memory to discribe it; only all I can say, it may well befitt the entering of so famouse an Emperour. And I had forgot to note downe that before the east gate of the temple of *Dibotes* stands a rownd hill of an endifferant biggnes, on the top whereof standeth a ston pillar, lyke the crosses in papistes churchyardes; w'ch hill, as I was tould, was made of the eares & noses of the Core-ans w'ch were slayne when Ticus Samme did conquer that cuntrey som 24 or 25 years past. In fine, we saw divers other monumentes & pagods, very sumptuous, w'th cloisters rownd about them lyke papistes monestaries, wherin the *bozes* or pagon pristes live in great pomp, lyke our frairs & monkes in Christendom, frõ whence it seemeth they had their origenall; for the pagan religion is of more anti-quetie, & as may sects or orders as the Xxrtians.[273)]

[fol. 153r.]

Capt. Adames came to Miaco this day, being well amend-ed, yet not w'thout paine in his shoulder.

Sonday. 03. This mornyng lowring wether, wynd W'erly, a stiff gale

---

Regent, was called *Taikō* 太閤 upon retirement.

273) Christians.

most p'rte of the day, but not soe much p'r night, the later p'rte being calme, yet dry wether day & night.

I bought 3 *chaw* cups coverd w'th silver plates;

	ta.	*m.*	[*co.*]
plate waynge ....*T.*	6:	3:	5
and for cups & workmanship, at 12 *mas* peec. ....*T.*	3:	6:	0
and for losse in plate, at 1 *mas tay*, is ....*T.*	0:	6:	0
Som totall paid for me p'r Mr. Eaton ....*T.*	10:	5:	5

ta. m. co.
10 : 5 : 5.

Silke sold for 312 *ta. pico.*

We sould our silk this day for 312 *tais* p'r *pico.*, it being reported the Emperours silk was now set at sale, yt being

Taffeties at pec.
Brod cloth.

deare. Also we sould the ordenary taffeties we had at 274) p'r pec. And we sent for our broad cloth frō Fushami to this place of Miaco, to make sale of it, our host of Sackay & others offring to buy it.

Pr'sent.

Albartus host, in his abcense, came to vizet me w'th a pr'sent.

Nota.

We agred to cary a pr'sent to morrow to Gonrock Dono, in respect he is the Emp'rs s'rvant & may be confered still

5 *tais* for corall.

at Langasaque, for ought we know. I rec. 5 *tais* plate bars for the corall sould the other day.

4. This mornynge calme cold wether, & littell wynd after S'erly, but calme p'r night very cold.

Pr'sent to Gonrok.

I went to Gonrock Dono w'th a pr'sent as followth, viz.:–

1 *tatt'y* blak cloth, Nọ .275)
1 Russia hide.
1 pec. Sleze land, Nọ D.
1 pec. diap'r napkins.
1 great hie gallepot, 6 *tt.*
1 great flat glapot[*sic*], 6 *tt.*
1 littell loe galet, 2 *tt.*
1 green ton.
1 gren porenger.

---

274) Not entered.
275) The number, not given.

November 1616

1 Duch jugg.

He was not a[t] home; so I left ye pr'sent & retorned. We

sould 5 halfe brod cloths to day at divers pr'ses to our host at Sackay for redy money, viz.:– 276)   [*fol. 153v.*]]

I wrot a lettr to our hoste at Bingana Tome to provize iron for me as followth, viz.:–

100 *picos* best flatt iron,

100 *picos* small square iron,

400 *picos* ordenary short iron;

& sent lettr p'r exprs.

Mr. Wickham paid Domingo, my boy, 5 *taies* p'r my order vpon acc? of his wagis, for my prop'r acc?

5. This mornyng calme cold wether w'th a hor frost, & littell or rather no wynd nether day nor night following.

I went to Gonrok Dono, accompanyd w'th Capt. Adames. He gaue vs frendly entertaynm't after the order of Japon; and amongst other matters asked vs the price of our lead w'ch the Emperour was to haue, telling me it was all one to hym what price we set, yet w'thall advized me that yf we put a hier price then the Hollanders, that it would be ill taken. I answerd that our lead was better then the Hollanders, and besids had cost vs much money in bringing it vp, & that our pr'velegis were such that, yf the Emperour bought any thing he was to pay the worth, & that at pr'sent it was worth 7½ *tais pico*. in this place; yet was I contended to let the Emperour haue it for 7 *tais*, & yf they pleased, would make the price allwais so hereafter, whether it were dearer or bettr cheape. He tould me he would adviz the Emperours offecers thereof. And for the steele he said the Hollanders set [*sic*] it to the Emperour at 2 *mas* p'r *catty*. So I condecended to set ours at same rate the Hollandrs doe theirs.

---

276) The detail, not entered.

340

November 1616

Capt. Adames ould host of this place, w'ch in tymes past would haue geuen hym a *higo*,[277] came to vizet me, & brought me a littell Japon box tronk lyke *makery*[278] work for a pr'sent, & our *makery* man brought me a littell scritorio of same work. I had rather be w'thout these pr'sentes, for, as the ould saying is, the[y] bring a sprat & look for a herring, &c.

6. This mornyng still cold wether w'th frost, & dry all day & lyke p'r night following, &c.

Nota.

Gonrock Dono sent for Gorezano our *jurebasso*, & tould hym that this day he would write to the Empero'rs Court about our lead & steele, but could not geue money for the lead aboue 5 *tais* p'r *pico.*, because the Hollandrs let the Emperour haue at same rate; soe I sent hym back to let me haue so much money as he thought fyt vpon the reconyng, & to com to acc? hereafter, & to will hym to lend me 2 or 3000 *tais* for 2 or 3 months. He sent me word he would looke ou'r his acc?, & what money he could spare he would lend me. [*fol. 154r.*]

7. This mornyng still cold calme wether w'th a hor frost, fayre wether all day, but rayne later p'rte night.

We sent pr'sentes to divers, as followeth, viz.:–

Pr'sentes.

To Sofo Dono, the *boz*,

1 *tatta*. black clo., N? .279)
1 Russia hid.
1 hie 6 *tt*. gallepot.
1 flat 6 *tt*. gallept.
1 flat 2 *tt*. gallept.
1 green tonne.
1 gren por'nger.
1 white jidgo[*sic*].

---

277) *Dar*, or *hacer, higas* (Span.), to ridicule —Thompson.
278) *Makie* 蒔繪, lacquer ware.
279) The number, not given.

And to Pedro Gozamon, Capt. Adames ould host,

2 single pec. chint bramport.

1 hie 6 *tt.* gallepot.

1 flatt same.

1 flat 2 *tt.* gallepot.

To   ,280) host howse wher cloth lyes,

1 pec. black silk grogren.

3 gallepot of Duch sort one.

To Yosio Dono, the Hollandes host,

2 pec. chint bramport single.

3 gallepotes of Duch sort 1.

Plate changed. We changed 850 *taies* ordenary plate for good plate, a 3 mas p'r 100 *taies.*

Boz pr'sent. The *boz* Sofo Dono brought me a pr'sent, 2 *barsos* wyne, 2 hense, & 2 bundelles sea weed.

Earthquake. A small earthquake this night past at midnight, but of small endurance, in Miaco.

8. This mornyng fayre clame wether, but sowne after a stiffe gale, wynd N?erly, most p'rte of the day w'th rayne p'r fittes, but dry p'r night, & not so much wind.

Pr'sentes. And host where cloth lyes,   ,281) brought me a pr'-sent, 2 *barsos* wyne, 3 fishes, a dish peares & an other of orenges *micanus*; & the Duch hose[*sic*], a pr'sent of figges. And Mr. Wickham reconed w'th Ric'd   ,282) m.r, & paid hym   283) for his diet, & 10 *taies* for teaching hym halfe a yeare.

Gerezano, our *jurebasso*, foolishly fell out w'th our host Torayemon Dono of Sackay, & went togeather p'r the eares w'th hym.   [*fol. 154v.*]

9. This mornyng fayre cold wether, wynd N?erly, fare

---

280) The name, not given.
281) The name, not given.
282) The surname, not given.
283) Not entered.

November 1616

wether all day & night foll'g, calme p'r night.

700 *tais.*   I rec. seven hvndred *tais* of Gonrock Dono, vpon acc?
for 100 *picos* lead, & 10 *picos* stile for themperour; & gaue
hym 2 billes of my hand, viz., 500 vpon lead & 200 vpon
stile, the place referred to Oyen Dono & Codgkin Dono.
The stile was del'd at Firando, & the lead I must del'r at
Osakay.

Nota.   The 10 of the ward where we lodged in Miaco, w'th 10
other principall men, came to vizet me w'th a pr'sent, *Nifon
cantange*, only to see the fation of our English habit & our
behavior. I vsed them in the best sort I could, they offering
me any kyndnes they could about our busynes.

Earthquake.   Also in the affore nowne there was an earthquake, but of
small contynewance.

Sonday.   10.   This mornyng calme wether w'th a hor frost, & littell
wynd after S'erly enclying to W'ward, but calme p'r night.

Quiksilu'r.   We sould the quicksiluer for 135 *tais pico.*, Priaman gould
at 13 *tais*   284) *mas, tay* wight, & brod cloth at div'rs
prices, &c.

54 Japon
bookes
8 *ta.* 9 *m.*   And I bought 54 Japon bookes printed, of their anti-
queties & cronicles from their first begyning, cost 8 *ta.*
9 *m.* 0, wherof Mr. Eaton paid me 8 *ta.* 4 *m.*; rest I paid.

Nota   Albartus, the Hollander, retorned from Osakay & came
to vizet me. He sayth how Codgskin Dono hath sent the
King of Firando word to com vp, sick or whole, although
he dye p'r the way.

11.   This mornyng calme cold wether, & litter [*sic*] or rather
no wind at all nether p'r day nor night following.

A lettr to
Firado.   I wrot a lettr to Firando to Mr. Nealson & Mr. Osterwick
of my arivall heare, & will com downe w'th as much hast
as I may, w'th other matters, as apereth p'r coppie; & sent

---

284) Not entered.

it p'r conveance of our host of Sackay p'r his man.

And I gaue host at Miaco a pec. corall of Mr. Tottons, poz. 8 *mas* 1 *condrin*.

So we dep'rted from Miaco & went to bed to Fushamy.

[*fol. 155r.*]] And ther was geven out in pr'sentes more, as foll'th, viz.:– 285)

To our host, Maqui n Dono,

1 *tatt.* black cloth, N.º .286)

2 pec. chint bramport, singell.

3 gallepotes, 1 of each sort.

1 gren ton.

1 gren podinger.

1 juge.

And to his wife,

1 pec. satten or grogren.

1 pec. Sleze land, N.º .

To his sonne,

1 pec. black satten.

To son in laws child,

1 single peec. chint bramport.

To the servantes of howse, in money 5 *taies*, and to our
host, for dyet & howserowne[*sic*], 80 *taies*.

And our host gaue me 20 salt cod fysh for present, and his wife gaue me a Japon *catabra* for a woman. And he met vs w'thout towne & brought vs a banket in good fation, for
w'ch we gaue his men w'ch brought it a bar of silver of 3 *tais*, and to the folkes of the howse where we eate it 15 *mas*. And after, our *makery* men met vs w'th an other banket in
state, for w'ch we gaue to them & the howse 3 *tais* 8 *mas* 8 *condrins*.

I went & vizeted Safian Dono at Miaco, & carid hym 2

---

285) In a space after this entry is written a later remark, reading "Leave Miaco."
286) This and the following numbers, not given.

barilles wyne & a fresh salmon, cost all 2 *tais*. He speake much about price lead, to let it go as the Hollanders; but in the end agreed at 6 *tais* p'r *pico*.

12.   This mornyng calme cold misty wether w'th a hor frost, but after nowne a stiff gale, wynd at S. W., w'th store of rayne after midnight, and much wynd, &c.

We gaue a pr'sent to our host of Fushamy & his wife 1½ *tatt*. black cloth, N?   287) [and] 1 pec. Sleze land, N?   , w'ch we did in respect he took our goodes into his gardong these trowblesom tyms (or embargo) when the[y] would not p'rmit them to ent'r into Miaco. And we gaue for dyet at Fushamy 8 *ta*. 0 *m*. 0 *co*., and for lodhier goodes 5: 0: 0, and for servantes in howse 1: 0: 0, and we dyned at Fraccata, & paid 3: 4: 5. And so went to bed to Osakay, &c., Mr. Eaton falling extreme sick of a fever p'r the way. Our host of Fushamy accompanid vs 3 leagues on the way p'r water, & brought vs a banket after the Japon fation. And a m'rchut of Osakay came after vs & brought vs an other, &c.   [*fol. 155v.*]]

13.   This mornyng overcast wether, w'th a stiff gale, wynd N?-erly, and so remeaned all day cold wether, but not so much wynd p'r night.

We sould the rest of our lead this day to our host of Osakay at 7 *tais* p'r *pico*, to pay ready money w'th 6 halfe pec. stamet at   ,288) but yet nether lead waid nor cloth measured, &c. And we agreed w'th a bark to goe to Firando w'th m'rch'ndz, to roe w'th 13 ores, for 30 *taies*.

I vnderstood Safian Do. past by to Sakay this day, & sent me word he would let me haue as much money as he could

Margin notes:
Fushamy.

Fraccata.
Osakay.
Nota.

Leades.

Cloth.
Bark.

287) This and the following numbers, not given.
288) Not entered.

November 1616

spare, but I know not yet vpon what conditions. I sent the Governor word I would com and vizet hym to morrow, &c.

Pr'sent to
Matsen
Dayre o.
Tayro
Cammy,
Gouernor
of Osakay.

14. This mornyng cold, overcast wether, littell wynd N?erly, and so remeaned all day & night following, cold dry wether.

We went & vizeted Shemash Dono,[289] the Governor, & carid hym a pr'sent, as foll'th, viz.:-

    1¼ *tatt.* black cloth, N?   .[290]

    1¼ stamet cloth, N?   .

    1½ *tat.* blac bayes.

    1½ *tat.* yelo bayes.

    1 pec. fyne whit bafta, N?   .

    10 gray cony skins.

    2 flat galepotes, of 6 *tt.*

    2 hie gallpotes, 6 *tt.*

    2 flat gallpot, 2 *tt.*

    2 white juges.

    2 green tonns.

    2 gren poringers.

    1 bar steele.

And to his secretary   Dono,[291] as foll'th, viz.:-

    1¼ *tatt.* black cloth, N?   .[292]

    1 peec. Sleze land, N?   .

    1 single pec. chint bram.

Nota. This Shemash Dono is Ogosho Sammas doghters sonne, & the Emperour now is his vncle. He vsed vs kyndly & promised to write to themperour for enlardging of our pr'velegese. & his secretary is a great man & doeth all. This prince accompanid me quite out of his castell, a thing w'ch he hath not donne hertefore to som kings w'ch came to vizet

289) Matsudaira Tadaaki, *Shimoosa-no-kami* 松平下總守忠明.
290) This and the following numbers, not given.
291) Perhaps the same person as Sadaye Dono seen in the entry for November 22, below.
292) This and the following numbers, not given.

Nota.　　　hym. Yisternight came a bark frō Firando, who bringeth
news the king is very sick & canot com to vizet the Emperour, but sendeth his brother Tonoman Samme in his place,
whoe is one the way coming vp, &c.　　　　　*[fol. 156r.]*」

  Capt. Adames & Mr. Eaton went to Osakay[*sic*]²⁹³⁾this
night to dispach som busynes, & to morrow Mr. Wickham
& my selfe to follow after to see what we can doe w'th Safian Dono, to take vp som monies at intrest to send for
Bantam.

 15.　This mornyng cold wether, littell wind Nº erly w'th a hor
frost, but after wynd vered W'erly, yet fayre wether all day,
but rayne in beg'ning of night w'th a gust wynd W. S'erly,
rest dry & calme.

A lettr.　　　I rec. a lettr frō Safian Dono to way out the lead to 2 men
Lead waid.　he sent, & they to del'r it vnto the Gouernor of Osakay for
the Emperour. Soe Mr. Wickham & my selfe, being ready to
goe for Sackay, left order w'th our host Feske Dono, & our
jurebasso Gorezano, & Wm. Sweetland to way it out to
them. The[y] would haue had it waid out in p'rcels of 50
cattis, but I would not; only in the end we agreed to way 5
Sakay.　　　small bars at a tyme. And so we dep'rted towardes Sakay,
where we fownd Capt. Adames & Mr. Eaton at our host
Pr'sent.　　Tozayemon Dono, our good frend. His wife pr'sented me
w'th a sleeping *keremon* of silk, & the lyke to Capt. Adames,
Mr. Wickhā & Mr. Eaton.

 16.　This mornyng fayre cold calme wether, & very littell
wynd Nº W'erly rest day & lyke p'r night.

A lettr.　　　I wrot a lettr to Wm. Sweetland to adviz me the wight
of the lead, w'ch he did in 1 lettr, but after, in an other,
advized of an error of 12 *picos* & od *cattis*, in 2 draught not
brought to accompt.

---

293) Sakai is meant here.—Murakami.

I got our host Tozayemon Dono to send his man to look out for our *goco* copp'r,[294] to haue it ready to lade to morow, as also to get 2000 *tais* in plate ready to carry along w'th me; for that I could not stay, tyme being past, but would leave Mr. Wickham a day or 2 to bring the logg & to acc? w'th hym. So he promised me all should be donne to content.

ta. ma. co.
4: 5: 0.
bason & vre.

Also I received a bason & vre from our *makey* man at Miaco; cost 4 *ta.* 5 *m.* 0 *co.* w'ch Mr. Eaton paid for one to his man w'ch brought it, of w'ch I advized hym in a lettr & sent it p'r his man, &c.   [*fol. 156v.*]]

Sonday.

17. This mornyng still cold calme wether w'th frost, & not much wynd after, nether p'r day nor night, but yt w'ch was at W. N?erly.

Nota.

One of the men w'ch Safian Dono sent to receve the lead came to Sakay this mornyng, enforming me of the error in the wight, so Mr. Wickham went w'th hym to Osakay to right it, & I stay heare till his retorne.

Nota.
Jorge
Durois.

Georg Durois retorned frō Edo, w'thout doing any thing, & came frō Osakay to this place to vizet me. He sayeth Safian Dono was com away before he arived at Edo, w'ch was the occation he could do nothing. I gaue hym councell that, when Safian Dono came to Langasaque, he should get som frendes to make way to hym, & to tell hym he had rather haue a littell w'th his faver then all w'th his all will, desyring hym to consider his pouertie.

Pap'r
10 būd'll.

We bought 9 bundells pap'r, comen sort, to writ lettrs, 100 sheetes in a bundell, for 3 *mas* 4 *condrins* p'r bundell, for w'ch Mr. Eaton paid.

18. This mornyng cold frostie wether, littell wind at W. N?erly, vering E'erly, fayre wether both p'r day & night fol-

---

294) *Goki-dō* ごき銅.

lowing.

Nota.

I went to Safian Dono to know whether he would lend me any money vpon intrest, as he promised me; but put me afe to Gonrok Dono his nephew, whome he said had charge of his busynes, & he droue me afe w'th wordes, ofring to deliver me money for all our sappon[295] w'ch was com in this junk, at 22 *mas* p'r *pico*. So I left of that matter & retorned to bed to Osakay, having first rec. in good changed plate

1200 *tas.*

of Tozayemon Dono, our host, one thousand two hvndred *tais*, vpon acc? of lead & other m'rch'ndiz, the lead at 7 *tais pico*; and gaue hym for a pr'sent, as followeth, &c.

2½ *tatta*. black cloth, N?   .296)

1½ *tatta*. stamet cloth, N?   .

1 pec. black si[l]k grogren.

1 whole pec. chint bramp't.

2 great gallepotes.

1 Duch jugg.

1 gren tonne.

1 gren podinger.

1 pec. blak si[1]k grogren, to his wife.

1 pec. Sleze land, N?   to her.

1 single pec. chint bramport to ther.

1 other same to his doughter.

[fol. 157r.]⌉

This Tozaemon Dono hath lent me 1000 *tais* gratis, besids all other favors donne in our busynes, he having donne more then all the rest.

18 *tais.*

Also we paid hym for our dyet in his howse 16 *tais*, and to the servantes of the howse 02 *tais*, paid out p'r Mr. Eaton.

Pr'sentes

And I gaue Mr. Eatons littell doughter Helena a silk coate, & to her mother a single pece chint bram.

---

295) Sappanwood, or *soboku* 蘇木.

296) This and the following numbers, not given.

November 1616

Our host sent 3 men w'th pikes to accompany vs to Osakay, w'th pikes because it was late.

19. This mornyng a whor frost, calme cold wether, but sowne after a stiffe gale, wynd W'erly, & towardes night rayne, but not of much durance, wind after vering N°.erly.

2 lettrs.

I wrot a lettr to our host of Sakay, Tozayemon Dono to com to Osakay forthw'th, to geue order for lading of copp'r, & to bring rest money along w'th hym, changd or vnchanged. Also an other lettr to Magazamon Dono, our host at Miaco, to send hether a chist of glas bottelles to carry downe w'th vs.

30 *tais.*

And ther was paid vnto Jorge Durois p'r Mr. Eaton, for money disburced at Langasaque for vs as foll'th, viz.:–

ta.

1 jar conservs of lemons & oreng flowers .....T.	04:	5:	0
1 jar consers of oreng flowrs & peaches.......T.	04:	0:	0
2 quince trees & 2 baskites onyons to sett ....T.	01:	1:	0
120 tallo candelles, cost ....T.	02:	0:	0
143 candelles, cost all ....T.	02:	2:	0
1 peare of milstons ....T.	01:	5:	0
Som totall for howse acc°, amonto vnto ....T.	15:	3:	0

More for my owne acc°, as foll'th.:–

2 peare silk stockinges ....T.	07:	0:	0
2 pear more rec. in way frō Shrongo, 1 blak, 1			
ashcoler................................T.	06:	4:	0
2 pear wollen or cotton yorne stockinges, 7 *mas* p'r			
....T.	01:	4:	0
Ther is 30 *tais* paid vpon this accompt ....T.	30:	1:	0

20. This mornyng cold wether w'th a stiff gale, wind N°.erly, but sowne after vered to W., & so remeaned a gale S. most p'rte day & night foll wing, &c.

Lettr.

I sent an other lettr to our host Tozayemon Dono to Sakay to com away for Osakay, for that we can do nothing

350

w'thout hym mor lade no copp'r.

Our host Tozayemon Dono came frō Sekay & brought me

800 *tais*. eight hvndred *tais* more, to make the other vp 2000 *tais* & Echo Dono[297] retorned frō Miaco w'th rest of the bar

50 *pico*. copp'r, being 50 *pico*., w'ch was laden abord the bark & the

bar cop'r. rest is in howse ready to lade to morrow.   [*fol. 157v.*]⌋

Domingo. Mr. Eatons boy Domingo is to make hym a new bond to serve hym 7 yeares, in these p'rtes, or at Syam, Cochin-china, or Patania, but not to goe for Bantam nor for Eng-land; & is for 10 *tais* plate del'd his father & mother a year

Susanna. past, &c. & p'r lyk agrem't he is not carry Susanna his sister out of Japon, w'ch is to serue the lyk tyme for 5 *ta.*, but he to fynd meate, drink, & cotes, to both, &c.

2 pec. corall. And I rec. the box corall back frō Mr. Wickham, poz. rightly & waid out 2 pec. to geue our host & hostis of Osa-kay, viz., 1 pec. poz. 3 *m.* 7 *co.*, & an other 2 *mas* 8 *condrin*.

21. This mornyng cold frosty wether, littell wynd W'erly, but sowne after a fresh gale, most p'rte of the day, but very littell wynd or rather calme p'r night.

Pr'sent. Our host of Osakay, Cuemon Dono, gaue me a silk *keremon* & 2 silk *catabras*, w'th 2 sacks rise, 5 sackes char-cole, 3 sackes salt, & 5 salted coddes, for a pr'sent; & gaue Capt. Adames, Mr. Wickham, Mr. Eaton, Fesque Dono our *bongew*, & Gorezano Dono our *jurebasso*, each of them a *keremon* of silk w'th other matters to our followers.

Nota. And sowne after the Governor sent me an other pr'sent, viz., 5 silke *keremons*, 2 *langanates*, & 2 barelles wyne;

2 pec. corall. and sent to buy 2 pec. corall, poz.   [298] w'ch I sent to hym as a pr'sent from my selfe, the other 2 pec. he re-torned. Also I gaue the man w'ch brought the present a pec.

---

297) Ichirō 一郎 (?), the old host of Wm. Eaton, seen as Echero in the entry for November 23, below.
298) Not entered.

1 pec.
grogren.
8 *tais.*

silke grogren. And I gaue the Maka Dono eight *tais* for a pr'sent, w'ch Mr. Eaton paid out. As also he del'd tow *oban* bars gould vpon acc? for thinges bought, *makary* ware, in forths, betwixt Capt. Adames, Mr. Wickham, Mr. Eaton &

110 *tais.*

my selfe, these 2 bars at 110 *taies.*

Gorezano our *jurebasso* haveing falne out w'th divers of my frendes by meanes of his fowle tong, espetially now of late w'th Tozayemon Dono, our host of Sackay, I willed hym to make peace w'th hym, or else I would not entertayne hym any longer; at w'ch my admonisions he set light, as well as at Capt. Adames, Mr. Wickham, Mr. Eatons, & others. Wherevpon I put hym away. This fellos fowle tong hath much iniured me & others, namely Capt. Adames, against whome he gaue out speeches at Empe'rs Court that he was an occation we gaue not a greater pr'sent to the Emperour & to others, w'ch hath procurd Capt. Adames much ill will, & the lyke to all of vs. This Gorezano had byn a dead man long agoe, yf I had not saved hym, & haue this reward for my labor.   [*fol. 158r.*]⌋

22. This mornyng cold calme wether, & littel or rather no wynd nether p'r day nor night foll'g.

A lettr to
Firando.

I wrot a lettr to Mr. Nealson & Mr. Osterwick as p'r coppie apereth, & sent it p'r Hollandes expres.

400 *tais.*

And I receved fowre hvndred *tais* of Mr. Wickham vpon acc? of Tozayemon Dono, & gaue Mr. Wickham vp a note

ta. m. co.
8846: 5: 8.

of all the monies I rec. to carry downe, since I arived at Miaco; w'ch amonted to eight thousand eight hundred forty & six *tais*, eigh[t] *mas* and seven *condrins*, wherof 7650 *tais* were packed vp in 6 chistes to goe for Firando, and the rest in an other chist to lay out for iron & other matters at Bingana Tomo, & 110 *tais* paid Mr. Eaton out of it to lay out vpon occations, as apeareth p'r coppie of note delivrd Mr. Wickham.

November 1616

Sedaye Dono.
Pr'sent
2 pistalles.

1 single pec.
chint
bramp't.

Nota.

Sadaye Dono, the Governors secretary, sent me 2 Japon pistalles for a pr'sent, & I gaue his man w'ch brought them a single peece of chint bramport. And sowne after came a servant of Calsa Sammes to vizet me w'th a pr'sent of frute, telling me (as frō his mr.) that he was sory he could not doe me any pleasure in respect he was in disfauour w'th the Emperour his brother; but, yf it were otherwais w'th hym hereafter, that then he would do that w'ch now he canot, &c.

Mr. Eaton & Tozayemon Dono, our host of Sakay, went to Mangasaque [sic] to receve the 100 pico. goco copp'r, & Capt. Adames went to Sakay vpon receapt of a lettr frō Safian Dono, to cleare acc? about the lead del'd the Emperour, &

rec. som 24 tais od money to ballan[ce] that acc?, yet rest a differrence of   299) tt. lead w'ch they wanted at Fushamy p'r kings wight.

Gorezano sent divers to me to p'rswane me to take hym into his place agane, but for many good reasons I denied them, whervpon he gaue it out he would retorne agane to Edo, &c.

23. This mornyng a hor frost, cold wether w'th a littell breth of wynd E'erly, but sowne after vered to the W., a stiff gale all day, but not so much p'r night.

I sent Co Jn?, our jurebasso, accompanid w'th our host of Fesque Dono, our bongew, to geue thanks in my behalfe to the Governor & his secretary for the pr'sentes they sent me, w'th offer of my service to them, w'ch they took in good p'rte, offring vs all favor that was in their power to do for our nation. And at night Mr. Eaton retorned w'th news our copp'r was laden & in way to be put abord, &c. I sent an

---

299) Not entered.

A lettr to
Firando

other lettr to Firando p'r Jor. Durois, [w'th] copy of other.

[fol. 158v.]⏌

Our host brought vs *cabuques*, 3, one the cheefe, w'th their mvsick, & staid all night. I gaue the cheefe a bar

1 bar *coban.*

Pr'sentes.

coban. And Echero Dono, Mr. Eatons ould host, brought me a pr'sent of a *bento*,300) or box for 5 p'rsons to eate in, & a fyre harth frō his wife; and Shroyemon Dono, a pike & 10 pap'rs fyne rise.

And late towardes night, Tozayemon Dono & 301)Dono, our hostes of Sakay & Miaco, came to Ozakay. And Neyemon Dono came to take his leave of me to goe for Edo.

Sonday.

24. This mornyng cold wether, littell wind W'erly, & not much after rest of day, but calme p'r night.

2 lettrs.

I wrot a lettr to Cacayemon Dono, secretary to Oyen Dono to Edo, to thank hym for his kyndnes in our affares, to be a meanes to solicet his m͛ that our mattrs the next yeare may be enlarged p'r the Emperour. Also an other to

Pr'sentes.

Mrs. Adames to thank her for our kynd entertaynm't, & sent her a gerdell w'th other littell trifels to her 2 children; lettrs & all sent p'r Neyemon Dono of Edo.

Nota.

And Gorezano made frendship w'th Tozayemon Dono, & would haue gladly gotten to be *jurebasso* agane; but I would not. Ther was pr'sentes geven as followeth, &c.:-

To Shroyemon Dono, our cloth seller,

1¼ *tatt.* black cloth, N͡o   .302)

1 pec. Sleze land, N͡o E.

1 pec. corall my selfe, poz. 2 *ma.* 5½ *co.*

To Echero Dono & his wife,

1¼ *tatt.* black cloth.

1 whole pec. chint bramport.

---

300) *Bentō* 辨當.

301) Perhaps Magoemon 孫右衛門, although the name is not given.

302) The number, not given.

November 1616

    & 1 pec. corall my self, poz. 2 *mas condrins.*

All the rest of our copp'r was laden abord this day, being 100 *pico.* of bars, & 100 *pico.* of *goco* copp'r.[303]

25. This mornyng a hor frost, littell wynd W'erly, & so re-meaned all day, but in the night vered N⁰.erly, & so remeand all night.

1 pec. chint.   I gaue   ,[304] the chife *caboque,* 1 single pec. chint bramport, & her mad 5 *mas* in plate, & to sent them away.

To Firado.   And we dep'rted frō Osakay towardes Firando in the afternowne, and gaue our host & hostis a pr'sentes as foll'-th, viz.:–

1¼ *tat.* black cloth, N⁰ .[305]

1 whole pec. chint bramport.

1 galepot judg & gren ton of ech sort.

1 pec. black silk grogren.

1 pec. Sleze land, N⁰ .

$$
2\ \text{pec. corall my selfe poz.}\ \begin{cases} m. & co. \\ 3: & 7: \tfrac{1}{2} \\ 2: & 8: 0 \end{cases} \quad \begin{matrix} ma. & co. \\ 6: & 5: \tfrac{1}{2} \end{matrix}
$$

& 120 *tais* for dyet 4½ *ta.* to sonne, & 6 *tais* to howse.

[fol. 159r.]]

We put our bar of Osakay at night & div'rs frendes came after vs w'th banketes, for a farewell, viz., hostes Osakey, Miaco, & others w'th the servant of Calsa Samme. We got

Taccasanga
20 leages. this night to a place called Taccasanga, 20 leagues frō Osakay.

26. This mornyng cold wether, wynd N⁰.erly, but after vered E'erly, somtymes a gale & somtymes calme. So we

25 leagues. [made] 25 leagues this day, & came to an ancor about mid-night, it be calme, & so stopped the tide.

---

303) In a space after this entry is written a later remark, reading: "Dep'rture frō Osakay."

304) The name, not given.

305) This and the following numbers, not given.

Bengo.
Pr'sent.

This day passed a *foyfone* by vs w'th 20 ores on a side, wherin went a *bongew* of the King of Biengos,[306] & came & spoke w'th vs, seeing we were strangers, & sent me a dozen of larkes for a pr'sent. So in requitall I sent hym a small *barso* of wyne & a salt cod, w'ch he took in good p'rte, sending me word, yf we put into any port of his m.ͬ province, we should be welcom & haue any favor shewed vs we stood in need of.

27. This mornyng fayre wether, wynd variable frō N.ͦ to S. E. w'th a gale somtymes, & somtymes calme.

We waid ancor an hower before day & rowed it vp, haveing somtyme wynd & somtyme calme. And so towardes

Bingana
Tomo.

night arived at Bingana Tomo, haveing met a bark of Firando p'r the way, whoe tould vs our 2 shipps & junk were all ready & attended our coming, wishing vs to make hast.

15 leagues.

We made this day 15 leagues.

Nota.

At my coming to Bingana Tomo, I thought to haue fownd

100 [*sic*] *pico.*
iron.

600 *pico*. iron ready bought & waid out, as I writ our hostis, but fownd nothing donne p'r meanes iron was soo deare, as the worst sort at 17½ *tais* p'r *pico*., & second at 21 *mas pico*., & non of best sort to be had. So I had thought to haue sent bark an expres to Osakay to Mr. Wickham to haue bought som theare, but vpon bettr consideration left it ofe, & thought it bettr to carry money then iron at so deare a rate. But in consideration our hostis said she had bought 100 *pico*., worst sort, at 17 *mas* 2 *condrins*, I took that & meane to send it to Syam, the king of that place haveing writ for iron; also a smith of this place haveing greate store of flat iron a span broad, mad of pvrpose for the Emperour, but durst not sell it w'thout consent of themperours *dico* or *bongew*, w'ch he would send vnto to know

---

306) Which this name suggests, Bungo 豊後 or Bingo 備後, is not clear.

the lowest price.   *[fol. 159v.]*」

Shimutsque.   28.   This mornyng fayre calme wether, or rather a littell
Japon mon.   wynd at N? W., variable after w'th calmes, both night &
day, &c.

A lettr Mr.   I wrot a lettr for Mr. Wickham, & left it w'th our hostice
Wick.   of Bingana Tomo, as apereth p'r coppie. Also I del'd fyftie
50 *tais.*   *tais* to the said hostice vpon acc? of wyne to be bought, &
sent p'r Mr. Wickham when he cometh.

250 *tais.*   More I deliverd two hundred and fyftie *tais* plate bars
vnto Mr. Eaton, to pay for iron at Bingana Tomo, viz.:–

		ta.	*m.*

168 fardes corse iron, at 65 *cattis* fardell, amontes to 109 *pico.*,
    20 cat. 185: 6: 4
016 fardes best iron, amontes all vnto nett
    012 po., 75 *cat.* 025: 2: 0
The corse iron at 17 *mas pico.*, & best at
    20 *mas cat.*.............................210: 8: 4

The rest of the money to disburse in other charges.

   29.   This mornyng calme wether, or rather a littell wynd
W'erly, but after variable, somtyms wynd somtyms calme
Pr'sentes.   both p'r night and day.

We dep'rted this mornyng from Bingana Tomo towardes
Firando, and, gaue our hostis for a pr'sent, viz.:–

1 pec. black silk grogren.
1 single peec. chint bramport.
   And to her sonne,
2 single pec. chint bramport.

And I gaue 2 women & hostis son in laws childe, 3 single
pec. chint bramport, borowd of Capt. Adames. And our
hostis gaue me a pr'sent of 5 bundelles figges, and her
son in law a barill wyne & 3 bundelles figges. And we
paid for our diet *T.* 9 *ta.* 0 *m.* 0 *co.*, and to servantes *T.* 1: 0:
0:, and I gaue an ould woman *T.* 0: 4: 5.

357

November 1616

Nota.

George Durois came to vs to this place, &c. We met 7 boates w'th the King of Fingos[307] provition, he, as they say, cominge after to goe vp to themperour. And, after them, mett as may w'th the King of Bongos,[308] in lyke

30 leages.

sort. So we made this day & night following, 30 leagues.

30. This mornyng a fresh gale, wynd at Nº W., but after ver'd

Camina
Seak.

to the W., & soe remeaned all night a stiff gale. So that we came to an ancor 3 leagues after we had past the strates of Camina Seak, & thear road all night, it prouing a very stor-

13 leag.

me, &c. So we made this day 13 leagues.   [*fol. 160r.*]

December 1616.

Sonday.

1. This mornyng wynd W'erly, & so remeand all day & night following, &c.

We waid ancor at break of day & road it vp w'th the tide

Mia Nots.
5 leages.
2 leages
7 leages.

to a villadg called Mia Nots,[309] 5 leagues from the place we came from, & after rowed 2 leagues more & came to an ancor againe, the sea being very greate. So we made 7 leages this day.

2. This mornyng fayre wether, wynd Nº.erly, & so vering to E., & so back, a stiff gale all day w'th som rayne towardes night, w'th dullard the wynd.

Shimina
Seak.
25 leages

We wayed ancor 2 howrs before day, & sett sayle & came to Shimena Seak 2 howrs before night, where we staid all night p'r meanes of the fowle wether; Capt. Adames coming in late same night. So we made 25 leagues this day.

---

307) Perhaps Katō Tadahiro, *Higo-no-kami* 加藤肥後守忠廣 of Kumamoto in Higo province.
308) Perhaps Takenaka Shigeyoshi, *Uneme-no-shō* 竹中釆女正重義, of Funai 府内 in Bungo province.
309) Miyanotsu 宮津.

358

December 1616

The King of Cokera was at this place w'th 50 seale barkes, ready to goe to vizet the Emperour.

3. This mornyng lowring droping wether, but littell wynd at S. E., but after brok vp fayre wether w'th a stiffe gale E'erly most p'rte day & night followinge.

W. waid ancor & put to sea w'th wynd provinge variable, & arived at Firando the morow mornynge at son rising,

55 leages. haveing made 55 leagues p'r day & night followinge.

Firando, And sowne after Ed. Sayer arived at Firando frō Sha-
Ed. Seyer. shma, where the king vsed hym kyndly, in respect of my

Nota. viseting hym as he passed by this place. I sent our *jurebasso* to adviz the king of my arivall & that I ment to vizet hym to morow. & he sent a man after to bid me welcom, as all the princepall of the towne did the lyke; & the neighbors came them selues & met me, after they heard the shipps shute of their ordinance.

And the Hollandes Capt. sent his *jurebasso* to bid me welcom & that he would haue com hym selfe, but that he was busy writing to send away their ship and junck, &c.[310)

[*fol. 160v.*]

4. This mornyng faire wether, wynd S. E'erly, fayre wether all day, but store of rayne p'r night.

2000 *tais.* The China Capt. tould me how he had 2000 *tais* in fyne plate ready to send in our ship, & that he would write to his

Nota. brother to provide more, but the worst was that Langasaque was belegered & all the passages stopt that no man might retorne frō thence. The occation he knew not; only som said it was to look out for on of Fidaia Sames consortes, & others that it was to look out for padres, &c.

Newes. Also he [*sic*][311) was reportes that 25 saile Hollandr shipps

---

310) In a space after this entry is written a later remark, reading: "Arriue at Firando."
311) There.

359

had taken the Molucas, &c.

5. This mornyng lowring wether, wynd S'erly, but after vered N°erly, fayre wether all day & night following.

I went & vizeted the King of Firando, in company w'th

Pr'sent. Capt. Adames & Ed. Sayer, w'th lettrs frō the King of Shashma & Safian Dono; & I carid the king a pr'sent of 2 barilles *morofack*, 2 salmons, & 5 p'rfumed fans. He took it in good p'rte, & I gaue hym thankes for the paynes that Fesque Dono his *bongew* had taken in going vp w'th me, &c.

Nota. And frō thence I went to the Hollandes howse to vizet Capt. Speck, to know yf he would send me 2 lettrs in the ship that went for Bantam & the junck that went for Syam, w'ch he promised me to do, as also to geue me a lettr to Bantam to send in our shipp, to signefie that it was falce the reportes geven out about carrying the ebony in the *Hozeander*, & that he was ready to do the lyke for vs vpon all occations offered, it being the States pleasure he should do soe.

2 lettrs. I wrot 2 lettrs, 1 for Bantam to Capt. Jourden p'r Duch ship, & the other to Syam to Mr. Beniamyn Farry p'r Duch junck, as p'r copie.

6. This mornyng fayre wether, wynd variable, w'th rayne most p'rte of the day, and lyke p'r night much wynd N°erly.

10 *kerymon* I sent the China Capt. brother a *keremon* & 2 salmons, & gaue the lyke to hym selfe, & a *keremon* a peec. to Mr. Sayer, Mr. Nealson, Mr. Osterwick, Mr. Rowe, Mr. Totton, Niquan the China, & Mat[ingas] father, & 1 to Mr. Wilmot;

Mianga. and *miangas*[312] of gerdelles & showes to Mr. Eaton, Mr. Sayer, Mr. Nelsons, Mr. Osterwickes, & Mat. women; and silver *chaw* pot & a fan to Capt. China wife; & a pear *tabis*

---

312) *Miyage* みやげ, souvenir.

w'th string & a fan to his doughter.

Nota.

The kyng sent for me & Capt. Speck, & shewed vs a lettr he had from the Concell to tell vs we should not trade into no other p'rte of Japon but to this towne of Firando & Langasaque, & to adviz hym eich yeare at ships coming what m'rch'ndiz we brought to the entent to signefie the Emperour thereof. *[fol. 161r.]*

Nota.

Pr'sentes.

I sent 2 salmons to Capt. Speck, w'th 1 to the junk they sent to Syam, & a barill of wyne w'th 1 salmon, mere to the m.ʳ of the *Black Lyon*. Also I sent a barill wyne & salmon to the cauelero of Shashma & Ed. Sayer carid hym the lettr he brought from thence, w'ch he took in good p'rte, &c.

Nota.

We fynd p'r experience that the King of Shashma hath shewed vs extraordenary fauor, & the Duch to the contrary non at all. The occation I think is the pr'sentes I gaue hym as he passed by this place to goe to the Emperour, the Duch not doing the lyke. So that now he let Matias stay allmost a month suing to speak w'th hym & might not haue admittance, &c.

Pr'sent.

313) Dono of Goto brought me a pr'sent 2 haches venison, & a baskit oringes, & supp'red w'th vs.

7. This mornyng lowring wether, wynd a stiff gale N.ºerly, and so remeaned all day faire wether, & lyke p'r night, cold frostie wether but not so much wynd, &c.

500 *tais*.

I del'd fyve hvndred *tais* plate bars to Mr. Osterwick of that I brought downe, & is to pay the Capt. & marreners of our junck the *Sea Adventure*, & for othe[r] matters, &c.

2 letters.

I wrot 2 lettrs, 1 to Albaro Munois for to send the + 314) & stones, & the other to Jor. Durois wife to certefie her how I saw her husband at Bingana Tomo.

---

313) The name, not given.
314) Crossbars (?). See also the entry for July 11,1616 above.

December 1616

A *mestiso*[315] called [316]came to demand passage in our junck for Syam, and tould me he went in the junck w'th Mr. Peacock & Walter Carwarden for Cochinchina, and related to me the death Mr. Peacock cleane contrary to the report I had before, saying that it was by mischance, an other boate rvning against them in a corant overthrowing theirs; & that Mr. Peacock was drownd by meanes of money he carid in his pocket, and that his host was in the boate w'th hym, & hardly escaped w'th swyming, being halfe dead when he came ashore; & that Walter Carwarden, their host, and he went afterward & fownd the dead body of Mr. Peacock, & brought it ashore & buried it; & that water remeaned in the contrey aboue a month after, not any one offering hym iniury, yet in the end embarked hym selfe in the same junck he went [*fol. 161v.*] in to retorne for Japon, carrying all matters left vnsould along w'th hym; w'ch coming to the knowledg of the King of Cochinchina, he wrot a lettr to Safian Dono, to signefie vnto hym that he was inocent of the death of the English or any other, & that, yf the[y] sent any of their nation to receve the money he owed them, he was ready to pay it.

I sent a bundell figes, a pap'r rise, & 2 p'rfumed fans to our neighbors, Japon manor, I retornyng from aboue, viz., to Tome Dono & his wife; to Cushcron Dono & his wife; to Zazabra Dō & his wife; to Skydian Dono & his wife; to China *jurebasso* & his wife; to Kitskin Dono & his wife, & a fan & a pap'r rise to his mother; and to China Capt. wife a *keremon*, she asking it.

Capt. Speck sent a *pico.* of tyn, to pay as we sell rest and to desyre to lend hym a barill gvnpolder, w'ch we did out

---

315) *Mestizo* (Span.), half-breed, especially between the Spaniards or Portugese and the Asian.
316) The name, not given.

December 1616

of Thomas, to retorn an other w'thin 3 or 4 daies.

Sonday. 08. This mornyng, cold frostie wether, wynd N°erly a fresh gale all day, but much rayne p'r night, wynd N° E., a stiff gale.

Nota.
P'r Gilbrt
Dickenson. I came to vnderstand that Gilbart Dickenson, being put in trust to way out the Companies Syam wood to Japons, did secretly consort w'th them to wrong the Company to benefit hym selfe: namely in 20 *pico.* del'd to one in [*sic*] gaue 22 *pico.*, & after went for money for the said 2 *pico.*, w'ch coming to the knowledg of Andrea Dittis, China Capt., he advized me therof & caused the money to be staid. He del'd or waid out much more to Tomo Dono & Cushcron Dono; but I canot fynd out out [*sic*] in what sort it was, only it was tould me he was seene rec. money of them & brought it back againe to chang for bettr, it not being good. Also he was accused p'r the chirurgion of the *Adviz*, called Robert Hawley, that he in secret tould hym he made acc° to put ten pownd in his purce p'r waying out of that wood, &c.

1000 *tais.* We rec. one thousand *tais* of Andrea Dittis, China Capt., in a chist to send for Syam good plate to melte, and as he sayeth bettr to send it thether as it is them to melt it heare.

[*fol. 162r.*]⌋

9. This mornyng lowring raynie wether, wind at N° E., so contynewed most p'rte of the affore nowne, but dyre [sic] wether the rest, & lyke p'r night following.

Lettr. I wrot a lettr to Soyemon Dono, & sent it p'r our *jurebasso*, to entreate hym to speake to the king for the 3000 *tais* he oweth, to send now in these shipps w'ch will be ready w'thin 5 or 6 daies.

Jor. Durois. Georg Durois came to this place, haveing past much danger at sea, staying 6 daies after vs, many barkes being cast away before his eyes.

Nota. The king sent Soyemon Dono & an other to know wether

363

I ment to send goodes to Miaco & those p'rtes; as he was enformed I did, contrary to themperours edict. Vnto w'ch I answerd that I ment to send goodes to our host of Sackay, w'ch I had sould hym for the vallu of 1000 *tais*, for w'ch I had rec. money of hym before hand; & that I might sell my goods to any man at Firando, w'thout geveng offence; & yt he had sent his man w'th his chap or marke to set vpon the goodes, & ment to com after hym selfe. So they took the answer in good p'rte. Also I desyrd hym to be ernest w'th the kyng for the money he owed vs, to send in these shipps, &c.

10.   This mornyng overcast wether w'th a stiffe gale at N°, & so remeaned most p'rte of day, but variable after, w'th rest of night, yet fayre wether, &c.

Concell.   We had a generall meeting & councell at English howse, wherat assested w'th my selfe, Mr. Ric'd Rowe, Mr. Jn°. Totton, Wm. Eaton, Wm. Nealson, Ed. Sayer, Wm. Nealson [*sic*], Jn°. Osterwick, Edmont Wilmot, Wm. Colston; where was handled the matter of the rvning away of Tho. Heath & Nic°. Wilson of th'*Advises* company, w'th Henry Blackcolles, Hewgh Hewes, Tho. Sommer, & Xporfer[317] Galsworthy of *Thomas* company, for rvning away w'th the *Tho.* skiffe, & 350 Rs. of 8 of Mr. Rowes in money; but [b]eing taken, we condemd them, w'th on Widger of the *Tho.* compamy, their consort, to be duckt at yard arme 3 tymes & whipt at capstayn each one 20 stripes; only Heath the gvner to be but duckt.   [*fol. 162v.*]]

Nota.   Also Jn°. Hawtery was brought in question by Mr. Eaton for goodes stolne at Edo & Osakay, w'ch he could not deny, but fell out in rayling termes against me, thretnyng me that he would make me to leape, &c. For w'ch Mr. Rowe

---

317) Christofer.

carid hym abord & put hym in the bilboes, &c.

The Hollandes junck went out for Syam this after nowne.

11. This mornyng fayre cold wether, littell wynd E'erly, after variable, yet fayre wether p'r day & night.

We went abord the *Tho*, and saw execution donne vpon the p'rsons aforsaid, according to order, only Galworthie & Widger were refered till an other tyme, they being both sick of the pox, & p'r the chirurgions opinion would be in danger of their lives yf they were ducked.

George Durois being ready to dep'rte towardes Langasaque, news came that the cheefe in that place we taken & bownd vpon suspition. So he staid till he heard ferther newes.

Capt. Adames entered into extraordinary hvmors, taking the p'rte of the scrivano of his junk w'ch one Miguell, 2 villans that have cozened the company, against me & all the rest of thenglish, to mentayne them before the justice. I take God to witnes I do what I can to keepe in w'th this man, &c.

I opened chist N? 4 and tooke out 100 *tais* plate and del'd it to Andrea Dittis, China Capt., for a m'rchnt of Miaco, according as he gaue me order.

News came frō Langasaque that men might enter but not com out againe; so we know not what will com thereof.

12. This mornyng fayre cold wether, wynd N? E., littell but rack W'erly, dry wether all day, but much wynd p'r night at W. N? W., or N? West, w'th store of rayne, very fowle wether.

N? 2.
N? 5.
2000 *tais*
China Cap.
600 *tais* to
Mr.
Osterwik

I opened chist N? 2, cont'g 1100 *tais* plate bars & del'd it to the China Capt. to melt or chang for fyne plate. Also I opened chist N? 5, cont'g 1500 *tais* same plate, & del'd 900 *tais* of it to said China Capt., Andrea Dittis, & rest being 600 *tais* to Mr. Jn? Osterwick to lay out on necessary occations, &c. I say [I] del'd two thousand *tais* to China Capt. & 600 *tais* to Mr. Osterwick, is all two thousand six hvndred *tais* plate bars.

Laurenzo
Sanzero.
7 *tais.*

We bought a slaue of George Durois, pownd [*sic*] vnto hym by one of Firando for 7 *tais* plate bars, w'ch money is now paid vnto hym. The slaues Christen name is Laurenso, & in Japon Sanzero, w'ch bill of Jorges & the Japons I del'd to Mr. Osterwick, &c.   [*fol. 163r.*]]

A jonck
out of
China.

Also this day arived a small China bark or *soma* from Hockchew,[318] laden w'th silk & stuffes in this towne of Firando. They bring news of the wars betwixt China & the Tartars.

Jor. Durois.

Jor. Durois dep'rted frō this place towardes Langasaque,

Mr. Wickham
retor. frō
Sakay.

1200 *tais.*
200 more

and Mr. Wickham arived from Osakay, & in his company Tozayemon Donos man, our host at Sakay, and Mr. Wickham brought a chist of money w'th hym of one thousand two hvndred *tais* plate of bars w'th 1400[319] *tais* I del'd imediatly to Mr. Jnº Osterwick to lay out about needfull occations.

Pilottes
for Syam.

50 *tais.*

Also we agreed w'th ould Mr. Burges of the *Thomas* & yong Mr. Burges of the *Adviz* to goe for pilottes in our junck for Syam. And ther was 50 *tais* plate bars geven to Skidayen Dono for to make his voyag to Syam, he being capt. of the junck, w'ch 50 *tais* Mr. Osterwick paid hym. Also we deliverd fowre thousand *tais* plate bars more to the China Capt., Andrea Dittis, to melt or chang into fyne plate: Chist Nº 1, cont'g 1100 *tais*, Nº 3, cont'g 1200 *tais*,

4000 *tais.*

Nº 6, cont'g 1400 *tais*; and Mr. Osterwick in ready money 0300 *tais*; is all 4000 *tais* plate bars.

Niquan the China retorned from Langasaque w'th 6000

318) Foochoo 福州.
319) The author originally wrote "1200" and upon giving a marginal note he corrected it as "1400."

tais fyne plate, sent frō Capt. Chinas brother for vs, and sent me word he would send 2000 *tais* same plate to morrow, w'ch he had taken vp of a frend for vs at intrest at 20 p'r c'nto according to my order, & would take vp more yf we stood in neede, &c.

13. This mornyng fowle rayny wether, much wynd at N? W. W'erly, but after nowne it brok vp fayre wethe[r], espetially p'r night it remeaned fare, not so much wynd later ende, &c.

Pr'sent frō a China.

A China called   320)came from Langasaque, and brought me a pr'sent of 4 boxes marmelaid, 3 pap'rs suger roles, 2 dozen suger cakes, and a dish of peares.

16 *cattans*.

I rec. 16 *cattans* of Mr. Eaton to send to Sir Tho. Smith, cost, viz.:–

	ta.	*m.*	*co.*
2 best sort long *cattans*, at 2½ *tais* p'r *cattan*, is .*T.*	05:	0:	0
6 second sort long *cattans*, at 1½ *tais* p'r *cattan*, is ......*T.*	09:	0:	0
8 short *cattans* at 8 *mas* p'r *cattan*, is ....*T.*	06:	4:	0
Som totall amontes vnto ....*T.*	20:	4:	0

2000 *tais*.

The China Capt. sent vs in 2 chistes plate bars good to melt, to send for Syam w'th the rendadors chape vpon it, cont'g in each chist one thousand *tais*, is tow thousand in all, desyring to haue the 100 *tais* sent back, w'ch he sent for that purpose before, as also 1000 *tais* more of our plate w'th it.   [*fol. 163v.*]⌋

14. This mornyng fayre wether, wind at N? W., a stiff gale, fayre all day, but rayne p'r fittes in the night w'th much wynd, &c.

Pr'sentes.

I sent 6 barill wyne w'th 6 salmons to Bongo Same, Semi Dono, Taccamon Dono, Oyen Dono, Torayemon Dono, & Soyemon Dono, w'ch were well accepted of, w'th much

---

320) The name, not given.

December 1616

complem't sent to me after p'r their servantes, &c.

Taccamon Dono paid all his ould score & desird to haue 50 pico. sappon vpon a new acc?, to pay next yeare as we sell the rest.

15. This mornyng overcast lowring wether, much wynd at N? W'erly, rack frō W., cold wether, snow & heele p'r fittes both day & night, blustring wynd espetially all day, &c.

I del'd one hvndred *tais* plate bars to Andrea Dittis, China Capt., to del'r to Skydayen Dono, capt. of the *Sea Adventur*, as his owne, for most advantage; but is for my selfe, &c.

Capt. Adames envited all thenglish to a banket w'th *kabokes*, &c.

16. This mornyng cold overcast wether, wynd still at N? W., rack from W., sleet or snow, cold wether both day and night.

We thought to haue gon out w'th junck, but co'ld not p'r meanes of much wynd, &c.

17. This morn'g still cold wether, slite of snow or heale, wynd st'll at N? W., rack frō W., fayre wether both day and night, & but littell wynd p'r night or rather calme.

I del'd fyftie *tais* plate bars to Ed. Sayer lent to hym to make his benefitt for w'ch he is to be acc? to me. And I deliverd tow thousand tow hundred *tais* to Mr. Eaton in plate, wherof 200 *tais* was in fyne plate, rest in bars, and is p'rte of cargezen sent p'r hym to Syam, rest being in severall sorte of goodes, amt. to *T.* 3043 *ta.* 6 *m.* 2½ *co.*

ta.
843: 3: 6: 2½
tas goodes
is all
3043: 6: 2½.
A lettr to ye
King
Shashma.

I wrot a lettr to the King of Shashma, to geue hym thankes for the good vsadg of Ed. Sayer & the rest in our junck, offring my service to hym in what is in my power. Soyemon Dono helpd me to endite & write my letter in good termes befyting so greate a prince. Also Soyemon

368

December 1616

Dono tould me that the King of Shashma did much esteem our Eng'sh nation, and would suffer vs to trade into the Liqueas or any other p'rtes of his domynions, but would not suffer the lyke to the Hollandrs, &c.   *[fol. 164r.]*

18. This mornyng foggy, calme wether, but sowne after rayne w'th wynd, a stiffe gale at N? E., and so remeand w'th rayny wether, rest day & night followinge.

2000 *tais.*

I del'd tw[o] chistes money to Andrea Dittis, China Capt., cont'g two thousand *tais* plate bars, for the 2000 *tais* same sort we had of hym to send for Syam. Also the

200 *tais.*

said China Capt. del'd two hvndred *taies* fyne melted plate to Mr. Eaton p'rte of his cargezen for Syam.

Yasimon Dono. Albaro Mu's

Yasimon Dono and Albaro Munois arived at this towne of Firando, one frō Xaxma & thother from Langasaque. & Yasi came & visited me, telling me how our nation were respected in Xaxma, & the Hollanders nothing exsteemed of, & that they were lyke to loose their processe w'th a China about red wood com in a junck from Syam put into Xaxma p'r contrary wynd.

19. This mornyng rayne wether, much wynd at N? W. after vering N?erly fayre wether after most p'rte of the day w'th the lyke p'r night, littell wynd.

200 *tais.*

I del'd two hundred *tais* plate melted to Mr. Eaton, whe'- of 100 *tais* to goe for my acc°, & rest lent to hym to adven- ture for Syam, to del'r p'r ext'a, &c. And I del'd ten *tais*

10 *tais* 2 *m.* 3 *co.*

2 *mas* 3 *condrins* plate bars to Mr. Eaton I lende to Domin- go, my man, to adventure to Syam, as apereth p'r remem- brance.

3 letters to Syam.

And I del'd my lettrs to Mr. Eaton, viz.:–

1 to **Mr. Beniamyn Farry**, cape m'rchnt at Syam w'th the cargezon goodes ther inclozed.

36 *tais.*

1 to **Jn? Ferrers**, to Syam, w'th his bill of 36 *pezos* or rialles of 8 I paid to Capt. Adams for hym, & send hym 3 shutes of

369

ap'rell by hym.

1 to Mr. Jn? Browne, to Pattania.

All w'ch 3 lettrs apeare p'r coppie.

Nota.

Two Spaniardes came to vizet me, of Andelozea, saying they were parentes of Harnado Ximines, enquiring for 2 or 3 men that were escaped out of the Spanish shipps &, they said, fled to the Hollanders; but after, Capt. Speck came to vizet me & tould me these Spaniardes had hanged an English man out of littell ship, &c.   [*fol. 164v.*]

20. This mornyng fayre wether, wynd at N? E., a fresh gale most p'rte of day and night following, &c.

Junk *Sea Adventr.*

Our junck the *Sea Adventure* went out of Firando to Cochi & there came to an ancor.

And Capt. Speck brought me a lettr to send to Syam, w'ch I did, & enclozed it to Mr. Fary w'th a word or 2. Also Capt. Speck went out w'th his boate after our junck to helpe to tow her out, and carid a pr'sent of wyne & porke; and shot afe 7 or 8 chambrs & pec. ordinance as she passed by, and our shipp shot afe each one 5 pec. of ordinance, &c.

Nota.

And being abord I fownd the capt. drunk, w'th others of Firando w'th hym, whoe demanded a writing of my hand to make good their pr'veleges, as also that I should lend hym 200 *tais* gratis at Syam, to pay the lyke som heare in Firando, at his retorne, w'ch I denyed to doe & so retorned ashore, offring hym that yf he were not content w'th that w'ch he had, that then he might geve ov'r the voyage, & I would send an other in his place. They had gon out this mornyng but that Mr. Eaton was not abord, but about midnight he dep'rted from hence, Mr. Wickham, Mr. Sayer, & Mr. Osterwick accompa'yng hym.

1 pec. of w't byram.

I had a pec. of white byrams to make Mat. shertes of 14 Rs., *corg*, but was spoked & staynd.

December 1616

21. This mornyng fayre wether, wynd at N? E., a stiff gale most p'rte of the day, but now & then a shower after p'r day & fore p'rte of night, yet not so much wynd p'r night.

Junck to Siam.

Our junck, *Sea Adventure*, put out of Cochi road towardes Syam this mornyng. God send her a prosperous voyage.

King of Goto.

The King of Goto[321] arived at Firando this after nowne, being bownd vp to vizet the Emperour, but came heare ashore and vizeted the King of Firando. So it is thought fit to cary hym a pr'sent, because our shipping & junck do still com & goe p'r his cvntrey, & somtymes p'r meanes of fowle weather enter into his harbors, and haue byn kyndly vsed, &c. [*fol. 165r.*]

Sonday.

22. This mornyng lowring wether, wynd at N? E. w'th rayne p'r fittes both day & fore p'rte of night following.

Pr'sent King Goto.

I went & vizeted the Kyng of Goto, & carid hym a pr'sent, in respect o'r shipps & junckes do daylie pas in & out p'r his kyngdom, viz., 1½ *tatt.* brodcloth, N?   ,[322] 3 syngle pec. chint bramport, [and] 1 chast fowling peece. He took it in good part, & after sent his man to vizet me (he being ready to dep'rte towardes Edo), to tell me his hast was such he could not com to thank me hym selfe, but assured me that, yf any of our shiping (juncks or other) came vpon his cost, they should be suckared w'th the needfull, & that instantly he would adviz me of the arivall of any that were to enter, for w'ch I thanked the messenger, telling hym I was sory his Highnes was dep'rted on such a sudden, because I ment to haue salutes hym w'th ordinance as he had passed out, the w'ch he said he would make knowne to the king, his m'r.

Pr'sent.

I went also & vizeted Yasimon Dono, and card hym a

---

321) Gotō Moritoshi, *Awaji-no-kami* 五嶋淡路守盛利.
322) The number, not given.

371

pr'sent of a barill *morofack* & a salmon, w'ch he took in

ta. m. co.
318: 0: 0.
6 tais.

good p'rtes. Semi Dono paid 318 *tais* plate bars on his old acc°, w'ch Mr. Osterwick receved, w'th 6 *tais* of an other for 6 pec. red zelas sould heretofore, &c.

23. This mornyng fayre wether, wynd a fresh gale at N° E, & so remeand all day & night following, &c.

Pr'sent.

I went & vizeted Songero Same,[323) ould Foyns sonne, & carid hym a pr'sent as followth, viz., 1¼ *tatta*. brod cloth, N° ,[324) 1 barill *morofack*, 1 salmon, [and] 3 p'rfumed fans. And Capt. Adames went w'th me, & carid hym 3 single pec. chint bramport of his owne. Yt is said that the king of this place is to goe vp to themperour forthw'th, and

Nota.

soe much Oyen Dono tould me, he comyng to vizet me yisterday, telling me the king was in great care to provide me money to send in these ships, he being now put to his shiftes in respect of his going vp to themperour, &c. Also it is said Sangero Samme is to go vp to themperour, but vpon what occation is not knowne, whether it be by comandem't of themperour, or of the King of Firando, his nephew. Yf themperour sent for hym, it is thought it is to make hym kyng, &c.

A clok of
Mr. Totton.

And I had an ould cloake of Mr. Totton, w'ch I gave to Capt. Whaw, China Capt. brother, at Langasaque.

[fol. 165v.]⌡

24. This mornyng still fayre wether, wynd at N° E., but not much wynd p'r night, yet cold wether, &c.

180 *pico.*
sappon.

We waid out 130 *picos* sappon to Semi Dono, and 50 *pico*. to Taccamon Dono. sould them at 25 *mas* p'r *pico*.

200 *pico.*
sappon.

Also we waid out 200 *pico*. sappon more to Andrea Dittis, China Capt., sould hym before at 24 *mas pico*. w'th a greter som.

---

323) Sangoro Sama. See Note 113) for 1615.
324) The number, not given.

December   1616

15 ba'iles gunpolder.	And we rec. 15 barilles gvnpolder from Langasaque from Capt. Whaw, China Capt. brother, poz. 325) *picos*.

2 per.
stocking.
68 candls.

18 caks
sope.
1191 bages
w't lyme.

15 *pico*.
sappon.

Chistmas.

Also I rec. 2 pear silk stockinges frõ Jor. Durois in p'rte of oyle and 68 tallo candelles vpon accᵒ howse cost. Also I had 18 caks Surat soape of Mr. Totton, cost   ,326) and we bought 1191 bagges lyme at 1 *condrin* 8 cash p'r bag, whereof 200 are for China Capt., cost all 21 *ta*. 4 *m*. 3⅘ *co*. And we sould of trust to Gorayemon Dono, our late *jurebasso*, 15 *pico*. sappon at 25 *mas* to pay at pleasure.

25. This mornyng a hor frost, littell wynd Nᵒerly to thest ward, and so remeaned all day & night following, gale encreasing, &c.

18 pec.
ordi.

Our 2 shipps, *Thomas* & *Adviz*, shot of each one 9 pec. of ordinance at son rising, in honor of Christmas Day.

Pr'sent.

And Andrea Dittis, China Capt., sent me a pr'sent of 2 pec. black taffeties, & 10 grete China cakes of sweete bread.

Nota.

We envited the m[as]t'rs, m[as]t'rs [*sic*] mates, & cheefe offecers of both shipp[s] to dyner & supp'r, being som 20 p'rsons, as also the China Capt., & our selus, m'rchntes, were aboue 30 p'rsons. And Mr. Rowe envited vs abord the *Tho*. to morrow to dyner. Mr. Totton being very sick, could not com, as Mr. Wilson, m[as]t'rs mate of *Tho*., the lyke. God send them health, &c.

26. This mornyng cold wether w'th a stiffe gale, wynd at Nᵒ E., and so remeaned all day & night following, fayre wether, only som small dropps rayne p'r night, &c.

Dyner ab'rd
Thomas.

We dyned abord the *Thomas*, & hat 3 pec. at entring abord, w'th 3 for a health to Honorable Company, viz. 2 out of *Tho*., and 1 out of *Adviz* w'th 5 orther [*sic*] single health, viz., 1 to Capt. China, 1 to Capt. Middelton, 1 to Capt. Jourden, 1 to Capt. Adames, & 1 to Capt. Saris;

---

325) Not entered.
326) Not entered.

w'th 7 pec. out of *Tho.* at going ashore, & 5 out of *Adviz,* w'th 3 out of *Tho.* for the women.

Caboque.

And we had the *cabokis* after supp'r ashre, whoe plaid and dansed till after midnight & then went away, being 8 women, & 6 or 7 men. *[fol. 166r.]*

27. This mornyng lowring wether w'th a stiff gale of wynd at N° E., all day, but not so much wynd p'r night, yet fayre wether night & day, &c.

8 tais.

I sent the *caboque* eight *tais* plate bars p'r our *jurebasso* w'ch money Mr. Osterwick paid vpon my accompt.

And in consideration of the frendship the China Capt. brother hath shewd vp to procure vs money, 3000 *tais* at intrest, & would let Mr. Wilmot nor his followers pay nothing for their diet at Langasaque, they lying theare aboue a month at a Chinas howse, we gaue to the China his host 1 *tatta.* black brod cloth N°   ,[327] & to Capt. Whaw

2 tat. bays.
1 tatt. black kloth.

2 *tatta.* stamet bays, 7½ *tay* wight best ambr beades, being 130 beades, 2 *tay* 9 *mas* wo[r]st ambr beades, being 10 beades.

A'ber beades.
130 beades.
10 beades.
Pr'sentes.

Yasimon Donos littell doughter came to vizet me, & brought me a pr'sent of oringes, & I gaue her a p'rfumed fan, a p'rfumyng bras balle, & a bundell of pap'r, &c.

28. This mornyng lowring wether, littell wind N°erly & not much all rest day following, w'th rayne towardes night, encreasing to a stiff gale N°., all night w'th much rayne, &c.

2 lettrs.

And I wrot two lettrs (p'r Andrea Dittis, China Capt., his direction) vnto 2 greate China lordes, viz., to Ffiokew, secretary of Estate, w'th 200 *tais* plate bars, del'd to his servant Liangowne, for provid charges p'r way; to Tykam Shafno, concellor of Estate; & yt I del'd 10 bars gould *oban* to same man for purpose afforesaid, as doth apere

---

327) The number, not given.

December 1616

200 *tais*.

p'r coppies of both lettrs. The 200 *tais* bars plate Mr. Oster-wick del'd to China Capt., but put vpon his acc?; but the 10 bars *oban* cont'g 44 *tay* wight gould, Capt. Whaw del'd

550 *tais*.

of hym selfe, amonting vnto 550 *tais* plate, all going for them prop'r accompt, yet they them selues haue wrot I sent it (or gaue it), as apereth to them in my 2 letrs. God grant good suckcesse.

3 lettrs.

Also 1 wrot 3 lettrs in Japon, viz., 1 to Safian Dono, and an other to his secretary 328) to desire Saf. to geue me a lettr of favor to the King of Cochinchina for paym't of such soms money, as he bought good for of Mr. Peacock. I say, to pay the money to Capt. Adames & adviz me how Mr. Peacock came to his end & what became of Water Carwarden. And the 3rd lettr was to our host, To-zayemon Dono, of Sackay, to buy 50 *pico. goco* copp'r to send me p'r first, w'th such money as he made of our good-es, &c.

Mr. Totton sick.

Also Mr. Totton being very sick, I put hym in mynd to make all matters stright, w'ch he promised me to do.

18 *mas* shews.

I paid the China sumaker 18 *mas* my selfe for 6 peare pantables, slippers, & pomps at 3 *mas* pec. for my selfe.

[*fol. 166v*]⌋

Sonday.

29. This mornyng a storme or gust of wynd N?erly, w'th much rayne most p'rte or rather all day following, but dry p'r night most an end, & not so much wynd vering to S. W., &c.

Nota.

Mr. Jn? Totton, m'r of the *Adviz* fynding hym selfe weake, sent for me, and in the pr'sence of Mr. Edmond Wilmot tould me he ment to make his will, & set matters in order, asking my opinion to whome he were best to make over his estate, that it might com to his littell son, his ould

---

328) The name, not given.

mother, & a sister he had, in respect he was now in these
forren p'rtes of the world of Japon & they in England; so
that yf he should put it into my handes or Mr. Wilmots,
we were mortall as well as hym selfe; so that he thought
it best to make over his estate to the Honorable Company,
our employers, leaving vs heare for witnesses of what past,
vnto w'ch his adviz I gaue comendacon, so that he went
on, & took an inventory of his estate of goodes, & monies,

ta. ma.
15: 2.

amonting to   .[329] Also he paid 15 *ta.* 2 *mas*
plate bars to Capt. Adames for rest of acc? betwixt them,
w'ch money I del'd Capt. Adames for hym in the pr'sence
of Mr. Willmot in our halle.

And I wrot 5 lettrs in Japons to severall men, viz.:-
1 to host at Osakay, Cuimon Dono.
1 to host at Miaco, Menguayemon Dono.
1 to Neyemon Don & his p'rtner at Edo.
1 to Capt. Adames wife.
1 to Cacozayemon Don, secretary to Oyen Dono.

30. This mornyng mild wether, lettell wynd at S. W., vering
after a fresh gale at N? W., & in the night N?erly w'th som
store of rayne both p'r day and night, &c.

2 lettrs to
Jor. Durois.
2 lettrs.

I sent 2 lettrs to Jor. Durois, 1 p'r Capt. Adames & the
other p'r Capt. Chinas man. And I wrot againe to Oyne
Dono, & Soyemon Dono to procure vs money frō the *Tono*
to send p'r these shipps.

31. This mornyng rayny wether, wynd N?erly, & so remeaned wet wether most p'rte of the day, but dry p'r night, &c.

I was geven to vnderstand that Tome. our *jurebasso*,
whome I ment to send for Bantam to haue done hym good
& haue geven hym 4½ years tyme he was to serue me. I
say I was enformed he owned 15 *tais* to the *coboquis* for
whoring, w'th other wild trickes he had don, as pawnyng

329) Not entered.

December 1616

his fellows weapons, & ap'rell. So I del'd hym vp his pap'rs
& turned hym away he haveing beaten his owne father
the day before, who came to vizet hym.[330]   *[fol 167r.]*

---

[330] Text continues at fol. 167v. to the entry for January 1, 1617[8], without
changing the leaf.